City of
Sedition

ALSO BY JOHN STRAUSBAUGH

The Village: 400 Years of Beats and Bohemians,
Radicals and Rogues, a History of Greenwich Village

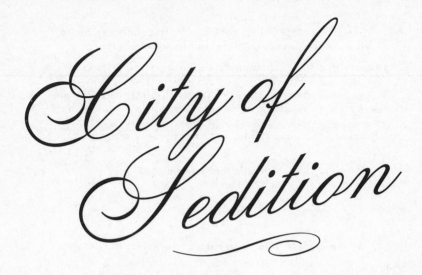

City of Sedition

THE HISTORY OF NEW YORK CITY DURING THE CIVIL WAR

John Strausbaugh

TWELVE

NEW YORK BOSTON

Twelve
Hachette Book Group
1290 Avenue of the Americas
New York, NY 10104
twelvebooks.com
twitter.com/twelvebooks

First published in hardcover and as an ebook in August 2016.
First trade paperback edition: July 2017.

Twelve is an imprint of Grand Central Publishing.
The Twelve name and logo are trademarks of Hachette Book Group, Inc.

The publisher is not responsible for websites (or their content) that are not owned by the publisher.

The Hachette Speakers Bureau provides a wide range of authors for speaking events. To find out more, go to www.hachettespeakersbureau.com or call (866) 376-6591.

Photo Credits: *Library of Congress:* 1, 2, 3, 4, 5, 6, 7, 9, 10, 11, 12, 13, 14, 15, 16, 17, 19, 20, 22, 23, 24, 25, 26, 27, 28, 29, 30, 31, 32, 33, 34, 35, 36, 37, 38, 39, 40, 41, 42, 43, 44, 45; *Kansas Historical Society:* 8; *New York Public Library:* 18, 21

The Library of Congress has cataloged the hardcover as follows:

Names: Strausbaugh, John, author.
Title: City of sedition : the history of New York during the Civil War / John
   Strausbaugh.
Description: First edition. | New York : Twelve, 2016. | Includes
   bibliographical references and index.
Identifiers: LCCN 2016001495| ISBN 9781455584185 (hardcover) | ISBN
   9781478909675 (audio download) | ISBN 9781455584192 (ebook)
Subjects: LCSH: New York (N.Y.)—History—Civil War, 1861-1865.
Classification: LCC F128.44 .S827 2016 | DDC 974.7/03—dc23 LC record available at
http://lccn.loc.gov/2016001495

ISBNs: 978-1-4555-8417-8 (trade paperback), 978-1-4555-8419-2 (ebook)

Printed in the United States of America

LSC-C

10 9 8 7 6 5 4 3 2 1

Contents

PART I
BEFORE: City of Confusion

PART II
DURING: City of Sedition

PART III
AFTER: City of Gilt

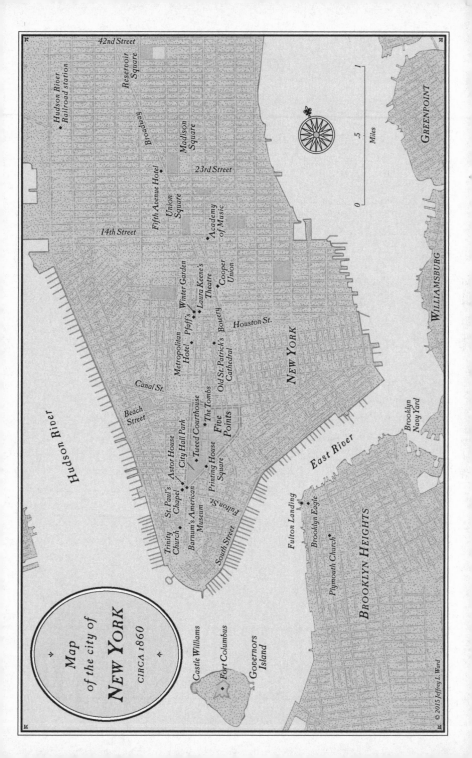

Map of the city of NEW YORK CIRCA 1860

© 2015 Jeffrey L. Ward

PART I

Before

City of Confusion

CHAPTER 1

My God, We Are Ruined!

The Civil War started in darkness. At 4:30 a.m. on Friday, April 12, 1861, batteries of the newly formed Confederate States of America commenced shelling the federal installation of Fort Sumter in Charleston harbor.

Telegraphed news of the bombardment began reaching New York City's newspaper offices late Friday afternoon. That night, a little before midnight, Walt Whitman strolled out of the Academy of Music on 14th Street, where he'd enjoyed a performance of Donizetti's *Linda di Chamounix*. He was walking down Broadway, heading for Fulton Street where he would catch a ferry home to Brooklyn, "when I heard in the distance the loud cries of the newsboys, who came presently tearing and yelling up the street, rushing from side to side even more furiously than usual." They were hawking late editions. "WAR BEGUN!" the *New York Tribune* cried. "FORT SUMTER ATTACKED!" *The Sun* chimed in.

Nearby, a group of prominent businessmen were meeting. No one in the country feared a war between the states more than New York's business community. They did a tremendous amount of trade with the South. Since the previous December, when South Carolina was the first state to secede after Lincoln's election, they'd been "studying with intense solicitude the means of preserving the peace." They'd held numerous meetings and rallies, petitioned their politicians, pleaded with their Southern partners. War, they knew, would not only mean the end of their highly profitable trade with the Southern states. It would leave the business leaders holding more than $150 million in Southern debt. That's the equivalent of about $4.5 billion in today's currency.

A messenger burst into the meeting and breathlessly delivered the news from Fort Sumter. "The persons whom he thus addressed remained a while in dead silence, looking into each other's pale faces; then one of them, with uplifted hands, cried, in a voice of anguish, 'My God, we are ruined!' "

That account was written by Morgan Dix, rector of the elite Trinity Church at the foot of Wall Street and son of the powerful political figure John A. Dix. He doesn't identify his fretful gentlemen, but their names are unimportant. They were representative of a large sector of New York's business elite at the start of the Civil War. As dismayed as they were, they could not have been startled by the Fort Sumter news. Conflicts between the North and the South had been festering for most of the century. Gloomy forecasts of ultimate disunion and civil war went back as far as the 1810s. Members of Congress had spent the entire decade of the 1850s alternately trying to bridge the widening sectional gulf and beating each other up over it. The moment the Republican Party nominated Abraham Lincoln in the spring of 1860, angry Southern "fire-eaters" (as Northerners dubbed the most radical and vocal pro-slavers) had made it unmistakably clear that they would consider his election tantamount to an act of war. In January, five more states joined South Carolina in seceding (Mississippi, Florida, Alabama, Georgia, and Louisiana); in February, the six formed their own separate nation. Five more would soon join. Overnight, federal installations like Fort Sumter had become foreign military bases. When Confederate troops surrounded and blockaded the fort, hoping to starve the garrison into a bloodless surrender, Lincoln had picked up the gauntlet and sent supply ships steaming out of New York harbor. Neither side had blinked, and now the Civil War had begun.

North and South had disagreed over many issues, but Civil War historian James McPherson argues that only one was combustible enough to ignite a war between them: slavery. In the first half of the 1800s, as Northern states were ending slavery, it expanded mightily in the South. Although only a third of white Southerners owned slaves, many were convinced that slavery was the foundation not just of their economy but of their culture, pride, and identity. And they believed that President Lincoln wanted to force them to abolish it. He had insisted many times in many ways that he had no such intention. "Wrong as we think slavery is, we can

yet afford to let it alone where it is," he said in his career-making speech to
New York Republicans in 1860. Southerners did not believe him. Through
the 1850s they had watched the movement to abolish slavery gain momentum in the North. The movement's bible, Harriet Beecher Stowe's *Uncle
Tom's Cabin*, published in 1852, had sold an astounding two and a half
million copies around the world in a single year, convincing Southerners that they were surrounded by enemies. The abolitionist John Brown's
attempt in 1859 to incite an armed slave rebellion had deeply alarmed
them. Though Lincoln and virtually all Northern political leaders had
denounced Brown as a mad fool, Northern abolitionists embraced him as
a sainted martyr. The more anxious Southerners saw this as a sign that an
all-out Northern attack, even military invasion, was imminent.

The truth was that to the majority of Northern whites, Southern slavery was not a pressing issue. It was certainly not one over which they
would fight and die. No matter how many tears they wept reading *Uncle
Tom's Cabin*, the majority of white Americans held some version of what
we'd now call a white supremacist view, on a scale from virulent to mild.
They believed that blacks were at best an intellectually inferior race, or
even an entirely separate species, closer to apes than to white people. This
held true in the North as well as the South, among abolitionists as well
as slave-owners. Stowe, whose novel did so much to stir up sympathy
for the slave, nevertheless considered blacks fit only for brute labor, and
she believed that if they were freed it would be best for them to "return"
to Africa. Lincoln came to emancipation in slow and halting steps. He
abhorred slavery on ethical and political grounds, but also favored blacks
leaving the country, and doubted that blacks and whites could live as
equals even as he issued his proclamation freeing them. Only a minority of New Yorkers expressed much interest in freeing slaves hundreds
of miles away, and many, from those fretful businessmen to immigrant
laborers, felt they had a personal stake in *preserving* Southern slavery.
Even Whitman, whose vision of America was as all-embracing and democratic as any white man's of his time, considered it dangerous extremism
when abolitionists pressed too hard for what he called "Settlement of the
Nigger Question."

Lincoln, the majority of Northern whites, and certainly most New
Yorkers did not and would not go to war to free a single slave in the South.
Except for radical abolitionists, they were, as Lincoln said on many

occasions, willing to let slavery remain there. The South was not. The United States went through a phase of astonishing growth in the first half of the nineteenth century, adding new territory and making new states at a ferocious clip. Ultimately, the war was not about Southern slavery but about whether or not to let slavery spread to all that new land.

The United States had begun the century an infant among the nations of the world, not yet twenty years old, still hugging the eastern coast of North America. The far frontier was the Ohio River; the Midwest was called the Northwest. Then the Louisiana Purchase in 1803—negotiated for Thomas Jefferson in part by a New Yorker, Robert Livingston—instantly doubled the country's territory, adding an immense swath of land from the Gulf of Mexico north to the Canadian border, and from the Mississippi west to the Rockies. It was an area that would become all or part of fifteen states. By 1850 the drive from sea to shining sea was complete and the country was four times larger than it had been in 1800.

To the South it was of vital political importance to spread slavery across that new land. From the very foundation of the republic, Southern states had been concerned with maintaining a balance of power with the richer, more populous North. To that end the South forced the three-fifths rule in Article I of the Constitution, which stated that for the apportioning of tax revenues and representation in the House each slave could be counted as three-fifths of a citizen. In 1800, there were nine slave states and eight free states. Since each state of any size was allotted two senators, the South actually dominated the Senate at this point.

After the Louisiana Purchase, Southern politicians, representing what came to be known as the Slave Power, expended a great deal of time and clout on maintaining a precise numerical balance of slave states and free. So, for example, when Indiana was admitted as a free state in 1816, Mississippi was added as a slave state the following year; when the free state Illinois was added in 1818, Alabama was added as a slave state. In 1820, Congress cobbled together the Missouri Compromise, admitting Missouri as a slave state and Maine as free, but thereafter prohibiting slavery north of a line extending from Missouri's southern border to the Pacific. The balance was maintained through the addition of Texas as a slave state in 1845 and Wisconsin as a free state in 1848. That brought the total to fifteen of each.

Winning its war with Mexico in 1848 earned the United States another vast parcel of territory that would eventually become California, New Mexico, Arizona, and parts of other states. Californians voted to be admitted as a free state in 1850. An enormous area of western territory was still up for grabs. Through the 1850s the fighting over this territory turned ugly. The Slave Power, feeling itself increasingly hemmed in by free states and losing its hold on Washington, desperately wanted to extend slavery's reach. That was something Northerners would not abide. Only the abolitionist minority among them opposed the extension of slavery on moral grounds. The rest resisted it not out of any sympathy for black slaves but because they believed that opening the West to slavery would ruin it for free labor. Congress passed the Compromise of 1850, a complex suite of laws meant to paste over the widening cracks by making concessions all around. It failed to please either side.

As the decade lurched on toward the precipice of war, decorum in the halls of Congress deteriorated shockingly. Fierce debate escalated into shouting matches and then physical violence. After a congressman pulled a pistol on an opponent, many came to work armed. The Kansas-Nebraska Act of 1854 turned the Kansas Territory into an actual battleground between free-state and slave forces. It came to be known as Bleeding Kansas. In 1856 a South Carolina representative took his cane to the venerable Massachusetts senator Charles Sumner over the Kansas issue, beating him so severely that he was permanently impaired. In the 1857 Dred Scott decision, a reactionary Supreme Court added fuel to the fire by declaring that, according to the Constitution, blacks were "so far inferior that they had no rights."

The following year, New York senator William Seward called the battle over slavery "an irrepressible conflict," which meant that "the United States must and will, sooner or later, become either entirely a slaveholding nation, or entirely a free-labor nation." When John Brown executed his raid on Harpers Ferry the year after that, hoping to inspire widespread slave insurrection in the South, it was almost the last straw. The last straw was Lincoln's election in November 1860.

The slave states immediately began seceding that December and formed their own confederacy. Lincoln resolutely believed that a United States from which individual states could withdraw at will was not united at all. They had to be brought back into the fold, by force if necessary. To preserve the Union, he reluctantly provoked a war.

Lincoln knew well that if he was going to win that war he needed the help of the biggest, wealthiest metropolis in the North. What he did not know was whether he could count on that help. In fact, he had good reason to doubt it.

New York City would play a huge role in the war, but it would be a hugely confused and conflicted one. No city would be more of a help to Lincoln and the Union war effort, or more of a hindrance. No city raised more men, money, and matériel for the war, and no city raised more hell against it. It would be a city of patriots, war heroes, and abolitionists, and simultaneously a city of antiwar protest, draft resistance, and sedition. As America fell into sectional conflict, New Yorkers fought their own civil war among themselves. It was even, in some ways, a localized clash between North and South.

From the South came cotton, far and away the city's most important commodity in the decades preceding the war. Cotton threads tied New York to the South and to plantation slavery in a long, intimate, and co-dependent relationship. From New England came Yankee émigrés who brought abolitionism with them, and were among Lincoln's most influential supporters.

The contest between these forces for the heart and soul of the city in the decades before the war helps explain why New York's actions and attitudes during the war can appear so schizophrenic. The same New York banks that funded the spread of plantation slavery across the Cotton South would provide the start-up capital for the Union war machine that ended slavery. New York merchants outfitted both. The port of New York, which was a hub of both the international cotton trade and the transatlantic slave trade up to the start of the war, became the chief port of the Union navy. New York City gave the Union army some of its bravest and most gallant officers, including the first one killed in the conflict; it also sent some of the most corrupt and insubordinate, including one who came within an ace of single-handedly losing the Battle of Gettysburg.

Without his New York supporters, it's highly unlikely Lincoln would have made it to the White House. Yet the majority of New Yorkers never voted for him and were openly hostile to him and his politics. Throughout the war New York City was a nest of antiwar "Copperheads" and a haven for deserters and draft dodgers. New Yorkers would react to Lincoln's wartime policies with the deadliest rioting in American history. The city's political leaders would create a bureaucracy solely devoted to helping New Yorkers evade service in Lincoln's army. Rampant war profiteering would create an entirely new class of New York millionaires, the "shoddy aristocracy." New York newspapers would be among the most vilely racist and vehemently antiwar in the country. Some editors would call on their readers to revolt and commit treason. A few New Yorkers would answer that call. They would assist Confederate terrorists in an attempt to burn their own city down, and collude with Lincoln's assassin.

CHAPTER 2

City of Slavery

The City of New York belongs almost as much to the South as to the North.

—*William Cullen Bryant*

In the first half of the nineteenth century, New York City had experienced its own surging growth at the same time as the rest of the nation, astonishing everyone who witnessed it. The metropolis owed much of its growth and success to its splendid geographical situation, nestled in one of the finest deepwater harbors in the world, with the East River on one side of Manhattan and the Hudson (or North) River on the other. The East River had year-round access to the Atlantic that, unlike the port's nearest rivals, Boston and Philadelphia, was very rarely blocked by winter ice. After the nearly disastrous War of 1812 ended, New York quickly made itself the primary American port trading with Britain and Europe, while its rivals fell far behind. The first four New York–built ships of the Black Ball Line, the first regularly scheduled "packet" ships carrying mail, news, cargo, and passengers between New York and Liverpool, started sailing in 1818. The crossing from New York, with prevailing westerly winds filling the sails, typically took three weeks; the trip back, against the winds, could take eight. Twenty years later, the first Atlantic steamships slashed the crossing to a miraculous twelve days.

Through the colonial period New England shipyards had dominated American shipbuilding. But by the 1830s shipyards on both sides of New York's East River were turning out more wooden vessels than any other port. They ran the gamut from large, world-crossing clippers to paddlewheel steamers to coastal schooners and sloops to canal boats and tugboats. Some of the largest and fastest wooden ships that ever sailed were launched on the East River. This industry provided work for "thousands of shipwrights, sailmakers, engine and boiler makers, carpenters, joiners, blacksmiths, riggers, chain and anchor makers," and other craftsmen. On the Brooklyn side of the river, the muddy Wallabout Bay, where hellish British prison ships had anchored during the Revolution, became the Brooklyn Navy Yard in 1806. It would play a large role in the Civil War.

By the early 1850s sixty piers ran up the east side of Manhattan, and on any given day they were crowded with upwards of nine hundred ships of all different types, their masts a forest, their bowsprits lancing over South Street, which ran along the waterfront. Local fishermen's boats jostled to get their catch into the Fulton Market. Ferries beetled over to Brooklyn and back; there'd be no East River bridges until after the war. South Street was a daily pandemonium of heaving, shouting longshoremen and crowding carts and wagons, busily hauling crates, boxes, barrels, and bales on and off the ships. The west side of South Street was lined with merchants' offices and warehouses, shipping company offices, sail lofts, sailors' taverns, and, as a writer put it in 1857, "those indescribable stores, where old cables, junk, anchors, and all sorts of cast-off worldly things, that none but a seaman has a name for, find a refuge."

On the other side of Manhattan, more than fifty piers spiked out into the Hudson as well. The wide and deep river connected the city to the state capital of Albany. Robert Fulton launched his first steamboat on the river from the Christopher Street dock in Greenwich Village in 1807. His wealthy backer was Robert Livingston, who had met Fulton in Paris while negotiating the Louisiana Purchase for Jefferson. Soon the Hudson was crowded with steamboat lines, whose owners—like Cornelius Vanderbilt, known as "the Commodore"—made and lost fortunes in their cutthroat and sometimes deadly competition to monopolize the river. The completion of the Erie Canal in 1825 linked the city by way of the Hudson to the frontier farms and forests of the Northwest. The farmers sent wheat, flour, whiskey, and lumber east to the city, which sent supplies—and more farmers—west.

In 1860 the port of New York was the nexus of a web of trade routes that stretched around the world; up to New England; down to the South and the Caribbean; and west to California. It handled a greater volume of imports and exports than all other American ports combined. That made the port of New York enormously important to Washington. The Custom House in New York was the single largest source of income for the government of the United States in the antebellum period. In the 1820s tariffs collected on imported goods in New York covered virtually all of the federal government's expenses. Of the roughly $65 million in annual federal revenues in 1860, $56 million came from tariffs on imported goods, and more than two-thirds of those imports came through New York. Small wonder the position of collector for the port of New York was one of the most prestigious of all presidential appointments, almost as much as a cabinet spot. Hiring for a bureaucratic fiefdom of some five hundred agents and clerks also made the collector a very popular man in the city, and some collectors were not above lining their own pockets through the odd graft and bribe.

Imported cotton cloth, lace, muslin, hats and umbrellas, fancy ladies' shoes, jewelry and jewels (brought in by Charles Tiffany from 1837 on), fine furniture, china, tea, wines and spirits, musical instruments, and an endless array of other luxury goods unloaded onto South Street went straight to New York merchants' warehouses and showrooms, which expanded in the antebellum years to take over more and more spaces in lower Manhattan.

New York became "the great commercial emporium of America," as its merchants bragged. Shopkeepers poured into the city from around the country to see and order their wares. Local shoppers perused the merchandise in retail stores, a new phenomenon, like the ones that lined Broadway. The fancier shops were on the west side of Broadway, the less expensive ones on the east; locals called them the "dollar side" and the "shilling side." (The silver shilling was a relic of colonial days that remained in diminishing circulation into the 1800s. Two shillings equaled a quarter.) In the late 1840s, A. T. Stewart, a Scots-Irish immigrant and importer of Irish linens, bucked tradition when he built the city's first department store, the magnificent "Marble Palace," on the shilling side at Broadway and Chambers Street.

With the spread of retail, shopping became a pastime. Hordes of promenading shoppers, mostly affluent women out to see and be seen, crowded the sidewalks of lower Broadway, while the cabs and carriages that brought them choked the street. Following Stewart's lead, stores began displaying their wares in large street-level windows for the first time, and the term "window shopping" was born.

As a natural corollary to New York's becoming dominant in shipping and commerce, the city also developed into the banking and stock market powerhouse of the nation—the "capital of capital," as it has been called. In 1815 there were five banks in the city, including the two rival institutions started by Alexander Hamilton and Aaron Burr. Eighteen more were founded over the next two decades. The prodigious growth of the city's merchant class spurred them. Buyers from the rest of the country rarely paid up front; most merchants let them go home with their goods after signing promissory notes to send payment in, for instance, ninety days. The merchant could wait to be paid, or now he could take the note to a banker, who'd lend him the amount minus a commission. Early banks pooled their wealthy board members' resources for capital.

A new type, the savings bank, appeared in the 1810s to take deposits from the average citizen. Banks' investments in state bonds funded the completion of the Erie Canal, which flowed more commerce into the city. New York banks attracted the majority of the investment capital that came from Britain and Europe, which was crucial in financing, among other things, the westward expansion of railroads. From 1830 on, there were more banks with access to more capital in New York than in the next several largest cities combined, or in the entire Deep South. Meanwhile, Wall Street was organizing itself from loose gaggles of speculators meeting on the streets and in coffeehouses into the nation's preeminent stock exchange. New York had become, as one journalist wrote, "the banking-house of the continent," which "holds the lever that moves the American world."

Pulsing with money and commerce, jobs and opportunity, New York attracted newcomers (nicknamed "greenhorns") like iron filings to a magnet. They poured down from New England, in from the countryside, and from across the sea. In the single decade of the 1790s the city's population doubled to about 60,000 people; by 1820 it had doubled again. Starting in the mid-1840s, huge waves of European immigrants, mostly poor Irish and Germans fleeing starvation and political turmoil, swelled the city's ranks. In 1850 the population topped half a million, and by the 1860 census the city was bursting at the seams with 813,660 residents. Philadelphia, the next largest city in the country, had some 200,000 fewer. With another 267,000 living in Brooklyn, then still a separate city, the combined New York–Brooklyn metropolitan area dwarfed all other urban centers. (Manhattan, Brooklyn, and the other three boroughs wouldn't consolidate into the Greater City of New York until January 1, 1898.)

At first everyone lived crammed together in the southern tip of the island. When City Hall opened in 1811 it stood on the city's uptown frontier. Beyond that was all farm, pasture, bog, and wilderness, dotted with a few suburban hamlets like Greenwich Village. By 1830 the city had sent tendrils up as far as 14th Street, though most everyone still lived below Houston Street. Then came a thirty-year building spree that pushed development up the island a little beyond 42nd Street, though it was sporadic and patchy up that far, and three-fifths of the residents in 1860 were still crowded below 14th Street. Beyond 42nd Street, in what's now midtown, was still mostly a wasteland of rocky promontories and forlorn gullies in 1860. Central Park was under construction, and a few pioneering finer homes were sprinkled around it, but otherwise midtown would resist development until steam shovels flattened it in the 1870s. Those New Yorkers who could afford it followed the leading edge of development up the island in their ceaseless quest to put a little distance between themselves and the poor and working-class masses, who lived densely packed into miserable tenements in areas like the infamous Five Points, considered the most dismal and deadly slum in the Western world.

From around 1820 until the start of the Civil War, by far the most valuable product New York shipped out was Southern cotton. New York City's central role in the huge international cotton market goes a long way to explaining many New Yorkers' attitudes about Southern slavery. The city was more than just complicit in maintaining the institution. The plantation system and New York City spurred each other's exponential growth in the first half of the nineteenth century.

One of the ironies of New York's deep involvement and investment in Southern slavery was that it occurred at the same time that the city was ending slavery at home. Black slaves had come to Manhattan with the first European settlers in the 1600s. New Amsterdam actively imported slaves both for local use and for resale to other colonies. In the 1700s, although the Yankee ports of Boston and Newport, Rhode Island, carried on more of America's transatlantic slave trade, the practice was also a cornerstone of New York's shipping business. Some of colonial New York's most prominent families, whose names are still seen around the city—the Livingstons, Wattses, and Schuylers, for example—made their fortunes in the slave trade.

In 1794, Congress began passing a series of laws aimed at curtailing and eventually abolishing American participation in international slave trafficking. Five years later, New York State started the gradual abolition of slavery within its borders. New York slaves were manumitted (freed) at a very leisurely pace, to ease the sting for owners and give them plenty of time to sell their human chattel to slave states if they wished. On July 5, 1827, black New Yorkers finally celebrated Manumission Day with prayers and parades, though their rights were still severely curtailed. Only one in two hundred black New York males could vote. Voting rights for all black New York males wouldn't come until the passage of the Fifteenth Amendment after the Civil War, and New York wouldn't approve women's suffrage until 1917. Churches, theaters, courtrooms, public schools, ferries, and omnibuses were all segregated. Limited job opportunities were open to blacks, and they had to compete for them with hostile white labor organizations. Still, they were technically free. Of the approximately 813,000 people living in the city in 1860, about 12,500 were free blacks.

By then New York was almost as economically dependent on plantation slavery as the Southern planters were. Cotton was the key. Before the 1790s, Southern farmers planted little of it. Cloth woven from cotton was known to be cheaper, more versatile and practical than wool or linen, and cotton was almost effortless to grow in the climate of the Deep South. But there were giant problems with harvesting it. First, it had to be hand-picked in the fields, requiring armies of laborers. Then the fibers had to be separated from the sticky seeds, which was maddeningly slow handwork. A slave could take almost a year and a half to make a single five-hundred-pound bale. It just wasn't economically feasible. So cotton remained a luxury item, used in only about 4 percent of the clothing worn in Europe and America. Southern planters stuck with tobacco, their primary earner, along with rice, indigo, and other crops. But tobacco was exhausting the soil, and wetland rice presented its own difficulties. The value of these crops declined as competition from the Caribbean increased. Because of the cost of buying and maintaining slaves to work these crops of decreasing value, it was widely assumed in the later 1700s that slavery would fade away of its own inutility.

Then in 1794, Eli Whitney, a New England schoolteacher posted to the South, patented an improved version of the cotton gin, a simple hand-cranked machine for combing the seeds out. Whether he actually invented the machine, as generations of American schoolchildren have been taught, is now in question. Regardless, this new gin quickly grew in popularity as planters recognized its potential. Where a slave could previously clean a pound of cotton a day, the gin produced fifty. With improvements over the next several years, the gin was churning out a mind-boggling one *thousand* pounds a day.

It would be difficult to overstate the transforming impact the improved cotton gin had on the country. In 1792 the South exported half a million pounds of raw cotton. The first year the gin was widely employed, the output tripled. By 1800 it was up to 18 million; by 1820, 128 million. In 1860, America exported more than two *billion* pounds. That was two-thirds of the world's cotton. The total value of American exports that year was $188 million; cotton represented $112 million of that, or roughly 60 percent. Flour and tobacco were only around $10 million each. By the end of the century nearly 75 percent of the clothes worn in Europe and America would be made of American cotton.

To Southern planters, cotton seemed a miracle plant. They came to call it King Cotton. The more they grew, the more the world wanted. All they needed was more land on which to grow it and more manpower to harvest it. Through the first half of the 1800s, despite rising land values in response to their nonstop buying spree, and falling prices per pound as they flung millions and then billions of pounds of cotton onto the market, planters kept expanding their acreage, transforming the Deep South from Florida to central Texas into one vast zone of plantations, some small, some huge. On the eve of the Civil War there were some seventy-five thousand of them.

All that cotton still needed to be handpicked in the fields—no machine for doing that effectively would appear until the 1930s. The falling price of cotton meant that the expenses of fielding armies of cotton pickers had to be kept as low as possible. Thus the improved cotton gin and the resulting spread of plantations made slavery seem not only viable again but absolutely necessary.

There were around seven hundred thousand slaves in the South in 1790. By 1860 there were more than four million, 40 percent of the total population of the South (and 95 percent of all blacks in the country). Seven of ten of them worked directly or indirectly in cotton. This explosive growth in the slave population was not fed from Africa, since Congress had banned the transatlantic trade. Rather, owners in the Upper South (states like Tennessee, Virginia, and Kentucky that were outside the cotton-growing zone) sold about a million of their slaves to planters in the cotton states. The saying "sold down the river" comes from this period. Slaves were in such demand that it was a seller's market. The price for a healthy slave tripled by 1830 to as much as $1,000 (roughly $30,000 today).

And yet the planters kept buying more land, and more slaves to work it. Ownership of land and slaves became not only a business proposition, but a foundation of pride and status. It developed into a kind of mania— and a program for perpetual debt. Traveling around the South for the *New York Times* in the 1850s, Frederick Law Olmsted noted the planters' "impulsive and unreflective" business methods and the "almost universal passion" among them "for increasing their negro-stock" no matter how much debt they incurred doing it.

That debt was one of the links binding the plantation South to New York City. To finance the continuing expansion of King Cotton's realm, the South naturally turned to the financial powerhouse of the nation. It was largely New York banks that provided them the loans to buy more land and slaves, as well as bridge loans to get them through lean years of bad weather, fluctuations in the market, and the often long lag time between sending off their crop and its final sale. Usually planters didn't deal directly with the New York banks, but through commissioned middlemen in Southern cotton seaports, who were called factors. Some factors were Southerners, but many were transplanted New Englanders and New Yorkers, and all had connections to New York's banks and merchants. Adding to planters' expenses, factors charged them a percentage to sell their cotton at the highest possible price, buy their goods and supplies for them at the lowest, and arrange their loans and lines of credit.

The South deepened its dependence on the North in other crucial ways. Instead of building their own mills, Southerners shipped the raw cotton up the coast or across the Atlantic. Spinning cotton stimulated the industrialization of New England, where nearly five hundred mills sprang up. England already had three thousand mills, which had been spinning cotton from the Mediterranean and Asia. They devoured every ounce of raw cotton the Americans could send them.

Almost all the cotton cloth spun in those mills for Americans to wear came to New York to be sold. Boston's merchants were closer to the New England mills, but since all the country's buyers of other merchandise were already coming to New York, the cloth was sent there as well. With all that cloth available, the city became the nation's center of the ready-made clothing industry. The Brooks brothers and future mayor George Opdyke were among the leaders of the field.

New York City also grabbed a significant share of the shipping of cotton, in what came to be known as the Cotton Triangle. The South had its own deepwater ports, including New Orleans, Mobile, Charleston, and Savannah, that had always shipped tobacco and rice directly across the Atlantic. New York's agents in the South made a good case that New York's regularly scheduled packet ships gave it the most timely intelligence on fluctuations in the cotton market overseas, making it the best port to ship from. Besides, the plantation economy had become so dependent on New York in other ways that the city could demand and get a share of the shipping as well. New Orleans shipped the bulk of its cotton directly to Boston or Liverpool, but New York was still able to reroute a quarter of it. Mobile, which was particularly thick with New York factors, shipped almost all its cotton to New York first.

By the 1820s the triangle was well established. Coastal schooners and sloops brought cotton up to the East River, where the bales were offloaded and stacked on South Street wharfs. They were then loaded onto larger New York ships to make the Atlantic crossing to Liverpool or head north to the New England mills. Cotton came to represent a whopping 40 percent of all the goods shipped out of the port of New York. Of course, each step of this process added various handling charges, tariffs, and insurance fees to the planters' costs. In Liverpool those ships were loaded with cotton cloth and other goods to carry back to New York's merchants. Southern plantation owners, eager to live like the aristocrats they felt they were, provided a ready market for the luxury items among these imports. New York merchants also sold them more utilitarian supplies, from farm equipment to food and furniture. The merchants, who also operated through factors in the South, offered long lines of credit at standard interest rates, another debt link.

A web of other businesses in New York City thrived on the cotton trade as well. Shipbuilders and outfitters, shipping companies, captains and seamen obviously benefited. Unloading and reloading the cotton meant jobs for thousands of dockworkers. Keeping track of it all employed a small army of clerks. Buyers from the South and around the country would stay a week or two, sometimes longer, in the hotels and in the boardinghouses, dining out at the city's restaurants, taking in its various entertainments.

Some Southerners deplored what one called the "unmanly and unnational dependence" on the North. "By mere supineness, the people of the South have permitted the Yankees to monopolize the carrying trade, with its immense profits," one Southern newspaper editorial complained. "We have yielded to them the manufacturing business....We have acquiesced in the claims of the North to do all the importing, and most of the exporting business, for the whole Union....Meantime, the South remains passive—in a state of torpidity." It was estimated that forty cents of every dollar paid for Southern cotton went to New York and the North. Yet calls for the South to diversify its crops and to start building its own cotton mills and factories mostly went unheeded. The South lacked the accumulated capital to invest in any large-scale industrialization projects, and many Southerners resisted the idea anyway. "We are an agricultural people; we are a primitive but a civilized people," one Alabama politician said with pride. "We have no cities—we don't want them."

Southerners didn't let that stop them from enjoying visits to the biggest, busiest city in the country. Especially in the hot summer months, New York filled up with Southern families wealthy enough to treat it as their summer home away from home. There were an estimated one hundred thousand Southerners in the city in the summer of 1860, when the resident population was a little more than eight hundred thousand. They filled the hotels, restaurants, theaters, music halls, and shops. They went with their well-off New York friends to the beach at Long Branch on the New Jersey shore, the yacht races at Newport in Rhode Island, and the horse races upstate at Saratoga. They joined the New York Yacht Club and other elite associations where they could hobnob with and exert influence on the city's civic leaders. They were allowed by law to bring their slaves with them, so that enslaved blacks were common on the city's streets long after slavery was abolished in New York State.

Taken altogether, it was estimated that on the eve of the Civil War the South was pouring at least $200 million a year into the city's economy. Many of New York's most prominent families made at least some of their wealth directly or indirectly from the cotton trade. Cornelius Vanderbilt shipped cotton, along with many other products, and passengers. The young J. P. Morgan studied the cotton trade in the South as part of his financial education. So did the son and grandson of Archibald Gracie, who built Gracie Mansion with cotton profits. George Opdyke, mayor for two years during the Civil War, started out selling plantation owners cheap clothing for their slaves. Lehman Brothers' founders were cotton merchants who moved to the city from Alabama in 1852 and would help found the New York Cotton Exchange.

The fact that the money some New York businesspeople made came directly from slave labor ruffled their consciences, though they still stuffed their pockets with it. Even the city's leading white abolitionist for a time, the dry goods merchant Arthur Tappan, did a large amount of his business with buyers from the plantation South.

Because of cotton, no city in the North was more pro-South, antiabolition, or anti-Lincoln. Many of New York's business, civic, and religious leaders defended the institution of slavery as staunchly as their Southern business partners did. Some New York newspapers were as ferociously racist and unwaveringly pro-slavery as any published in the South. One of the most stridently white supremacist papers anywhere was the *New York Day-Book*. Begun in 1848 to promote the interests of Southern slavery, it billed itself as "The White Man's Paper" and was filled with supposedly scientific and medical proofs of the inferiority of blacks and the rightness of enslaving them. It was widely read in both the North and the South.

⁓

Cotton wasn't the only way New York profited from slavery in distant places long after it ended at home. Right up to the start of the war, the city was a major American port for the international trafficking in African slaves.

On paper, this practice could get you killed. In 1808, Congress declared any ship found to be bringing African slaves into American ports liable to seizure and sale. In 1820, Congress made slave-running an act of piracy, a hanging offense. Banning the trade was an easy political gesture by then. America's domestic slave population was stable and growing. There was little need to import more slaves.

Conditions were the opposite in Cuba and Brazil, however, where slaves working on the vast sugar plantations and in the gold mines perished at appalling rates. Constantly hungry for new slaves from Africa, Cuba and Brazil bought at least two million of them in the first half of the nineteenth century. Running slaves to those countries was an extremely lucrative business: A single voyage might net over $100,000, about $3 million in today's dollars.

Americans found the lure irresistible—especially since the risks of being caught, convicted, and hanged were infinitesimal: Congress could pass its laws, but the rest of the government was extremely blasé about enforcing them. After all, the buying and selling of domestic slaves was perfectly legal in half of the country—including Washington, where a major slave market thrived within sight of Capitol Hill. No other country in the world held as many slaves. And it was very big business. The market value of the South's four million slaves was nearly $3 billion, "more than the value of land, of cotton, or of anything else in the slave states," James McPherson notes. Like most white Americans, the majority of government officials, from presidents (ten of the fifteen who preceded Lincoln were slaveholders) to customs officials and harbor marshals to judges and prosecutors, considered the forced removal of some black savages from the jungles of Africa to those in Brazil a trifling issue. Banning entrepreneurial Americans from making a dollar at it struck many as downright hypocritical and un-American. As *Harper's* noted at the end of the slave trade in the 1860s, "the sympathy of the Government and its officials has been so often on the side of the criminal, and it seemed so absurd to hang a man for doing at sea that which, in half the Union, is done daily without censure on land, that no one has ever been punished under the [1820] Act."

As the port of New York grew into the largest and busiest in the country, its involvement in the illegal Atlantic slave trade increased proportionally. By the 1850s it was an open secret that New York was the North's major slaving port. New Yorkers owned and invested in slave ships and financed their voyages. New York shipyards fitted them out. New York's corrupt and easily bribed port authorities turned a blind eye. In 1865 the *Evening Post* published a list of eighty-five slave ships that had sailed from New York bound for Africa in 1859 and 1860. The *New York Leader* claimed that two slavers a week left the harbor, and the *New York World* estimated that ships fitted out in New York carried up to eighty thousand slaves from Africa to Cuba each year.

At sea, slavers had little to fear from the small U.S. Navy. When England banned the slave trade in 1807, the Royal Navy became the main enforcer on the high seas, boarding slave vessels under any flag and impounding their human cargoes. It looked high-minded, but it was in fact a clever way to deny slaves to competitor nations and colonies. The Africans "freed" from other nations' slavers weren't sent home but taken to work in Britain's colonies in the Caribbean or West Africa.

The United States refused to cooperate with the British navy and expressed high indignation at the very idea of Crown warships stopping and boarding any U.S. vessel, slaver or not. America put to sea its own grandly named African Squadron, originally only four ships, patrolling off the West African coast. In the 1840s, the British seized five hundred slave ships carrying thirty-eight thousand Africans. The African Squadron caught seven.

In 1858, President Buchanan authorized a significant increase to the squadron, adding four fast steamers on the African side of the Atlantic and four more in the Caribbean. Ramping up the squadron was mostly an effort to challenge British dominance on the high seas. Whatever the motive, it resulted in the squadron's seizing twenty-eight ships from 1858 into the spring of 1861, when it had been averaging only one a year. During the Civil War, the United States finally agreed to cooperate with the Royal Navy's antislaver efforts, so that the squadron could be recalled and put to work blockading Confederate ports.

Most American slavers who were caught in the act were hauled to New York City to stand trial. They didn't have much to fear there either. Up to 1861, 125 slave ship captains and crewmen came to trial in New York City's federal courtrooms, where two judges in particular, Samuel Betts and Samuel Nelson, were notoriously lenient. The prosecutors were lackadaisical, and the juries of twelve white males were extremely loath to convict. The great majority of those 125 defendants were acquitted, or jumped bail, or otherwise disappeared. Only twenty of them drew convictions, and despite their obvious acts of piracy under the law were sentenced not to hang but only to an average two years' prison time. Of those twenty, ten received presidential pardons.

Of all the slavers tried in New York courts, only one of them would ever hang for piracy under the 1820 law, and he was as much a victim of poor timing as of judicial probity. One of the very last slavers to be arrested, he had the bad luck to be convicted after Lincoln entered the White House and the Civil War was under way.

CHAPTER 3

City of Confusion

New York City was not only the biggest, busiest city in America in the first half of the 1800s. It was also extraordinarily diverse. Drawing all those immigrants from all those places into the tiny speck of real estate that was lower Manhattan created a Babel densely crowded with languages, cultures, races, ethnicities, religions, and political opinions. Although a white Protestant elite dominated its society, and preserving pro-Southern business concerns loomed large in its politics, from the 1830s on it was a city often at war with itself, fighting in microcosm over the same issues that were driving the country at large to war.

When New York zoomed past Boston as a shipping and commercial center in the early 1800s, large numbers of New England merchants and entrepreneurs started to migrate there. They formed a noticeable Yankee subculture in the city of "Yorkers." Coming from a milieu of Puritan piety and Calvinist self-denial, they tended to be appalled by what a cauldron of sin and vice New York was. From its very start in the 1600s, New York had always been a party town. As it grew in the 1800s it was becoming as dangerous, sinful, and lawless as any Wild West town would be, a city of brothels, gambling rooms, opium dens, and a plethora of places to get a drink, from classier taverns to lower-class porterhouses to the lowest basement dives and the back rooms of grocers. Whores, muggers, pickpockets, and roving, brawling street gangs ruled much public space. The city's few score night watchmen and constables provided very little law enforcement. The Municipal Police wouldn't be organized until the mid-1840s, and they'd be so ineffective and corrupt that Albany would replace them with the state-run Metropolitan Police in the late 1850s.

Where the Yankees' ancestors may simply have condemned and avoided all that sin, this generation attacked it. They were inspired by the Second Great Awakening, the evangelical revival movement that swept through the country in the early decades of the century. In the South and West, Methodists and Baptists, with their energetic and ecstatic services, led the revivals. The Great Lakes corner of New York State saw so many revivals and new religious communities—including the Latter-day Saints, the Shakers, the Millerites, and the Oneida Society—that the evangelist Charles Finney dubbed it the "burnt region," also known as "the burned-over district," meaning that there were no more unconverted souls left to be fired up with the spirit. Even the staid Presbyterians and Congregationalists in New England leavened their grim Calvinism with the evangelical spirit.

Yankee evangelicals didn't limit themselves to reforming Christianity. Their reformist spirit spread in broad ripples through American culture. Evangelicals threw themselves into the temperance movement, trying to wean Americans from their admittedly ruinous levels of alcohol consumption. They burrowed into the destitute slums of the big cities with Bible tracts and the best intentions to reform the lives of the poor. They lobbied for universal education, arguing that ignorance bred sin. They became feminists.

And they were on the leading edge of the movement to abolish slavery in America. In New York, the white abolitionist movement would largely be identified with Yankee émigrés. Two of the most celebrated and vilified white abolitionists in the city were the Yankee brothers Arthur and Lewis Tappan. Arthur was born in 1786, Lewis two years later. They grew up in an evangelical household in Northampton, Massachusetts. Arthur moved to New York in 1815, drawn by the mercantile opportunities in the bustling port. By the time Lewis joined him in 1828, Arthur was one of the country's largest importers of silks and other dry goods—stockings, parasols, gloves, hats—that came back on the ships that had carried slave-grown Southern cotton across the Atlantic. He operated out of an imposing three-floor building of granite on Pearl Street facing the fashionable Hanover Square. Crates of goods shuttled to and from the nearby East River docks all day long. Buyers, many of them from the South, perused samples in the ground-floor shop, where Arthur allowed no haggling and, very unusual among New York's merchants, offered no long-term credit, which to him smacked of usury. He acted as a pious and strict patriarch to his young clerks, most of them Yankees entrusted to him by their parents for business training. They had to live in properly religious boardinghouses (Lewis himself took lodgings in one when he arrived), avoid liquor and tobacco and the theater, and hand in written proofs of regular church attendance. A room on the third floor at Pearl Street was used for prayer and readings of inspirational texts. Arthur was just as strict with himself, lunching daily on a few crackers and a glass of water.

In 1827 Arthur founded a newspaper, the *Journal of Commerce*, which combined business and shipping news with a mission of morally uplifting the wicked metropolis. Its primary targets, he wrote, were "the theatres, and particularly the indecent dancing there; and the desecration of the Sabbath, and the use of intoxicating drinks." The Sabbatist argument was a very tough sell in New York City, where most workers had only Sundays off and resented anyone trying to close their bars and places of entertainment. The *Journal* appeared every day except, of course, the Sabbath, and refused advertisements from any establishments Tappan considered bad influences. After a couple of years he would sell it to two of its editors, Gerard Hallock and David Hale.

As he prospered, Arthur became one of the city's most generous philanthropists, backing a wide variety of reformist causes and missionary movements. He was a significant donor to seminaries that trained evangelical missionaries, including Lane Theological Seminary in Cincinnati, where his future pastor Henry Ward Beecher would be trained. He funded the American Bible Society and the American Tract Society, which distributed millions of pages of Protestant literature from the western frontier to the big eastern cities. Lewis himself regularly marched through Wall Street and the Five Points handing out this literature. He was a principal in the Magdalen Society, a home for the reform of prostitutes, which published a report on widespread vice in the metropolis that city boosters denounced as wildly exaggerated slander. In the late 1820s Arthur led the fund-raising drive for the construction of Clinton Hall at Beekman and Nassau Streets; it was a new home for the Mercantile Library, a reading room and lecture hall where Yankee clerks evaded the licentious lures of the wicked city.

Even though plantation slavery was, directly or indirectly, a foundation of his business, for a white man of his time Arthur Tappan was unusually sympathetic to and friendly with black New Yorkers. He first came to abolitionism through his associations with the city's black church leaders. From the 1600s on, black New Yorkers had carried out a very pragmatic form of abolitionism, buying their own freedom, then working hard and saving up to buy it for family and relatives. It says much about the era that the first white abolitionist societies refused membership to blacks, even to leading black abolitionists such as the Reverend Peter Williams Jr., one of Tappan's guides into the movement. Williams was born into slavery in the city in the 1780s. His parents bought their freedom and his father established a small tobacco factory and shop on Liberty Street in what's now the financial district. They were also principals in founding what became the flagship Zion African Methodist Episcopal Church. Peter grew up to be a leading spokesman for abolition, and overcame resistance from white church leaders to become the rector of the Episcopalian Free African Church of St. Philip. He was also a cofounder, in 1827, of *Freedom's Journal*, the first black-owned and -run newspaper in the country, published in Greenwich Village.

With Williams and other black church leaders, Tappan founded the Phoenix Society for young males and the Dorcas Society for females, basically a book and lecture club "to promote the improvement of the colored people in morals, literature, and the mechanical arts." Tappan often collaborated with and financially backed Samuel Eli Cornish, founder of the First Colored Presbyterian Church. Tappan and Cornish once strolled together into a service at Samuel H. Cox's all-white Presbyterian church on Laight Street. It caused a ruckus among the congregation, but helped turn Reverend Cox into an abolitionist.

For all that, Arthur was never one of abolitionism's radicals. Sounding too strident on slavery would jeopardize his business and make him a lot of enemies, not just in the South but among his fellow New York businessmen. Early on he backed the American Colonization Society, which was founded on the conviction that blacks and whites would never learn to live freely and equitably with each other, so it was better for blacks to "return" to Africa and populate Liberia. While the ACS drew support from a variety of well-intentioned white leaders, few black leaders ever endorsed it, only small numbers of black Americans opted to go to Liberia, and many of them died as a result of the miserable conditions there.

In 1830, when he heard that a young New Englander named William Lloyd Garrison had been jailed in Baltimore for slander—he'd accused a man of owning a slave ship—Arthur bailed him out. Garrison was already becoming the nation's most fiery white abolitionist when he came to New York for a private meeting with Tappan. Impressed by Garrison's ardor, Arthur funded the start-up of Garrison's Boston newspaper, *The Liberator*, and began a milder New York sister paper, *The Emancipator*. He also backed the creation of Garrison's New England Anti-Slavery Society.

When Great Britain moved in 1833 to begin ending slavery in its colonies, Garrison felt emboldened to press more passionately for its instant eradication in America, which he called "immediatism." Tappan followed his lead, gingerly. He announced a meeting at Clinton Hall to form a New York Anti-Slavery Society. This meeting would result in the straitlaced businessman's first close call with an angry antiabolitionist mob.

⁓

Early one morning in August 1831, the young Horace Greeley stepped off a Hudson River steamboat onto the dock at Whitehall in lower Manhattan. He was twenty years old, "knew no human being within two hundred miles," had ten dollars in his pocket and all his belongings "tied up in a pocket-handkerchief." No one who saw him could have guessed what a famous and influential man young Greeley would become, though they might have divined how eccentric and often inscrutable he'd be. Brilliant, excitable, and extremely flighty, he was going to found the most loved and hated newspaper in America. In a city where so many business, civic, and religious leaders were pro-South and pro-slavery, he would be the loudest and often shrillest voice of the opposition. In a city that would never vote for Abraham Lincoln, he'd be Lincoln's champion, if also one of his most bedeviling gadflies.

Called "Hod" by his family, Greeley had barely survived his birth in 1811 on a New Hampshire farm where his father struggled to scratch a subsistence out of the pebbly soil. "I was for years a feeble, sickly child," he wrote in his 1872 autobiography. He grew up pale and frail, with squinting watery blue eyes, his voice a nasal whine, his nerves so highstrung that he was "unable to watch, through a closed window, the falling rain, without incurring an instant and violent attack of illness." He was probably bipolar, flying high through periods of superhuman workloads, then plunging into blackest depression, known in his time as "brain fever." He was an intellectual prodigy, and became a classic example of what his hero Henry Clay called the Self-Made Man. Though wretchedly poor and haphazardly schooled, he was "an eager, omnivorous reader" who devoured new ideas, especially political and social ones, like they were food or air.

When Hod was fifteen his father apprenticed him to a Vermont newspaper, the *Northern Spectator*, while he hauled the rest of the family west to Erie County, Pennsylvania. Western Pennsylvania was still on the frontier in the 1820s. Mr. Greeley and other pioneers hacked small farms out of the forest one tree stump at a time, using the trees to build their log cabin homes. Horace toiled on the *Spectator*'s big, ancient hand-cranked printing press until 1830, then rejoined his family, traveling hundreds of miles on foot and by canal boat to reach them. A few years later he would help make the image of the humble log cabin at the edge of the primeval forest an enduring American symbol.

At the end of the summer of 1831, Hod said goodbye to his family again. Determined to make his own way in the world, he headed back across the state of New York by the new Erie Canal to Albany, then down the Hudson to New York City. The country lad with the fragile nerves was barely prepared for the brutal physical assault that was the nation's most dense and bustling metropolis in summertime. Much of the city's population of roughly 250,000 was still crowded into lower Manhattan below Houston Street, where they rushed around at a hectic pace remarked on by every visitor. The skyline was squat and unlovely, spiked here and there with church steeples. A five-story building was a skyscraper. This was just as well, because the hand-pumped water from the volunteer firemen's hoses couldn't reach any higher, and the city was a tinderbox where fires were a daily hazard.

Just the noise alone must have been agony to Hod—the clatter of iron-banded wheels and clopping of hooves on granite paving stones, the shouts of hundreds of drivers and peddlers, the fire bells and church bells, the clangor and din of workplaces and warehouses and shipyards and docks, the never-ending rumble of tens of thousands of feet. It was a filthy place as well, and in the summer it reeked. The inhabitants dumped their garbage in the streets, where roaming brown-backed pigs were the only removal service. There was no indoor plumbing; everyone used chamber pots or outdoor privies, the noxious contents of which often spilled into the streets as well, where the human waste mixed with the droppings of the thousands of horses that pulled omnibuses, cabs, carts, and carriages. Sidewalks of wooden blocks, introduced in the 1830s, scarcely helped to lift one's heels or hem out of the muck. In heavy rains knee-deep puddles swirling with unspeakable things blocked many streets. There were no sewers; thirty years later, at the start of the Civil War, still only a third of the city would have them, and they often backed up into the streets anyway. Adding to the miasmal stench were the clouds of disgusting odors billowing out of the many slaughterhouses, rendering facilities, and tanneries packed into the lower end of the island.

The Collect Pond, once a major source of fresh water, had become so polluted that it was nicknamed the Colic Pond and was filled in shortly before young Greeley arrived. The site remained soggy and pestilential, and the infamous Five Points slum was growing on and around it. Construction of the Croton Aqueduct wouldn't begin until 1837, so fresh water was at a premium. People drew hard, brackish well water from pumps on street corners at their peril, or bought fresher water, drawn from wells up the island, for two cents a pail from vendors who trundled wooden casks marked "Tea Water" around the town. Residents who had the space collected rainwater in cisterns; homemakers preferred this softer water for washing fine clothes. When the midtown Croton Reservoir finally opened in 1842, the whole parched city joined the celebration. But many of the poor jammed into the slums would have no access to Croton water; theirs still came from wells often fouled by their leaky outhouses. At the same time, what passed for milk was a thin, sickly liquid squeezed out of diseased cows in dank back-alley pens. Vendors stirred in chalk to whiten it. It's no wonder New Yorkers preferred to drink distilled and fermented liquors morning, noon, and night.

Even the ferries across the rivers were deplorably unsanitary. The *New York Mirror* in 1836 would complain that they were usually "jammed with a heterogeneous mass of live and dead stock; hucksters and their miscellanies; milkmen with their pans; hay-carts, wagons, drays, men, women, children, pigs, sheep, ducks, pigeons, geese, eggs, hens, clean and unclean things, all promiscuously huddled together."

Given these crowded, filthy, soggy conditions, outbreaks of cholera and yellow fever (a.k.a. yellow jack) were regular summer occurrences. The summer after Greeley arrived, a great cholera epidemic ravaged the city. The city's wealthy elite escaped to suburban Greenwich Village and beyond, leaving the workers and poor to sicken and die on their own. All businesses except for "Doctors, Undertakers, Coffinmakers, &c" shut down, according to one newspaper, reducing the city to a grim ghost town.

Although Greeley would become one of the most recognized figures in this roiling, stinking city, he was never quite at home in it. To sharp-dressed New Yorkers he would always seem a bumpkin and an odd-ball. They smiled to see him shuffling around the crowded streets, tall but stooped in his rumpled clothes, his pockets stuffed with papers. His friend P. T. Barnum would describe him as a "gangling, wispy-haired, pasty-cheeked man, high-domed and myopic, with the face of somebody's favorite grandmother." Yet, like Lincoln, Greeley would turn his lack of physical grace into an asset, winning a huge national following by play-ing, as cultural historian Constance Rourke put it, "the avowed rustic, the homely sage." He took to wearing long, loose overcoats of white Irish linen in all seasons, with a crushed white hat to match. He looked more like a coachman than a newspaperman. It became his ridiculous, disarm-ing signature look, often remarked on, captured in photographic portraits and in Thomas Nast's cartoons. When he could afford it in the mid-1840s, Greeley would buy a house on ten woody, gloomy acres in Turtle Bay, now the site of the United Nations complex, then still remote and rural. To get down to his office in the city he took one of the horse-drawn stages that ran on the Boston Post Road (now Third Avenue) once an hour. In the 1850s he would also buy a farm up the Hudson in Chappaqua, where he would seek retreat from the cares and stress of city life.

For his first couple of years in the city he picked up short-term typeset-ting and printing work at various newspapers. He eventually took a room in a respectable boardinghouse run by devotees of Sylvester Graham, a fellow New England transplant and inventor of the graham cracker. Mix-ing religion with the "science of health," Graham advocated a spartan regimen—no meat, spices, alcohol, tobacco, caffeine, or sweets; no sex; no corsets; hard mattresses; lots of sunshine and fresh air and exercise. Greeley met his future wife, Mary, at the boardinghouse. Her lifelong devotion to the bland and dusty Graham diet would come to dismay him—and their dinner guests—but he did remain a fresh air and exercise fiend, as well as an antismoker and temperance man.

Greeley arrived in New York at the start of an interesting period for the city's newspapers. They were about to renovate themselves, and he'd be one of the pioneers. The first half of the nineteenth century saw a rev-olution in printing technologies. At the start of the century, the hand-cranked printing press, like the one Greeley labored over in Vermont, had not changed much since Gutenberg's time. It had an output of about five hundred pages an hour. In the 1810s the steam-powered press, pioneered in England, increased that capacity by a factor of five. It was a big leap, but an even bigger one would come in 1843, in New York City, when Richard M. Hoe added the innovation of the rotary drum. Hoe's machine, aptly called the Lightning, boosted output to ten thousand pages an hour per cylinder. By the 1850s it would come in a variety of sizes, from the basic one-cylinder model to a ten-cylinder behemoth that stood two stories tall. Big newspapers would construct their buildings around their mammoth Hoe presses.

Steam also propelled the development of the railroads, which carried big-city newspapers out to the frontier. Weekly digest editions of New York papers would travel by train to huge and wide-flung readerships around the country, making them the first national newspapers.

By the mid-1840s telegraph lines would be linking New York to other East Coast cities from Washington to Boston; by the start of the Civil War, coverage would spread through the South and Midwest, some fifty thousand miles of lines, owned and operated by half a dozen competing companies. The telegraph speeded up the transmission of news—newsmen called it "the lightning" as well—though it was so expensive that newspapers mostly used it for short news-flash dispatches before the war.

These industrial advances incited an explosive growth in newspapers. There were two hundred in the country in 1800. By 1850 there would be twenty-five hundred. That year New York City alone would boast more than one hundred newspapers and periodicals with a combined annual circulation of nearly eighty million copies.

Greeley helped start one critical phase of this revolution in the 1830s: the rise of the populist press, the "penny daily." When he arrived, New York had eleven daily papers—seven morning editions and four in the evening. They were all "six-cent journals," also known as blanket sheets, both for the size of their pages and for the soporific effect of their gray, dull columns of business and political news. Sold by subscription to the city's elite, they had a combined daily circulation of under twenty-seven thousand. The longest-lived was the august *New York Evening Post*, founded by Alexander Hamilton in 1801. In 1828 the New England poet William Cullen Bryant ("To a Waterfowl") began fifty years as its editor in chief. The two big morning dailies were the *Democratic Chronicle* and flinty Colonel James Watson Webb's *Morning Courier and New York Enquirer*. There was also Arthur Tappan's *Journal of Commerce*.

The idea of a daily newspaper for a general readership, priced at an affordable penny or two or three, floated on the rising tide of populist politics that swept through America in the 1820s and 1830s. Although most Americans, like Greeley himself, got only a few years of schooling, it was enough to lift the level of basic literacy quite high. Alexis de Tocqueville, who was beginning his famous travels around the country at the same time Greeley came to New York, was surprised to find that the "motley multitude" of Americans were far more likely to know at least their ABCs than were their counterparts in Europe.

On January 1, 1833, Greeley and two young partners gave the motley multitude of New York their first daily, the *Morning Post*. The partners priced it at two cents, and innovated the use of newsboys to hawk it on the street. (New York gentlemen had their blanket sheets delivered.) Unfortunately, a blizzard hit the city that day, clearing the streets of pedestrians for the next several days. The partners quickly dropped the price to a penny, but it didn't help. After less than a month they folded the paper.

So Greeley was watching with interest when Benjamin Day, another young printer recently arrived from New England, launched the first issue of his penny daily, *The Sun*, nine months later, on September 3, 1833. Working out of a small room on William Street, a couple of blocks east of City Hall, Day was publisher, editor, writer, typesetter, printer (on an old hand-cranked machine), and mail clerk, with one assistant. He filled much of his first four eight-by-eleven-inch pages with copy and ads clipped from the established blanket sheets. He printed a thousand copies. A typo on the masthead gave the date as September 3, 1832.

Where Greeley's paper had failed, *The Sun* caught on instantly. Already by December it was up to four thousand copies a day, rivaling the biggest papers in the city. By 1835 it was at twenty-two thousand. The hollering of Day's newsies around City Hall and Wall Street annoyed upper-crust New Yorkers, but attracted the milkmen, cartmen, barbers, and ferrymen who were *The Sun*'s prime audience. Day filled his columns with poetry, stories, fluff like "Wonderful Antics of Fleas," theater and book reviews (*The Sun* judged Dickens's new novel *Nicholas Nickleby* just as good as *Oliver Twist* and "not so gloomy"), and local police blotter items with added commentary. ("SUDDEN DEATH—Ann McDonough, of Washington Street, attempted to drink a pint of rum on a wager, on Wednesday afternoon last. Before it was half swallowed Ann was a corpse. Served her right.") It was much livelier and more entertaining than the copy that filled the gray established papers, whose editors responded by slagging *The Sun*; Colonel Webb of the *Courier and Enquirer* sneered that it was "penny trash."

Greeley meanwhile started a weekly, *The New-Yorker* (no direct lineage to the magazine), a mix of literary and theater reviews, poetry and stories, and his editor's column. He was for restricting the sale of alcohol, for opening up public lands in the West to settlers rather than speculators, and against capital punishment. On slavery he wrote, "We entertain no doubt that the system of slavery is at the bottom of most of the evils which afflict the communities of the south," yet he did not call for its immediate abolition, but rather the gradual and "ultimate extinction of the evil." He did not believe that freed blacks and whites could ever live in harmony, and he backed the efforts of the American Colonization Society.

⌒

Greeley also arrived in New York at the same time as waves of new Irish Catholic immigrants. The Irish had been coming to America since colonial times. But they were mostly Irish Protestants, educated professionals and skilled artisans who worked their way into and up the city's social hierarchy. This new group was another class entirely: poor, uneducated Catholic peasants and unskilled laborers, predominantly young males. They came fleeing poverty and prejudice, and found more of the same. Taking any kind of brute labor they could find, they lived crowded into the tenements and "vile rookeries" of the Lower East Side and the Five Points. There, in a curious quirk of history, they developed an intimate love-hate relationship with poor black New Yorkers. They lived together, worked together, played together, learned each other's music and dances, and slept together despite the authorities' constantly passing ordinances against race-mixing, called "amalgamation" at the time. They clung together to the very lowest rung of the city's social ladder. Racist stereotypes, bandied about with a complete lack of conscience by other New Yorkers, were startlingly similar for the Irish and the Negro: Both were lazy, drunken, sex-crazed, stupid, and apelike.

An early product of the intimacy of blacks and Irish on the Lower East Side was the rise of America's first pop music to go international: blackface minstrelsy. For all that minstrels went on about the plantation and My Old Kentucky Home, minstrelsy was a Northern, urban phenomenon. It was launched in the variety theaters on and around the Bowery in the late

1820s. Its first superstar, Thomas Dartmouth Rice, was the son of Irish immigrants, born and bred in the Five Points. Rice was minstrelsy's Elvis, and his hit song-and-dance routine, "Jump Jim Crow," was its "Hound Dog," played and sung around the world. To extend that metaphor, minstrelsy's Beatles, Dan Emmett's Virginia Minstrels, were also launched to stardom on the Bowery, a decade after Rice.

Early minstrelsy was far from the purely racist stereotyping that would characterize the giant minstrel shows after the Civil War. It was, like early rock and roll, much more a black-and-white mix, and expressed a confusion of imitation and insult, envy and mockery. Rice's Jim Crow character, for example, is a lame and clownish figure, but simultaneously a hero, a two-fisted frontiersman and ladies' man, a black Davy Crockett. Minstrelsy was the sound of young Irish men struggling to distinguish themselves from both their black neighbors and their white Protestant enemies in the big eastern cities. It would grow into the most popular music in America. Even abolitionists loved it. It was Abraham Lincoln's favorite music. Stephen Foster deplored slavery even as he wrote a number of blackface minstrels' greatest hits, which can be performed today only with sanitized lyrics. His contemporary Henry Clay Work was an abolitionist and son of abolitionists, yet still used many minstrel tropes in his songs, along with caricatures of Irish and German immigrants Americans would find appalling today.

As the numbers of Irish Catholics entering the city reached thirty thousand a year, the city's Protestants feared they were being overrun. They saw Catholicism as not only heretical but fundamentally antidemocratic and un-American, since all Catholics swore allegiance to a "foreign power," the pope in Rome. To evangelicals, the new Catholics were the Vatican's slaves, just as truly as blacks in the South were the plantation owners'. Lewis Tappan and other evangelicals fanned out through the Lower East Side handing out the Bible tracts Arthur paid to print, trying to convert the immigrant and break his bondage to Rome. The Irish deeply resented being treated like savage heathens. By association, if the Tappans were for abolition, the Irish decided they were against it. For all their good intentions, the Tappans and other abolitionists in the city helped to drive a wedge between poor blacks and the poor Irish that would have dire consequences in the coming decades.

While the abolitionists were making enemies of the Irish workers, antiabolitionist forces in the city were wooing and exploiting them. One of their favorite tactics, which they would use right into the Civil War years, was to scare workers with terrible predictions that if the millions of enslaved blacks in the South were freed they'd flood into northern cities and take away all the work.

When Arthur Tappan announced his meeting at Clinton Hall on October 3, 1833, to form a New York Anti-Slavery Society, James Watson Webb responded in the *Courier and Enquirer* by denouncing the abolitionists' "crusade against the white people of the United States" and calling for "patriots" to protest. The hall's worried administrators asked Arthur to hold his meeting elsewhere. Lewis proposed an alternative site. A year earlier he had rented a theater near City Hall that had gone through many names and managements over the previous decade. It had started out as the respectable Chatham Gardens Theatre and deteriorated into the low-class Blanchard's Amphitheatre, which presented equestrian and circus acts, featured a rowdy saloon, and was known for the prostitutes who trolled the all-male audience in the cheap third-tier balcony. No one missed the symbolism when Lewis "converted" this low Yorker resort into the Chatham Street Chapel and lured Charles Finney, one of the leading evangelists of the day, to serve as its first preacher.

While the abolitionists were meeting there, an angry mob of workingmen roused by Webb's rants, many of them but not all Irishmen, marched on Clinton Hall. By the time they'd redirected themselves to the chapel, the New York Anti-Slavery Society had been formed, with Arthur Tappan as its president and Lewis and the Reverend Peter Williams on its central committee. As the mob surged in the front door, the abolitionists escaped out the back. The mob dubbed a black man who happened to be on the premises "Arthur Tappan," demanded a speech, and then jeered and laughed him down. A couple of months later in Philadelphia, the larger American Anti-Slavery Society formed and elected Arthur as president, with Lewis and Williams on the executive committee.

The battles were just beginning.

CHAPTER 4

The Great Riot Year

Samuel F. B. Morse has come down to us as the man who won the inventors' race to patent the electric telegraph in 1837. Before that, though, he was known as a gifted portrait painter and a cofounder of the National Academy of Design. He moved to New York City and opened his first studio there in 1825.

Morse and his brothers Richard and Sydney were more transplanted New England evangelicals, born a preacher's sons in the Boston suburb of Charlestown. They were fiercely anti-Catholic. In 1834, Samuel wrote a series of articles for the *New York Observer* (no relation to today's), a religious weekly founded by his brothers, that was published as the widely read pamphlet *Foreign Conspiracy against the Liberties of the United States*. It described a supposed Vatican plot to take over America. Many Protestants believed it.

That same year, a rumor spread in Boston that a young Protestant woman was being held against her will at the Ursuline convent school in the Morses' hometown of Charlestown. Whipped into a conspiracy-theory frenzy by preachers like Lyman Beecher, father of Henry Ward Beecher and Harriet Beecher Stowe, a Protestant mob burned the convent and attacked nearby Catholics' homes in August 1834.

It wasn't an isolated event. There were so many instances of mob violence in 1834 that it came to be known as the Great Riot Year, and many sober city dwellers feared that full-on anarchy in the streets was imminent. Although New York outstripped all other cities, it wasn't the only one growing larger and more diverse at breakneck speed by the 1830s.

Cities from New Orleans to Boston suffered growing pains. Besides the conflicts between Protestants and Catholics, which were simultaneously conflicts between the new immigrants and the so-called Native Americans or nativists, the growing presence of the abolitionist movement brought increased racial tensions. The beginnings of industrialization came with mounting worker unrest and attempts to organize labor unions—which also led to racial tensions, as white workers froze black laborers out of job markets. Social stratification by class became more glaringly obvious. One way it expressed itself was in the escalating efforts by the upper orders to clean up the rampant drinking, whoring, gambling, and petty crime they identified as exclusively lower-class pathologies. The lower orders fiercely resented these meddling efforts. And competition between political parties, reflecting all these issues, turned more pugnacious.

New York, as usual, led the way. Of some two dozen outbreaks of urban mob violence around the country in 1834, thirteen occurred on New York streets.

The Tappans were again at the focal point of one of the more violent outbursts, which occurred in July of that year. White hooligans forced their way into the Chatham Street Chapel and started a fight with a black group meeting there. The next night a mob chanting Colonel Webb's praises and denouncing the Tappans broke into Lewis's home on Rose Street (now lost in a spaghetti of Brooklyn Bridge ramps, but then a quiet residential lane). Tappan had wisely moved his family up to Harlem that day, so the rioters entered an empty house. Arthur, his features disguised, watched as the mob smashed his brother's belongings in the street and then torched the house. When a mob surrounded Arthur's store, he armed his clerks for its defense. Rioters also caused such damage to Peter Williams's church that the city's Episcopal leadership demanded he renounce his association with the Tappans. The rioting continued through the week. The mayor finally called in the militia to restore order.

Arthur Tappan was shaken by the violence. He began to distance himself and his organizations from Garrison and the more radical abolitionists, but it was too late. His own brother got him into more hot water. In 1835, Lewis organized a massive publication campaign that mailed more than a million pages of antislavery literature around the country. The citizens of Charleston, South Carolina, broke into the post office, seized mailbags from New York, and made a bonfire of the contents, over which they hanged and burned effigies of Garrison, Reverend Cox, and Arthur Tappan. Southern courts indicted the Tappans for trying to incite Negro insurrection, and demanded their extradition to stand trial. A boycott against Arthur's wares spread through the South, and there was much talk of shifting trade away from all New York businesses. Committees of alarmed New York merchants pleaded with Arthur to give up the abolitionist cause before he ruined them all. Webb railed at the brothers almost daily in his editorials, boys jeered and spat at them on the street, and they both received death threats in the mail. Someone mailed Lewis a severed Negro ear. When Arthur moved from Manhattan to Brooklyn Heights (Lewis would as well), the mayor of Brooklyn personally kept watch at night outside his house. The loss of his Southern business would force Arthur to declare bankruptcy in 1838.

Lewis soldiered on. From 1839 into 1841, he organized the defense in the *Amistad* trial, working indefatigably to help African slaves who had revolted and taken over the slave ship to win their freedom.

~

On Lispenard Street, across town from the Chatham Street Chapel, a young associate of the Tappans named David Ruggles had an abolitionist bookshop. The 1834 rioters strangely left it unmolested. A year later, however, an unknown arsonist burned it down. Given the tenor of the times, it seems inevitable—because Ruggles's store was not only an abolitionist bookshop, but the first black-owned bookshop in the country.

Ruggles was a remarkable young man. He was born in 1810, the son of a blacksmith and a cook who'd been set free by their owner, Grover Cleveland's great-grandfather. David grew up in Norwich, Connecticut, a Congregationalist town with a significant free black community that during his childhood had relatively good relations with whites. That would end with the backlash against abolitionists in the 1830s. He went to sea at fifteen, shuttling up and down the coast, and settled in New York City in 1827, the year slavery officially ended in New York State. At eighteen he opened a small corner grocery shop at Broadway and Cortlandt Street and ran ads in *Freedom's Journal* with lines like, "Sugars above mentioned are free sugars—they are manufactured by free people, not by slaves." He embraced the temperance movement and stopped selling spirits, which set his store apart from many other grocery stores in the city that were actually just fronts for backroom grog shops.

After a fire ruined the grocery store, Ruggles traveled around the East as an agent for the Tappans' Anti-Slavery Society and *The Emancipator*. Then, while still in his early twenties, he started his bookshop. It was on Lispenard Street near St. John's Park, a spot he must have chosen with care. Recently carved out of the old Lispenard Meadows, it was in the 1830s a posh residential area for the city's elite. (It's now a cheerless roundabout jammed at rush hour with Holland Tunnel traffic.)

Among the works he displayed were his own pamphlets, arguing against the Colonization Society and calling for women's suffrage, and one collecting a few lectures and writings by another notable figure of the time, Maria Stewart. Born in Hartford, Connecticut, around 1803, she'd been orphaned as a child and indentured to a preacher. What book learning she acquired came in Sunday school. In 1831, Garrison published her first essay on abolition as a pamphlet, *Religion and the Pure Principles of Morality*. At events set up by Garrison she began giving public talks in 1832. Women didn't engage in public speaking in the 1830s. The feminist author Fanny Wright had created a huge flap by doing so in 1828. Stewart is believed to be only the second woman in America to speak publicly, made all the more controversial because she was black, speaking to mixed audiences of whites and blacks. In her second talk she exhorted black men to show more gumption in defense of their rights; they responded with angry shouts and tossed vegetables. Disheartened, she moved to New York City and apparently did no more public speaking, continuing her education and becoming a teacher instead.

After his shop was burned down, Ruggles opened a new one. He went on to help form the New York Committee of Vigilance, a group of black and white citizens who directly opposed "blackbirds"—bounty hunters who roamed the city trying to catch runaway slaves or, failing that, kidnapping free blacks and shipping them south into slavery, as happened to Solomon Northup, author of *12 Years a Slave*. Ruggles risked serious reprisal by publishing the names of known blackbirds operating in the city, and of New Yorkers, black and white, who assisted them.

In 1836 he fed the *Evening Post* information that a Portuguese slave ship had docked in the harbor. The captain, a well-known slaver named de Sousa, had about a dozen Africans on board and was slipping them off a few at a time to slavery in the South, unmolested, as was usual, by harbor authorities. The *Post* article led to de Sousa's arrest. His case went to Judge Samuel Betts, who, characteristically, set him free. Enraged, an armed black mob boarded the ship, which still held five Africans, and freed two of them at gunpoint. The specter of armed black men deeply disturbed white New Yorkers, who blamed Ruggles. One night some men tried to break into his home, claiming that they'd come to apprehend him as a fugitive slave. Constables arrived—and arrested Ruggles. He was quickly released, his already high esteem in the city's black community greatly enhanced.

At the same time, Ruggles was a key figure in the city's Underground Railroad. Slaves throughout the South came to know him as the man to see if they could escape to New York. He put up hundreds in his home at the corner of Lispenard and Church Streets (still standing), while arranging for them to continue north to greater safety. In 1838 a young fugitive from Maryland, Frederick Bailey, made his way by train and ferry to lower Manhattan. He'd been told to find Ruggles, but the city so frightened and confused him that he spent his first night hiding on the dock, just a few blocks from Ruggles's home. Ruggles found him there the next morning. Anna Murray, a free black woman from Baltimore with whom Bailey had fallen in love, joined him a few days later. They were married in Ruggles's home by the Reverend James Pennington, himself an escaped slave from Maryland. Ruggles gave the couple five dollars and sent them north to New Bedford, Massachusetts, a safe haven known as "the Fugitives' Gibraltar." There Bailey gave himself a new name: Frederick Douglass.

Not long after that, Ruggles's health and eyesight began to fail. In 1842 the New England abolitionist Lydia Maria Childs arranged for him to move to a commune in Northampton, Massachusetts. He died in 1849, at the age of thirty-nine.

The Chatham affair was not the first riot in the city in 1834. In April, New York City citizens had gotten to vote for their mayor for the first time. It was also the first time that the dominant Democratic Party, known colloquially as "the Democracy," and the new Whig Party went head-to-head in the city. Many heads were cracked.

Traditionally, municipal politics had been something of a sideshow in New York. From its start as a tiny fur trading post in the 1620s, the city was a company town, created for business and profit. It generally had a weak and laissez-faire local government, designed to stay out of the way of the business community and the flow of revenues to distant bosses—first in Holland, then in Britain, then in the state capital in Albany and the federal government in Washington. Despite its spectacular boom, New York City in the 1830s was still politically organized, as one historian has put it, like "an overgrown town," with a government unable to provide even minimal services. The lawless, filthy, disease-racked state of the city when the young Horace Greeley arrived was a direct result.

The more depraved and anarchic the city looked to its remote-control administrators up the Hudson, the more they tightened the reins, convinced that the locals could not be trusted to run it for themselves. The governor appointed the mayor until 1822, and the Common Council (city council) did so for the next twelve years after that. The mayor's office was a weak ceremonial position anyway. The real power to run the city was dispersed among the state legislature, the city's individual department heads, and the members of the Common Council, all with their own fiefdoms and agendas, and often with their eyes on as much spoils as they could grab. The mayor was most often a businessman who served at first for only one year, then for two, spending that short time leading parades and giving speeches at banquets before gracefully relinquishing the post to the next figurehead.

A giant city with a puny local government was a power vacuum waiting for a political machine to fill it. That machine was Tammany Hall. In the Revolutionary period the Sons of King Tammany, also known as the Society of St. Tammany and the Columbian Order, was little more than a patriotic wassail club, a Raccoon Lodge for artisans and small businessmen. "Tammany" came from the legendary Delaware chief Tamanend. Members were braves, and their elected chiefs formed a Committee of Sachems (chiefs), who chose from among themselves a grand sachem. The meeting place—usually a back room or upstairs of a tavern—was called a wigwam. Their main public function was to dress up as Indians for parades on July 4, Columbus Day (Tammany men were the first to celebrate it), and Tammany Day (May 12).

By the early 1800s, Tammany was fading away everywhere but in New York City, where it thrived. For a few years the New York lodge met in a hall at Martling's Tavern, on the corner of Nassau and Spruce Streets. This long room came to be known as Tammany Hall, which became synonymous with the organization. In 1812, Tammany built its first stand-alone wigwam a short way up Nassau at Frankfort Street, a corner that disappeared when the Brooklyn Bridge was built. It was five stories tall and featured a large meeting hall that could hold two thousand. The rest of the building operated as the Tammany Hotel.

Tammany might never have developed beyond a fraternal organization were it not for two sharp-witted outsiders who pushed its development for their own ends. First, Aaron Burr began molding Tammany into a machine in 1800, using it as a base in his competition with Alexander Hamilton for political control of the city. Then Martin Van Buren came along in the 1820s to complete the process.

Van Buren and Tammany rode the wave of populism that transformed democracy in America in the 1820s. The original republic was an oligarchy of landed gentry. The founding fathers were all landowners, and in many cases slave-owners. Only landowners could vote. As the founding fathers died off, the next generation—the first generation of Americans born in the republic—demanded more participation. As universal suffrage for white males spread in the 1810s and 1820s, the expanding base of voters totally changed the nature of politics. To tap and organize the new mass of voters required new mechanisms. Professional politicians, campaigning, two-party partisanship, and urban political machines all began to fall into place.

The machines grew because what was not in place yet was anything like a civil service exam, or a merit system for political appointments, or rigorous oversight of how politicians awarded government contracts and spent government money. For much of the 1800s governments from the municipal level up to the federal operated on spoils and patronage. The party in power rewarded the machine and loyalists who put it there with jobs (judge, postmaster, sheriff, and so on) and contracts (construction, printing, street sweeping, and so on). The more crooked politicians skimmed some off the top through kickbacks and other forms of graft. It's this era that gave us the quote "To the victors belong the spoils."

The wily son of an upstate tavern keeper, nicknamed "the Little Magician," Van Buren was a chief architect of the Albany Regency, a machine that manipulated power and patronage on the state level in the 1820s and 1830s. When he came to New York City, he saw that Tammany also had the makings of a powerful and profitable machine, and he began to shape it. With Tammany's support he got the state to amend its constitution in

1821 to expand suffrage broadly among white male citizens, as well as some free black males who owned property.

Nothing signaled the dawn of this new populist era like the 1824 and 1828 presidential campaigns of General Andrew Jackson, "Old Hickory," the roughest of rough-hewn frontiersmen, hero of the War of 1812, slaughterer of Indians and Brits and sometimes his own soldiers, duelist, slave-owner, whoremonger, gambler, drinker, and implacable foe of the eastern elite who had run the young nation until then. In 1824, Van Buren and his machines backed John Quincy Adams for president, who won. But when Jackson ran again in 1828, Van Buren put a finger to the wind and switched sides. His Albany Regency carried the state for Jackson, while Tammany delivered the city.

Tammany's efforts on Jackson's behalf were as rough and rude as their candidate. Tammany operatives illegally registered voters who included teens, and paid them to "vote early and often" for Old Hickory. Some "repeaters," as they were called, hit the same polling place over and over through the day, using a new false name and address on each visit. A bearded repeater was good for at least four votes. After voting once, he'd go get shaved down to a mustache and muttonchops, and vote again under a new name. Then the mustache would go, then the muttonchops. Tammany combed the cemetery rolls for dead men to resurrect on polling day, stuffed ballot boxes with false Jackson votes, and destroyed ballots for Adams. According to Tammany's rivals, they even got prisoners released from jail and escorted them to the polls. They also stationed goons with hickory sticks outside polling places to scare Adams voters. (Voting was not as private as we know it now. Before the late 1880s, when New York adopted the "Australian ballot" with all candidates printed on one form, each party had its own separate ballot. On entering the polling place in 1828, the voter requested either a Jackson or an Adams ballot, thus openly declaring his allegiance.) All this became election-day standard operating procedure in the decades leading up to the Civil War.

In 1832, Van Buren got his reward when the reelected Jackson made him his vice president. Tammany men planted a hickory tree outside the wigwam and watered it with beer to celebrate all the spoils they expected to come their way.

After Adams, Jackson's main opponent was Henry Clay, who formed the National-Republican Party to go up against him. Clay was a slave-owner from the South who adopted the West and often agreed with the prevalent politics of the North. Where many politicians of his time saw themselves as representing their particular region of the country, Clay had a truly national vision of all sections cooperating and making such sacrifices and concessions as needed for the good of the whole nation. Recognizing that slavery was the issue that could blow the union apart, he spent much of his long career trying to broker peace between the extremists on the pro- and antislavery sides. They called him "the Great Compromiser."

It's a measure of how hard it was at the time to sell a national vision that Clay went down to humiliating defeat in 1832 (not for the last time), and the National-Republicans fell apart. From the wreckage a new anti-Jackson party formed, calling themselves Whigs in the antimonarchical tradition (because, they said, Jackson was as despotic and autocratic as any monarch). Clay was a leading spokesman, along with the great orator from New Hampshire Daniel Webster, and three New Yorkers: the politician William Seward; his chief backer Thurlow Weed, editor of the *Albany Evening Journal*; and James Watson Webb. A loose coalition, the Whigs were more unified in whom they were against than in what they stood for. Abolitionists gravitated to them, for instance, but by no means were all Whigs abolitionists. Webb certainly was not.

In New York City, the Whigs—and the Republicans who came after them—were largely WASP and patrician, the party of the Yankees, a minority but a well-placed opposition to the Yorkers' Democracy and its larger base of immigrants and workers. The Whigs knew that to take the city they had to win over some of those workers, and both sides courted them with large rallies and raucous parades. Tammany had a virtual lock on the immigrants, so the Whigs wooed the nativists. That alone was enough to guarantee trouble. The balloting took place over three days, April 8–10, 1834. On April 8 in the contested Sixth Ward on the Lower East Side, Tammany toughs shoved their way into the Whigs' neighborhood meeting room and attacked the assembled with clubs and knives, even stabbing one man to death. Those "who escaped injury reached the street hatless, and with coats half-torn from their backs," according to J. T. Headley in his 1873 *The Great Riots of New York, 1712 to 1873*. Mobs of several thousand Whigs and Democrats clashed in the streets on the third day of voting, swinging fists and cudgels and hurling brickbats.

When the sitting mayor arrived and pleaded for calm the crowd pelted him with stones. He declared the city in a state of insurrection and called in the militia, who appeared on foot and horseback to disperse the mob. The voting yielded more confusion. Tammany took the mayor's office for their Democrat, but the Whigs won a dominant position on the Common Council.

⟶

Two years later, when the Democrats ran Tammany's friend Vice President Van Buren to follow Jackson in the White House, the Whigs were still too new and unformed to agree on a single candidate to oppose him. They ran four, each backed by his own faction, handing the victory to Van Buren.

Van Buren ran into trouble in his first year in office. Jackson had spent his second term warring with the East Coast establishment and what he saw as their most pernicious instrument, the central Bank of the United States. He withdrew federal funds from it and redistributed them among hundreds of smaller banks around the country, all of which issued their own banknotes. Jackson also opened large tracts of western land for sale, feeding a dangerously inflationary real estate bubble. Then he decreed that this land could be bought only with gold and silver, and the value of all that paper the banks had issued plummeted. When Van Buren took over, he inherited a time bomb that went off in the Panic of 1837, a wave of bank failures that brought widespread unemployment and six years of depression. Since he did little to ameliorate the disaster, people took to calling him "Van Ruin."

The Democrats' disaster was a potential windfall for the Whigs. In 1837, Thurlow Weed appeared unannounced at the cramped, cluttered *New-Yorker* office and found Greeley with his sleeves rolled up helping to set type. Weed was another self-made man who'd risen from log cabin poverty on his wits and ambition. Growing up near Albany a hardscrabble farmer's eldest son, he got his first job working a blacksmith's bellows at the age of eight, then was a cabin boy on a Hudson River sloop. At twelve he began working for a long line of printers and newspapers upstate and in New York City. He and Seward met when both were state assemblymen in the mid-1820s. By the time he founded the *Evening Journal* as a Whig organ in 1830, Weed was much more than just a newspaperman;

he was a cunning political strategist who wielded great power in the state and availed himself of all the spoils that came with it. They called him the Warwick of New York politics. In his autobiography Greeley would remember him as "shrewd, resolute, and not over-scrupulous."

Weed was promoting Seward for governor and had long-range plans for him to go all the way to the White House. He wined and dined Greeley to convince him to edit a weekly Whig campaign paper, *The Jeffersonian*. Through 1838, Greeley shuttled between New York and Albany, by horse-drawn sleigh in the winter, by the Hudson otherwise, producing two weekly papers. Seward won handily, and would serve as governor until 1843, establishing a record as a progressive antislavery and anti-nativist leader. At the same time, the "firm," as Greeley would put it, of Seward-Weed-Greeley grew very powerful in national Whig politics.

The Whigs now looked to the 1840 presidential contest. They went into their national convention in Harrisburg, Pennsylvania, still agreeing more on what they hated about the Democrats than on what they stood for. Southern and Northern Whigs were divided on slavery, and there was much other regional infighting. Greeley went there to support Clay. A thirty-year-old delegate from Illinois named Abraham Lincoln also attended, but apparently he and Greeley took no notice of each other yet. As both a proven failure and a slaveholder, Clay was anathema to Weed, Seward, and the party's abolitionists. To Clay's bitter chagrin, the party decided to go with a popular figurehead, the sixty-eight-year-old Indian fighter General William Henry Harrison, a political cipher whose claim to fame was having beaten Tecumseh's Indian warriors on the Tippecanoe River in Indiana in 1811. John Tyler, his running mate, was also a nonentity; a slave-owning Virginia plantation aristocrat and former senator, he had come over to the Whigs from the Democrats in reaction to the Democrats' increasing populism.

Greeley was disconsolate about the ticket but went to work. It was he who came up with the meaningless yet evocative slogan "Tippecanoe and Tyler Too." He developed Harrison's image as a rough-hewn man of the frontier—never mind that the old general had grown up on a Virginia plantation—and published a new weekly campaign newspaper, *The Log Cabin*, with an image of said cabin and a jug of hard cider on the cover. Its circulation peaked at a very impressive one hundred thousand, with many readers on the frontier in log cabins of their own. The whole campaign was folksy and of-the-people, featuring a *Log Cabin Songbook* and mass sing-alongs, parades, Tippecanoe buttons, Tippecanoe shaving soap. Harrison clubs in every town built their own log cabins in the town square.

The Whigs won a stunning upset. But Old Tip was in office only a month when he died of pneumonia on April 4, 1841, the first president to expire in the White House, making the startled Tyler president. Greeley nicknamed Tyler "His Accidency" and despaired that the Whigs had inadvertently put a slave-owning Southern aristocrat in the White House. Despised by Democrats and Whigs equally, Tyler would spend an ineffectual time in office.

CHAPTER 5

The War of the Pennies

On April 10, 1841, the same day that New York City held a somber funeral parade for Old Tip, Horace Greeley published the first issue of his new penny daily, the *New York Tribune*, to go up against *The Sun* and its first serious contender, the *New York Herald*, launched by James Gordon Bennett in 1835. Born into a relatively prosperous Roman Catholic family in the Scottish Highlands in 1795, a college graduate who'd studied for the priesthood before losing his faith, Bennett had sailed to America in 1819. In Charleston, South Carolina, he worked as a reporter and picked up the Southern affinities that would mark him as a "doughface," or Southern sympathizer, when he had his own newspaper. In New York in the mid-1820s he joined Tammany Hall but was put off by "the hollow-heartedness and humbuggery of these political associations and political men."

In 1832, after a few years of reporting for and feuding with Colonel Webb at the *Courier and Enquirer*, he quit and started his own daily, the *New York Globe*, which lasted only a month. In 1835 he tried to talk Greeley into starting another one with him. Greeley turned him down, so Bennett did it on his own, starting the *Herald* as a penny daily with five hundred dollars he'd scraped together. His first office was a moldy basement on Wall Street, his work surface some planks laid across barrels. Like Day, Bennett did most of the work himself at first. The *Herald* took off quickly, and in a few months was in the black. Within a year he moved to marginally better digs on Nassau Street and was gunning for Day. In an early editorial he vowed to "extinguish the *Sun* and put out the light thereof, to the great gratification of all persons of taste, good sense and judgment in this city." Day jabbed back that Bennett's "only chance of dying an upright man will be that of hanging perpendicularly upon a rope."

The era of objective journalism was still far in the future. Antebellum newspapers were highly personal affairs that reflected their editors' characters, politics, and prejudices. Editors freely expressed their low opinions not just of one another but of any public figure, especially politicians. Character assassination was routine. Sometimes the aggrieved victim of a particularly vile slur would sue for libel, but it was just as common to seek out the writer and settle it like men. In 1836, Bennett wrote that Webb was engaging in illegal speculation on Wall Street. The colonel found him on the street and gave him a public thrashing that went on for twenty minutes while bystanders gawked. Over time Bennett would take so many public beatings from men he'd somehow insulted or slandered in his paper that P. T. Barnum (no friend of the *Herald*) wrote in his memoir that "gentlemen were in the almost daily habit of cuffing, kicking and cowhiding Bennett in the streets and other public places for his scurrilous attacks upon them."

Bennett did more than sling calumny and get whipped for it. Being a former reporter himself, he valued actual newsgathering, rather than simply reprinting and pontificating, and was thus a chief inventor of modern professional journalism. As the *Herald* grew he would hire a small army of correspondents, forcing competitors to do the same. He would be the only New York editor to send a correspondent to the Mexican War in the 1840s, and would put more men on the front lines than any other during the Civil War.

Politically, Bennett aligned with the Democrats' most conservative wing. As early as 1835 he forecast that Northern agitation against slavery was going to pull the nation apart someday. He lashed abolitionists. In his more obstreperous editorials of the 1850s he would tend to use "Republican" and "nigger worshipper" interchangeably. Like most whites he took white superiority as self-evident. Blacks were slaves "simply because the great Creator has made them an inferior race," he wrote. "In the same community with the white man, the black, enslaved or emancipated, must forever occupy a degraded position." He argued that abolitionists would do better to concern themselves with the struggles of poor white workers than worry about "the sleek, well fed, fat negroes" in the South.

In 1838, partly as a victim of the Panic of 1837, Day was forced to sell

The Sun to his bookkeeper and brother-in-law, Moses Yale Beach. Meanwhile, Bennett's *Herald* sailed on. Bennett and Beach were not very far apart in politics, both pro-Democrat and antiabolition, and Greeley was disgusted with them both.

With money borrowed from friends, Greeley rented a decaying attic at 30 Ann Street for his offices. George Jones, who had worked with him back in Vermont, handled the business end. His all-purpose assistant, the twenty-one-year-old Henry J. Raymond, was a former farm boy like Greeley, from western New York. Unlike his boss, Raymond was a university graduate. A quiet young man, he was as steady and undemonstrative as Greeley was flighty and prone to excess.

Bennett's *Herald* and Beach's *Sun* were not pleased to be sharing the market with Greeley, and the sniping began right away. Greeley sneered that *The Sun* was "slimy and venomous" and the *Herald* "a very bad paper," while Beach accused Greeley of publishing "dirty, malignant" lies. Street fights broke out among their rival newsies.

Despite all the backbiting, they could cooperate when it was in their mutual interests. In 1849, Greeley, Bennett, and other newspapermen set aside their differences and pooled their resources to lease their own dedicated telegraph lines. They called it the New York Associated Press.

Their papers weren't just read in New York; taking advantage of special postal rates, they mailed significant numbers of copies to subscribers around the country. Weekly editions, like nineteenth-century versions of *Time* or *Newsweek*, became extremely popular. Out on the frontier, it was said, the weekly *Tribune* was as well read as the Bible. Frontiersmen lined the walls of their log cabins and outhouses with it, leading to the popular expression "reading the walls." By the time of the Civil War, Greeley's daily and weekly *Tribune* editions had a combined subscribership of around three hundred thousand throughout the North and Midwest. Given the way papers were passed around, he may well have had a million readers, from the working-class neighborhoods of New York to the edge of the prairies. In Illinois, Lincoln was a devoted reader. Greeley became known as "Uncle Horace," one of the highest-profile Americans of his time.

Besides the Whig Party, Greeley made the *Tribune* a platform for a wide range of new and progressive ideas that caught his flitting fancy. He promoted vegetarianism, temperance, spiritualism, socialism, phrenology, and feminism. He was a key conduit for Yankee intellectual and literary movements in New York City. He hired the Boston feminist Margaret Fuller, an inspiration to Susan B. Anthony and Elizabeth Cady Stanton. He was the earliest and most enthusiastic New York booster for the Boston Transcendentalists and the Brook Farm commune. He introduced the writings of Emerson and Thoreau to New York, which had a huge impact on at least one young New York writer, Walt Whitman. When the Brook Farmers disbanded in 1847, Greeley brought George Ripley from there to be his literary editor and Charles A. Dana as managing editor. Dana would take over the bulk of the day-to-day chores, freeing Greeley to write his eccentric editorials, travel, and pursue his political interests. Dana went to Europe to report on the failed 1848 republican uprisings in the German states. He introduced Greeley to the writings of Karl Marx, whose *Communist Manifesto* was published that year. The *Tribune* would print Marx's writing through the 1850s. Greeley was a most energetic promoter of the "communal socialist" movement called Fourierism, for the French philosopher Charles Fourier. Brook Farm was organized along Fourierist principles; Greeley helped found one of the longest-lived Fourierist communes, Sylvania, in what is now the township of Greeley, Pennsylvania.

Greeley believed that the vast lands of the West held the answer to the "filth, squalor, rags, dissipation, want, and misery" in the slums of the big eastern cities. When he was starting out he'd lived near the Five Points, and "saw extreme destitution more closely than I had ever observed it, and was able to scan its repulsive features intelligently." He believed the federal government should make it easy for the urban poor to acquire modest plots of land on the frontier, which they could work the way his father had. Much of his opposition to allowing slaves into the new lands stemmed from his conviction that opening the frontier to slavery would close it to free men. In the 1850s, proponents of this "free soil" position and those wanting to expand slavery would clash murderously in Kansas, and the *Tribune* would be closely involved.

⌒

One evening in June 1844, near the end of his time in office, President Tyler came to New York City and, in a private ceremony at the Church of the Ascension on Fifth Avenue at 10th Street, married Julia Gardiner. It was a union of Old New York and Old Virginia dynasties, highly symbolic of New York City's close ties to the plantation South. The Gardiners had settled Gardiners Island out at the forked tip of Long Island in the 1630s. Down through the generations the head of the household was known as the Lord of the Isle. Slaves worked on the island until slavery ended in the state in 1827. Born in 1820, Julia would easily adapt to her role of plantation mistress as Tyler's wife.

Tyler declined to run for reelection in 1844. The Democrats ran a Jacksonian from Tennessee, James K. Polk. Henry Clay secured the Whig nomination. Greeley stumped tirelessly for him. He filled the *Tribune* with pro-Clay editorials, started a separate *Clay Tribune*, wrote a steady stream of letters, and gave almost daily speeches, until he was covered with nervous boils and on the brink of complete physical collapse. Polk won by the slimmest of margins. Clay, who was used to defeat, took it stoically. But Greeley, declaring himself "the worst-beaten man on the continent," suffered one of the attacks of brain fever that would drag him down periodically throughout his life.

The Tylers quietly boarded a boat for Richmond on the night of Polk's inauguration. Although she missed New York and Washington, Julia fit right in as mistress of Sherwood Forest, Tyler's plantation near the James River on the Virginia Peninsula. She'd still be there when Union troops, including several units from New York, invaded the Peninsula in 1862.

Greeley and the Whigs protested when Polk welcomed Texas as a slave state in 1845. It was to be the last slave state admitted to the union, but no one knew that yet. The following year, Whigs howled when Polk used border disputes between Texas and Mexico as a pretext for war. They saw it as an excuse to spread slavery even farther in the West. In the *Tribune*, Greeley cried, "People of the United States! Your Rulers are precipitating you into a fathomless abyss of crime and calamity!...Awake and arrest the work of butchery ere it shall be too late to preserve your souls from the guilt of wholesale slaughter!" He sent himself as the *Tribune*'s correspondent to an anti-Polk political convention in Chicago. It was his first time that far west. Also in Chicago was a fellow Whig whom Greeley described as "a tall specimen of an Illinoian," Abraham Lincoln. He'd just been elected to Congress for the first time. They still apparently did not meet, but Greeley was impressed enough to note in the *Tribune* that this Lincoln fellow "spoke briefly and happily" at the convention.

In 1848, at the age of seventy, Henry Clay sought the Whigs' nomination one last time. Younger Whigs groaned, convinced that the old man simply could not win. Weed and other powers in the party found a new version of Old Tip: General Zachary Taylor, the somewhat dubious hero

of Polk's highly dubious war. When not fighting, Taylor lived on his Louisiana plantation with two hundred slaves. Greeley, fearing that Taylor
would support expanding slavery to the territories, rallied New York City
Whigs for Clay, but the party chose Taylor. Greeley denounced his nomination as "a slaughterhouse of Whig principles" and refused at first even
to print the Whig ticket in the *Tribune*.

To get Greeley on Taylor's side, Thurlow Weed cunningly offered him a
small but juicy plum. A New York congressman had vacated his seat, and
Weed offered to arrange for Greeley to fill it the last three months of the
congressman's term if he'd speak up for Taylor. Greeley's ambition outran
his scruples, as it would a few times, and he came over to help with Taylor's campaign. It wasn't easy. The general was so mute and inscrutable
a candidate that one cartoonist depicted the famous phrenologist Orson
Fowler reading the bumps on his head "to ascertain what his political
principles are," while Greeley takes notes.

With Greeley's help, Taylor made it into the White House, and Greeley
got to go to Washington, where he sat on the Whig side of the aisle with
Lincoln. Although he was there only three months, he managed to startle
and enrage his fellow congressmen by accusing many of them—including
Lincoln—of padding their travel expenses. He also backed a bill to allow
settlers on the western frontier to acquire federal land through home-
steading. When another congressman asked why Greeley cared about
frontier squatters, he replied that coming from New York City he represented "more landless men" than anyone else in Congress. The bill was
tabled; it would resurface in 1862 as the Homestead Act, which President
Lincoln would sign. After the Civil War it would be a key instrument in
the settling of the West.

∽

In September 1851, a new daily paper joined the penny wars: the *New
York Times*. Henry J. Raymond was its founder and editor. He had left
the *Tribune* after years of Greeley wrangling, especially put out by Greeley's promoting social experiments that struck him as fringe and faddish.
To start the *Times* he partnered with George Jones, who'd also left the
Tribune. They stole more than a dozen workers from Greeley, who took
to calling Raymond "the Little Villain." They put together the first issue
in a "raw and dismal" loft in an unfinished brownstone on Nassau Street,
working all night by candlelight, no glass in the windows yet. A new Hoe

Lightning below them rumbled and spat out the unevenly inked sheets. Like most dailies, it was a four-page one-sheet. The first issue summarized the latest news from Europe, briefly mentioned a revolt of fugitive slaves in Pennsylvania, and noted that women had been spotted in Greenwich Village wearing the shocking new garment called bloomers.

Raymond pointedly set an editorial style that was quieter and more sober than his rivals'. In his first editorial he promised that "we shall make it a point to get into a passion as rarely as possible. There are very few things in this world which it is worth while to get angry about; and they are just the things that anger will not improve." The measured tones of the *Times* contrasted well with Greeley's high-strung crackpotism and Bennett's crudities. By the end of the first year Raymond and Jones could raise the price to two cents.

Like his former boss, Raymond also got into politics. He went to Albany as a Whig assemblyman for Greenwich Village's Ninth Ward in 1849. By January 1851 he'd risen to the state's Speaker of the House. Horace Greeley had enjoyed his brief time in public office and wanted more. In 1854 he asked Thurlow Weed to help him run for governor, or at least lieutenant governor. Weed demurred, thinking Greeley was a loose cannon best lashed to the deck of the *Tribune*. Instead, he helped Greeley's nemesis Henry Raymond win the lieutenant governorship. Finding this "bitterly humbling," Greeley wrote Weed and Seward, "It seems to me a fitting time to announce to you the dissolution of the political firm of Seward, Weed, and Greeley, by the withdrawal of the junior partner." From then on the triumvirate was Seward-Weed-Raymond, with Greeley playing the increasingly erratic and sometimes hysterical spoiler.

CHAPTER 6

Immigrants and Know-Nothings

> We deny that it is a crime, or a wrong, or even a peccadillo, to
> hold slaves, to buy slaves, to sell slaves, to keep slaves to their
> work, by flogging or other needful coercion.
>
> —*John Mitchel*

Already one of the most densely packed and demographically mixed urban environments in the world, New York was inundated by a tsunami of new immigrants between 1845 and 1860. The bulk of them were new Irish Catholics, fleeing starvation at home. Another large contingent were Germans. In the decade of the 1840s the population of the city swelled from around 300,000 to more than 500,000. By 1850 a quarter of the city's population was Irish, while Kleindeutschland (Little Germany) in today's East Village was the third-largest German community in the world after Berlin and Vienna. By 1860, New York City's population had ballooned to about 813,000, *half of them* foreign-born. Racing to catch up, the city launched into a feverish building spree, throwing houses up as quickly as possible and surging up the island. Still, most of the newcomers were cruelly packed into the same tenements and slums that were already stuffed with immigrants. The new housing mostly went to New Yorkers trying to get some distance from them.

While the city's nativists and Whigs reacted to the new immigrants with revulsion, hostility, and alarm, harnessing this enormous bloc of potential new voters would give Tammany Hall a power base to sustain it for decades.

The crush of new Irish Catholics was instigated by a fungal blight that began destroying Ireland's staple potato crops in 1845, devastating the already fragile economy and producing nightmarish famine. As Ireland's English overlords barely lifted a finger to help, the population plummeted by 25 percent, with a million Irish dying of starvation and attendant diseases and another million fleeing in the "Great Migration" to North America, England, and Scotland. These "Famine Irish" were mostly Catholic, mostly desperately poor, uneducated and illiterate, many of them speaking only Gaelic; they were starving serfs, brutalized and demoralized by their English overlords back home, unskilled and terribly ill-equipped for life in the great metropolis. Few came willingly, and many were packed off by their landlords, who found it cheaper to get rid of their starving tenants than to keep them. The infamous "coffin ships" that hauled them were as dismal as any slave ship.

In the city, unemployment among these immigrants was desperately high. New York's almshouses, lunatic asylums, and private charities were soon overwhelmed. So were the jails, as many Irish males turned to alcohol and opium, thievery and thuggery, and filled the ranks of the city's most notorious street gangs, giving rise to slang terms like "paddy wagon" and "donnybrook." Thousands of Irish women turned to prostitution, and unwed births soared, so that the orphanages bulged with illegitimate and abandoned Irish children. Thousands more lived on the streets in an almost feral state, bereft of family, education, or community except their own. Called "guttersnipes," "urchins," "strays," "street rats," and "Arabs," they were a constant presence for the rest of the century. They found work as bootblacks, street sweeps, and newsboys, and also pickpockets, panhandlers, petty thieves, and prostitutes. Middle-class citizens grumbled at all the crime and depravity; shopkeepers complained about the unfair competition from street peddlers; and they all grimaced at the tax hikes levied on them by a municipal government that had already done a very poor job of providing basic public services.

With the flood of Famine Irish into the Lower East Side in the 1840s and 1850s, the immigrants' struggle to set themselves apart from blacks and be accepted by whites turned mean and hard. The Irish now developed a fierce strain of antiblack and antiabolitionist sentiment. Clinging desperately to their low-level jobs, Irish workers hated the abolitionist movement they feared would unleash millions of freed black workers to flood the city and replace them. The irony is that exactly the opposite happened: The Famine Irish who poured into the city soon greatly out-numbered the city's blacks, and it was Irish workers who took jobs from the blacks from the moment they arrived. Before the immigration wave of the mid-1840s, the majority of the city's menial and unskilled workers—including longshoremen, coachmen, brickmakers, barbers, porters, boot-blacks, and domestics—had been black. The poor Irish offered to work for lower wages, displacing many black workers and depressing earnings for everyone. By the mid-1850s, to give one example, just about all the longshoremen in the city were Irish, and blacks were roughly excluded.

The city's pro-South politicians, businessmen, and newspaper editors encouraged and exploited the widening rift between Irish and blacks. It was a tactic that would blow up on them in the vicious draft riots of the summer of 1863.

⌒

German-speaking immigrants had been coming to New York from early on. There was no united Germany until after the Civil War; they came as Bavarians, Westphalians, Hessians, Badeners. The large surge in their immigration from the mid-1840s on was driven by their own crop failures and economic upheavals. The repression that followed the failed republi-can uprisings that swept across Europe in 1848 also sent a number of pro-gressives and revolutionaries fleeing. They were called "Forty-Eighters." The Germans faced their own language barrier and were isolated in Klein-deutschland. Anglo New Yorkers routinely called them "Dutch," a cor-ruption of *Deutsch*, and stereotyped them as cruelly as they did the Irish. Still, the Germans fared better in the city than the Irish did. Far more German immigrants were skilled workers, artisans, or professionals. They brought with them a tradition of community organizations the Irish lacked and set up their own businesses, lending institutions, libraries, and cultural associations that thrived in Kleindeutschland.

Along with nearly all of the Famine Irish, a third of the German immi-grants were Catholics. There'd been fewer than one hundred thousand Catholics in America at the start of the century. During the 1840s their numbers soared toward two million. Anti-immigration forces, already hysterical about a papist takeover, now formed an organized resistance. In 1844 the nativist American Republican Party was strong enough to take almost every seat on New York's Common Council and get its candidate elected mayor. He was James Harper of the giant Harper & Brothers publishing firm. The other brothers were John, Joseph, and Fletcher. Raised in a strict Methodist home on Long Island, they were deeply conservative, though Fletcher, the youngest, would later migrate to a progressive point of view as editor of *Harper's Weekly.*

James served only a single two-year term, but a precedent had been set. Nativist secret societies sprang up in the city. They were patriotic fraternal organizations, with secret rites and mysterious rituals like the Freemasons. The Order of United Americans, the most popular, began with thirteen men in 1844 and grew to fifty thousand members in sixteen states within a decade. They came from all walks of life, from skilled laborers to James Harper's brother John. Members of the Order of the Star Spangled Banner, begun in 1850, pledged to respond to any questioning from outsiders with the statement "I know nothing." Greeley dubbed them Know-Nothings. It was the common name for nativists as they grew in numbers and disruptive strength through the decade.

Into this melee waded New York Catholics' first great champion, Bishop John Hughes. He'd begun in humble circumstances himself, born in 1797 on a small farm in County Tyrone in Ulster, where life for Catholics was bitterly harsh. This background left its mark on a militant, feisty man who came to be known as "Dagger John" and was said to act more like a Roman gladiator or an Irish chieftain than a meek follower of Christ. He sailed for Baltimore in 1817, was ordained a Jesuit in Philadelphia in 1826, and in 1838, in the original St. Patrick's Cathedral between Mott and Mulberry Streets above Prince Street, was consecrated bishop of the New York diocese. When the diocese became an archdiocese in 1850 he'd be its first archbishop.

A compact and vigorous man (and a vain one, given to wearing bad toupees as his hairline receded), Hughes got started on building up Catholicism's institutional foundation. In 1840 he turned his attention to the city's public schools, state-funded but run by a private organization, the Public School Society. Although the religious indoctrination in the classrooms was minimal, it was definitely Protestant, and teachers felt free to voice their anti-Catholic, anti-immigrant, and anti-Semitic opinions. Hughes led the movement to organize independent parochial schools, and to petition the city and state for a share of the funds that went to public schools. Governor Seward agreed with him, but New York City's

Protestant hierarchy howled. Bennett and other newspaper editorialists spat virulently anti-Catholic and anti-immigrant rants. Greeley's *Tribune* was one of the few voices of moderation.

Despite death threats, Hughes thundered back at mass rallies of Irish and German Catholics. Street fights broke out between Catholic and Protestant gangs. The result was a compromise that pleased neither side: Religious instruction was banned from public schools, but no funding would go to parochial ones. A Protestant mob stoned Hughes's residence. When they threatened to burn down St. Patrick's, Hughes called on the city's Irish Catholics to defend it, and a few thousand showed up armed. He famously warned that if a single Catholic came to harm, "we shall turn this city into a second Moscow," a reference to Moscow's residents burning down their city in 1812 rather than let Napoleon have it.

Even while defending his flock against the nativists, Hughes conceded that they were "the scattered debris of the Irish nation." Borrowing a page from the city's evangelicals, he turned his priests and nuns into an army of reformers teaching abstinence, discipline, and obedience. He brought Father Theobald Mathew, the French "apostle of temperance" who invented "the pledge," to New York, and twenty thousand swore off drink. From the Germans he adapted the notion of mutual aid societies and an Irish bank. He helped found the Society for the Protection of Destitute Catholic Children. In the late 1850s he would buy land and lay the cornerstone for a grand new St. Patrick's Cathedral, strategically placed well uptown on the classiest thoroughfare in Manhattan, Fifth Avenue. It wouldn't be completed until after his death.

Bishop Hughes reflected the interests, or at least the sentiments, of his Irish constituents in another way: his views on slavery. Where the American Catholic Church tended to maintain a "studied silence" on the issue, not wishing to alienate Catholics in either the North or South, the irrepressibly opinionated Hughes was far more forthcoming. He lashed abolitionism as dangerous "mischief." He argued that as long as slavery was lawful where it existed, owning slaves was not sinful, though mistreating them was. Like others, he forecast dire consequences for his working-class Irish flock if millions of abruptly freed Negroes should inundate the North.

In 1846, Bishop Hughes took over the management of a struggling Catholic weekly newspaper, the *Freeman's Journal and Catholic Register*, a merger of two earlier ones. When that proved to be one job too many, he sold it two years later to a disputatious twenty-eight-year-old and recent convert, James Alphonsus McMaster.

McMaster was born upstate to Scots-Irish immigrants in 1820. The family spelled their name MacMaster, but James would drop the "a" to make it look more Irish to his readers. His father was a Presbyterian minister. James moved to New York City in 1839 and converted to Catholicism in 1845. During the ceremony a candle he held lit a priest's hair on fire. People later thought it prophetic. After studying for the priesthood for a year in Belgium, he returned to New York set on a new course, journalism, assuming the ownership and editorship of Hughes's paper in 1848.

Under McMaster, the *Freeman's Journal* would extend and expand on Hughes's views against abolition. In 1861 it would be among the first New York newspapers suppressed by the Lincoln administration. Before the war was over, McMaster would go all the way to plotting actual treason.

New York's Irish got their own version of Forty-Eighters in the personages of Thomas Francis Meagher, John Mitchel, and John O'Mahony. Born into Ireland's tiny elite of upper-class Catholics in 1823, Meagher was studying law in Dublin when the famine hit. He fell in with the Young Ireland protest movement that included Mitchel, an incendiary Protestant political writer, and the Catholic scholar O'Mahony. By his early twenties Meagher was being celebrated as "Meagher of the Sword" for fiery speeches advocating political violence against the English if necessary. "Abhor the sword? Stigmatize the sword? No, my lord," he cried, for if peaceful means failed to redress Ireland's dire plight, "then up with the barricades and invoke the God of battles!" He designed what became Ireland's tricolor flag, inspired by the flag of France. At the same time, Mitchel was matching him in the press with his own seditious statements against the Crown.

In 1848, as republican revolt broke out all over Europe, Meagher and O'Mahony led a small and pitifully ill-conceived armed rebellion that resulted only in hardening the already cold hearts of the British. O'Mahony slipped out of the country and settled in France. Meagher was caught, tried, and convicted for treason, a hanging offense. Mitchel was convicted separately for his writing. Their supporters took to the streets in angry mobs to protest their impending executions. The furor reached New York, where Horace Greeley presided over a "Friends of Ireland" protest rally that drew a crowd of five thousand. Rather than execute them, the British decided to banish Meagher and Mitchel to Tasmania, then called Van Diemen's Land. Meagher had the run of the island, even marrying a Tasmanian girl, then paid for his escape on a merchant ship, leaving the wife behind. He arrived in New York City in 1852; Mitchel made his own escape and arrived a year later, and O'Mahony came from France the year after that.

The New York Irish greeted them as heroes. They wrote a polka for Meagher. (The polka was then a new dance craze; Julia Gardiner is said to have introduced it to Washington society during her short time as First Lady.) They sang jolly ballads about him, with lyrics like "From Van Diemen's Land, he gave them leg bail, / And he sailed to New York on the back of a whale." They threw gala dinners and parties for him, and arranged a multistate lecture tour.

Probably the most prominent Irish Catholic layman in the city, Judge Charles Patrick Daly, and his sharp-tongued wife, Maria, accepted Meagher into their circle. Charles was born to Irish Catholic immigrants in 1816, in the Lower East Side hotel his father managed. His mother died soon after. He got at best two years of schooling. After his father died, Charles, thirteen, ran away from his hated stepmother, all the way to Savannah, where he shipped out as a cabin boy on a merchant vessel. In the next few years he sailed around the world, accumulating tales of shipwrecks and Barbary pirates he'd tell for the rest of his life, to sometimes skeptical listeners.

When he returned to New York at sixteen he took a clerk's job in a law firm, where he studied at night and slept on the floor. At the time, experience was often substituted for law school, and he passed the bar in 1839. He joined Tammany and went to Albany for one term, then got appointed, at twenty-eight, as one of three judges on the Court of Common Pleas, then the highest court in the city. Meanwhile Daly was also teaching himself history, the arts, and science. He would found New York's Shakespeare Society; fund libraries; be the president of the American Geographical Society, the Athenaeum Club, and the Friendly Sons of St. Patrick; and write an authoritative history of the Jews in America. He also studied how to make money, and by speculating wisely in western land he made for himself a comfortable financial situation.

He was thirty-nine and still unmarried when he met Maria Lydig. The Lydigs were old German Protestant money. When she and Charles started courting, Maria was unmarried at thirty-two, which was considered well into spinsterhood. For close on a year she courted Charles as assiduously as he did her, while fighting to overcome her father's objections. Mr. Lydig liked Charles personally—most everyone did—but marriage to an Irish Catholic, even so successful a one as Judge Daly, was a step down the social ladder. Eventually she won his assent, plus a handsome dowry and a nice house on West 8th Street. Maria's Civil War diary, first made public in 1962, offers wonderful insights into the lives and minds of New York's top Democrats of the era.

With all the toasting and feting, Meagher began to show a weakness for strong drink that would mar his reputation for the rest of his days. When his Tasmanian wife reached New York in 1853, Archbishop Hughes— who had originally held "a hearty contempt" for the Young Irelanders, according to an early biographer, accusing them of "big words and small deeds"—met her at the dock and squired her around town. But she was a country mouse who didn't fit Meagher's glittering new life, and he packed her off to live with his father in Ireland. Six months later she died after giving birth to a son. In 1855, at Archbishop Hughes's house, Meagher married someone better suited to his new station, the Fifth Avenue social-ite Elizabeth Townsend, whose family's ironworks had made the massive steel chain that barred the Hudson to British ships in the Revolutionary War. Her father wasn't thrilled that she converted to Catholicism to marry an Irishman.

The following year Meagher started a weekly paper, the *Irish News*, which took a mildly pro-South and antiabolition stance. O'Mahony meanwhile cofounded the Fenian Brotherhood in New York. It was an international organization for funding, recruiting, and training fighters to make rebellion against the British back home. Despite serious misgivings about helping to emancipate black slaves, many Fenians would fight in the Civil War.

John Mitchel settled in Brooklyn but didn't tarry long. In 1854 he started his own newspaper, the *Citizen*, in which he was soon picking fights with Rome and Archbishop Hughes, alienating New York's Irish Catholics. Mitchel also declared himself for the South and slavery, but far more obstreperously than Meagher did. "We are not abolitionists; no more abolitionists than Moses, or Socrates, or Jesus Christ," he wrote. "We deny that it is a crime, or a wrong, or even a peccadillo, to hold slaves, to buy slaves, to sell slaves, to keep slaves to their work, by flogging or other needful coercion.... [We] wish we had a good plantation stocked with healthy negroes in Alabama."

Meagher stood by his outrageous friend as many in New York's Irish community turned against him (for his anti-Catholicism, not his racism). James McMaster, who shared Archbishop Hughes's low opinion of Young Ireland, railed against them in *Freeman's Journal* as a "vain, blustering set of braggarts" who were out to "make Ireland a laughing-stock to the world." Meagher found McMaster outside his home on East 6th Street near First Avenue and proceeded to beat him with a riding crop. They must have made quite a sight. Meagher was of average height and build, while McMaster was tall and well assembled, with forbiddingly hawkish features. Nevertheless McMaster resorted to yanking out a pistol and got off a shot that grazed Meagher's forehead. Meagher took the gun from him and beat him some more, then went to surrender to a cop. They each drew a fine of five hundred dollars.

By 1855, Mitchel decided he'd had enough of New York. He moved to Tennessee and started a newspaper, the *Southern Citizen*. When war broke out he would relocate to Richmond and take over the editorship of the *Richmond Enquirer*; two of his sons would die fighting for the Confederacy.

CHAPTER 7

A Trio of Tammany Rogues

The city's Irish and German immigrants gained another powerful ally in the form of Tammany Hall. As a patriotic club, Tammany had always rejected immigrants and Catholics. But as a political machine, it now saw the tens of thousands of newcomers as potential votes and reversed its position, welcoming them with open arms. Tammany men greeted immigrants at the docks and helped them find homes. They negotiated for them with their landlords, bailed them out if they landed in jail, and found them jobs on the city payroll—for example, stuffing the Municipal Police with tough Irishmen. They helped them through lean times and frigid winters with gifts of food and fuel. They sped them through the naturalization process so they could register to vote. The newcomers naturally voted Tammany's way, giving Tammany Democrats a power base from which to oppose the nativists on one hand and Greeley's Whigs on the other. The immigrant vote would sustain Tammany into the next century.

From the 1840s on, Tammany was also a training ground for tough, usually crooked men who knew how to serve themselves very handsomely while at least putting on a show of serving the public. Three who rose up through the ranks in the 1840s and 1850s would loom large in Civil War New York. As mayor and congressman, Fernando Wood would be one of New York City's most outspoken opponents of Lincoln and his war. The outrageous Daniel Sickles would go from being one of the city's most notorious political figures to one of its most controversial military officers, and back again. And William Tweed would exploit New Yorkers' opposition to the war for immense personal and political gain.

⌒

Fernando Wood was born into a family of poor Philadelphia Quakers in 1812, the third of five sons, with two sisters. His mother gave him his exotic-sounding name for a character in a popular gothic novel from 1800, *The Three Spaniards*. His father was a struggling dry goods merchant who was ruined, like many others, by the economic stagnation that came with the War of 1812. He then dragged his ever-expanding family all over the map seeking and never finding success—from Philadelphia to Kentucky, New Orleans, Havana, and finally New York City in 1821. When his small cigar shop there failed after a few years, he left the wife and kids and headed south again. He never returned, dying in a boarding-house in Charleston in 1831.

Fernando grew up driven to find success, by any path necessary. He and his brother Benjamin, eight years his junior and born when the family was in Kentucky, decided that in a hard, cold world they could trust and depend only on each other, a partnership they continued for life. Tall and handsome, with shockingly blue eyes, Fernando flirted for a while with becoming an actor on the stage. (A third brother, Henry, would become a minstrel impresario.) He was most punctilious in dress and etiquette, and in debate he had a way of making the most outrageous statements with a calm, almost supercilious politesse that could drive his opponents to frothing conniptions. His contemporaries considered him cold and Mephistophelean, an "elegant brigand" and a "brilliant desperado," and under no circumstances to be fully trusted. A political opponent later remembered him as "the handsomest man I ever saw, and the most corrupt man that ever sat in the Mayor's chair."

By nineteen Fernando was married and supporting not only his own wife and child but his widowed mother and younger siblings, all living together on Greene Street below Houston Street. He opened a tobacconist shop downtown on Pearl Street that failed along with many others in the Panic of 1837. The following year he opened a grog shop on the East River that also failed. Benjamin meanwhile left school early and went wandering around the states, to South America and the Caribbean, to Louisiana. When he came back to New York he sold Louisiana state lottery tickets, a just barely legal and not very respectable form of numbers running.

By twenty-four, Fernando was leading Tammany's Young Men's

Democratic-Republican General Committee, through which the Hall groomed members for future leadership. Tammany sent him to Congress in 1840, at the age of twenty-eight. Questions about his ethics were already beginning to dog him. A few years earlier a bank clerk had mistakenly credited the considerable sum of $1,750 to his account. Always struggling financially, he had kept his mouth shut and spent the money. The Whigs learned of it and puffed up a scandal, but Tammany pulled him through on a squeaker. He served only one term.

In the second half of the 1840s, Wood reached his goal of financial success through investing in the city's go-ahead housing market, buying land uptown and selling it off in small plots. He also organized a cartel of investors to ship supplies to the forty-niners panning for gold in California. (Much of the gold rush was funded by investors in New York.) Wood was accused, apparently with good cause, of swindling his backers, furthering his reputation as a sharper.

~

Rising up through the Tammany ranks a little behind Wood came a fun-loving, hot-tempered young egomaniac who would be one of the most notorious characters in a city lousy with them. Daniel Edgar Sickles was so gossiped and argued about during his lifetime that biographers have struggled to extricate facts from lore ever since. Even the date of his birth is unclear. It was probably 1819, definitely in Manhattan. The Sickles family were what Washington Irving called Knickerbockers, descendants of the Dutch settlers of New Amsterdam, when they'd been Van Sicklens. Dan's father, George, was a patent lawyer who made good money speculating in the city's booming real estate. Dan, an only child, was slightly built, bright, handsome, and headstrong. According to one biographer, he ran away from home a few times as a boy after disputes with his parents. They sent him up the Hudson to a boarding school, but he ran away from there too. Next George bought an estate in New Jersey and tried to interest Dan in the quiet life of the gentleman farmer. He ran away again.

Finally George found a setting his teenage son liked: the rollicking, cultured household of the Da Ponte family on Spring Street. The patriarch, Lorenzo Da Ponte, was one of the most colorful and unusual characters in New York. He was a Venetian Jew who later converted and became a Catholic priest, which didn't stop him from marrying, which didn't stop him from being Casanova's friend and rival in libertinage. When his exploits got him banished from Venice he went to Vienna, where he became Mozart's librettist on *Don Giovanni, Cosi fan tutte*, and *Le nozze di Figaro*. He came to New York in 1805 to escape debts. Chronically short of cash, he ran a bookstore, a boarding school, and a grocery. Then, through a young scholar and poet he met at the bookstore, Clement Clarke Moore (author of "A Visit from St. Nicholas," which begins, " 'Twas the night before Christmas…"), he became the first professor of Italian literature at Columbia University. In 1833 he founded the first opera house not only in New York but in America, the Italian Opera House at Church and Leonard Streets. He was a terrible businessman and Italian opera was still foreign to New York ears, so the venture soon failed.

In many ways this cultured old reprobate seems a more fitting father figure to Sickles than George was. The Da Pontes' threadbare but lively home was open at all hours to the city's artists, writers, and scholars. "Bohemian" was a term not yet in use in New York, but it suits the Da Pontes and their circle. It was the sort of crowd Herman Melville would describe in his novel *Pierre* as "bread-and-cheese adventurers, and ambiguously professional nondescripts in very genteel but shabby black, and unaccountable foreign-looking fellows in blue spectacles," who gather "like storks in Holland" and "sit and talk like magpies." Young Dan heard aesthetics and philosophy argued in a dozen languages and became moderately proficient in a few. He drank red wine and ate spaghetti, a rare and exotic dish in New York in the 1830s. Lorenzo's son, also named Lorenzo, was a teacher at NYU and took Dan under his wing. Dan doted on an adorable, dark-eyed toddler named Teresa, Lorenzo senior's granddaughter by an adopted daughter. In 1838, nearing the age of ninety, the older Da Ponte, with characteristic flair, wrote an ode to his own mortality, "Parti de la Vita" (Farewell to Life), and died the next day. His friends and fans threw him a big funeral at St. Patrick's. Just a few months later, his son died of pneumonia. Dan, apparently unhinged by the double loss, went so wild with grief at this second funeral that he had to be carried out of the churchyard. It would not be his last public outburst.

As a young man in the 1840s, Dan became the subject of much gossip around town as a dashing and dissipated rake, what New Yorkers called a "sporting lad." He toured the gambling dens and whorehouses. He liked to treat his pals to big dinners at Delmonico's, the high rollers' eatery of choice, and was such a sport that they didn't often complain when he had to borrow money from them to cover the bill. At the Astor House, the flagship of Broadway's luxury hotels that dominated the block between Vesey and Barclay Streets, he often sat in with an erudite circle that included Horace Greeley, Mathew Brady, Martin Van Buren's son John (nicknamed Prince John), and the eminent Shakespearean Edwin Forrest. Politically, this was an interesting crowd: Greeley the excitable Whig; Brady, whose portrait of Lincoln would later help him win the White House; Sickles and Van Buren the Democrats; and Forrest, whom the Democrats used in effect as a celebrity spokesperson, one of the first in American history. In the late 1830s, the handsome Forrest had whipped up audiences of cheering workingmen and swooning ladies with his fiery speeches for the party.

When Sickles followed his father into patent law, he was accused more than once of defrauding clients to get the cash to fund all this high living. He was never convicted—probably because he also followed his father into the ranks of Tammany Hall, and Tammany-backed judges had a way of making such matters melt away.

There were a great many thugs in Tammany's ranks when Dan was coming up there in the 1840s, and they tended to settle political arguments with knuckles and cudgels. A smallish man among the bruisers, with an attractive pan he didn't want dented, Dan reputedly took to attending meetings armed with a pistol and bowie knife for self-defense.

Fernando Wood liked him and got him elected to the state assembly in 1847. Dan instantly scandalized Albany by bringing a high-class hooker, Fanny White of Mercer Street, up the river with him. Dan showered Fanny with jewels and furs, and Fanny was rumored to have given him a percentage of the money she made on her back to help fund his lifestyle. His colleagues in the assembly branded him a pimp, or a "cadet" as they were then called, and passed a vote of censure.

Meanwhile, Teresa, the dark-eyed baby he'd dandled at the Da Pontes', was growing up into a lovely, doll-like young lady. He courted her over the objections of both families. According to the gossips, when Fanny learned of it she horsewhipped him in a fit of jealous rage. In 1852, Teresa left convent school to be his bride. She was sixteen, he almost thirty-three. He soon made it evident that his apparently genuine devotion to his bride wasn't going to curtail his sporting nightlife. It was on its way to being one of the most tattled-about marriages of the century.

Corralling the immigrant vote gave Tammany control of the Common Council by the early 1850s. The council was comprised of twenty aldermen and twenty assistant aldermen. They were unpaid, a holdover from the days when gentlemen of wealth considered a little public service an honor and duty. For Tammany's aldermen, few of whom were wealthy or gents, serving on the council was a license to steal. The ever-expanding and more crowded metropolis presented them a galaxy of opportunities for personal gain. They accepted bribes for licensing the growing city's new streetcar and ferry lines. They authorized the city to buy needed property, such as a new potter's field on Ward's Island; instead of the fair price of $30,000, they paid more than $100,000, and the seller split the overage with them. Contractors on city construction jobs typically padded their bills by 15 percent, which they kicked back to the councilmen. If you wanted a job in the burgeoning bureaucracy, you bribed the council. If you wanted a bill before them killed, you bribed them. The graft was so rampant that Greeley dubbed them "the Forty Thieves."

The Thieves were kicked out in the mid-1850s, but by then a crooked tradition had been set. The city's debt more than doubled between 1855 and 1862, yet its public services and spaces—docks, ferries, markets, streets—deteriorated shamefully. Everyone knew where the money really went. "Our city legislators, with but few exceptions, are an unprincipled, illiterate, scheming set of cormorants," Bennett's *Herald* complained, "educated in barrooms, brothels and political societies." Greeley's *Tribune* for once agreed: "Our Common Council is probably as utterly shamelessly corrupt as any such body ever was on earth. It is a stench in the nostrils of the whole city."

Serving as an alderman among the Thieves, William M. Tweed first learned how to line his pockets at the public's expense, a practice he would take to outrageous extremes during and after the Civil War. Born of Scots-Irish parents in 1823, Tweed had grown up in Cherry Hill on the Lower East Side, an area all but obliterated by the construction of the Brooklyn Bridge, which he would help to fund. After a few years in school he went into his father's chair-making and brush-making business. He got married in 1844 and started what grew into a large family. Politically, like most everyone in his neighborhood, he leaned toward the Democracy, though he was briefly infatuated with the Know-Nothings and voted for James Harper in 1844.

He was a husky lad who would sag to pear-shaped fat as an adult, smart, sociable, and well liked by other men in the neighborhood. He joined the Order of Odd Fellows and became a volunteer fireman. Late in the 1840s he and some other brawny fellows formed their own Volunteer Fire Company No. 6, the "Big Six," with a firehouse on Gouverneur Street. They named it the Americus Engine Company and gave it a logo, a Bengal tiger, copied from a lithograph they admired that hung in a neighborhood store. They painted it on their helmets and on the flanks of their shiny silver engine. The others elected Tweed their foreman.

Fire was a constant danger in a crowded city dense with flammables. Vast conflagrations in 1835 and 1845 had laid waste to much of the Wall Street area, right in Tweed's backyard as it were, and smaller fires happened daily all over the city. It's estimated that as many as half were set by arsonists paid by landlords and developers to make space for new buildings. New York wouldn't organize a paid municipal fire department until the end of the Civil War. Before then, all firemen were volunteers. Fighting fires was an exciting sport for strapping "fire laddies," whose 125 neighborhood fire companies, comprising some four thousand volunteers, were a cross between social clubs and street gangs, and the competition among them was fierce. They were famously fussy about their engines, hoses, and ladder carts, dazzlingly shined and bright—"like a new set of cutlery," Dickens wrote after his time in the city. They gave them names like Neptune, Oceanus, Knickerbocker, and Eagle, with appropriate logos painted on their sides. "Dressed up like a fire engine" became slang for looking sharp. At the sound of bells rung by watchmen posted at the tops of buildings and towers located around the city—one in the cupola of City Hall, one each above the Jefferson and Essex Street markets, and so on—they'd run to the firehouse in their red shirts and helmets. Then they'd race to beat their competitors to the scene. They hauled their equipment through the streets themselves, refusing to use horses as a matter of honor, and pumped the water themselves as well, disdaining to use steam pumps until very near the start of the Civil War. When competing companies met at a fire, as they often did, fights broke out. Over the years, as animosities and old grievances piled up between this company and that, these fights could turn into all-out street battles, bloody and vicious, while the fire raged forgotten and untended, crowds of young boys cheered on their favorite warriors, and the distraught owner of the burning home or business stood there in his nightshirt pulling out his hair.

Tweed's leadership of the Big Six, and his lusty way with an ax handle in a street brawl, brought him to the Democracy's and Tammany's attention. He also caught the eye of an immigrant boy named Tommy Nast. Tommy was born in an army barracks in Bavaria in 1840; his father played trombone in a regimental band. In 1846 the Nasts fled the political upheavals in Europe. They came to a New York roiling with its own political and social strife. The nativists were at their anti-immigrant, anti-Catholic peak in the city, and the Nasts abandoned their Catholicism. As an adult, Tommy would go all the way to being virulently anti-Catholic. He grew up on William Street on the Lower East Side, struggling with English, an indifferent student, but drawing and painting from the start. Short and chubby all his life—he would earn the nicknames "Roly Poly" and "Little Piggy"—he developed a healthy fear of the gangs of Irish kids who patrolled the neighborhood streets spoiling for a fight. But he loved running after the fire laddies, and Big Six was his favorite company. William Tweed knew nothing of the boy at the time, but would come to know the name Thomas Nast all too well in years to come, when they were two of the most famous men in New York.

Like many Tammany men, Tweed got into politics not so much to make policy, which generally bored him, but to get ahead and make money. In 1851, when he was twenty-eight, he was elected to the Common Council as alderman for the Lower East Side's Seventh Ward, the area from Division Street to the East River. In 1853 the voters of his ward sent him to Congress. He found politics in Washington terribly dull, summing it up as "hearing a lot of snoozers discuss the tariff." When he returned to New York in 1855, Tammany got him a spot on the Board of Education. It was a minor position, and unpaid, but Board of Ed members made decent graft from the sale of textbooks and from taking kickbacks from the teachers they hired, charging them as much as seventy-five dollars for a job that paid three hundred dollars a year. Tweed also arranged to sell the schools some chairs. For reformers like Henry Raymond at the *Times*, the board was all "second, third and fourth rate hacks...selling their friends and their principles for the smallest mess of pottage."

Tweed proved Raymond wrong. He never settled for small messes of anything.

CHAPTER 8

Lurching Toward the Precipice

Through the decade of the 1850s, many people saw New York senator William Seward's "irrepressible conflict" coming. Some tried to divert it. Others cheered it on as the biblical apocalypse that would finally show whose side God was on, North or South. Whether the vast new western territories should be carved into slave states or free-soil wasn't the only issue that divided North and South, but it was the one around which they drew their battle lines.

In July 1850, Zachary Taylor died of an intestinal ailment after sixteen months in the White House. The Whigs had now gotten two men elected who died in office. His vice president, Millard Fillmore, an upstate New Yorker with Southern sympathies, took over. Taylor's death paved the way for the passage of the Compromise of 1850, which he had opposed. Fillmore signed it into law in September 1850. It was a complex suite of new laws meant to paste over the widening cracks in the nation by making concessions all around. It was so unwieldy that before he died Taylor sneered that it was like an omnibus, a vehicle on which any piece of legislation could ride. Henry Clay, old and dying himself, had started the process but failed, after months of deal-making and fountains of oratory, to build the bipartisan coalition he needed. It was his last defeat; he left Washington and would pass away in 1852. The Democrat Stephen Douglas, "the Little Giant of Illinois," broke up the omnibus into separate bills and pushed them all through. The Compromise settled border disputes between Texas and New Mexico; admitted California as a free state, while allowing New Mexico, Nevada, Utah, and Arizona to apply for statehood without declaring themselves either slave or free; and abolished the slave markets in Washington, while allowing slavery itself to continue there, which it would until 1862.

Most controversially, the Compromise included a new Fugitive Slave Law. A prohibition on aiding runaway slaves had been written into Article IV of the Constitution and backed by a 1793 law that levied moderate fines on anyone assisting the escapees. Northerners had ignored or resisted it, and several states passed laws of their own contravening it. This new version was meant as a crackdown and went much further. It committed the federal government to help slave owners pursue and capture any runaways in nonslave states. It required all citizens in those states to assist as well, under penalty of harsh fines and possible jail terms.

It was a sop to slave owners, who had always hated that the North was a haven for their runaways. To all blacks in the North it was a terror. To white abolitionists and others in the North it was an outrageous incursion of the "slavocracy" (a Greeley word) into the land of democracy. Seward, who had gone from being New York's governor to one of its senators, gave his first speech in the chamber denouncing the Compromise in general and the Fugitive Law in particular. He declared that any compromise would be "radically wrong and essentially vicious." He famously invoked "a higher law" than the Constitution or any laws of men.

The Whigs would dump Millard Fillmore in 1852 for signing the bill into law. In his stead they would run yet another old warhorse, General Winfield Scott. When the Democrat Franklin Pierce trounced Scott, Greeley declared that "the Whig party is not merely discomfited, it is annihilated." He turned out to be right. The party would fall apart into its various factions over the next few years, and a new party would be born to take its place.

In New York City, abolitionists held a big annual meeting in 1850 in the context of the debate over the Compromise. All the leaders of the movement were scheduled to speak, along with a rising new star: the Reverend Henry Ward Beecher, pastor of Plymouth Church in Brooklyn Heights.

In 1847 some of the Tappans' Brooklyn Heights circle had decided to start a new Congregationalist church in the neighborhood. The principals were David Hale; John Tasker Howard, another Yankee who'd moved to New York and thrived in the import-export business; and Henry Chandler Bowen, a former clerk in Arthur's firm who had started his own successful import firm and married Lewis's daughter Lucy. Howard and Bowen shared strong antislavery views. Hale was antislavery but in a more moderate way—he didn't think abolitionist rabble-rousing should interfere with making money.

Situated on a windswept bluff with spectacular views of Manhattan and the harbor, Brooklyn Heights had been farmland in 1814 when Robert Fulton's regular steam ferry service made commuting to and from Manhattan easy. Soon after, enterprising Heights property owners began to sell off plots for new homes, advertising the area to Manhattan's wealthy as "the nearest country retreat." Although the waterfront below was as wild and seamy as all waterfronts, the Heights in the late 1840s was a sedate patrician suburb of unpaved, tree-shaded streets, with more than a touch of the bucolic to it still.

The Tappan circle bought an old Presbyterian church on Cranberry Street, rechristened it Plymouth Church as a nod to their shared Yankee heritage, and recruited a congregation of about fifty members. It was as much a business venture as a religious one. "The whole process was a recognized and highly profitable industry in that day," Paxton Hibben explains in his gimlet-eyed *Henry Ward Beecher* of 1927. "Church property was tax free, and readily rentable for lectures during the week, as well as for Sunday services." Members of the congregation also paid rent on their pews. ("Free" churches, in which anyone sat anywhere, were a new, populist response to this practice.) And a church tended to raise the value of other properties around it, so that wise investors in churches also bought parcels near them. Hale was financially involved in the Broadway Tabernacle, the cavernous Congregationalist hall in Manhattan between what are now Worth and Leonard Streets. Open and well lit, the Tabernacle was more an auditorium than a conventional church. It could fit three thousand. From investing there and in several other churches, Hale knew how to make one a going concern.

The group next searched for a pastor who could quickly attract parishioners. They thought first of Lyman Beecher. The venerable New England Congregationalist was one of the most famous preachers in the country, and could easily draw Brooklyn's Yankees to the church. He had collaborated previously with the Tappans on some of their reformist projects. When Arthur helped found the Presbyterian Lane Seminary in Cincinnati, Beecher moved his wife and twelve children from Boston to the frontier to be its first president in 1832. He was a moderate on the slavery issue, which must have appealed to Hale.

When Lyman Beecher proved unavailable, the Plymouth group turned their thoughts to his son Henry. Born in 1813, in the middle of Lyman's large brood, as a boy Henry had been chubby, sweet-natured, shy, and afflicted with "a thickness of speech arising from a large palate, so that... I used to be laughed at for talking as if I had pudding in my mouth." Elocution lessons at Amherst helped with that. Henry was a student at Lane when the abolitionist movement swept onto the campus in the early 1830s. His father agreed that slavery was wrong, but had declined to support Garrison; at Lane, he pleaded with the more fanatical abolitionist students to be less outspoken. Henry followed his father down the middle of that road. So did his sister Harriet, who at first considered abolitionists "moral monomaniacs."

By 1847, Henry had been making a name for himself preaching out west for several years. The Plymouth group paid for him to come to a kind of audition at the Broadway Tabernacle, which he passed. They then wooed him intensely with handsome salary offers, and Beecher came to Brooklyn Heights. Henry Ward Beecher was a new phenomenon in the staid suburb, and Brooklynites didn't quite know what to make of him at first. "His personal appearance is neither prepossessing nor commanding," the *Brooklyn Daily Eagle* noted shortly after his arrival. "He is short in stature, rather stout, and clumsily built." In the late 1840s, New York and Brooklyn men of any substance wore black frock coats pinched at the waist, tight trousers in wide checks or stripes, silk top hats, and bushy beards or whiskers. Beecher looked and dressed like a westerner: floppy pants, no top hat, clean-shaven, with his long and wavy hair tumbling over an open collar.

Then there was his preaching style. While out west he'd been startled and impressed by the Methodists' lively services, so different from the dour affairs he'd known in New England. Frontier preachers put on a great show and roused their congregations to laughter, tears, twitching, and barking. By the time he hit Brooklyn Heights, Beecher was quite a showman himself, more the preelectronic version of a televangelist than the stuffy ministers Brooklynites were used to. Sinclair Lewis would call him "a combination of St. Augustine, Barnum, and John Barrymore." Instead of the usual dry homilies, his sermons were rambling, extemporaneous monologues on topics of the day, delivered in conversational language laced with jokes and slang that scandalized a few bluenoses but delighted everyone else. Mark Twain, who caught a Plymouth service in the 1860s, described how Beecher "went marching up and down his stage, sawing his arms in the air, hurling sarcasms this way and that, discharging rockets of poetry, and exploding mines of eloquence, halting now and then to stamp his foot three times in succession to emphasize a point." He also noted that the reverend was "a remarkably handsome man when in the full tide of sermonizing" but "homely as a singed cat when he isn't doing anything."

When the original Plymouth Church burned in 1849, Beecher's employers immediately started work on a new one behind it on Orange Street. Although his congregation included only around two hundred members, Beecher convinced them to build the new space to hold two thousand. Inspired by the Broadway Tabernacle, he wanted a wide-open, well-lit space with no columns obstructing anyone's view (of him), semicircular pews and balconies for an almost theater-in-the-round effect, and no pulpit, but rather a curving stage. When it opened in 1850, the new church, still in use today, was the largest auditorium in Brooklyn. Soon New Yorkers were taking the ferry across the East River to the Fulton Street landing below the Heights to see what the fuss was about. Sunday ferries came to be known as Beecher Boats.

Beecher's first steps toward a more abolitionist stance seemed motivated mostly by his innate showmanship. James Pennington, who had married Frederick and Anna Douglass in Ruggles's home, had been living as a free man in New York and Brooklyn for years when he revealed himself to be a runaway slave in his autobiography *The Fugitive Blacksmith*, published in London in 1849. Like Douglass, he was born a slave on Maryland's eastern shore and given the name Jim Pemberton. When he was twenty he ran away, leaving his parents and ten siblings behind. He eventually made his way to Pennsylvania and was taken in by Friends. When he came to New York and Brooklyn in 1829 he was using the Quaker name Pennington. He got a job teaching school and was the first African American allowed to audit classes at Yale, though he had to sit in the back.

In September 1848 he was the pastor of the First Colored Presbyterian Church and was deeply involved in the abolition movement and Underground Railroad. Paul Edmonson, "an aged coloured man of tall and slender form," came to him. "I saw depicted on his countenance anxiety bordering on despair." Edmonson was also from Maryland, a free man married to a slave, which meant his children were slaves. Two of his daughters had been purchased by the Virginia slave-trading firm of Bruin and Hill. Anguished by the thought that his daughters would be sold into prostitution, Edmonson was trying to raise the considerable sum of $2,700 Bruin and Hill would charge to buy their freedom.

Pennington, the Tappans, and others organized a fund-raiser at the Broadway Tabernacle. To fill the hall, Pennington sent Edmonson across the river to Brooklyn Heights to seek Beecher's help. Henry's sister Harriet later wrote that Edmonson "inquired his way to his door—ascended the steps to ring the door-bell, but his heart failed him: he sat down on the steps, weeping!" Beecher found him there, heard him out, and agreed to speak.

Beecher worked the packed Tabernacle into a "panic of sympathy," as he put it, by getting his white audience to put themselves in the Edmonsons' place, then conducting a mock slave auction to buy the girls' freedom. The results were spectacular. The women in the hall wept, men with shining eyes and trembling hands shoved cash in the collection plate, and the Edmonson girls were freed. The showman in Beecher was thrilled by his triumph.

Shortly after that, Hale died, leaving Beecher surrounded by Plymouth's more ardent abolitionists. His course was set. Beecher held many more mock auctions through the 1850s, at his own church and elsewhere. The most famous would occur in 1860, when he roused his congregation to buy the freedom of a pretty nine-year-old from Washington, Sally Maria Diggs, called "Pinky" for her light complexion. Passing the collection plate, they raised nine hundred dollars. Congregants gave jewelry as well as cash. In a theatrical flourish Beecher fetched a ring from the collection plate, slipped it onto Pinky's finger, and declared, "With this ring, I thee wed to freedom." If there'd been a stage curtain in the church it would have dropped at that moment to thunderous applause. Beecher's adoring congregation increased his salary and gave him a fine home and carriage.

The abolitionists' annual meeting was held on May 7 and 8, 1850, at the Broadway Tabernacle and the hall of the New York Society Library nearby. With most of the speakers New Englanders, the city's antiaboli-tionist forces reacted to it as though it were a Yankee invasion. In the con-servative, pro-slavery *Herald*, James Gordon Bennett denounced the event for several days in advance, calling it "The Annual Congress of Fanatics—The Disunionists, Socialists, Fourierists, Communists, and other Aboli-tionists. May the seventh has come, and with it a host of fanatics, worse than the locusts of Egypt." He charged that the "demonic" William Lloyd Garrison, full of "malevolence and unblushing wickedness," "urges the utter overthrow of the churches, the Sabbath, and the Bible. Nothing has been sacred with him but the ideal intellect of the negro race." Bennett also expressed the sly hope "that there are those who will enter the arena of discussion, and send out the true opinion of the public."

As the platform of the Democracy and the Irish, Tammany was anti-black and antiabolition. Tammany also had grown very adept at marshal-ing the Lower East Side's street gangs and other hoodlums to act as muscle and "shoulder-hitters" when needed on election days and other occasions. A gang of these toughs packed one corner of the Tabernacle for the morn-ing session on May 7, prepared to cause whatever trouble they could. Their ringleader was the colorful and much-ballyhooed Captain Isaiah Rynders. It was said he was born in the Hudson River town of Waterford in 1804 and left home by the age of twelve. On Mississippi riverboats he became a gambler and reputedly a brawler with fists, pistols, and the bowie knife. He was said to have murdered a man or two during his years wandering the South, though from his activities in New York he sounds more like a garden-variety bully than a mankiller. He picked up the hon-orific "Captain" along the way. He was in New York City by the mid-1830s and began working his way up the ladder as a Tammany enforcer and vote-getter. By the early 1840s he owned a saloon on Park Row fre-quented, according to his obituary in the *Times* in 1885, by "drunkards, thieves, gamblers, and ruffians." These he organized under the rubric the Empire Club, which the *Times* described as "any number of soap-lock, black-muzzled customers, who wear their hats very much on one side, turn up the bottom of their pantaloons, carry their cigars in the corner of their mouth, with the end projecting upwards, and call Isaiah Rynders 'Cap.' These fellows generally have strong red hands and weak red eyes, and smell like a whiskey barrel." (A soap-lock was a spit-curl pasted down on the forehead with soap, a fashion affected by some Bowery lugs at the time.) As his influence in the Five Points and on the Lower East Side grew, he was credited with playing a major hand in delivering New York City for Democratic presidents Polk and Buchanan.

On May 7, Garrison, the first key speaker of the Tabernacle meeting, hadn't gotten far into his speech when Rynders's mob rushed the stage. To placate them, one of them was allowed to offer a pseudoscientific argument that Negroes were not men but a type of monkey. Frederick Douglass spoke next. "The gentleman who has just spoken has undertaken to prove that the blacks are not human beings," he said mildly. "I offer myself for your examination. Am I a man?" Rynders cried out, "You are not a black man—you are only half a nigger." Douglass responded, "He is correct. I am, indeed, only half a Negro, half-brother to Mr. Rynders." Beecher spoke that afternoon, similarly trading barb for barb, and all but daring Rynders to step up and tussle. Walt Whitman wrote a brief piece about the event for the Whig *Brooklyn Daily Advertiser*. Although he liked Beecher's "bold masculine discourses," comparing them to the average preacher's "emptiness and something very akin to effeminacy," he thought he should show "more coolness."

Rynders's gang turned up in full voice at Library Hall the next morning, booing, heckling, jumping up on the podium, preventing the New Englander Wendell Phillips from speaking. Police arrived and shut down the proceedings. Beecher hastily talked the Plymouth trustees into letting Phillips speak there. He had to threaten to resign to sway a few trustees worried that their beautiful new building would be burned down. Thousands of Brooklynites and New Yorkers streamed through the Heights' quiet streets that evening and packed the church to the rafters. Although some in the crowd booed and heckled, the evening went off peacefully.

⌒

Henry was becoming the most famous Beecher in the land. Then his sister Harriet upstaged him. The Fugitive Slave Law propelled her, like other moderate Northerners, toward the abolitionist movement. A move away from Cincinnati, a largely pro-slavery environment, back to New England, the hotbed of abolition, also contributed to her change of heart. In 1851 she began writing *Uncle Tom's Cabin*, which the abolitionist paper *The National Era* serialized. Published as a book in Boston on March 20, 1852, it sold a dumbfounding two and a half million copies worldwide in its first year, some three hundred thousand of those in the United States. Millions more people first encountered the story in a variety of performed adaptations, from lavish musical productions to small "magic lantern" shows, an early form of projected images.

A production at the National Theatre in Chatham Square starting in 1853 played to packed houses for an unprecedented 325 performances and moved Edwin Forrest to tears. At the start of act 5, Tom (a white performer in blackface) sang a new Stephen Foster song, "My Old Kentucky Home." It's possible Foster caught one or more performances. He had recently moved from his hometown Pittsburgh to New York City to try to arrange better deals with his song publisher Firth, Pond & Co. on Broadway, and with the minstrel groups like E. P. Christy's who plugged his songs onstage. For several years he'd been struggling, and largely failing, to make his living solely as a popular music songwriter. His worldwide hits like "Oh! Susanna," "Camptown Races," and "Old Folks at Home" had made him famous, yet at this stage in the music business a songwriter had virtually no way to determine if his sheet music publisher was paying him honestly, no means to collect fees for performances of his work, and little protection against copyright theft. With the meager royalties Foster received he was barely able to feed his wife and daughter. He'd go home to Pittsburgh as poor as he'd come, then return to New York to try again at the start of the war.

Harriet Beecher Stowe, on the other hand, quickly became famous, infamous, *and* rich. She was an overnight celebrity, mobbed everywhere she went. Henry was delighted for her, and enjoyed basking in her reflected glory. When she visited him in Brooklyn Heights, members of the Plymouth congregation acted as her bodyguards on the streets, shielding her from the crowds. While reading or seeing *Uncle Tom's Cabin* did not turn the average white Northerner into an overnight abolitionist, it did stir up a Beecherian "panic of sympathy" for the Negro—or at least for the fictional Negroes in the story—which the movement was pleased to exploit. Coming in the midst of the furor over the Fugitive Slave Law, *Uncle Tom's Cabin* compounded the hardening of Northern opinions toward the South. At the same time, its mammoth popularity went some way to convincing many Southerners that their differences with the North were irreconcilable. Both the book and staged adaptations were banned in the South. Harriet's bags of hate mail included an envelope containing yet another severed Negro ear. Newspapers in the South denounced her as a liar and fraud. So did the Morse brothers' conservative *New York Observer*.

Horace Greeley got himself so worked up over the Compromise of 1850 and the Fugitive Slave Law that in 1851 his managing editor Dana sent him on an ocean voyage to cool down and avert another bout of brain fever. Greeley went to London to see the opening of the Exhibition of the Industry of All Nations, a world's fair. The setting was the Crystal Palace, a mammoth steel frame holding a million square feet of glass. It was the architectural wonder of the age, and Greeley was as impressed as any of the fair's millions of visitors. As soon as he returned he started organizing a New York industrial exhibition, unofficially the city's first world's fair. New York's own Crystal Palace rose on Reservoir Square, behind the Croton Reservoir in what's now Bryant Park (named in 1884 for William Cullen Bryant).

P. T. Barnum was among the investors Greeley successfully wooed. As fellow Yankees in the big city, they had become friends when Barnum opened his American Museum at Broadway and Ann Street at the same time that Greeley was starting the *Tribune* a block away. They were both temperance men and antislavery, and each had his own genius for appealing to mass audiences. Greeley was supportive of Barnum's museum when many other papers in the city were disdainful. They remained friends even when Barnum tried publishing his own newspaper. Partnering with Moses Beach's sons Henry and Alfred, he created the weekly *Illustrated News*, filled with large engravings. It was short-lived but paved the way for the immensely successful *Frank Leslie's Illustrated Newspaper* and *Harper's Weekly*.

President Pierce came to open Greeley's exhibition on July 14, 1853. He brought his secretary of war, the former Mississippi senator and Mexican War veteran Jefferson Davis. At a banquet, Colonel Davis was introduced as a hero who had "won imperishable honors" fighting for his country. "It is true that I have marched beneath that striped and starred banner of my country," Davis orated to many huzzahs. "It is true that the warmest feelings of my heart always gather about it. From boyhood to mature life, it was my fortune to serve beneath that banner, and to watch it as it waved, from the morning to the setting sun. It was the flag for which my father had fought in the Revolutionary War. It has been my fortune to see it in peace, and it has been my fortune to see it in triumph." The mordant irony of his remarks wouldn't come clear for a few years yet.

But the exhibition was a bust. Barnum blamed the location, which, "being four miles distant from the City Hall, was enough of itself to kill the enterprise." Visitors gawped at the Crystal Palace and the adjacent Latting Observatory, an Eiffel-like tower of wood and iron that at 315 feet was the tallest structure in the country, with magnificent views over to Queens and New Jersey from observation platforms reached by Elisha Otis's new steam-driven vertical railway, or elevator. But paid attendance lagged far behind expenses. Barnum took over the operation in 1854, but even he couldn't save it. The observatory burned to the ground in 1856, the Crystal Palace in 1858.

CHAPTER 9

Riot and Outrage

Despite what it was called, the 1850 legislation created as much conflict as compromise. Arguing over it not only drove North and South further apart, but created angry factions inside both the Whigs and the Democratic Party. In New York, Tammany's rank and file, always a fractious and brawling bunch to start with, split into warring tribes with colorful nicknames like the Barnburners, Hunkers, and Locofocos (for a type of match). The sachems turned to the smooth-talking Fernando Wood to broker a temporary peace among them. When he succeeded, they rewarded him by securing him the Democratic candidacy for mayor. Greeley's *Tribune* reminded voters about Wood's having conned his gold rush investors, and the Whigs soundly defeated him.

When the elections came around again in 1852, the Democracy went with more of a sure thing: Jacob Westervelt, one of the city's most successful and prosperous shipbuilders, of a Knickerbocker family whose roots went back to New Amsterdam. His grandfather Jacobus was a patriot of the Revolution who died in one of the British prison ships in Wallabout Bay. When young Jacob was learning the shipbuilding trade he spent a few years in a Charleston shipyard directing the work of slaves. On the East River his shipyards churned out hundreds of vessels, from one of the first ocean-crossing steamships to record-setting clippers that supplied the California gold rush. A patriot like his grandfather, he would put many ships at the service of the U.S. Navy when the war broke out.

Street disturbances by Know-Nothing gangs increased during his term. One Sunday afternoon in December 1853 an itinerant street preacher who roamed the Hudson and East River waterfronts delivering screeds "against popery" "planted himself upon a pile of timbers" at Westervelt's shipyard and drew a crowd the *Times* estimated at ten thousand. Word reached the mayor in his home at East Broadway and Grand Street, and he dispatched a squad of police who took the preacher into custody. The crowd now marched over to the Westervelt home and "startled" Westervelt with demands that the preacher be released or "they would burn down the Mayor's house, or blow it up." A "strong body of the police force" arrived to disperse the mob.

Westervelt, as was customary for New York mayors, declined to run for reelection in 1854. Fernando Wood saw his opening and, despite the *Tribune* and the *Post* denouncing him as a crook, he squeaked into the mayor's office on a wisp of a plurality. In 1849 a Whig-dominated state assembly in Albany, anxious to clip the Democracy's wings in the city, had piled new restrictions on the mayor's office, further weakening it. Fernando Wood had other ideas. He declared that the mighty metropolis, with all its complexities and problems, cried out for strong, dynamic "one-man rule." He brushed aside cries from Whigs that he planned to become a despot: "Better have an iron rule than no rule at all, as it is now."

At first it looked like he might actually be the city's white knight. He made a great public show of trying to curb the graft and patronage that riddled the municipal government, clear the streets of their hordes of prostitutes and pickpockets, close the bars on Sundays, and shut down the gambling halls. Grateful New Yorkers cheered these long-overdue reforms. Then, gradually, they saw that most of it was just for show. Mayor Wood kept the graft and patronage to himself, let the prostitutes and gambling dens simply move to other locations, and looked the other way when many bars ignored the blue laws. And he fought constantly with Albany.

He'd been in office a little over a year when a book called *Biography of Honorable Fernando Wood, Mayor of New York City* appeared in the stores. The author "portrayed Wood as a brilliant descendant of a respectable colonial family, a man with a deep sense of public service, destined for greatness, perhaps the presidency." Wood not only paid for the publication but evidently wrote much of the self-serving copy.

It was one way of announcing that he intended to run for reelection, something few of his predecessors had done. With Tammany more or less falling in behind him, the electioneering turned ugly. The Dead Rabbits, one of the street gangs in Tammany's service—their leader, John

Morrissey, was a protégé of Isaiah Rynders—roved the streets, busting up Whig rallies. They guarded the polling stations on election day, while Tammany functionaries stuffed ballot boxes, marched repeaters around town, and lost opponents' ballots. Wood even dragooned the Municipal Police to serve as campaign aides. He tithed them a percentage of their pay for campaign funds; any officer who complained found himself demoted. Then on election day Wood gave them a few hours off to go vote for him and strong-arm opposing voters.

Wood won in a stroll—the help of the Municipals alone was said to add fifteen thousand votes to his tally—but he had made enemies on all sides in the process. His second term proved a disaster. He lost the support of the Tammany sachems, who grumbled that he was keeping all the graft to himself. In Albany the Whigs rescheduled the next election to reduce his term to one year.

They also decided to take control of the Municipal Police force away from him, folding it into a new state-run Metropolitan Police force. Wood refused to obey, and two-thirds of the Municipals, most of whom had gotten their jobs directly from him, stuck by him. For a month or so in 1857 the city was in the ludicrous position of having two rival police forces who, like volunteer firemen, spent more time fighting each other than fighting crime. When Metropolitans went to City Hall to arrest the mayor, Municipals fought them off with fist and club. The 7th Regiment came to the Metropolitans' aid, and Wood gave himself up.

On July 4, 1857, the Dead Rabbits reduced a chaotic situation to near anarchy. Fired up by righteous anger and copious amounts of liquor, they launched an all-out attack on some Metropolitans, then turned on a rival gang, the Know-Nothing, anti-Catholic Bowery Boys. The two gangs, adding up to as many as a thousand fighters, blocked Bayard Street in Chinatown with makeshift barricades of bricks, street vendors' wagons, and mattresses, from behind which they began to blaze away at each other with muskets and pistols. A *Tribune* reporter saw one rioter shot through the head and several others going down wounded or dead, including a few gawking bystanders. A small detachment of Metropolitans arrived and promptly retreated under what the *Tribune* reporter described as "a shower of stones, bricks, oyster-shells, fragments of ironware, and in some instances whole pots and kettles" hurled by the fighters' Irish girlfriends, wives, and mothers from the windows and rooftops of the surrounding tenements.

Over two days the fighting grew and spread out to other streets. "Civil War in the Bloody Sixth," the *Tribune* cried out. "Awful Riots and Bloodshed." At one point Isaiah Rynders appeared and tried to convince the fighters to make peace. It was a foolish misstep on his part. He had lately been flirting with the Know-Nothings, enraging Morrissey and his Irish gang. They beat him up. He told the cops to call in the militia. When Metropolitans, Municipals, and militia finally cleared the littered and bloody streets, ten people were reported dead and hundreds more wounded. The *Times* and many New Yorkers blamed Wood.

~

Tammany's young hellion Dan Sickles meanwhile was causing trouble of his own—not in New York but in London.

In 1853, Franklin Pierce appointed James Buchanan his minister to Queen Victoria's court. Buchanan had run unsuccessfully against Pierce for the Democratic nomination; before that, the tall, genteel Pennsylvanian had been Polk's secretary of state and Jackson's envoy to Russia. Like most Democrats, he was friendly to the South and pro-expansionist. A lifelong bachelor, leading to speculation then and now that he was gay, Buchanan enjoyed being around hard-partying, fun-loving younger people like Sickles, and he invited him to join him as his personal secretary in London. In the *Herald*, James Gordon Bennett denounced the appointment. Bennett already had ugly history with Sickles. Among other things there was the humiliating rumor that Sickles was the actual father of Bennett's son James Gordon Jr., born in 1841.

When he sailed for England, Sickles left his sweet, innocent, and pregnant Teresa back in New York—but took Fanny White along. Allegedly he had the astounding gaucheness to bring Fanny with him to a reception in Victoria's drawing room, where he introduced her to the queen as "Miss Bennett of New York." It's unclear this actually happened, but Bennett heard and believed it and went apoplectic. For the next few years the *Herald* rarely missed a chance to shower Sickles with obloquy. Teresa later joined Dan in London, where "the Little American," as they dubbed her, charmed the court.

Too willful and intemperate for diplomacy, Sickles committed a few other gaffes. He organized a London banquet to celebrate July 4, at which he wanted only Americans. When Brits showed up as well, then rose to toast a portrait of Victoria, he remained glued to his seat, fuming. The

British were deeply offended. Then he helped Buchanan frame an impru-
dent document called the Ostend Manifesto. Now that the United States
had expanded from sea to sea, some Americans—especially Democrats—
were looking to the Caribbean and South America for new lands to annex.
Cuba seemed an especially rich and fat prize. It lay just ninety miles from
Florida; it already did considerable business with America; Spain's grasp
on it looked weak; and pro-slavery forces liked it because it would add
more slave territory to the ledger. The Ostend Manifesto argued that
if Spain would not sell Cuba to the United States, it should be taken by
force. It caused an international uproar.

Leaving few friends and several unhappy creditors behind, Sickles
returned to New York in 1855. Tammany made him chair of its executive committee and he got elected to the state senate. He was a leading
organizer in the creation of Central Park—not least, he readily admitted,
because he hoped to make a bundle speculating on the surrounding real
estate. He did not. Dan Sickles would always be much better at spending money than at making it. In 1856 both Sickles and Isaiah Rynders
stumped for Buchanan's successful presidential campaign. Tammany got
Sickles sent to Congress as his reward, and Buchanan would appoint Rynders as federal marshal for New York, a classic example of handing the fox
the keys to the henhouse. In the *Herald*, Bennett continued to denounce
Sickles, including an accusation that he'd committed mail fraud. Sickles
sued for libel, but the case never made it to court.

At Buchanan's festive inaugural ball on March 4, 1857, held in a cavernous wooden shed thrown up on Judiciary Square to accommodate all
his celebrating "Buchaneers," Dan buttonholed various men of influence.
Teresa, generally acclaimed one of the premier belles of the ball, chatted
and danced with Washington's district attorney, the handsome, dashing
Philip Barton Key. He was Francis Scott Key's son, a nephew to the arch-
conservative chief justice Roger B. Taney, and a scion of Washington's
pro-slavery elite. In 1848, he had prosecuted two white men for "stealing"
seventy-six Washington slaves in a failed mass escape attempt. Key won
his case and the men spent four years in prison.

Key and Teresa made a pretty couple as they danced. Eyebrows went up
and tongues wagged. Dan, politicking at the other end of the hall, seemed
not to notice. He wouldn't catch on for another two years.

CHAPTER 10

From New York to Bleeding Kansas

We are not one people, we are two people. We are a people for Freedom and a people for Slavery. Between the two, conflict is inevitable.

—*Horace Greeley*

In 1854, Stephen Douglas shepherded new legislation through Congress, which was dominated by Democrats as the Whig Party fell apart. The ostensible issue was where to lay the tracks for the first transcontinental railroad west from the Mississippi. At stake were all the federal subsidies and real estate opportunities that would come with the project. Illinois senator Douglas wanted a northern route, which required organizing the territory of Nebraska for statehood. Southern Democrats balked, since the old Missouri Compromise mandated that Nebraska be admitted as another free state, the last thing they wanted. Douglas needed their support, so he proposed nullifying the Missouri Compromise and splitting the sparsely settled region into two territories, Nebraska and Kansas. The residents of each would decide for themselves whether to go slave or free, a principle he gave the eminently democratic-sounding name "popular sovereignty." The presumption was that the more northern Nebraska would probably go free-soil, but Kansas, next door to Missouri with its ninety thousand slaves, might well go slave. Southern Democrats, who'd never expected to see any slavery introduced north of the 1820 demarcation, were delighted by this new opportunity for expansion and agreed.

As the debate went on in Congress in early 1854, protest rallies flared up throughout the North. Greeley railed against the plan as "measureless treachery and infamy" and "infernal rascality." In the *Times*, Henry Raymond predicted that passage of the bill would promote "a deep-seated, intense, and ineradicable hatred" of slavery in the North "which will crush its political power, at all hazards, and at any cost." In the *Herald*, Bennett supported the bill, scoffing that it was sophistry to distinguish between black slavery and "white slavery"—a popular term for wage labor—except that in his estimation black slaves were treated better than white ones.

The bill made it through the Senate in March. That month, by no coincidence, the Republican Party, started by abolitionists and free-soilers, was born in the ashes of the Whigs. Greeley named it. When Seward, Weed, and Raymond also came over, Greeley's personal rivalries with them would often get the better of his politics, shaping his stormy, on-and-off relationship with the party.

Franklin Pierce signed the act into law in May. Kansas became the first actual battleground between pro- and antislavery forces. Only about a thousand settlers lived there when the act became law. Some twelve hundred abolitionists, mostly from New England, headed to Kansas as settlers in 1855, intent on voting to keep it free-soil. Thousands of pro-slavery Missourians flooded across the border to oppose them. The pro-slavers, dubbed "border ruffians" by the Northern press, came armed and angry. The free-soilers armed themselves as well. Bloodshed was inevitable.

New York abolitionists and antislavers couldn't resist getting involved. In March 1855, Henry Ward Beecher went up to Hartford's North Church to speak at a rally for a contingent of abolitionist colonists headed to Kansas. He was now preaching that when it came to ending slavery there was "more moral power" in a rifle or sword "than in a hundred Bibles." As he worked the crowd into a froth, many of them Yale students and faculty, a professor stood up and pledged to buy the colonists a Sharps rifle, renowned for its large bore and accuracy. Beecher went into auction mode and raised twenty-five pledges. One was from a man named Killam, which struck Beecher as funny. Returning to Brooklyn, Beecher raised funds for another twenty-five rifles from the Plymouth congregation. The young men of the colony, each armed with a shiny new weapon, dubbed themselves the Beecher Bible and Rifle Company. In New York, the papers leaped on the story, calling Sharps rifles "Beecher's Bibles" and Plymouth "the Church of the Holy Rifles."

Charles Dana, Horace Greeley's managing editor at the *Tribune*, also raised money to send rifles; New Yorkers even purchased an old howitzer and shipped it. In the paper, Dana kept up such a fierce barrage of editorials supporting the free-soilers and denouncing the border ruffians that Greeley privately begged him to cool his rhetoric. Greeley had appointed himself the paper's Washington correspondent, and Washington was effectively a Southern city. Greeley knew that *Tribune* readers around the country assumed that Uncle Horace wrote all the editorials. His antislavery opinions had already made him a hated figure in the South. Now he feared for his life on the streets of the nation's capital.

Dana did not relent. In 1855 he sent an idealistic young correspondent named James Redpath to Kansas. Redpath went not just to cover the conflict, but to get involved. Born in 1833, he came as a teen with his family from Scotland to America in the late 1840s. They settled in Michigan. He was nineteen when Horace Greeley saw his writing in a Detroit paper and brought him to New York in 1852. Brilliant, restless, the ginger-haired young Scotsman—"Red" to friends—was taking the first steps in an amazing career with many surprising turns. He soon chafed at toiling in the bowels of the *Tribune* as an anonymous cub reporter and decided that Greeley, off gamboling in the fields of politics, was a "sham."

About the time that Redpath came to New York, Frederick Law Olmsted began a series of long tours of the cotton South, writing dispatches for Raymond's new *New York Times*. Although he's remembered today as the codesigner of Central Park, a project that would begin in 1858, Olmsted made his first impact through these *Times* articles on slavery and the South, collected in several bound volumes that were widely read in the years leading up to the war.

Bored with his office job, Redpath decided to follow in Olmsted's footsteps. He traveled extensively in the South beginning in 1854. Warned that Southern whites might react hostilely and even violently to the presence of a "Greeley spy" among them, he traveled under assumed names and mailed his dispatches to friends in the North, who relayed them to Dana at the *Tribune* and to the *National Anti-Slavery Standard*, the weekly organ of the American Anti-Slavery Society. In 1859 the New York abolitionist publisher A. B. Burdick would collect Redpath's articles as *The Roving Editor; or, Talks with Slaves in the Southern States.*

Redpath's personal, epistolary writing is sometimes witty and sarcastic— he had fun reporting Southerners' very low opinions of the "d——d rascal" Greeley—other times angry. He surreptitiously interviewed slaves, poor whites, plantation owners. He saw slave auctions in New Orleans, caught services in both white and black churches, and toured Charleston's infamous slave pen the Sugar House, where slaveholders too squeamish or just lazy to whip their slaves themselves could pay a small fee to have it done for them. Whites, he reported, almost uniformly insisted that their slaves were happy and content. The slaves themselves consistently told him otherwise. What Redpath saw and heard in the South converted him not just to abolitionism but to the conviction that with the right incentives slaves could easily be roused to armed insurrection.

Now he headed west with Dana's blessings to put his convictions into practice on the Missouri-Kansas border. That's where he met the grand old man of armed slave revolt, John Brown. Brown was born in 1800 into a Congregationalist and abolitionist household in Connecticut and raised on the frontier in Connecticut's Western Reserve (northeast Ohio). He was one of the rare white men of his time, even among abolitionists, who sincerely believed that blacks and Native Americans were his equals. In 1849 he and his wife moved to North Elba, New York, to be near Timbucto, the wealthy abolitionist Gerrit Smith's ultimately failed experiment to establish a farming colony for free blacks. Meanwhile, his son John Jr. moved to New York City to work for the abolitionist publisher Fowler & Wells, which had offices on Nassau Street and a shop on Broadway.

By the passage of the Fugitive Slave Law, Brown was formulating a plan to lead a guerrilla army into the South and encourage slaves to armed revolt. First, though, there was Bleeding Kansas. In 1854 four of Brown's grown sons moved their families to a small community of free-soilers there. John Jr. was soon writing Brown, asking him to bring weapons. He arrived in 1855 with rifles, swords, and other supplies. Pro-slavers from Missouri were by then crossing the border in armed guerrilla squads and executing raids on free-soil settlements. A particularly fearsome posse who called themselves the Kickapoo Rangers burned the free-soil town of Lawrence on May 21, 1856.

The next day a Democratic congressman from South Carolina, Preston Brooks, sought out the venerable Massachusetts abolitionist senator Charles Sumner on the floor of the Senate. Sumner had delivered a thundering speech denouncing the "Crime Against Kansas," in which he vilified Stephen Douglas as a "noisome, squat and nameless animal" and also mocked South Carolina senator Andrew Butler for taking up with "the harlot, Slavery." Brooks, who was related to Butler, found Sumner at his desk and beat him about the head and back with a cane of gutta-percha. Although it was a light cane used for whipping dogs and slaves, he so severely whaled on Sumner, as colleagues stood and watched, that the senator was permanently impaired.

Reactions in the North and South showed how far apart they had grown. The *Tribune* observed that a young Southerner "trained to knock down his human chattels for 'insolence'—that is, for any sort of resistance to his good pleasure—will thereafter knock down and beat other human beings who thwart his wishes...and human society becomes a state of war, diversified by interludes of fitful and hollow truce." As he had predicted, Greeley was assaulted in Washington for these sentiments. A drunken congressman from Arkansas accosted him on the street and gave him a beating, then followed him to his hotel room and beat him up some more.

Preston Brooks was lionized in South Carolina, presented with several silver-tipped canes, and promptly reelected. The future Mississippi senator and Supreme Court justice Lucius Quintus Cincinnatus Lamar II would argue that the fault was all Sumner's—that if Sumner "had stood on his manhood...and struck back," the "blow need not have been the opening skirmish of the war....We are men, not women."

The sack of Lawrence on May 21 and the caning of Sumner on May 22 drove John Brown "crazy—*crazy*," according to his son Salmon. Brown decided it was time to fight terrorism with terrorism. On May 24, he led seven others, including three of his sons (but not John Jr.), on a retaliatory raid, dragging five pro-slavers from their cabins and brutally hacking them to death in what became known as the Pottawatomie Massacre.

Brown and his small band then went into hiding to evade federal troops and Missouri vigilantes. On June 2 they surprised a vigilante squad, killing four and taking two dozen prisoners. Brown's name was now on every lip in Kansas and Missouri. To pro-slavers he was a feared and hated bogeyman. Most Kansans, including John Jr., were appalled by Pottawatomie and terrified of pro-slavery reprisals, while a few others saw Brown as a righteous avenger.

Redpath was already of the latter opinion when he rode out from Lawrence to find Brown. He discovered his band camped in a wooded creek bed, roasting a pig. Redpath came away from this first meeting convinced that Brown was "the predestined leader of the second and the holier American Revolution."

A young man who had made his way from Brooklyn to Kansas also showed up at Brown's camp in early June. John E. Cook was a slight, swaggering, irrepressible chatterbox who dressed flashily even in the wilderness. With his soft skin, long blond curls, and deep blue eyes, he radiated an erotic, androgynous magnetism that men found unsettlingly feminine and women found irresistible, to judge by his string of conquests wherever he went. Further confounding Brown's men, for all his pretty looks Cook cursed like a heathen, told wild tales of his exploits as a hunter of buffalo, and augmented his fancy duds with a fourteen-inch bowie knife, a brace of shiny Colt pistols, and a hunting rifle, with which he was a crack shot.

Cook was born in 1829 in a prosperous Congregationalist household in the town of Haddam, Connecticut. After briefly studying law at Yale he moved in 1854 to Williamsburg, an independent township about to be incorporated into greater Brooklyn, to clerk for a law firm. He sometimes taught Sunday school at a Dutch Reformed church in Bushwick, and may well have attended some of Henry Ward Beecher's antislavery sermons in Brooklyn Heights. He headed for Kansas in 1855.

In August 1856, when some three hundred Missourians burned the settlement of Ossawatomie, they shot and killed Brown's son Frederick. "The shot that struck the child's heart," Henry Ward Beecher would later say, "crazed the father's brain." Brown led the defense in an all-out battle and killed some thirty of the attackers. He was known as "Ossawatomie Brown" from then on.

With both federal troops and Missouri vigilantes scouring Kansas for him, Brown slipped away. He traveled around the Northeast seeking help with his planned guerrilla incursion in the South. Both Redpath and Cook stayed in Kansas. Redpath went from writing about the armed abolitionists to fighting alongside them in several skirmishes with the pro-slavers. On Brown's orders, Cook led a small band who called themselves the Freestate Marauders on night raids across the border in Missouri, dragging slave-owning families out of their beds and threatening to hang them if they didn't leave the area. When Brown sent Cook to scout out Harpers Ferry, Cook impregnated and married the daughter of the woman who ran his boardinghouse.

The *Tribune* was by now a virtual nest of Brown sympathizers and co-conspirators. Along with Redpath the staff included Richard Hinton, an English journalist and abolitionist who had met and befriended Redpath and Brown in Kansas. Another Englishman, Hugh Forbes, worked for the *Tribune* as a translator of European news items. Forbes boasted a swashbuckling record as a mercenary who had fought with Garibaldi in Italy and spent some time in an Austrian prison before coming to New York. He was also a quarrelsome and untrustworthy alcoholic. Brown hired him to train his guerrilla army, and Greeley kicked in some funds. Forbes never trained a soul. He merely tried to extort more money out of Brown by threatening to go public with the insurrection plans.

In Boston, Brown met with Samuel Gridley Howe, the physician who founded the Perkins School for the Blind. He was also a leader in prison reform and the antislavery movement. Today he's probably better known as the husband of the writer and feminist Julia Ward Howe. She was born in New York City in 1819 and grew up in "a fine house on the Bowling Green, a region of high fashion in those days," she would write in her 1899 *Reminiscences*. Her father, Samuel Ward, descended from Revolutionary patriots, was a partner in Prime, Ward & King, the largest private bank in the city. Ironically, considering Julia's sympathies, it got that way financing the international cotton trade. As a young lady, Julia enjoyed teas and balls, rounds of visits to the Astors' and other drawing rooms on holidays. She took Italian lessons from the younger Lorenzo Da Ponte and music lessons from European maestros. Howe, whom she married in 1843, was eighteen years her senior. It was not a happy union; for all his antislavery activism he was an authoritarian patriarch as a husband and tried to quash both her free spirit and her writing. So her first volume of poems, *Passion Flowers*, was anonymous. Despite her husband's efforts she also wrote plays, a biography of Margaret Fuller, travelogues, and a number of pieces for Greeley and Dana at the *Tribune*.

In *Reminiscences*, Julia remembered the day John Brown came to their house. "He looked a Puritan of the Puritans," she recalled, "forceful, con-centrated, and self-contained." Hearing his plans to raise an armed Negro insurrection, she wrote, "I confess that the whole scheme appeared to me wild and chimerical. None of us could exactly approve an act so revolu-tionary in its character, yet the great-hearted attempt enlisted our sympa-thies very strongly."

Early in the war, she'd take a song sung for Brown and adapt it with new lyrics into one of the Union's most popular anthems.

CHAPTER 11

Leaves of Grass

Through me forbidden voices,
Voices of sexes and lusts...voices veiled, and I remove the veil,
Voices indecent by me clarified and transfigured.
                                        —Walt Whitman

When John Brown Jr. was working at Fowler & Wells in the early 1850s, it's quite possible he saw Walt Whitman there. Walt never committed himself to abolition as ardently as, say, the Browns did; he had come to Fowler & Wells not to read their abolitionist literature but to have the famous phrenologists read the bumps on his head. Still, in 1855, amid all the furor over slavocracy versus democracy, he would launch a slim volume of verses that expressed the most unreservedly democratic vision yet penned in America, while also utterly revolutionizing American letters. The problem was that very few people read *Leaves of Grass* at the time, and few of them were in the mood to hear its message.

Walt was born on Long Island in 1819, the second of six sons. His father, Walter Sr., was of English stock, his mother, Louisa, Dutch; both families were yeoman farmers, and also slaveholders until Manumission Day in 1827. "The hard labor of the farm was mostly done by them," Walt would recall of his grandfather's slaves, "and on the floor of the big kitchen, toward sundown, would be squatting a circle of twelve or fourteen 'picka-ninnies,' eating their supper of pudding (Indian corn mush) and milk." Louisa was Quaker, Walter a radical Democrat with a pronounced streak of revolutionary individualism. He was thrilled to meet Thomas Paine when the latter, by then widely reviled for his antireligionism, was an outcast dying in Greenwich Village. Walter taught his children to read other radicals such as Fanny Wright, the feminist, abolitionist, and free-thinker. Although not serious churchgoers, the Whitmans took Walt as a boy to hear Elias Hicks, the abolitionist Quaker who exhorted his listen-ers to reject authoritarian religion and follow their own "inner light"—"pointing to the fountain of all naked theology, all religion, all worship, all the truth to which you are possibly eligible—namely in yourself and your inherent relations," Walt wrote many decades later. All of this had obvious influence on the poet who would sing the "Song of Myself."

Walt grew up in a dozen homes of decreasing size on Long Island and then in Brooklyn as Walter Sr., a carpenter, struggled to provide for his family. As he grew up, Walt would become the family's principal bread-winner, and play the father figure to his younger brothers and sisters after Walter Sr.'s death in 1855.

Like many other American kids in his time, Walt had haphazard schooling but was an avid reader and autodidact. At eleven he was run-ning errands for a Brooklyn law office, and at twelve he apprenticed at the first of a long list of Brooklyn and New York newspapers for whom he'd work as a typesetter, writer, or editor. In 1842 he was transfixed by a series of lectures given in Manhattan by the New England Transcenden-talist Ralph Waldo Emerson, whom Horace Greeley had been extolling since the first issues of the *Tribune* for his "profound and luminous per-ception, forcible expression, and a fervid, innate eloquence." Emerson's call for a truly American poetics, not beholden to England, a homegrown poetry that captured "our log-rolling, our stumps and their politics, our fisheries, our Negroes and Indians, our boasts and our repudiations," was another profound influence on the budding poet.

Whitman spent the 1840s and early 1850s as a journeyman journalist. The myth of Walt as a loner and outsider, which he himself would later help to build, fits him better as a poet than as a newspaperman, when he was a well-known member of the trade. He got to know Greeley and Dana; the *Tribune* published a few of his pieces and would be the first daily to review *Leaves of Grass*. Walt also became friends with William Cullen Bryant of the *Evening Post*. The two of them took long walks in Brooklyn. In 1845, Walt wrote two pieces for the *Broadway Journal*, the literary magazine Edgar Allan Poe bought for fifty dollars—a loan from

Greeley—and quickly drove into the ground. Thirty years later, when Poe's grave in a Baltimore churchyard belatedly got a proper monument, Walt was the only writer of note to attend the ceremony.

Walt's politics were never deep; they were more emotional and reflexive than reflective. In his early twenties he flirted for a while, as did many other young white New Yorkers, with the nativist movement. When he edited a Democrat two-penny daily, the *Aurora*, at the height of the controversy over Bishop Hughes's parochial schools in 1842, his editorials railing against the Irish "bog-trotters" were as nasty as anyone's. After editing the *Brooklyn Daily Eagle* from 1846 to 1848, he was fired for his free-soil opinions. He later published his own very short-lived free-soil paper, the two-page weekly *Freeman*. Like Greeley, he opposed expanding slavery into the territories because he wanted them kept open to white settlers, rather than out of any great sympathy for Negroes.

In 1849, Whitman walked into the Fowler & Wells Phrenology Cabinet, a bookshop on Broadway near City Hall. Lorenzo and Orson Fowler (who'd been depicted in the 1848 cartoon reading the bumps on Zachary Taylor's head), with their brother-in-law Samuel Wells, were the leading publishers and distributors in America of books and periodicals on "Phrenology, Physiology, Psychology, Hydropathy, Phonography, Spirit-rapping and Women's Rights." Among their titles were books by Greeley and Margaret Fuller. Phrenology had come to America in the 1830s and had not yet been ridiculed out of all favor. Whitman, Greeley, Henry Ward Beecher, and many other progressive thinkers explored it as a path to self-knowledge. Whitman wrote for the Fowlers' magazines and did some work for them as a book agent. Since the Fowlers were also abolitionists, Walt now began to move in that direction as well.

In 1855, about to turn thirty-six, Whitman self-published the twelve unnamed poems in the first version of *Leaves of Grass*, an astonishing volcano of visionary free verse. It was utterly unlike anything that had been written in America before—or anything that would be written again until the twentieth century. Ecstatic and mystical, earthy and erotic, modernist before modernism, its imagination vaulting from a single atom to the whole whirling cosmos, it was rampantly egoistic and idiosyncratic at the same time that it championed the most truly democratic ideals America had yet produced. *Leaves* was the poet declaring his love for the whole nation, from its big eastern cities to its farthest frontier, North and South, and every type of person in it, whom he catalogued. "I am the mate and companion of people, all just as immortal and fathomless as myself; / They do not know how immortal, but I know. / Every kind for itself and its own." He included blacks, if awkwardly, along with everyone else in his democratic fervor, something he might not have done a few years earlier.

Whitman published *Leaves* in an edition of 795 copies, helping to set some of the type himself in a Brooklyn Heights print shop a couple of blocks from Plymouth Church. He arranged with Fowler & Wells to distribute it. They displayed it in their shops in Manhattan, Philadelphia, and Boston, and ran small ads in the *Tribune*. A couple of other shops in Manhattan and Brooklyn took it, though the Manhattan one quickly sent it back when the proprietor actually read some of it.

It helps to grasp what a shaggy and unruly sport of nature *Leaves* was in 1855 to know that Henry Wadsworth Longfellow's metronomic *Song of Hiawatha* appeared the same year. *Hiawatha* sold upwards of fifty thousand copies. Whitman later said that *Leaves* sold only ten. But it was not ignored. Whitman and the Fowlers put complimentary and review copies in many hands. Reviewers reacted more to Walt's egoism, his joyous earthiness and undisguised eroticism, than to his democratic visions. In the *Tribune*, Dana noted that *Leaves* contained "bold, stirring thoughts" but considered it "disfigured with eccentric fancies...uncouth and grotesque." At the *Times*, Raymond would hold back a review for a year, saying privately that the book's "sundry nastinesses...will and *ought* to keep it out of libraries and parlors." When the lengthy review finally ran in November 1856, it asked, "Who is this arrogant young man who proclaims himself the Poet of the Time, and who roots like a pig among a rotten garbage of licentious thoughts?" Yet it also conceded, "With all this muck of abomination soiling the pages, there is a wondrous, unaccountable fascination" to it, and "a singular electric attraction." Other reviewers were much harsher, simply damning *Leaves* as obscene "rowdyism" or the ravings of a lunatic.

Walt sent a copy to his distant and unaware mentor Emerson, and when Emerson wrote back a very encouraging letter—with the famous "I greet you at the beginning of a great career" line—Whitman and Dana had it printed in the *Tribune*, to the older poet's unhappy surprise. Emerson would quietly back away from Whitman as the poet's notoriety spread, but for the time being his apparent stamp of approval persuaded other progressives and Transcendentalists to come to Whitman's defense. Henry

David Thoreau recognized something of a kindred spirit, though their egos clashed and Walt's eroticism embarrassed him. James Parton, who had just written the first book-length biography of Horace Greeley, came on board—but, far more important, so did Parton's soon-to-be wife, Sara, who, writing as Fanny Fern, was one of the most popular authors and highest-paid newspaper columnists in the land. She'd been educated at the Hartford Female Seminary, founded by the feminist Catherine Beecher, sister to Reverend Henry and novelist Harriet. Her 1853 collection of columns—notably titled *Fern Leaves*, in a woodsy typeface Walt would borrow—had been a gigantic bestseller, as was her children's book *Little Ferns for Fanny's Little Friends* and her autobiographical novel *Ruth Hall*, which took its share of abuse because it was considered unladylike at the time for women to write autobiographically. She had just started writing for Tammany's *New York Ledger*, where she devoted two bold columns to championing *Leaves*. Soirees and salons around New York and Brooklyn got buzzing about Whitman and his scandalous verses.

Still, *Leaves* didn't sell. A second edition in 1856 fared no better, even with a quote from Emerson's letter emblazoned in gold leaf on the cover, Fowler & Wells backing it, and Walt writing his own anonymous reviews hailing the author's genius. He kept feverishly writing new poems and was hoping to put out a greatly expanded third edition when a sharp economic downturn forced Fowler & Wells to suspend all publishing efforts. They had been disappointed with Walt's sales and embarrassed by the vicious reviews, and probably wouldn't have handled the third edition anyway.

In 1859, forty and despondent—a "year all mottled with evil and good—year of forebodings!" he called it—Whitman started hanging around New York's first celebrated bohemians, who gathered to eat, drink, and carouse in a basement rathskeller called Pfaff's on Broadway near Bleecker Street. This colorful group was mostly poets and frayed-cuff journalists (so much so that newspaper people were frequently called, and called themselves, bohemians), plus some theater people and general bons vivants. The scene revolved around Henry Clapp Jr., a lapsed temperance man from New England and editor of the weekly *Saturday Press*, in effect the house organ of the crowd. The Pfaff's crowd was also behind the humor magazine *Vanity Fair*. Clapp was renowned for his dry wit; one of his best-known quips was that Horace Greeley was a self-made man who loved his maker.

James Redpath met Walt at Pfaff's and they became lifelong friends.

Others in the circle included the free-spirited writer Ada Clare and her notorious actress friend Adah Isaacs Menken, and a two-fisted Anglo-Irish writer, Fitz-James O'Brien, who in many ways was the quintessential bohemian on the scene—or as the *Tribune*'s Junius Browne put it, "one of the cardinals in the high church of Bohemia." Born in Cork in 1828 and raised in Limerick, O'Brien was the son of a prosperous lawyer and landowner. When his father died, O'Brien grabbed his handsome inheritance and ran with it to London, where he promptly squandered it living the high life. He came to New York penniless in 1852. A prolific writer of journalism, poetry, plays, and short stories (most notably gothic horror, for which he was dubbed "the Celtic Poe"), he spent what he earned partying with his friends. "O'Brien had a warm heart, a fine mind and a liberal hand," Browne wrote, "but he was impulsive to excess and too careless of his future for his own good." His Pfaff's friend William Winter, a theater and literature critic for the *Tribune*, noted O'Brien's "utter and unaffected irreverence for various camphorated figure-heads which were then an incubus upon American letters." When drunk, O'Brien often escalated a literary argument into a bout of fisticuffs and ended the night in the nearby Jefferson Market jail. He was proud of his broken nose and always ended a fight with a handshake. When the Civil War broke out he would leap immediately into the fray.

Other newspaper and magazine men, including Henry Raymond, also went to Pfaff's, friendly with if not inside the Clapp circle. Here Whitman found acceptance. He tended to sit to one side and bask quietly in the gaiety the bohemians generated.

By the time he had the third edition of *Leaves* ready, it had ballooned to five hundred pages. He would come to his next publisher in a way that would again link his name to John Brown's.

CHAPTER 12

Hard Times and High

While we seek mirth and beauty and music light and gay,
There are frail forms fainting at the door;
Though their voices are silent, their pleading looks will say
Oh! Hard times come again no more.

—*Stephen Foster*

Another panic hit New York's banks and Wall Street in the fall of 1857, with devastating impact. As depression swept out from New York to engulf the North, Stephen Foster's plaintive and beautiful ballad "Hard Times Come Again No More," published by Firth, Pond & Co. in 1854 and already popular in parlor rooms everywhere, was sung with a new depth of feeling. In New York's financial district, the Panic of 1857 drove businessmen into the arms of the Lord—and King Cotton.

The trouble stemmed from a welter of sources. Significant among them was a loss of conviction in the western expansion that had been attracting much speculation, both in railroad stock and in western land, since the Missouri Compromise. Guerrilla war in Kansas shook investors' optimism. Then, in the spring of 1857, the Supreme Court shattered their confidence with its extremely reactionary decision in the Dred Scott case. Scott was a slave from the South who sued for his freedom when his master moved to free soil north of the old Missouri Compromise line. In denying Scott's right to freedom, the high court declared the Missouri Compromise unconstitutional. Chief Justice Roger B. Taney, Philip Barton Key's uncle, wrote that according to the Constitution *no* blacks in America, wherever they lived, had any rights under the law whatsoever—they were "beings of an inferior order, and altogether unfit to associate with the white race, either in social or political relations, and so far inferior that they had no rights which the white man was bound to respect." In one stroke Taney and the other judges—six of whom were pro-slavery—seemed to render all the debate over whether the territories should be free or slave moot. According to them, slaves were property, like furniture or farm animals, and their owners were free to take them anywhere they liked.

The decision shocked the North. In New York, it stoked real fear among investors that the entire West could become one vast Bleeding Kansas. Land and railroad stock values plummeted over the summer. The New York headquarters of Ohio Life Insurance & Trust Company, which had speculated heavily in western railroads, failed in August, triggering a run on other banks' gold reserves, forcing many to suspend payments, call in loans, and shut off credit. This had a ripple effect that spread around the North and even as far as London and Paris, which had, through New York, been investing in western expansion as well.

Most New York banks and Wall Street recovered relatively quickly. Canny investors bought up cheap railroad stocks. Cornelius Vanderbilt, for instance, used the occasion to begin augmenting his shipping empire with strategic rail connections. The rest of the city, however, suffered a deep recession that cut across all sectors, from the waterfront to the shop floor to domestic service, even street peddlers and organ grinders. Estimates put the number of New Yorkers and Brooklynites who lost their jobs as high as one hundred thousand. An estimated forty thousand were thrown out on the streets by their landlords that winter—and it was a harsh winter. Some froze to death. A thousand merchants closed their stores. Construction projects went dormant.

Mayor Wood responded by proposing a grand campaign of public projects to put New Yorkers back to work. But he had made too many enemies to push it through. Tammany formed a fusion People's Party with the Republicans and Know-Nothings to oppose him. Wood lost his bid for reelection that November.

In their dismay that fall, many men of the city's financial district turned to God for succor, sparking what became a nationwide religious revival. By 1850 the wave of evangelism that had carried the Tappans, Beechers, and others along during the Second Great Awakening had ebbed. Then in September 1857 a former businessman named Jeremiah Lamphier began holding a noontime prayer meeting in a third-floor classroom of the North Dutch Church at Fulton and William Streets, a few blocks up from Wall Street. Lamphier had spent twenty years on Wall Street before giving up "mercantile pursuits" to be a lay missionary. His timing couldn't have been better. Only six men joined him the first day, but by October his flock had increased a hundredfold. By February, Bennett's *Herald* was running page-one stories about the "Great Revival of Religion in New York" and "Remarkable Conversions Among the Unrighteous." The *Times* reported that five thousand Wall Streeters of all Protestant denominations were praying together every workday. Many churches around the financial district were filling up for evening meetings as well. The movement, called the Third Great Awakening and the Businessmen's Revival, spread throughout the city and around the country that spring.

One strange young man drawn to the Fulton Street meetings was a bit too fervent in his devotions for the staid businessmen around him. Thomas "Boston" Corbett was born in London in 1832, came to New York City with his family as a boy in the early 1840s, then worked upstate in Troy as a hatter, during which time it's likely that he contracted the mercury poisoning that caused his mental problems. (The felt for hats was dipped in a mercury solution that accumulated in the workers over time. Dementia among them was common enough to give rise to the saying "mad as a hatter.")

After a street-corner conversion to Methodism in Boston, Corbett took the city's name as his own, grew his hair very long in imitation of Jesus, and became a street evangelist himself. At the age of twenty-six, after being approached by a prostitute, he went to his room in a boardinghouse and castrated himself with a pair of scissors so that he could avoid forever the temptations of the flesh.

A few weeks later he moved back to New York City and became an unwelcome regular at the Fulton Street meetings, shouting "Amen!" and "Glory to God!" and preaching at the other men in ways that made them uncomfortable. None of them had any inkling that in 1865 this odd young fanatic would become a national celebrity.

❧

While New York's economic ties to the expanding West suddenly weakened, the Cotton South, feeding a steady world market, was relatively unscathed by the Panic. This made New York's merchants and bankers all the more aware of how crucial their business ties to the South were. In Washington, South Carolina senator James Henry Harrison crowed that it was not the South that was dependent on the North, but vice versa. "The South [has] sustained you in great measure. You are our factors. You fetch and carry for us. One hundred and fifty million dollars of our money passes annually through your hands. Much of it sticks; all of it assists to keep your machinery together and in motion. Suppose we were to discharge you; suppose we were to take our business out of your hands; we should consign you to anarchy and poverty." He jeered at the North's westward expansion. "The great West has been open to your surplus population, and your hordes of semi-barbarian immigrants, who are crowding in year by year. They make a great movement, and you call it progress. Whither?" He added for good measure that without Southern cotton, "England would topple headlong and carry the whole civilized world with her, save the South."

New York's businessmen had little doubt that he was right. From this point right into the war years they, as well as the politicians and newspapermen who served them, defended the South and slavery even more passionately than they had before. At the same time, the widespread unemployment caused by the Panic redoubled workingmen's fears about emancipated blacks flooding the city and taking from them what work they could find. They joined the businessmen in fierce antiabolitionism.

⁓

The heterogeneous metropolis was rarely of one mind about anything. Even in times of economic woe and moral panic, it continued to offer myriad pleasures and entertainments for those who could afford to seek mirth and beauty and music light and gay.

Thus at around the same time that Boston Corbett was discomfiting New Yorkers on Wall Street, a twenty-three-year-old Shakespearean actor named Edwin Booth was dazzling them on Broadway. They were about the same age, but in no other way alike. Yet in a manner that no one, certainly not the two of them, could possibly have imagined, their lives would intertwine at the end of the Civil War.

Booth had come to the city to make his Broadway debut in *Richard III*. The Broadway theater district was then still strung on either side of Houston Street. Booth's venue was Tripler Hall, also called the Metropolitan Theatre, on the west side of Broadway in the middle of the block between Bleecker and West 3rd Streets. It was built in 1850 specifically for the arrival of the Swedish soprano Jenny Lind, whom Barnum brought to New York with unprecedented ballyhoo. Edwin's arrival generated its own hullabaloo, which Edwin Forrest, long touted as America's leading homegrown Shakespearean, suffered with much grumbling and gritting of the teeth. Forrest, now in his early fifties, understood that he might be expected to pass the baton to Booth. He gripped it tightly instead.

The Philadelphia-born Forrest was bitterly jealous of competitors. In 1849, his feud with the British Shakespearean William Charles Macready had been the pretext for the Astor Place Riot, the deadliest public disturbance in the city's history to then. Forrest's fans were associated with the lower-class Bowery Theatre, Macready's with the ritzier Astor Place Opera House. On May 10, 1849, a mob of Forrest's fans, some led by Isaiah Rynders, marched up to the Opera House, where Macready was performing for an audience of the city's elite. The mob tossed paving stones through the windows and set the building alight. When police failed to quell the disturbance, the 7th Regiment was called out. Made up mostly of toffs and scions of wealthy families themselves, the 7th opened fire on the crowd of ruffians, killing twenty-three and wounding many others. Isaiah Rynders was tried for being an instigator of the riot; his attorney "Prince John" Van Buren got him off. Judge Daly heard the cases of other instigators and (no doubt partly because he was such a huge Shakespeare fan) handed down harsh sentences. "Disaster Place" lost its audience, turned into a minstrel house, and closed a few years later.

Although this was Edwin Booth's Broadway debut, it was not actually his first time playing Richard III in New York. He had first performed the role at the National Theatre on Chatham Square, at the foot of the Bowery, in 1851. He had been a last-minute stand-in for the star, who had refused to go on an hour before curtain time. The audience at the National, as at the nearby Bowery Theatre, was a rough crowd. They liked slam-bang melodrama and dazzling spectacle, and if an actor didn't deliver, they responded with hoots, stamping feet, and hurled produce.

Edwin was terrified. He was, after all, only seventeen years old. The crowd was startled into quiet when, as the humpbacked Richard, he lurched onto the stage. By the end of his performance they were cheering wildly. The boy-king had escaped bodily harm. His triumph was all the more noteworthy because the actor he'd subbed for was the most celebrated Shakespearean in the land: Junius Brutus Booth. His father.

Born in England in 1796, of Jewish and Welsh heritage, Junius Brutus Booth had skyrocketed to stardom on London's stages, specializing in a florid and highly physical portrayal of Richard. At the height of his renown he suddenly decamped for America in 1821, leaving behind a wife and bringing a pregnant lover, a flower girl from the streets. Before the year was out he was barnstorming American stages from New Orleans to New York to thunderous ovations. He made up for his stumpy, bow-legged physique with his giant acting style and an offstage reputation as a prodigious drinker and satyr. He sired ten children in America, bastards all—he wouldn't marry their mother until the 1850s—and raised them in an expanded log cabin, which he named Tudor Hall, north of Baltimore. Junius Brutus Jr. was born in 1821. Edwin, the seventh child, was born in 1833 during a meteor shower, and with a caul. The family's black servants predicted he'd have the second sight, and he would later claim to experience accurate premonitions. Ironically, Booth Sr. named him for Edwin Forrest. John Wilkes came ninth in 1838. He was his parents' favorite. His father named him after the eighteenth-century English radical who was charged with sedition for railing against tyrannical kings and princes. It was a legacy John would take all too seriously.

Junius Brutus Booth may have been the star Shakespearean actor in America, but gradually the alcoholism and a festering disturbance of the mind made him one of the most unpredictable as well. In the middle of a performance he might break into a bizarre rant or a bawdy song, upbraid the audience, or decide to do the part on tiptoe or in a whisper. Sometimes he'd refuse to go on at all. Theater managers tore their beards out trying to handle "the Mad Tragedian," but he packed their houses with audiences drawn as much by his antics as by his acting.

By the mid-1840s Junius's drinking and profligate spending had grown so out of hand that Edwin, at the age of twelve, was delegated to tour with him. His job was to keep the bottle hidden before performances, pocket as much of his father's pay as he could, and take his elbow on the way home from a night of carousing afterward. Edwin would later call this "my punishment." They returned often to New York, where Junius's impassioned acting and wild reputation guaranteed box-office success at the Bowery and National. To a young Walt Whitman, who would see him many times at the Bowery, Junius's "genius was to me one of the grandest revelations of my life, a lesson of artistic expression. The words fire, energy, *abandon*, found in him unprecedented meanings."

At eighteen, Edwin sailed with his father from New York by way of Panama to San Francisco, where Junius Jr. had moved. After some engagements there, Edwin toured the rough stages of the West while Junius Sr. headed home. Mr. Booth took sick in New Orleans and died on a Mississippi riverboat at the age of fifty-six. "What, Booth dead?" a contemporary cried. "Then there are no more actors!"

All three of his sons followed him onto the stage. Junius Jr., known as June, was uninspiring, but Edwin and John Wilkes, in their very different ways, would dazzle. Slight, pale, melancholic, his romantic dark curls hanging to his shoulders, Edwin seemed born to play Hamlet. John Wilkes was his opposite, noted for his dark good looks and his athleticism, given to leaping off balconies, dangerously violent swordplay, and "boisterous declamations." After a performance he would bathe in oysters to soothe the bruises. When he injured his right arm he switched the swordplay to the left and made up for the clumsiness with demonic aggression. He first became popular in the South, where the gentlemen admired his manliness and the belles swooned in bevies. Ravenous for fame, John would compete with Edwin always.

In San Francisco, Edwin shared the stage with the pretty, ambitious Laura Keene, a British actress newly arrived in America. Her path would cross with the Booths' more than once. Born Mary Frances Moss in London seven years before Edwin, she had married a man named Taylor at eighteen, lived with him over a pub, and probably worked there as a barmaid. By 1851 she had left Taylor and was making her way up in London's theaters. Because it was considered immoral for a wife to leave her husband even under the greatest duress, she billed herself as Miss Laura Keene and instructed her two young daughters to refer to her in public as their aunt. In 1852 she was spotted by the theatrical agent J. Hall Wilton, who a couple of years earlier had convinced the reticent Jenny Lind to tour America for Barnum. He brought Keene to New York, whence she headed west.

Keene took Edwin for a lover, but wasn't too impressed with his acting—a rebuke he joked hurt him "Keenely." They sailed together anyway with a small troupe for Australia. It took seventy-two days to get there, and when they arrived Australia was in an economic slump. Keene blamed the poor box offices on Edwin's youth and inexperience. Then she discovered that her husband was living in Australia, and quickly sailed for home rather than be outed as a wayward wife. That was it for Edwin and

Laura's affair. Edwin and the rest of the company sailed on to Honolulu, where they were delighted to find that Shakespeare was a big hit with the native Hawaiians.

When Edwin came to the Metropolitan in 1857, Laura had preceded him there. She had taken over the space for a year to produce the popular *Laura Keene's Varieties*. Although many actors at the time doubled as theater managers, she was the first woman in America to do so. By the time of Edwin's arrival she was producing, managing, and acting in her own brand-new Laura Keene's Theatre, a mammoth, opulent white-and-gold wedding cake of a building just across Broadway from the Metropolitan.

For his Broadway debut Booth was billed, to his chagrin, as "Son of the Great Tragedian." He dreaded comparisons to his illustrious father. On tour in the West he'd asked managers to bill him as "simply Edwin Booth." One manager plastered Detroit with posters trumpeting "Simple Edwin Booth." To get out from his father's shadow, Edwin was developing a less bombastic, more naturalistic acting style. New York audiences loved it, much to the teeth-gnashing of older, old-school hams like Forrest.

Among Edwin's most devoted fans was the theater critic and aesthete Adam Badeau, who as "Vagabond" wrote a column of arts reviews and high-society gab for the weekly *Sunday Times*, which was not affiliated with the *New York Times*. "I am a Vagabond," he declared in the introduction to a collection of his columns published in 1859. "I care not who knows it, nor who is frightened from perusing my papers because of the announcement." Born in New York City in 1831 and raised up the Hudson in what's now Sleepy Hollow, Badeau returned to the city in 1856 with an excellent education, a comfortable inheritance, and an undisguised preference for members of his own sex. He went to *Richard III* with all his critical barriers up, and was instantly and irrevocably smitten with Booth. Although he found the twenty-three-year-old's performing style "undeveloped, chaotic, plastic," he gushed, "Young Booth has the unmistakable fire, the electric spark, the god-like quality, which mankind have agreed to worship." Not surprisingly, the two struck up a close, lifelong friendship, with Badeau serving as both promoter and aesthetic adviser.

Laura Keene meanwhile was having a great success of her own. In 1858 she debuted *Our American Cousin*, a silly parlor farce about an American bumpkin in England. It was an instant hit. It ran for 150 nights, then went on to tour America and England.

In 1860, Edwin Booth married the actress Mary Devlin; John Wilkes and Badeau were the witnesses. Edwin was doing well enough financially that they could take an apartment in the new, very stylish Fifth Avenue Hotel, a giant marble palace uptown at Madison Square, the first hotel in the country with one of Elisha Otis's vertical railways. Life was as comfortable and secure as a pair of antebellum actors could hope it to be. Even with his second sight, Edwin had no inkling of the bizarre and shattering turns it was going to take.

CHAPTER 13

Murder and Rebellion

I would sing how an old man, tall, with white hair, mounted the scaffold in Virginia.

—*Walt Whitman*

Most Tammany men who went to Washington found both the politics and the pleasures there terribly dull compared to New York City. To them the nation's capital was Podunk, small and Southern and provincial, set in a dismal fen that heated up intolerably in the summer.

Not Dan Sickles. He liked the South and Southerners, and was sympathetic to their cause. He loved involving himself in national and international affairs, hobnobbing with his friend President Buchanan, partying and philandering to his heart's content. He left Teresa alone at home more and more. As he did, Washington gossips noticed that Philip Barton Key's much-admired iron-gray horse was often seen hitched to the post outside the mansion Sickles had rented on Lafayette Square. Teresa and Key had started an affair. Key rented a house from a discreet "colored" man where they met in secret, but as two of the most easily recognized figures in town—Key the tall, athletic squire, she like a new doll right out of the gift box—they were inevitably spotted.

The gossip circulated and escalated for two full years before finally reaching Sickles. When he was told by a friend, he played the enraged husband to the hilt, although he must have known how hypocritical he was being. In a stormy scene he confronted Teresa, forced her to sign a tearstained confession, and banished her from his bed.

In February 1859, the hapless and clueless Key stood outside the Sickles mansion and, looking up at a bedroom window, waved a white hanky, watching through opera glasses for a responding signal from his lover. But it was Dan Sickles peeking from behind the curtains. He rushed down to the street, where, according to the *Times*, he waved a pistol and shouted, "You have dishonored my bed and family, you scoundrel—prepare to die!" The *Tribune* rendered it more succinctly: "Sir, you have dishonored me; prepare to die!" Key begged him for mercy and, pitifully, used the only weapon he had on him—he tossed the opera glasses at him. Sickles fired, and in a moment Key dropped dying into the gutter, shot three times, one ball piercing his chest and another his groin. According to witnesses, Sickles pressed the pistol to Key's head to deliver the coup de grâce, but it misfired. Then, standing over him, breathing heavily, he growled, "Is the scoundrel dead?" "Mr. Key's friends are quite indignant, and talk about shooting Mr. Sickles at sight," the *Tribune* noted.

It was one of the most sensational murders of the century. Sickles's friends and cronies, including President Buchanan, rallied behind him. The public and press largely did as well, "the provocation being deemed ample justification for the deed," the *Times* observed. There were a few holdouts. The Brooklyn *Times* thought that a true gentleman would have called Key out to the field of honor for a proper duel, not murder him like a dog in the gutter. And there was William Cullen Bryant in the *Evening Post*, who had been denouncing Sickles as a wicked scoundrel for some years by then. Now he railed that Sickles, "a person of notorious profligacy," "who, in his own practice, regards adultery as a joke and the matrimonial bond as no barrier against the utmost caprice," had "little right to complain when the mischief which he carries without scruple into other families enters his own." Bryant was correct, of course, but he leaned into a strong headwind of common antebellum morality, by which it was one thing for a husband to stray, something quite a bit more damnable when the wife did it.

Edwin M. Stanton, later Lincoln's secretary of war, led Sickles's defense team in a Washington courtroom that April. The press followed what the *Times* called the "intensely exciting" and "exceedingly impressive" proceedings in minute daily detail. Scores of potential jurors were disqualified because as married men they couldn't possibly render an impartial judgment. Stanton used a then novel defense, arguing that his client was not guilty due to temporary insanity. When on the eighteenth day the jury acquitted Sickles after a little more than an hour's deliberation, "the decorum of the Court went off at once in a most irregular but irrepressible cheering," the *Times* reported, and Sickles was "carried off in triumph by his friends."

Dan Sickles basked in nearly universal approbation for three months; then, as though he couldn't help himself, he plunged headlong into a pit of infamy once again by forgiving Teresa and taking her back. Now the public and press turned against him en masse. The moral standards of the time insisted that adulterous wives were to be scorned and abandoned; for Sickles to take Teresa back was to condone her actions, a more severe violation of the marriage code than any of his own "mischief." He would serve out his term in Congress, but his public career, all agreed, was over.

They were very wrong about that.

On the night of October 16, 1859, John Brown led twenty-one followers in a raid on the federal arsenal at Harpers Ferry, Virginia (soon to be West Virginia). He intended to liberate weapons and munitions with which to arm slaves for revolt. While his detachment took the arsenal, he sent John Cook and others to nearby farms to kidnap local slavers. So Cook was away when hundreds of local militiamen came rushing into Harpers Ferry and penned up Brown's small force at the arsenal. Cut off from Brown, Cook and his raiding party headed for the hills. On the night of the seventeenth, U.S. Marines led by Colonel Robert E. Lee and Lieutenant Jeb Stuart arrived. They took the arsenal back in a bloody siege the next morning. Fifteen people had been killed, including two of Brown's sons, the mayor of the town, and one local black man Brown's men mistakenly shot.

The first journalist to make it to Harpers Ferry didn't get there until a few hours after the fighting ended. David Hunter Strother wrote and illustrated for *Harper's Monthly* and *Harper's Weekly* under the nom de plume Porte Crayon. He was a local, born and raised in Martinsburg, just twenty miles from Harpers Ferry. After moving to New York in the 1840s he'd studied oil painting under Samuel F. B. Morse, then started a long and mutually fruitful association with the Harper brothers' empire in 1853. Strother happened to be in Martinsburg on the night of Brown's raid and got to Harpers Ferry by train. By the time he arrived the scene was in deplorable chaos. Many of the victorious marines were drunk and celebrating. Dead bodies strewn on the street had attracted a crowd of gawkers. Strother overheard one young man complain, "Gentlemen, just give room here. Can't you stand back and let the ladies see the corpses?"

Strother had little love for Brown, abolitionists, or Negroes. The November 19 *Harper's Weekly* would print a quartet of his drawings under the rubric "Effect of John Brown's Invasion at the South"—rude caricatures of male slaves brandishing pitchforks and hatchets, and a mammy wielding a knife. Yet at Harpers Ferry that day he also made sensitive sketches of Brown in defeat.

Because *Harper's* was a weekly, Strother's article didn't appear until November 5. The New York dailies had been all over the story by then, though much of what they'd reported was wildly inaccurate rumor. The *Herald* declared that an "Extensive Negro Conspiracy in Virginia and Maryland" was afoot on October 18; nothing like that materialized. As late as October 22, *The Sun* was still reporting that a mob of Negro insurgents, "all armed," had taken over the entire town and barricaded all the roads, rails, and bridges, and that "all the principal citizens have been imprisoned, and many have been killed."

Southerners, whose worst nightmares revolved around the threat of armed slave revolt, denounced Brown as an agent of the Republican Party and its mouthpiece Horace Greeley. The Republicans had made remarkable strides since starting up five years earlier. They had fielded their first presidential candidate in 1856, the abolitionist and explorer John C. Frémont. He ran a respectable second to Buchanan. Republicans had actually achieved a majority in the House by 1859 and were gaining on the Democrats in the Senate as well. The party could look to 1860 with real optimism, and no one in it wanted an association with the mad Brown to derail them. William Seward, the presumed front-runner for the nomination, condemned Brown. So did a dark horse well back in the pack, Abraham Lincoln. In the *Times*, Raymond decried the raid as "irresponsible anarchy or wild and reckless crime." Greeley wrote, "The whole affair seems the work of a madman." Greeley's enemies, including Weed, accused him of having known and backed Brown's plan; Greeley lied and denied it.

The state of Virginia remanded Brown to nearby Charles Town and hastily arraigned him on charges of murder, treason, and inciting insurrection, all hanging offenses. He was convicted on all charges and hanged on December 2. As a friend of the presiding judge and the nephew of the prosecutor, Strother got special treatment throughout the proceedings.

He was even allowed to climb the gallows after Brown's body had hung twisting for half an hour, lift the hood that covered the old man's head, and sketch his face in death. Northern opinion was such that *Harper's* decided not to run Strother's less than worshipful account of the hanging. It would not in fact appear in print until a 1955 issue of the magazine *American Heritage*.

Another witness to the hanging was the twenty-one-year-old actor John Wilkes Booth. He'd been performing in Richmond when the raid took place. Seeing troops of the Richmond Grays, the city's elite militia, boarding a train for Harpers Ferry, he convinced a pair of officers to lend him a uniform so he could tag along. As much as he despised Brown's abolitionism, he was impressed by the old man's calm courage as he mounted the gallows. He nearly fainted at the sight of the actual hanging.

~

After the hanging, the governor of Virginia allowed Brown's wife, Mary, to ship his body out of the state for burial in North Elba. When the train carrying the coffin reached Philadelphia, large crowds, both black and white, had gathered around the station. To avoid trouble, the mayor had the coffin secretly shifted to a steamboat. Theodore Tilton, an abolitionist from Brooklyn Heights and acolyte of Henry Ward Beecher, was sent to ride with the coffin up to its next stop, New York City. It arrived on the evening of Saturday, December 3. Leaving the coffin on board, Tilton crossed over to Brooklyn to meet with Jacob Hopper, a Quaker, abolitionist, and undertaker, who agreed to take charge of the body. Hopper rented a private room at the undertakers McGraw & Taylor at 163 Bowery near Delancey Street and had the coffin quietly moved there. When Hopper opened the rough walnut box he found Brown's corpse carelessly tossed inside, the noose still around his neck, still wearing the battle-tattered clothing he'd been hanged in. Hopper treated the corpse, gave it new clothes and a more presentable coffin. The undertakers' staff cut up the noose and snipped locks of Brown's hair to hand out as souvenirs. Thirty years later, Hopper revealed to the *Brooklyn Eagle* that he still had Brown's ragged clothes.

Word got out on Sunday, and a crowd gathered outside McGraw & Taylor wanting to see the corpse. To keep the crowd from getting out of hand, the police decided that if they would form a quiet line they could enter the premises and file past the body. Here several lives weave together in an only-in-New-York convergence. Two journalists joined the line. One was Richard Hinton, the English abolitionist who wrote for the *Tribune*. John Swinton, an editor at the *Times*, was the other. Both of them knew Walt Whitman. Viewing Brown's corpse, Hinton casually remarked on a resemblance to Walt. This stray thought put him in mind to recommend Walt to a new abolitionist publishing house just starting up in Boston, Thayer & Eldridge.

A month later, Thayer & Eldridge published its first title, *The Public Life of Capt. John Brown*, which James Redpath had hastily thrown together with Hinton's assistance. A worshipful biography of the "warrior-saint," it was soon a bestseller.

That May, Thayer & Eldridge published as its second title Whitman's much-expanded third edition of *Leaves of Grass*. It was far from a bestseller. In the five years since the first edition, *Leaves* had grown five times in length, including new sections extolling physical love between men and women and just between men. Encouraged by Henry Clapp, Whitman's friend from Pfaff's, Thayer & Eldridge sent review copies to New York papers of all political stripes, on the theory that any review, good or bad, would be useful. Most were bad, though often with a grudging grain of praise buried in them. The white supremacist *Day-Book*, for example, declared Whitman's poetry to be "disfigured by the most disgusting beastiality [*sic*] we remember ever to have seen in print," and the poet "vigorous, coarse, vulgar, indecent, powerful, like a great strong, filthy bull, delighting alike in his size and his strength, and his filth; full of egotism, rampant." Then it concluded, "The book is, in many respects abominable; in many respects the maddest folly and the merest balderdash that ever was written; but it unfortunately possesses these streaks of talent, these grains of originality, which will probably preserve the author from oblivion."

Once again, no bookstore would stock it and sales were terrible. For decades the librarians at Harvard would keep their copy under lock and key with the pornography. Thayer & Eldridge went bankrupt before the year was out. Whitman wouldn't try again with *Leaves* until after the Civil War.

⌒

After fleeing Harpers Ferry, John Cook, with a thousand-dollar bounty on his head, made it a hundred miles cross-country before he was nabbed in Pennsylvania. Hoping for leniency, he wrote out a twenty-three-page confession but drew a death sentence anyway. He was hanged two weeks after Brown.

His body was also brought by train to Jersey City, then across Manhattan to Brooklyn, where his Haddam family members and his young Harpers Ferry widow had gone to await it. It was taken to the premises of the Brooklyn mortician Dr. Thomas Holmes. Holmes would come to be known as "the Father of Modern Embalming." Reputedly he'd been practicing phrenology on Egyptian mummies when it occurred to him that the ancients had developed better methods of preserving bodies than were known in his day. He invented what are considered the first effective modern embalming fluid and pump. Cook's would not be the last famous corpse he preserved.

Cook's open-casket funeral took place at the Bushwick church where he'd sometimes taught Sunday school. Church elders worried that the service might attract an unruly crowd, but the funeral went off without incident. Cook was buried first in the Cypress Hills Cemetery nearby, then later moved to Green-Wood Cemetery.

⁓

When Fernando Wood lost his reelection bid in 1857, he was out but in no way down. Fernando Wood was nothing if not a survivor. Because the Tammany sachems had turned against him, he broke away with his supporters and formed his own rival machine, called Mozart Hall for the Broadway hotel where they held meetings. They fashioned themselves the true friends of the workingman, as opposed to the fat-cat sachems. He bought the *New York Daily News* (no lineage with today's paper of that name), which had started up in 1855 and was failing. His brother Benjamin took on the editorship and in a few years would be the principal owner. The *News* was Mozart Hall's house organ, sparring with the *New York Leader*, edited by Tammany sachem John Clancy. Benjamin promoted the wisdom and benevolence of Fernando Wood while railing against Clancy and Tammany's leadership as "a kid-glove, scented, silk stocking, poodle-headed, degenerate aristocracy."

Wood ran again for mayor in 1859. To oppose him, the Republicans nominated a wealthy textiles merchant, George Opdyke. Born in New Jersey in 1805, as a young man Opdyke had moved to New Orleans and innovated the mass production of cheap, ready-to-wear clothing, which

Louisiana plantation owners bought for their slaves. He brought that expertise with him to New York City in 1832 and built the city's first large-scale clothing factory, on Hudson Street, continuing to sell mostly to the Southern market. His closest competitors were the Brooks brothers, who were starting out around the same time. By the mid-1840s Opdyke was a millionaire and becoming a power in state politics—interesting, considering how he made his fortune, as a free-soiler and abolitionist. He joined the Republican Party when it started up, was elected to the state assembly, and would be a stalwart Lincoln supporter when the time came.

The shocking news of John Brown's raid on Harpers Ferry in October gave Fernando Wood an excuse to add a strongly pro-South, antiabolition tenor to his speeches. He called Brown a "fiend" and the South the city's "best customer," and repeated the by now familiar warning to white workers that abolishing slavery in the South would flood the North with millions of freed slaves competing for jobs. It worked. Fernando Wood was mayor again. He would still be in office when the Civil War began. Opdyke would be heard from again as well.

CHAPTER 14

Slave Ships

Through all the uproar over domestic slavery of the previous three decades, the port of New York had gone on quietly but openly serving as a major American hub of the illegal transatlantic slave trade. In 1858, when President Buchanan tripled the size of the African Squadron, slavers responded with a flurry of activity, trying to get in a few more profitable voyages before the end. The squadron bagged more than two dozen slavers between 1858 and 1861. Three had ties to New York.

Launched from a Long Island shipyard in 1857, the *Wanderer* was the most impressive racing yacht of its time. With its sleek, revolutionary design it could make an astounding twenty knots, outrunning any ship at sea, including steamers. It was also sumptuously appointed, because it was a rich man's toy. The owner, Colonel John Johnson, was a member of the New York Yacht Club. He was not a New Yorker but a Louisianan, owner of a cotton plantation, who, like many other plantation gentry, treated New York City as a home away from home.

In 1858, Johnson sold the *Wanderer* to another Southerner, a Charleston man named William Corrie, and got him admitted to the Yacht Club. Corrie was acting as a front for yet another Southerner with New York connections: Charles Augustus Lafayette Lamar, of the wide-flung Lamar family that included the former president of the Republic of Texas, Mirabeau Buonaparte Lamar, and Lucius Quintus Cincinnatus Lamar II, the future Supreme Court justice who approved when Sumner was whipped in the Senate. Charles's father, Gazaway Bugg Lamar, was one of the wealthiest men in Savannah, an innovator in steamboat shipping, a cotton factor with large interests in several plantations and warehouses, and director of Savannah's Bank of Commerce. In 1846, Gazaway moved to Brooklyn and helped found the Bank of the Republic, originally on Hanover Square and then on Wall Street. Among other transactions, the bank sold Georgia state bonds (the Georgia governor was an in-law) to New York investors.

Like most Southern gentry, his son Charles harbored uncompromising opinions about slavery. He felt it was the height of hypocrisy that buying and selling domestic slaves was perfectly legal, but bringing new slaves over from Africa carried the death penalty. His adventures in the African slave trade were less about making money—he had that to burn—than about proving a point and defying laws he considered unjust.

In New York, Corrie had no trouble hiring a crew. At Port Jefferson on Long Island the *Wanderer* was provisioned as though it were heading on a world cruise, including water tanks with a capacity of fifteen thousand gallons. Everyone on the waterfront could see what was going on, and when the yacht sailed out of Port Jefferson a navy revenue cutter (a vessel used to stop smugglers, slavers, and, during the war, blockade runners) intercepted it and forced it to dock at the Battery in Manhattan. There an assistant district attorney came aboard, with the U.S. marshal for New York—Isaiah Rynders. Corrie treated them to a splendid luncheon at the rosewood captain's table, they left in a jolly mood after a cursory glace around, and the *Wanderer* was free to make for Charleston.

From there, Corrie sailed across the Atlantic to the mouth of the Congo, where he shoved more than four hundred captured Africans, mostly boys, belowdecks. The *Wanderer* effortlessly outran British and African Squadron interceptors to make it home. At the end of November 1858 it reached Jekyll Island off the coast of Georgia, and the Africans were percolated into the existing slave population of the area. All Savannah buzzed with excited rumors. A slave ship from Africa was something no Georgians had seen in some time. Folks gawked at the Africans as though they were celebrities.

The press in New York and Washington picked up the story, forcing Buchanan's government to a reluctant show of action. Federal marshals in Georgia impounded the *Wanderer*, arrested a few of the crew, and went looking for the Africans. A district attorney brought indictments against Charles Lamar and a handful of the others the following spring. It wasn't easy bringing Lamar to trial in Savannah, where he was not only local royalty but now a hero for having so brazenly defied the Yankees.

He played the role to the hilt and had a grand time doing it. When the government auctioned the *Wanderer*, as it usually did with impounded slave ships, Lamar bid on it. Only one Savannah man dared to bid against him. Lamar outbid this rival by one dollar, then reputedly gave him a beating for his impudence. Now that he was the owner (again) of the ship, Lamar claimed that everything it had held was also his property, including not only its incriminating logs and other paperwork from the trip, but its cargo of Africans as well. A local judge actually ordered that two of them be handed over to him. In New York, Greeley and Raymond wrote flabbergasted editorials, Raymond marveling that "a slave-dealer, a kidnapper of negroes, a felon guilty of an act equivalent in the meaning of the statute to piracy" was allowed "to snap his fingers in the face of the law" in an act of "cowardly pilfering and spiritless piracy." Lamar fired off letters to both the *Tribune* and the *Times*, challenging Raymond and Greeley to duels. When the American Colonization Society raised $50,000 to send some of the rounded-up Africans to Liberia, where it promised to find them gainful employment, Lamar offered to match the sum, joking that he'd find work for them too, right at home. He took to going everywhere with one of his new boy slaves, whom he called Corrie. Meanwhile in Charleston, three grand juries refused to bring charges against the real Corrie for his part in the escapade.

The arrested crewmen stood trial late in 1859 and won acquittals. In 1860, facing the high improbability that any jury of Southern men would convict Lamar of a capital offense, the government dropped its case against him. Lamar would join the Confederate army, attain the rank of colonel, and be one of the last Rebel officers to die in battle.

The *Nightingale* began life in 1851 as a sleek luxury clipper meant to carry upper-crust passengers to London and back. It was named for the soprano Jenny Lind, Barnum's "Swedish Nightingale." An unusual full-length wooden figure of her adorned the prow. In February 1860, Captain Francis Bowen, an infamous "Prince of Slavers," bought it in New York, then sailed it to Liverpool, where, despite the great public show England made of interdicting the trade, it was an open secret that he was outfitting it and recruiting a crew to make a slave run. Off the coast of Angola the African Squadron's USS *Saratoga* boarded and found nearly a thousand African men, women, and children chained in the hold. Bowen somehow escaped. After sailing it to Liberia to release the Africans—minus 160 of them who died en route—the navy brought the *Nightingale* back to New York, where Bowen's three mates stood trial and faced the death sentence.

All three would get off. The one who earned the most press was the twenty-five-year-old Minthorne Westervelt, a relation of former mayor Westervelt. Minthorne was also well-born on his mother's side. His mother's father was Daniel Tompkins, a former governor and James Monroe's vice president. Tompkins Square Park on the Lower East Side was named for him.

Why was this wealthy and well-connected young man serving as the third mate on a slave ship? The prosecutor argued that he did it on a lark, for the adventure. His lawyers offered the dubious excuses that he hadn't known it was a slaver when he signed on and had no opportunity to jump ship once he found out. From his long instructions to the jury, printed in full in the *New York Times*, it's clear the notoriously lax judge Samuel Nelson did not want to see a Westervelt hanged. He stressed several times that the jurors "should look very deliberately and astutely into the facts and circumstances, and, before a conviction, should be satisfied that [Westervelt] acted freely, voluntarily, willingly, and without any restraint."

The jury deliberated overnight and declared themselves deadlocked at eight for conviction and four for acquittal. "This is not, perhaps, a matter of surprise," the *Times* commented, adding that it was "very sad" that a young man of privilege, who "has had about him the influences of the centre [*sic*] of civilization upon this continent...has barely escaped conviction of being engaged in the Slave-trade." The *Times* laid it to "the demoralization of public sentiment" in a city that had supported the trade for so long. Ten days later, Judge Nelson released Westervelt on bail, with the remarkable statement, "The prisoner is a young man—I think a little over twenty at the time he was charged with this offence—and it was proven on the trial that down to the commission of it he had borne a respectable and unblemished character, that his antecedents in that respect had stood unimpeached. He is now in Eldridge-street Jail, among felons and criminals, and undoubtedly among associations that are unfriendly to good principles and character—tending rather to corrupt and deprave a young mind." The defense had asked for bail to be set at $10,000. Nelson thought $5,000 was sufficient.

Westervelt was never retried. When the war came he enlisted and served for a year as a lieutenant in the 1st Regiment Marine Artillery, a New York unit also known as Howard's Artillery, which saw action in the Carolinas. While in the service he contracted chronic diarrhea and died in December 1862.

The navy pressed the *Nightingale* into service during the war. After that it was bought by Western Union. It apparently ended its career in Norway in the 1890s. One hundred years later, a Swedish antiques dealer discovered what he believed to be the *Nightingale*'s figurehead being used as a farmer's scarecrow. Although there was some question about its authenticity, it was sold at auction by Sotheby's in New York for $100,000 in 2008.

⌒

There was nothing unusual about the case of the slave ship *Erie* except for the way it would end. In August 1860, the African Squadron's *Mohican* seized the *Erie* and found 897 men, women, and children in the hold. Captain Nathaniel Gordon of Maine, already an experienced slaver in his midtwenties, was brought to New York. Awaiting trial in the Eldridge Street jail, Gordon was allowed out on the town at nights, on the promise he'd return in the morning. He could easily have bolted, as so many others did, but had no reason to fear the trial. It was clear that neither the presiding judge, Nelson, nor the original prosecutor, James Roosevelt, had any intention of seeing him hanged.

Then the political tide turned on him. With Lincoln's election that November, the spoils system dictated that Democrats give up their federal appointments to Republicans. Both Roosevelt and Rynders were out. The new marshal, Robert Murray, moved Gordon from his cushy digs on Eldridge Street to the dank and miserable Tombs, the city jail built on the swampy site that had formerly been the Collect Pond. The new prosecutor, E. Delafield Smith, who was also the chairman of the state's Republican central committee, had Washington's backing to press hard for a conviction.

Gordon would rot in the Tombs until June 1861 before seeing a courtroom. The outcome of his trial would send a dire message to all New Yorkers engaged in the Atlantic slave trade.

CHAPTER 15

The Tall, Dark Horse Stranger

If he had not come to New York, or if his speech there had been a failure, the Lincoln of history would not have existed.

—James McPherson

On Saturday, February 25, 1860, Henry Bowen was in Manhattan catching up on some work at the *Independent*, a religious weekly he and other Plymouth founders had started back in 1848, with Reverend Beecher and Theodore Tilton as star columnists and editors. The offices were at 6 Beekman Street, just off Printing House Square. In the middle of the quiet afternoon an unsettling figure materialized across his desk from him. A battered stovepipe hat exaggerated his improbable height. He was dark and thin as a shadow, with swarthy, deeply lined cheeks and hooded blue-gray eyes. He wore a rumpled black suit and carried a carpetbag. He stood there for a few heartbeats radiating diffidence. Then, almost apologetically, in a thin and nasal voice, he introduced himself as Abraham Lincoln and held out a giant hand.

Bowen was startled. All New York Republicans had read Lincoln's debates with Stephen Douglas when he unsuccessfully competed for Douglas's Senate seat in 1858. But only Horace Greeley and a few others had ever seen or heard the man. Lincoln had passed through the city in 1848, and then briefly visited it once again with his wife, Mary, in 1857. The latter had been a business trip for him—he tried, unsuccessfully, to collect some $5,000 owed him for legal services by the Illinois Central Railroad, which had offices in the city. Mary, a pathological shopper, had loved strolling Broadway.

Bowen was not on the committee that had invited Lincoln to come speak at Plymouth Church the following Monday, which would be Lincoln's first public speaking engagement in the metropolis. Although Lincoln had not yet declared himself a candidate, some Republicans were beginning to promote the prairie lawyer as a viable competitor to New York's statesmanlike Seward, whom Bowen, and most everyone else, favored to lead the party in the upcoming presidential race.

From Springfield, Lincoln had traveled by train to Philadelphia and then Jersey City. From there he'd taken a ferry to Cortlandt Street in Manhattan and walked the few blocks to Bowen's office. As the weary traveler asked Bowen's indulgence to drape his long legs across the couch for a little rest, Bowen felt "sick at heart" over Lincoln's prospects before a big-city audience.

The Plymouth committee had developed cold feet themselves. Invited speakers generated important revenue for the church, and they began to doubt that Lincoln, to whom they'd offered a very nice fee of two hundred dollars plus expenses, could fill the hall. Horace Greeley had pounced. He and William Cullen Bryant were on the board of an organization called the Young Men's Central Republican Union. It had begun in the 1850s as a pro-Frémont group; Greeley was now pushing it to become an anti-Seward one. The group gladly took over sponsorship of Lincoln's visit, and moved the venue to the Great Hall of the new Cooper Union for the Advancement of Science and Art in Manhattan. Lincoln didn't know of the venue change until Bowen told him.

In the *Tribune*, Greeley exhorted all Republicans in the city to come hear "a man of the people, a champion of free labor, of diversified and prosperous industry." In the *Evening Post*, Bryant was predicting that Lincoln would utter "a powerful assault upon the policy and principles of the pro-slavery party, and an able vindication of the Republican creed." Because Henry Raymond was in Seward's camp, the *Times* barely noticed Lincoln's arrival.

After resting up awhile in Bowen's office, Lincoln walked a short way over to bustling, clattering Broadway. Towering above the jostling crowd, a full seven feet from his heels to the top of his beaver hat, he turned into the Astor House. The Astor, which had been the jewel of luxury hotels when young Dan Sickles hobnobbed with Greeley and others there in the 1840s, had now been overtaken by newer, more deluxe competitors—the nearby Metropolitan; the St. Nicholas up at Broadway and Broome Street, featuring steam heat, which may be why it was a favorite of Southern visitors; and the Fifth Avenue uptown, where Edwin Booth lived. But the Astor was the dowager empress, still the favorite of visiting politicians and writers, who enjoyed bending ears and elbows in its top-notch restaurant and bar. The Lincolns had stayed there in 1857.

After a bellboy got a fire going in his room's fireplace, Lincoln sat long into the night working on his speech. The next morning, at Bowen's invitation, he joined the crowds streaming to the Fulton Street ferry landing. The Beecher Boats left every five minutes on Sunday mornings, and they were packed. Stepping off at the landing in the area now called DUMBO (Down Under the Manhattan Bridge Overpass), the crowd surged up the hill and onto Orange Street, where doormen kept them milling outside while members with rented pews took their seats. Only then were visitors allowed to pack the galleries. Bowen easily spotted Lincoln in the crush and escorted him to his family pew. Lincoln, with his ridiculously long legs, took the aisle seat. A small brass plaque still marks the spot. Bowen introduced him to Beecher after the service. Lincoln, never the most comfortable extemporaneous speaker himself, greatly admired the show Beecher put on. Beecher was too impressed with himself to think much of Lincoln; like many others in New York, he considered him coarse and not very intelligent. Like Horace Greeley, he would be both an ally and a gadfly.

On Monday a delegation of local Republicans met Lincoln at the Astor House. They spent some time fussing with the new black frock coat he'd bought for the trip; the sleeves were too short, and it had wrinkled in his trunk. They also gave him a new silk top hat to replace his worn-out beaver. Then they led him uptown to Mathew Brady's photography studio to have his portrait taken.

Brady's early years are obscure. Evidently he emigrated from Ireland but claimed to have been born upstate in the early 1820s. By the 1840s he was in New York City, making jewelry cases. It's believed that Samuel Morse introduced him then to the new daguerreotype miniature on copper plate, the first viable form of photography. In 1844, Brady opened his first daguerreotype gallery at Broadway and Fulton Street, diagonally across Broadway from Barnum's museum. He developed a reputation as the daguerreotypist to the stars, cannily wooing the celebrated figures of the day to sit for him, from John James Audubon and James Fenimore

Cooper to Daniel Webster and Henry Clay. In 1856 he hired the Scotsman Alexander Gardner. While Brady, whose eyes were failing, concentrated on business and promotion, Gardner took over the technical end of things and helped Brady make the crucial move from daguerreotypes to glass-negative photographs printed on paper. In 1858, Brady opened the National Photographic Art Gallery on Pennsylvania Avenue in Washington, and Gardner went there to run it for him. In the waiting room on any given day one could find some of the most powerful political and military figures in the country impatiently waiting their turn to have their portraits done. Besides *cartes de visite* (a combination postcard and calling card), many of these portraits would be reprinted as lithographs in newspapers and in *Harper's*—the editors there said that nine of ten portraits they ran came from Brady studio images—solidifying and furthering the great men's national celebrity.

When Lincoln came to him Brady had just opened his fourth studio in New York, at Broadway and 10th Street, three blocks up from the Cooper Union. A natty five foot six, Brady gazed up at the odd-looking giant with his mule ears and long neck and considered how to pose him. He decided on a pose he'd used before—for Senator Jefferson Davis. He had Lincoln stand at a slight angle to the camera with the fingertips of his left hand resting on a stack of books, which both suggested erudition and helped keep the body still during the camera's long exposure time. He also hiked up Lincoln's shirt collar to hide the neck. He couldn't do much about the wrinkles in Lincoln's coat, which are clearly visible in the photograph. Because of that long exposure time, portraitists clamped a brace to the subject's neck to keep the head still. For Lincoln, Brady had to lift his brace on a stool to reach. Like many subjects of the era, Lincoln looks self-conscious and ill at ease, even a little melancholy, in the resulting portrait. Nevertheless, it would be the most important photograph not only of his life but maybe of the century.

The Cooper Union, which had just opened the previous autumn, was the industrialist, inventor, and philanthropist Peter Cooper's great gift to the people of New York. Cooper was yet another of the era's self-made men, a poor grocer's son born in 1791 on Little Dock Street (later Water Street) in lower Manhattan and apprenticed to a coach-builder in his teens. By the age of thirty he owned a prospering glue factory, and at forty he introduced the Tom Thumb, the first practical steam locomotive in America. His Trenton Iron Works rolled out steel used in the first transatlantic telegraph cable. Other inventions ranged from a remote-controlled torpedo boat to the gelatin dessert that became Jell-O to bifocal spectacles with hinged lenses. In 1857 he'd bought the North American Telegraph Company, progenitor of AT&T, and invented ways to improve signal transmission. Meanwhile he'd been active in city politics, serving his first term as a non-Tammany Democrat on the Common Council in 1828 and running unsuccessfully for mayor in 1845.

Beginning in the 1840s he'd bought up small parcels of real estate below Astor Place to create Cooper Union, a school of applied sciences and technology that was a progressive marvel with its free admission and open enrollment (the first private college in the city to admit blacks, Jews, and women), a free library, a curriculum independent of any religious instruction, and an outstanding series of lectures in the Great Hall. With plush seating for two thousand and glittering gas lighting, it was the grandest auditorium in Manhattan.

Fifteen hundred people, "the pick and flower of New York" according to one correspondent—most every paper had a writer there—braved a slushy snowstorm to come to the Great Hall on Monday evening. Greeley, Bryant, and sixteen other prominent New York Republicans sat on the stage behind Lincoln; Beecher's young friend Theodore Tilton, who had accompanied John Brown's body to New York, was thrilled to sit among them. Bryant gave Lincoln a rousing introduction. He was one of the few New Yorkers besides Greeley who'd actually met him before. While traveling in Illinois in 1832 he'd encountered Lincoln as a gangly young captain of the state's Indian-fighting militia.

Lincoln was well aware of how much he had riding on this one performance. In a wide field of potential Republican presidential candidates he knew he appeared, on paper, one of the least qualified. He'd been a state legislator out in the boondocks, an undistinguished one-time congressman, and a celebrated but failed senatorial candidate. Despite all the interest his debates with Douglas had generated, newspapers still frequently misspelled his name as Abram, or called him Abe, which he hated because he thought it sounded too cornpone, or just went with A. Lincoln. He had nothing like Seward's public record or oratorical suavity. He'd later say he never felt so nervous in his life as he did on the Great Hall stage. He fidgeted in his new outfit, rattled his foolscap pages, and began to read his painstakingly worded speech in his thin, twangy voice. The first words out of his mouth, according to a witness, sounded like "Mr. Cheerman." The crowd gawked. Some tittered. This was the man who'd held his own against Douglas? Who was challenging the mighty Seward?

But a few minutes into it he found his footing, and for more than an hour he held the audience so spellbound that the only sound other than his voice was the hissing of the gas lamps—and the increasingly frequent bursts of applause. Lincoln was never a comfortable extemporaneous speaker; he preferred to read his speeches. He wrote himself some masterful ones, lawyerly in their precision and logic, and breathtaking, for the time, in their plainspoken concision. This night he went straight to the key issues of the hour, slavery and the threat of secession. He took no extreme abolitionist stance but offered a moderate, measured statement of conviction that while slavery was "an evil not to be extended" to new territories, the Constitution demanded that it be "tolerated and protected" where it already existed. "Wrong as we think slavery is, we can yet afford to let it alone where it is," he said. Knowing that Southerners would be reading his words in newspapers over the next few days, he spoke directly to them: "Do you really feel yourselves justified to break up this Government[?]" Addressing their fears of slave rebellion, he argued, "John Brown's effort was peculiar. It was not a slave insurrection. It was an attempt by white men to get up a revolt among slaves, in which the slaves refused to participate. In fact, it was so absurd that the slaves, with all their ignorance, saw plainly enough it could not succeed." Finally, rallying all Republicans, he concluded with the famous line, "Let us have faith that right makes might, and in that faith, let us, to the end, dare to do our duty as we understand it."

The audience exploded in cheers and tossed their hats in the air. It was an unalloyed triumph, not just for Lincoln but for Greeley, who now knew he'd found his champion in his battle with Seward, Weed, and Raymond. Greeley made a few closing remarks. Afterward, Lincoln went for a victory meal at the Athenaeum Club, farther uptown at Fifth Avenue and 16th Street. It was a club for "gentlemen of literary tastes," including Bryant, publisher George Putnam, and the lawyer and future president Chester A. Arthur.

Then Lincoln rode a streetcar down to the Astor House, reportedly "alone, the sole occupant of the horse-drawn vehicle." Near midnight, he walked over to the *Tribune*'s offices at Nassau and Spruce Streets, where an eighteen-year-old proofreader showed him the transcript of his speech.

Lincoln, who loved hanging around newspaper offices, lingered for quite a while, carefully reading the text and chatting with the young worker.

When Lincoln went down to the lobby of the Astor House the next morning, he saw that the *Tribune*, the *Herald*, and the *Times* had all run the speech in full. It also appeared later that day in Bryant's *Evening Post*, and Greeley would publish it as a pamphlet. Telegrams arrived with a flurry of offers to come speak elsewhere in the Northeast. Strangers approached him to shake his hand. He even got a job offer: Erastus Corning, one of the state's leading conservative Democrats, asked if Lincoln would consider doing law work for his New York Central Railroad. Lincoln politely declined. He left New York that day for a whirlwind tour of New England, giving speeches in eleven cities over the next two weeks. Although he still did not declare his candidacy, he admitted privately to a friend that "the taste of it is in my mouth a little."

⌒

When the Republicans met for their convention in Chicago that May, in a cavernous space called, coincidentally, the Wigwam, Seward was still the front-runner. Like Seward and the other more prominent candidates, Lincoln stayed away. At the time, men still "stood" for the office of the presidency rather than openly running for it; it was a lingering holdover from the early republic, when patrician gentlemen were expected to surrender to the public will without appearing too eager for power and glory. Even with the rise of political parties and machines, candidates still maintained a dignified distance from the fray and let their supporters do their campaigning.

From Springfield, Lincoln closely monitored the convention by telegraph while his forces busily worked the floor. They introduced the popular image of him as "the Rail-Splitter"—which prompted guffaws in the South, where rail-splitting was menial labor assigned to slaves. They packed the convention hall with supporters who shouted and cheered on cue every time an organizer waved a white hanky. They cut backroom deals. And they had a secret weapon: Horace Greeley. Weed and Raymond had frozen Greeley out of the New York delegation to the convention, but he wangled himself a spot as an alternate delegate for Oregon. Greeley was at least as famous as any of the candidates, and even Raymond admitted he "made a great sensation here. He is surrounded by a crowd wherever he goes." Greeley was wearing his long white duster, and Raymond couldn't resist adding, "Some foolish wag pinned to his coat tail a paper bearing an inscription, 'For Wm. H. Seward,' and for several hours he unconsciously carried the irrepressible badge with him." The *Times* listed the large field of candidates with Seward at the top and "Mr. Lincoln" last. In the *Tribune*, Greeley placed Seward first, with Lincoln next. Arguing that Seward was too radical to take the White House from the Democrats, Greeley helped swing delegates toward Lincoln. Seward won the first two ballots but failed to get enough votes for the nomination. Lincoln came in second. On the third ballot, he narrowly won enough votes to carry the nomination.

It was as big an upset as there ever was. Seward was bitterly disappointed. Weed reportedly broke down in tears. Raymond denounced Greeley's actions as "the long-hoarded revenge of a disappointed office-seeker." James Watson Webb called Greeley a "viper." But they were loyal Republicans, and after licking their wounds they all got to work for their candidate. Henry Bowen came around as well; Lincoln rewarded him with an appointment as collector for the port of New York. With Bowen came his preacher, Henry Ward Beecher. Although still not impressed with Lincoln on a personal level, he had come to see him as the most likely vessel through which the great work of ending slavery would be accomplished.

The platform the conventioneers unanimously ratified came out swinging, attacking the Democrats for their "measureless subserviency" to the Slave Power, denouncing "the threats of disunion so often made by Democratic members," and condemning as "a dangerous political heresy" the Taney court's "dogma that the Constitution, of its own force, carries slavery into any or all of the territories of the United States."

Lincoln did not personally hit the campaign trail. He remained in Springfield, while an army of Republicans did his stumping for him. His Cooper Union speech and his Brady photograph, both reproduced tens of thousands of times during the campaign, represented him. Engraved and lithographed copies of the photo appeared in newspapers and magazines around the country, including the cover of *Harper's Weekly*. Fletcher Harper, the youngest of the four Harper brothers, had founded the weekly in 1857. Originally a conservative Democrat like his siblings, he gradually went over to the other side with the coming of disunion and war. With a circulation of more than one hundred thousand by 1860, his magazine was a highly influential Republican platform.

Brady and a distributor also had the photo printed on thousands of *cartes de visite*. Lincoln's handlers printed the portrait on campaign buttons, banners, and flyers. Now all Americans had an image to put with his words. In the end, it could be said that no day in Lincoln's political career was more pivotal than Monday, February 27, 1860, the day he made his speech and got that picture taken in New York City.

Behind the scenes in Springfield, Lincoln monitored and micromanaged the campaign. He and his team were fully aware of how critical the nationally distributed New York papers could be to his chances. Although Greeley was always a wild card, they felt they could count on the *Tribune*, the *Times*, and the *Post*. They wrote off the *Daily News*, where Benjamin Wood told his readers that if Lincoln won "we shall find negroes among us thicker than blackberries." That left the mighty *Herald*. They had little hope there either. When Lincoln was nominated, a Bennett editorial sneered, "Abram Lincoln is an uneducated man—a vulgar village politician, without any experience worth mentioning in the practical duties of statesmanship, and only noted for some very unpopular votes which he gave while a member of Congress. In politics he is as rabid an abolitionist as John Brown himself, but without the old man's courage." Like Wood, Bennett warned his Irish and German readers about "hordes of darkeys overrunning the North and working for half wages." Nevertheless, Lincoln sent out feelers to "his Satanic Majesty," as Bennett was known. His Majesty would not be wooed—not yet.

The Democrats, meanwhile, did Lincoln the great favor of falling to pieces all on their own. They had gone into their national convention in Charleston that April hopelessly divided over slavery. Hard-line Southern delegates wanted a platform that mandated extending slavery to the territories. Northerners leaned toward Stephen Douglas and the popular sovereignty approach. Fernando Wood, who had just stumped for Douglas in the Northeast, went to the convention hoping that his friends among the Southern delegates would secure him a spot as Douglas's vice presidential running mate. But the Southern delegates walked out rather than back any compromise on slavery. Douglas led a field of candidates who included Andrew Johnson and Jefferson Davis, but after an exhausting fifty-seven ballots the delegates gave up and agreed to reconvene in Baltimore in May. A large cadre of Southerners walked out of that convention too; the remaining delegates chose Douglas but not Wood. The Southerners formed their own Congregational Democratic Party and nominated John Breckinridge of Kentucky. Another Southern party, the Constitutional

Union Party, made up mainly of former Whigs from the border states who opposed secession, nominated Tennessee senator and plantation owner John Bell. And there were a few other Democratic splinters.

Both parties knew that winning New York State with its thirty-five electoral votes—more than any other—was critical. Lincoln's strategists calculated that they'd have to win the state without much help from New York City. The "moneybags of Wall Street" and the "rich Jews and other moneylenders" would side with the slaveholders, Greeley predicted. Seward agreed.

To ensure that outcome, the Democrats sent their most fiery, rabble-rousing speakers to the city. Breckinridge's man earned laughter and applause when he asked his audience not to let the Republicans "steal away [the South's] niggers." Ohio's fiercely pro-slavery congressman Clement L. Vallandigham, who bonded with the Wood brothers, used similar language stumping for Douglas. The *Herald*, the *Day-Book*, and the *Daily News* all cheered. So did the *Journal of Commerce*, which after the death of the Tappans' friend David Hale had turned increasingly against abolition through the 1850s. It was never as outrageously racist as the other papers, but disapproved of ending slavery because of the potential impact on New York business.

The squabbling among the various Democrat factions deeply troubled the city's Democrat elite, many of them prosperous merchants and financiers. They were convinced that Lincoln's election would push the South into secession, which would spell financial ruin for them. Chief among them was August Belmont, the Rothschilds' German-born agent in New York, son-in-law to the illustrious Commodore Perry, sportsman for whom the Belmont Stakes would be named in 1867, and a big player in the Democracy. Belmont brought together New York's backers of Douglas, Breckinridge, and Bell and proposed a fusion slate, hoping to cobble together enough electoral votes to defeat Lincoln. Many of the city's merchants backed the idea, as did Fernando Wood.

In October they held a rally at Cooper Union to ratify a Douglas-Breckinridge-Bell slate. The evening began with parades through the streets, fireworks, and the incessant firing of Captain Rynders's cannon, called the Baby Waker. Blazing tar barrels filled Cooper Square with eye-watering smoke. Speechmakers riled up the crowds both inside and outside of the Great Hall. One referred to the Republican Party as a "hybrid monstrosity," a Cyclops with its one eye fixed on slavery, and declared that "however the Republican candidate, as a lawyer, might split hairs, or however, as a backwoodsman, he might split rails, he should not be permitted, as President, to split the Union." Another lambasted Lincoln and his "Black Republicans" in language that sounds astonishingly racist now, but had the crowd laughing and cheering then. A *Times* reporter glossed his speech:

> The engrafting of negrology upon their political stock, produced its natural fruit—nigger—the eternal nigger. [Laughter.] They ate nigger—they drank nigger—they—at least the amalgamationists—slept nigger. They saw him in their dreams— they saw him in their waking hours—all over, everywhere, they saw the sable gentleman. Ubiquitous, this black principle was becoming attenuated through the exhaustion of mere extension. But the Convention at Chicago rescued their party from this new peril. When nominating a rail splitter for the Presidency they really resolved that they saw a nigger in the fence. [Great cheering.]

Cartoonists joined in mocking the Black Republicans. New York's Currier & Ives published a cartoon of Greeley and Lincoln with the "next Republican candidate"—a microcephalic black man Barnum was currently promoting as the "What-Is-It?"

The Republican campaign rolled on. It included two aspects that seem odd now. One was the unofficial but ubiquitous campaign song—"(I Wish I Was in) Dixie's Land," better known simply as "Dixie." We think of "Dixie" as the theme song of the Confederacy, which it was. But the song was hugely popular in the North as well. Dan Emmett, performing with Bryant's Minstrels, introduced it at Mechanics' Hall on Broadway in 1859. He claimed to have written it in his damp and chilly Bowery rooms, pining away one night for sunnier Southern climes. His account was contested by a pair of black musicians, Dan and Lew Snowden, who'd been Emmett's neighbors when he lived in Ohio and claimed to have taught him the tune. Whoever wrote it, "Dixie" was an immediate hit. Other minstrel groups added it to their repertoire; Firth, Pond & Co. produced the sheet music, and it spread quickly throughout the country. Lincoln pronounced it "the best song I ever heard," and he was just one of its very many fans. Both Union and Confederate troops would march to it.

The other unexpected aspect of Lincoln's campaign was a pseudomilitary organization of young Republicans who called themselves the Wide-Awakes. They looked rather like a militia, only carrying torches rather than muskets, and provided protection at rallies and at the polls. The first club formed in Hartford in March 1860, and soon new ones opened in cities and towns throughout the North. In big cities like New York they had thousands of members by the fall. Wide-Awakes wore uniforms that included military-style caps and shiny capes. They marched through the streets in neat regimental style, carrying banners with their logo, a staring eye. Although their parades always started out peacefully, there were frequent clashes with fans of the Democracy.

On the night of November 2, Seward addressed a Lincoln rally in the hall of the Palace Garden, one of the city's last indoor-outdoor pleasure gardens, opened in 1858 on 14th Street at Sixth Avenue. The room was so densely packed that "there was hardly room to wedge in another finger," the *Times* reported, and an even larger crowd flattened the lawn outside. After Seward spoke to lusty cheers, a glee club sang "Dixie." Then "several thousand" Wide-Awakes formed up and, torches blazing, marched Seward all the way from 14th Street down to the Astor House where he was staying. Along the way a gang of volunteer firemen rushed the procession "with clubs and wrenches, which they used freely upon the heads of the Wide-Awakes, of whom several were knocked down, and dispossessed of their torches." Seward was eventually delivered safely to his hotel. When the war started, Wide-Awakes who were of age would volunteer for the Union army in great numbers.

Lincoln's election that November was anything but a resounding national mandate to govern. He won just under 40 percent of the popular vote, almost all from the Northeast, the upper Midwest, and the far West. None of the fifteen slave states went for him; he wasn't even allowed on the ballot in ten of them. Douglas polled just under 30 percent. Breckinridge and Bell divvied up the South. Had the Democrats not split their votes they surely would have won. Although Lincoln took New York State (as did the Republican gubernatorial candidate Edwin Morgan), he lost by a landslide in both New York City, where the fusion slate outpolled him better than two to one, and Brooklyn.

CHAPTER 16

City of Secession

The gloomy lull of the early part of the winter of 1860–1,
seeming big with final disaster to our institutions.
—*Herman Melville*

No one doubted what the stark North-South divide in the presidential voting presaged; newspaper editors throughout the South made it painfully clear. "Devotion to the Union is treason to the South," the *Oxford Mercury* thundered. "The South should arm at once," the *Augusta Constitutionalist* counseled. The editor of the fire-breathing *Charleston Mercury* described Lincoln as "a Northern white-washed octoroon mulatto." Correspondents for New York papers were advised to get out of the South or they might be hanged as "Lincoln spies." Now more than ever it was especially dangerous to be identified as a reporter for Greeley's *Tribune*, the Northern paper Southerners hated the most. But even the pro-South *Herald* and *New York World* (begun in 1860) had come under suspicion.

Now that secession seemed imminent, the erratic Greeley lost heart. On November 10 he editorialized, "If the cotton states shall become satisfied that they can do better out of the Union than in it, we insist on letting them go in peace." But the prospect panicked New York's business and banking community. Commerce with Southern clients had already begun to fall off. The factors in the South were having trouble collecting on debts. Secession, they feared, would mean the cataclysmic end of the city's hugely profitable involvement in the international cotton trade. It would also close Southern markets to their goods.

The city's Southern partners in the trade did nothing to lighten the mood. In the May 1859 issue of *De Bow's Review*, the widely read and influential journal of Southern politics and commerce, editor James De Bow had called for secession and offered dire predictions of the economic catastrophe that would strike the North if the South cut its ties. In cotton, the South "possesses a weapon more formidable than all the inventions of modern warfare," De Bow wrote. If the cotton trade were cut off, he mused, "What would become of the great metropolis, New York? The ships would rot at her docks; grass would grow in Wall Street and Broadway; and the glory of New York, like that of Babylon and Rome, would be numbered with the things that are past!"

More than a few in New York City's business elite believed it. On December 15, Richard Lathers, one of the city's most prosperous cotton merchants, hosted an emergency meeting of his fellow businessmen in his offices at 33 Pine Street. An Irish Protestant, Lathers had grown up in South Carolina, where he was a colonel in the state militia, and moved to New York as a cotton factor. He was, not surprisingly, a staunch pro-slavery Democrat.

Lathers and the meeting's other organizers sent written invitations to the top two hundred of their colleagues in the city; two *thousand* worried businessmen showed up and spilled out onto the street. Among them were August Belmont; Erastus Corning; John Jacob Astor's son William; A. T. Stewart; former president Millard Fillmore; and John A. Dix, a leading Democrat. In his opening remarks Lathers called on Southern planters to remember their responsibilities to "their Northern brethren whose sympathies have always been with Southern rights and against Northern aggression."

The Southern brethren clearly weren't listening. South Carolina seceded five days later. More states followed in the next few weeks. Early in 1861, Lathers and his wife would embark on a lonely, quixotic goodwill tour of the South, as though the two of them could personally stave off the inevitable. Meanwhile, forty thousand of the city's businessmen and their employees signed a petition to Congress to please make peace with the South before it was too late. Congress did not respond.

Since the South could not be persuaded to remain in the Union, Mayor Wood offered New Yorkers an alternate plan. On January 7, he addressed a message to the city's newly elected Board of Aldermen. "It would seem that a dissolution of the Federal Union is inevitable," he grimly noted, and continued: "With our aggrieved brethren of the Slave States we have friendly relations and a common sympathy. We have not participated in the warfare upon their constitutional rights or their domestic institutions." If the South seceded, he asked, "why may not New York disrupt the bands which bind her to a corrupt and venal master"—that is, Republican-run Albany, which had "plundered her revenues" and "attempted to ruin her commerce." He concluded, "Amid the gloom which the present and pro-spective condition of things must cast over the country, New York, as a Free City, may shed the only light and hope."

The idea of New York becoming a free and open port city was not new. Dan Sickles had argued for something similar. Privately, Belmont and other prominent Democrats in the city thought it might become necessary. As far back as 1857, when Wood was fighting to keep the Republicans in Albany from stripping him of power, his Irish and German supporters had proposed that the city cut its ties with Albany to become an independent state and "add a new star in the East to our glorious national constel-lation." But to raise secession in January 1861, just a month before the Confederacy was formed, was brazenly provocative. Except for Benjamin Wood's *Daily News*, most of the papers in the city howled that the notion was an "absurdity" (*The Sun*) and a gaggle of "miserable sophistries and puerilities" (the *Times*). Greeley characterized it as "treason" proposed by a "blackguard."

~

In January 1861, as President Buchanan's lame-duck cabinet members were abandoning him one by one, he appointed John A. Dix to be the replacement secretary of the treasury for the last three months of his term. It was one of several interesting roles Dix would be called on to play. Orig-inally from New Hampshire, he'd fought in the War of 1812, then moved in the 1820s to New York State, where he became a member of the Albany Regency. He'd held a long list of state and federal positions, and was one of the grand poobahs of the Democracy in both the state and New York City, where he lived on West 21st Street.

Dix was already serving as Buchanan's postmaster for New York City. Early in 1860, the previous postmaster, Isaac Fowler—who also happened to be Tammany's grand sachem—had been accused of embez-zling $155,000. Isaiah Rynders, still U.S. marshal for New York at the time, was ordered to arrest him. Rynders went to the New York Hotel, where Fowler had been living in grand style for some time, "but tarried at the bar and by his loud announcement of his intent, allowed word to be taken to Fowler, who forthwith escaped," Gustavus Myers wrote in his 1917 *History of Tammany Hall*. "He subsequently made his way to Mexico." Fowler's brother John, a Surrogate Court clerk, also ran off "with $31,079.65 belonging to orphans and others."

Although Dix's new role as Buchanan's treasury man was short-term, he took it very seriously. He was a conservative Democrat, and still hoped for a peaceful resolution of the secession conflict, but he was also a patriot and strong unionist. So he ordered all U.S. revenue cutters that were stationed in the South to sail north before they could be confiscated. Learning that one cutter captain had refused his order, he fired off a famous telegram instructing that the captain be treated as a mutineer, adding, "If any one attempts to haul down the American flag, shoot him on the spot." It became a favorite Union slogan.

On January 15, Rynders and a large group of workingmen—which the *Times* characterized as "composed mainly, and indeed almost entirely, of the rough-spun sons of the Celtic Isle"—held a rally at Brookes' Hall on Broome Street to protest the way Lincoln, Seward, and the other Republicans were "rushing us into the horrors of civil war." It was the usual rowdy affair. The crowd gave three cheers for South Carolina, three groans for Horace Greeley and Reverend Beecher. Rynders was loudly cheered for declaring that the workingman would never go to war for "the damned and lying Black Republicans.... Who brought this trouble on our land? Not ourselves. We had no hand in dissolving the Union. We did all we could to avoid these troubles. But if war comes, and I have to fight, I will fight to the death for South Carolina." A dissenter called out that Rynders was "a political demagogue." The crowd tossed him out.

A week later, John A. Kennedy, the Republican superintendent of the Metropolitans, sent men to board the cargo steamship *Monticello* at Pier 12 on the Hudson. They impounded thirty-eight cartons containing twenty-five muskets each, bound for Savannah. An arms manufacturer in Troy had sold them to the state of Georgia through a New York intermediary—Gazaway Bugg Lamar, who made other such purchases in the months leading up to the war. The Georgia governor warned New York's Governor Morgan that he'd seize all New York merchant ships in Savannah's harbor if the shipment was not released into Lamar's custody. It was, and the *Monticello* sailed. Mayor Wood apologized to Georgia for the "outrage," noting that he had no control over the Metropolitans.

~

While it was highly unlikely that New York would actually declare itself a free city, just the suggestion of it was worrisome to Lincoln as the Confederate States of America voted itself into existence on February 4. Lincoln pondered all this as he remained in Springfield until February 11. At the *Herald*, Bennett dispatched a twenty-five-year-old named Henry Villard to cover Lincoln's activities out there. He was born Heinrich Hilgard, the dreamy and discontented scion of a respectable Bavarian family, and had sailed away to America at the age of eighteen in 1853, arriving in New York with a new name and no English. Over the next few years he wandered around the Midwest and South, hopping from one German community to the next, picking up English, working odd jobs. Though not a citizen, he became involved in the Republican Party and the abolitionist movement, and in a few years he would marry William Lloyd Garrison's daughter Fanny.

By 1857 he was back in New York, writing freelance for the *Staats-Zeitung* despite his personal quibbles with its Democratic slant. He first encountered Lincoln when the *Staats-Zeitung* sent him to Illinois to cover the 1858 Lincoln-Douglas debates. Now he leapt at the opportunity to cover the president-elect in Springfield, though he was no fan of Bennett or "his shameful record as a journalist, and particularly the sneaking sympathy of his paper for the Rebellion, and its vile abuse of the Republicans for their antislavery sentiments." He agreed to write for Bennett only on the condition that his copy would not be tinkered with, to which Bennett agreed.

Liking the young immigrant personally—and hoping to get Bennett's support—Lincoln gave Villard more access than any other reporter. In Springfield, Villard watched as Lincoln patiently met with a daily stream of party stalwarts seeking jobs and other handouts; as one by one the Southern states seceded; as every day's mail brought death threats and gifts of poisoned fruit; as the creases in Lincoln's already craggy face seemed to deepen into fissures. The *Herald* shared Villard's articles with the rest of the Associated Press papers, so that hundreds of thousands of Americans got to know their new president through the eyes of an immigrant who was still not a citizen. As the weeks passed, Villard warmed to Lincoln, though in his stiff Teutonic way he never did get over being scandalized by Lincoln's barnyard parables, low country humor, or his bizarre habit of drawing his bony knees to his chin and cackling at his own jokes. Then again, many of the president's closest advisers would be dismayed by these same antics.

Villard was among the group riding on the Lincoln Special, the train that left Springfield on Monday, February 11, and made whistle stops in five states before reaching New York City on Tuesday, February 19. He noted that Lincoln's friend Ward Hill Lamon, a lawyer and later U.S. marshal for D.C., "brought a banjo along, and amused us with negro songs." He also noticed that as the train drew nearer to New York City, Lincoln grew pensive and withdrawn, "his face and forehead furrowed by a thousand wrinkles, his hair unkempt...his clothes illy arranged." When the train stopped in Albany on February 18, a man in the crowd growled, "That Negro-lover will never get to the Executive Mansion." Another man punched and kicked the speaker senseless. John Wilkes Booth was in Albany that day, performing a monthlong run. He did not go to see Lincoln, and kept his opinions to himself.

Lincoln knew he was in effect entering enemy territory when the train arrived at the new Hudson River Railroad station between Ninth and Tenth Avenues at 30th Street. Unlike in previous cities and towns on the route, the mayor did not come to greet it. Fernando Wood would make Lincoln come to *him* the next day at City Hall. Instead, Metropolitan superintendent Kennedy met the train. A line of open carriages brought the entourage three and a half miles down to the Astor House. The city had declared a holiday, and large crowds lined both sides of Broadway, but the mood was not terribly festive. Kennedy had cleared the route of all other traffic and lined it with thirteen hundred cops to keep order.

There was no official reception when Lincoln stepped out of his carriage in front of the Astor House. He'd chosen to stay there not only because he had fond memories of it, but because other hotels, many of which had long thrived on Southern visitors, didn't want him. Watching from atop an omnibus, Walt Whitman recorded an uncomfortable moment as Lincoln and the "vast and silent" crowd gazed at each other. "There were no speeches—no compliments—no welcome—as far as I could hear, not a word said," Whitman wrote. "Still much anxiety was conceal'd in that quiet. Cautious persons had fear'd some mark'd insult or indignity to the President-elect—for he possess'd no personal popularity at all in New York city, and very little political.... The result was a sulky, unbroken silence, such as certainly never before characterized so great a New York crowd."

The next morning, the president-elect had a private breakfast meeting with one hundred business and political leaders including Thurlow Weed, James Watson Webb, and the shipping magnate Moses Grinnell. That afternoon, while Mrs. Lincoln and the boys visited Barnum's American Museum, Lincoln went to City Hall to meet with a cool but civil Mayor Wood and his city council. Wood used the occasion to lecture Lincoln: "Coming to office with a dismembered government to reconstruct, and a disconnected and hostile people to reconcile, it will require a high patriotism and an elevated comprehension of the whole country and its varied interests, opinions and prejudices to so conduct public affairs as to bring it back again to its former harmonious, consolidated and prosperous condition."

"I can only say that I fully concur in the sentiments expressed by the Mayor," Lincoln replied. "In my devotion to the Union I hope I am behind no man in the Union.... It shall be my purpose at all times to preserve it."

That evening, the Lincolns caught Verdi's new opera, *Un ballo in maschera*, at the Academy of Music on 14th Street. Some of the sophisticates in the audience smirked to see him wearing black gloves, when all the other gents wore white; a Southerner in the crowd snickered that Lincoln must be "the Undertaker of the Union." *Un ballo in maschera* is about the assassination of a king who is shot by a political conspirator while attending a masked ball.

The Lincolns left the Astor House early the next morning and took the Cortlandt Street ferry over to Jersey City, where they boarded the train that took them through New Jersey to Philadelphia. From there they were to go on to Baltimore, where Lincoln was to attend a luncheon and then board another train for the last leg to Washington, or Washington City as it was commonly called at the time. But Maryland, a border slave state, was teetering on the brink of secession, and Baltimore was seething with angry pro-Southerners. Of the roughly thirty thousand votes cast in Baltimore in November, only about a thousand were for Lincoln.

In Philadelphia, Lincoln heard, from two separate investigations, reports of plots to assassinate him as he moved between trains in Baltimore. The first report was from the railroad detective Allan Pinkerton. Hired in January by the president of the Philadelphia, Wilmington, and

Baltimore Rail Road to investigate secessionist plans to sabotage his lines outside Baltimore, Pinkerton and five of his detectives had gone undercover in the city and come upon credible evidence of an assassination plot.

The other report came in a letter from William Seward, brought to Philadelphia by Seward's son Frederick. Independent of Pinkerton's investigation, of which they were unaware, Seward and General Winfield Scott had asked John A. Kennedy back in January to send detectives from New York to Baltimore—where Kennedy, the son of immigrants, was born and grew up before moving to New York. Like Pinkerton, Kennedy had personally led some of his best operatives to Baltimore, and they too learned of the plot.

Pressed by Pinkerton, Seward, and Lamon, Lincoln reluctantly agreed to change his travel plans. He passed through Baltimore in the middle of the night and arrived in Washington, disguised under a slouch hat (given to him in New York) and shawl, at 6 a.m., with Pinkerton and Lamon at his side. The Democrat newspapers made great sport of what one called Lincoln's "wretched and cowardly" sneaking into Washington, much to his chagrin.

PART II

During

City of Sedition

Four years of lurid, bleeding, murky, murderous war.
—Walt Whitman

CHAPTER 17

The Tempest Bursting

Since Andrew Jackson's time, the arrival of a new president in Washington had always brought with it a horde of office-seekers. As the civil service had grown in the first half of the 1800s, the opportunities for graft, nepotism, punishing the rival party, and paying off one's own expanded with it. The diplomatic service, the courts, customs, the treasury, the military and postal services—all departments were fat with plums.

The secession crisis did nothing to deter the plague of office-seeking locusts that descended on Washington with Lincoln's inauguration. Southerners had begun fleeing the city when the secession movement started, leaving many jobs vacant. Also, as the first president of the young Republican Party, Lincoln was expected to clear out old Democrat appointees and fill their jobs with party loyalists. Some ten thousand applicants came for post office jobs alone. They filled every nook and cranny of the hotels and boardinghouses and camped out on the streets and in the parks. They formed long lines snaking in and out of the front door of the White House and lounged by the dozens in the halls. "I've got more pigs than I have tits," Lincoln said.

Robert Henry Newell headed down to Washington from New York for the specific purpose of observing and satirizing the job-seeking masses for the *Sunday Mercury*. A New York native, he was a journalist by twenty-two and hanging out at Pfaff's with the bohemians. Now he started a very successful series of humorous letters to the *Mercury* signed "Orpheus C. Kerr"—Office Seeker. "I am living luxuriously, at present, on the top of a very respectable fence, and fare sumptuously on three granite biscuits a day, and a glass of water, weakened with brandy," Kerr wrote in an early dispatch. He used a handkerchief for a sheet, "and I never go to bed on my comfortable window-brush without thinking how many poor creatures there are in this world who have to sleep on hair mattresses and feather-beds all their lives." He also "boarded exclusively on a front stoop on Pennsylvania Avenue, and used to slumber, regardless of expense, in a well-conducted ash-box.... I tell you, my boy, we're having high old times here just now, and if they get any higher, I shan't be able to afford to stay."

Several nonfictional New Yorkers also came with their hands out. One of them was Horace Greeley. For his cabinet Lincoln chose the four men who had run closest to him at the convention. He made Seward secretary of state, Simon Cameron secretary of war, Salmon Chase secretary of the treasury, and Edward Bates attorney general. Greeley made it quite clear he'd love a place in the cabinet too, and many people thought he deserved one. Even Bennett said so—not least because it would get his chief rival out of town. But Lincoln felt there was too much bad blood between Greeley and Seward, who was the senior statesman in the cabinet and would become one of Lincoln's most influential advisers. Greeley took his rejection as another humiliating slap, and his wounded ego colored his attitude toward the president from then on.

While Greeley's hopes for an appointment were dashed, another New York newspaperman had more success. In 1861, James Watson Webb was approaching sixty and ready to retire from publishing. He sold the *Courier and Enquirer*. When war broke out in April, he would play up both his army experience and his long service to the Whigs and Republicans, and lobby Lincoln for a commission as a major general in the Union army. Lincoln offered him a brigadier generalship instead, which Webb haughtily rejected. He asked Seward to get him a diplomatic post somewhere, and was appointed minister to Brazil. He would serve there throughout the war and later cause problems for the Grant administration.

Probably the most inept and diffident of the New York office-seekers who descended on Washington that March was a novelist whose brief heyday of commercial success was now well behind him. In fact, he had by this time given up writing novels altogether. At forty-one, Herman Melville was forced to admit that he was incapable of supporting his wife and children as a writer, and he had come to Washington hoping that his family's political connections might snag him a diplomatic posting of his own.

It was a desperate and forlorn act for a man who had never been very political himself and whose instinctive response to times of crisis was to withdraw, brood, and write. He was born in 1819 in a boardinghouse on Pearl Street at the tip of Manhattan. A plaque and a bust mark the spot now, site of a skyscraper. His mother's family, the Gansevoorts, were prominent (and slaveholding) Knickerbockers whose name still dots New York City and State. In 1830 the bottom abruptly dropped out of his father's import business. Mr. Melville moved the family to Albany and died when Herman was twelve. Mother Melville, as she was called, and her seven children remained a tight unit within an extended network of cousins and, later, in-laws.

With no other job prospects in the wake of the Panic of 1837, Herman went to sea in 1839 and for five years accumulated the experiences that went into *Typee*, *Omoo*, *Mardi*, and *Moby-Dick*. *Typee* sold well in 1846, feeding a popular hunger for South Seas adventure stories. *Omoo*, published by Harper & Brothers the following year, sold fairly well too, and Melville's star was on the rise. With his bushy beard and muscular build hardened by his years before the mast, he looked the part of the seafaring adventurer and enjoyed a certain celebrity. But with *Mardi*, published in 1849, Melville's writing took a turn toward the metaphysical and murky, and readers and reviewers began to abandon him. By 1850, when he and his wife moved to the Berkshires to make a poor show of farming, his most successful years as a commercial author were already behind him. *Moby-Dick* appeared to mixed reviews and poor sales in 1851. His next novel, *Pierre*, with its shocking theme of incest, doomed his career as a novelist for good.

In the 1850s *Harper's* and *Putnam's* published some of Melville's fictions, including the short novel *Israel Potter* and the stories "Benito Cereno" and "Bartleby, the Scrivener," but one could hardly make a living from that. *The Confidence-Man*, in some ways his most confounding novel, appeared on April Fools' Day 1857. A broad, doleful satire of "that multiform pilgrim species, man," it earned scathing reviews and had sold little when its publisher went bankrupt a month after releasing it.

Melville gave up on fiction and started writing poetry—dark, ruminative, reflecting the grim mood of a young nation falling apart:

> *When ocean-clouds over inland hills*
> *Sweep storming in late autumn brown,*
> *And horror the sodden valley fills,*
> *And the spire falls crashing in the town,*

I muse upon my country's ills—
The tempest bursting from the waste of Time
On the world's fairest hope linked with man's foulest crime.

No one read his poetry either. Despondent and at wit's end, Melville ran back to the sea. He shipped out as the Republicans were nominating Lincoln in May 1860, sailed around Cape Horn to San Francisco and back, returning to a fretful New York as Lincoln was elected in November. As the national mood sank over that bleak winter, Melville's gloom deepened and he succumbed to the impulse to run away again: He decided to ask the new administration for a posting to the American mission in Florence. Family members, worried about his mental state, helped. Like Whitman, Melville was not a particularly political animal. To the extent that he had politics, he leaned toward the conservative and the Democrat, which didn't make him the likeliest candidate for a Republican posting. His older brother Gansevoort had been a rising Tammany Democrat who helped Polk get elected; Polk rewarded him with a diplomatic post in London, where he died in 1846, only thirty-one years old. Another older brother, the prosperous lawyer Allan, was also a Tammany man. Herman was related by marriage to, and friendly with, Richard Lathers. On the other side, an uncle, Dr. Amos Nourse, was a prominent Republican from Maine and close friend of Lincoln's vice president, Hannibal Hamlin.

The family helped Herman put together letters of recommendation, and he left in March for Washington, where Uncle Nourse, as he was known in the family, squired him around. At Lincoln's inaugural levee they stood in the reception line for ninety minutes watching Lincoln shake hands, Melville said, "like a man sawing wood at so much per cord." It was as close as Herman came to lobbying. He loitered in the city for a couple of weeks, sitting on park benches, gazing balefully at the Capitol dome and Washington Monument, both of them unfinished and ominously broken-looking. At the end of March he went back to the Berkshires, jobless.

John Wilkes Booth was in the audience for Lincoln's inaugural address on March 4, 1861, and afterward boasted that he was close enough that he could easily have shot Lincoln. Greeley was in the audience as well, seated next to Stephen Douglas, when Lincoln assured the Southern states that "I have no purpose, directly or indirectly, to interfere with the institution of slavery in the States where it exists. I believe I have no lawful right to do so, and I have no inclination to do so."

Greeley met with the president afterward. He was dismayed, he wrote, by the president's "obstinate calmness" and "dogged resolution not to believe that our country was about to be drenched in fraternal blood." That same day, John Tyler's nineteen-year-old granddaughter Letitia was raising the Confederate flag in a counterceremony at the new capital of Montgomery, Alabama.

The *Tribune* had a writer below the Mason-Dixon that day. Born into an old Puritan family in 1833 and raised on their Massachusetts farm, the stocky, bushy-bearded Albert Richardson had disappointed his parents by heading west, seeking adventure and a writer's life. In 1857 he'd moved with his wife to Bleeding Kansas to cover the battles there for a Boston paper. Like James Redpath, he sided with the free-soilers. In 1859, in a tiny Kansas town that happened to be named Manhattan, he stepped up into a stagecoach, bound for Pike's Peak to cover the gold rush there, and met an odd-looking man with squinty eyes and white Quaker whiskers— Horace Greeley. Greeley was on his first extended tour of the West. By the end of their trip—interrupted when the coach flipped down a ravine, leaving Greeley battered—Richardson was a *Tribune* correspondent.

In February 1861, with civil war on the horizon, Richardson talked Dana into letting him go south as a secret *Tribune* correspondent. Like Redpath, he traveled incognito and employed various subterfuges to get his reports back to Dana across the Mason-Dixon. A number of Southerners told Richardson they were against secession. In Memphis he was told, "The masses have been stirred into a vague, bitter, 'soreheaded' feeling that the South is wronged; but the leaders seldom descend to particulars. When they do, it is very ludicrous.... You can hardly imagine how bitterly [Southern aristocrats] hate the Democratic Idea—how they loathe the thought that the vote of any laboring man, with a rusty coat and soiled hands, may neutralize that of a wealthy, educated, slave-owning gentleman."

In March, Richardson noted:

President Lincoln's Inaugural, looked for with intense interest, has just arrived. All the papers denounce it bitterly. The *Delta*, which has advocated Secession these ten years, makes it a signal for the war-whoop: "War is a great calamity; but, with all its horrors, it is a blessing to the deep, dark, and damning infamy of such a submission, such surrenders, as the southern people are now called upon to make to a foreign invader. He who would counsel such—he who would seek to dampen, discourage, or restrain the ardor and determination of the people to resist all such pretensions, is a traitor, who should be driven beyond our borders."

For all the saber-rattling in the South, Lincoln wasn't the only new president hoping to avoid war if possible. In Montgomery, Jefferson Davis didn't want one either. Lincoln still hoped the Southerners would get over their fit of pique and peacefully rejoin the Union. Davis hoped the North would peacefully let them leave. Neither president could claim a strong mandate to govern. Lincoln had barely slipped into the White House; Davis was only nominally ruling over a pack of states' rightists giddy about their new independence.

Militarily speaking, neither side was equipped for war. The standing U.S. Army was a little more than sixteen thousand men, led by a thousand trained officers. If war came, some would choose to fight for the South, some for the North, making for two very puny armies. The officers in particular were largely Southerners, because commander of the army General Scott, the New Yorker from Virginia, had been giving them preferential treatment for twenty years. When war did come, West Point graduated its class of 1862 a year early to provide thirty-four new junior officers to feed into the hungry Union army. A rambunctious Cadet George Armstrong Custer, with poor grades and numerous discipline problems, would rank thirty-fourth. The U.S. Navy, meanwhile, was tiny—some ninety vessels—and antiquated. Almost half of them were in dry dock in Portsmouth, Virginia, in 1861.

Both presidents knew they'd have to call on their state and local volunteer militias. This was a dismal prospect, especially in the North. All men of military age were required to serve in their state militias, but by 1861 service was more theoretical than a reality, and many militias were more patriotic drinking clubs than anything resembling trained military units. There were a handful of crack militia regiments in the North, including New York's elite 7th, but most were "a peacetime joke." Conditions were slightly more favorable in the South, where attendance at military academies was a proud tradition among the gentry.

The South was desperately unprepared for war in other crucial ways. The North could field vastly more men, with its population base of twenty-one million as opposed to only six million whites and four million slaves in the South. The population of New York State alone was almost half that of the entire Confederacy. The Confederacy almost completely lacked the necessary industries like iron foundries, arms manufacturers, and medical suppliers. New York City produced as much manufactured goods as the entire South. As the secession movement gathered momentum, Gazaway Lamar was far from the only intriguer shipping weaponry to the South. Arms manufacturers in the North sped up production of rifles, pistols, cannons, powder, and shot to ship south, knowing that once war commenced this market would be shut off to them. The first cannon fired at Fort Sumter would be charged with gunpowder from Connecticut.

Lincoln was determined not to let the South simply walk away. "We must settle this question now," he said, "whether in a free government the minority have the right to break up the government whenever they choose." Southerners, and their supporters in the North, argued that any state that had voluntarily joined the union had the right to leave it. Neither side could cite the Constitution; it was silent on the issue.

Davis could barely restrain his fire-eaters and war hawks. As Southern states started commandeering federal installations within their borders, Fort Sumter in Charleston's harbor had become the sticking point. Lincoln couldn't let the Confederates impound it, and Davis couldn't let what was now a "foreign" base remain. Davis built up his forces around it, hoping to starve out the small garrison led by Major Robert Anderson, a protégé of General Scott, and Captain Abner Doubleday from upstate New York—nine officers and some seventy soldiers. Davis hoped they could be forced out without a shot fired.

Lincoln tested the South's resolve by announcing that he was sending an unarmed ship to bring Anderson food and other supplies, but no troops. The Tuesday, April 9, *Times* noted the bustle of activity in New York harbor as the chartered steamship *Baltic*, a large luxury liner that had been launched on the East River a decade earlier, was loaded up with "immense quantities of bacon," flour, soap, "all kinds of preserved meats and vegetables, packed in boxes, vinegar and molasses in portable kegs, stove-coal...and every other article that can be reckoned among Quartermasters' stores. There were also many cases, evidently containing United States muskets, and fixed ammunition by the ton, packed in snug boxes, most of it marked as shrapnel for heavy twelve-pounder boat howitzers." A crowd of idlers took bets on where it was all heading. The *Herald* thought it knew: Its article about the activity on the *Baltic* ran under the headline "Invasion of the South—Inauguration of the Civil War." Bennett condemned the "bloody mission."

The *Baltic* sailed that day, flanked by the navy warships *Pawnee* and *Harriet Lane*. By late on the afternoon of Thursday, April 11, they were standing off Charleston harbor. Bradley Osborn, a reporter for the *World*, climbed up the mainmast of the *Harriet Lane* for a better view. At 4:30 on Friday morning, he watched the fireworks as General P. G. T. Beauregard commenced shelling the fort. Thousands of Charlestonians also watched from wharves and rooftops as the relentless bombardment continued all through Friday. A *Times* writer among them described their expressions as "sad, anxious, preoccupied."

CHAPTER 18

War! War!! War!!!

Good soldiers, brave men, hard fighting, will do more toward
quiet than all the compromises and empty, wagging tongues in
the world.

—*Henry Ward Beecher*

Telegraphed news of the Sumter bombardment began to reach New York
late Friday afternoon. A thoughtful crowd gathered in Printing House
Square, where the *Herald* and other papers posted the latest ripped-from-
the-wires news on message boards outside their offices.

But as anxious and preoccupied as the city had been for weeks, it was
still the start of a spring weekend and people went out that evening for
some fun. Edwin Booth was starring at the Winter Garden (the Metropolitan, renamed), hailed as "the sensation of the city" by *Harper's*. Across
the street, Laura Keene was starring in another grand success. For the
1860–61 season she followed *Our American Cousin* with *The Seven Sisters*, a musical "burletta" very loosely about the diabolical daughters of
Pluto, king of the underworld, wherein one of them comes to New York
and falls in love at Coney Island. The sketch of a plot was just an excuse
for a spectacle that managed to be both patriotic and titillating, extolling
the values of national unity just as the country was falling apart, with
flag-waving chorus girls in gauzy outfits singing and dancing their way
through historical tableaux. Among the songs in the show was "Dixie."
Keene was pioneering the sort of gaudy leg show Flo Ziegfeld would
supercharge in the next century. *The Seven Sisters* ran from the fall of
1860 straight through to the summer of 1861, 250 consecutive nights,

selling some four hundred thousand tickets. She would reopen it in the fall and tour a road-show production from Boston to Washington.

Farther down Broadway, Nixon's Circus was at Niblo's Garden at Prince Street. At the American Concert Hall, a variety theater at 444 Broadway near Canal Street—known colloquially as "The 444"—a young song-and-dance man named Tony Pastor was amusing an audience of mostly working-class men. Admission was fifteen cents and vendors hawked cigars; historian Mark Caldwell notes that "even the violinists in the orchestra could be seen smoking cigars, cigarettes and pipes as they played." Born around 1837 in a small house on the future site of the World Trade Center, Pastor by the age of nine had performed as a child prodigy in blackface at Barnum's American Museum, and at ten he had hit the road, touring with a minstrel troupe and then with a circus, first as a clown, then as ringmaster at age fifteen. Now he did all types of ethnic novelty songs—Irish and Cockney character songs, Dutch songs like "The Goot Lager Beer," minstrel songs. As the war got under way he would cleverly start loading his act with patriotic material like "The Star-Spangled Banner"—he's thought to be the first performer to sing it on a variety stage.

At the Academy of Music up on 14th Street, the soprano Clara Louise Kellogg was singing the lead in Donizetti's *Linda di Chamounix*. Kellogg was nineteen and had just made her debut at the Academy in February. Although she'd been living and training in New York for several years, she was born and spent her first few years, as it happens, in South Carolina. In her *Memoirs of an American Prima Donna*, published in 1913, she recalled that she had "a negro mammy to take care of me, one of the real old-fashioned kind, of a type now almost gone. She used to hold me in her arms and rock me back and forth, and as she rocked she sang." The family soon moved north, where Clara's ongoing love of Negro spirituals and minstrel songs "horrified" her father, and she was quite probably the only opera diva who could pluck a banjo. She would become good friends with a dashing Civil War cavalry officer, George Armstrong Custer.

Walt Whitman, who loved opera, caught her performance that night. Afterward, near midnight, he was strolling down Broadway when he encountered the newsies hawking the Sumter news. He walked into the Metropolitan Hotel at Broadway and Prince Street, "where the great lamps were still brightly blazing, and, with a crowd of others, who gather'd impromptu, read the news, which was evidently authentic." As someone read aloud, "all listen'd silently and attentively. No remark was made by any of the crowd, which had increas'd to thirty or forty, but all stood a minute or two, I remember, before they dispers'd." Whitman continued on his way downtown to the Brooklyn ferry slip at Fulton Market, which Caldwell describes as "always alive all night, with passengers boarding and leaving the ferryboats, pickpockets preying on them, and rows of 24-hour oyster restaurants."

Businessmen "devoted to the interests of the South" had planned a rally in City Hall Park for the following Monday, where they intended to call on Lincoln yet again to negotiate a peaceful settlement with the secessionists. They now scuttled those plans as obsolete.

That night, up in Portland, Maine, Edwin Booth's brother John was ending a successful monthlong run. From there he'd go to Albany, where his barroom rants in favor of the Confederacy would anger some locals. They demanded that he be banned from the stage for his "treasonous statements," but his fans would prevail.

⌒

The shelling of Fort Sumter continued without cease through Friday night and Saturday morning, until Major Anderson finally surrendered at 2:30 on Saturday afternoon. He and his men were allowed to evacuate aboard the *Baltic*. They brought the fort's large, tattered American flag with them as the *Baltic* steamed for New York City on Sunday.

By that Sunday morning the news of Fort Sumter's fall had galvanized and transformed Brooklyn and New York. A huge crowd filled Printing House Square, ravenous for the latest news from the wires. The *Herald* printed 135,000 papers that day, the largest print run in American history to then.

For all their pro-South and anti-Lincoln inclinations, New York and Brooklyn reacted to the news with an explosion of patriotic outrage. The bluster would fade as they tasted the actual horrors of war, but for a brief time men of the metropolis were as gung-ho as anyone in the North.

Beecher preached an abolitionist war sermon that roused a packed Plymouth Church to thunderous cheers. "I hold that it is ten thousand times better to have war than to have slavery....Let every man that lives and owns himself an American take the side of true American principles."

For the next two years Beecher would express impatience with Lincoln's conduct of the war and his reluctance to move on slavery. The Emancipation Proclamation would finally mollify him.

American flags appeared on windowsills and rooftops all around Manhattan. Banners hung along Broadway with sayings like "Trust in God, and keep your powder dry" and "Jeff. Davis, Jeff. Davis, beware of the day / When the Seventh shall meet thee in battle array." Large crowds of men and boys wandered the streets and massed hooting and jeering in front of any building that did not display a flag. Mayor Wood called out the Metropolitans to protect his home and Benjamin's *Daily News* offices from angry crowds. A crowd gathered in Printing House Square noticed that no flag flew from the *Herald* building. Bennett had hammered away at Lincoln right up to the weekend. He warned that "only by conciliation and compromise" could Lincoln avoid "a civil war of five, ten or twenty years' duration." But he doubted that Lincoln was statesman enough to keep the peace, so he argued that "our only hope now...seems to lie in the overthrow of the demoralizing, disorganizing, and destructive" Republican Party, "of which 'Honest Abe Lincoln' is the pliant instrument."

Worried about the *Herald*'s influence in Europe, Lincoln summoned Thurlow Weed to the White House and asked him to meet with Bennett on his behalf, to try to woo His Satanic Majesty again. Weed and Bennett had known and intensely disliked each other since the 1820s, but he went to have dinner with Bennett in his mansion in Washington Heights and delivered Lincoln's message. In his autobiography, Weed recalled that "Mr. Bennett replied that the abolitionists...had provoked a war, of the danger of which he had been warning the country for years, and that now, when they were reaping what they had sown, they had no right to call upon him to help them out of a difficulty that they had deliberately brought upon themselves."

Now the crowd demanded to know why no flag was flying from the *Herald* building. Bennett sent an office boy out a back door to run over to Broadway and buy one. It was hung from a window and the crowd dispersed. Still, Bennett bought a supply of rifles to keep in the office just in case.

The day after the mob's visit, Bennett asked Henry Villard to come dine with him at Washington Heights. He had now rethought his position on the war and had two messages for Villard to convey to Lincoln. First, he'd decided "that the *Herald* would hereafter be unconditionally for the radical suppression of the Rebellion by force of arms, and in the shortest possible time, and would advocate and support any 'war measures' by the Government and Congress," Villard wrote in his memoir. Second, he offered the treasury the use of his son James Jr.'s sailing yacht the *Henrietta* as a revenue cutter, if Junior could be commissioned as an officer. With Lincoln's blessing, the yacht was equipped with a few guns, and James Jr. spent a year serving as a third lieutenant aboard it, patrolling from Long Island down to the Carolinas.

John Dix and other prominent men hastily organized a patriotic "monster meeting" to be held the following Saturday in Union Square. The square was not yet the popular gathering place it would become. But it was a big space and the name seemed propitious, even though it was so called because it was the union of two streets, Bloomingdale (now Broadway) and the Bowery (now Fourth Avenue). It also featured an equestrian statue of George Washington, which seemed appropriate.

The *Baltic* reached New York and anchored off the Battery at one o'clock on the afternoon of Friday, April 19, one week after the shelling of Sumter began. News of its arrival "created great excitement in the streets," the *Times* reported, and "a large concourse of people rushed toward the Battery." An estimated hundred thousand New Yorkers thronged Union Square that Saturday for Dix's monster rally. The *Times* called it the "largest meeting, without exception, that was ever held on this continent." An exhausted-looking Major Anderson was the rally's guest of honor, and his tattered flag fluttered from Washington's statue. The very long list of notables who addressed the cheering multitude included both Republicans, like Henry Raymond, and Democrats, like the Brooklyn state senator and commissioner of New York harbor Francis B. Spinola. He sounded a familiar theme of nonpartisan patriotism when he said, "Truly, my fellow-citizens, this is no time for words. We must act. Act now, act together, or we are lost." Tammany Hall came out foursquare for the war. Even Mayor Wood put his finger to the gale-force wind and changed his tack. Greeted with a mix of cheers and boos, he actually draped himself in his own American flag as he told the crowd, "I am with you in this contest. We know no party now."

The headline of the next day's *Sunday Mercury* hollered "WAR! WAR!! WAR!!!" Orpheus C. Kerr added a poem that summed up his scathing opinion of Southerners:

'Neath a ragged palmetto a Southerner sat,
A-twisting the band of his Panama hat,
And trying to lighten his mind of a load
By humming the words of the following ode:
"Oh! for a nigger, and oh! for a whip;
Oh! for a cocktail, and oh! for a nip;
Oh! for a shot at old Greeley and Beecher;
Oh! for a crack at a Yankee school-teacher;
Oh! for a captain, and oh! for a ship;
Oh! for a cargo of niggers each trip."
And so he kept oh-ing for all he had not,
Not contented with owing for all that he'd got.

Southern businessmen who until this time had always treated New York as their second home now felt ill at ease on its streets. Gazaway Bugg Lamar would leave the city in May, claiming that his life "had been repeatedly threatened by mobs." Back in Savannah, he would become a major stockholder in the Importing and Exporting Company of Georgia, set up to run Union blockades. He would buy and warehouse a huge cache of cotton, predicting that the price would soar as war drastically reduced production and shipping.

Recalling the martial fever in Brooklyn and New York in these first weeks of the war, Whitman later wrote:

> Even after the bombardment of Sumter... the gravity of the revolt, and the power and will of the slave States for a strong and contin- ued military resistance to national authority, were not at all real- ized at the North, except by a few. Nine-tenths of the people of the free States look'd upon the rebellion, as started in South Caro- lina, from a feeling one-half of contempt, and the other half com- posed of anger and incredulity.... A great and cautious national official predicted that it would blow over "in sixty days," and folks generally believ'd the prediction. I remember talking about it on a Fulton ferryboat with the Brooklyn mayor, who said he only "hoped the Southern fire-eaters would commit some overt act of resistance, as they would then be at once so effectually squelch'd, we would never hear of secession again—but he was afraid they never would have the pluck to really do anything."

He also remembered Brooklyn volunteers who "were all provided with pieces of rope, conspicuously tied to their musket-barrels, with which to bring back each man a prisoner from the audacious South, to be led in a noose, on our men's early and triumphant return!"

There were dissenters from all the patriotic brio. The coming of war created a schism among Northern Democrats. The majority of Democrats in the North, like Dix and Spinola, grudgingly agreed with Lincoln that the United States must be preserved and the secessionists put down. They came to be known as War Democrats. The antiwar Democrats were a minority, but a highly vocal and visible one. They opposed every aspect of the war effort from the start to the finish. Some simply spoke out against it in speeches and in newsprint. Others went all the way to committing acts of treason. This antiwar faction was politely known as Peace Democrats, less courteously as Copperheads, as in deadly snakes in the grass. The epithet may have derived from a story in the *New York Times* that ran two days before the firing on Fort Sumter. When postal workers in Washington opened a mailbag from the South, "a box fell out and was broken open, from which two copperheads, one four and a half and the other three feet long, crawled out. The larger one was benumbed and easily killed; the other was very lively and venomous, and was dispatched with some difficulty and danger. What are we to think of a people who resort to such weapons of warfare." By 1862, Peace Democrats were calling themselves Copperheads, but with a different meaning. "Copperhead" was slang for a penny, which had an image of Lady Liberty on it. Copperheads took to wearing pennies as pins, signifying that they were the true defenders of liberty.

In New York, one of the most outspoken Copperheads was Benjamin Wood. Through the spring and summer of 1861, his editorials would render the *Daily News* one of the most vehemently and persistently antiwar papers in the North. He blamed radical abolitionists for having goaded Lincoln into the "insane strife." For engaging in the war, he accused Lincoln of "high treason, and for similar conduct Charles I of England lost his head."

James McMaster begged to differ as well. Prior to the fall of Sumter, *Freeman's Journal* had been a relatively moderate, mainstream platform of conservative dissent. His editorials had come out for popular sovereignty in Kansas and for states' rights in the South. He had blamed radical abolitionists for making "African slavery" a national issue. He endorsed

Douglas in 1860 and warned that if Lincoln and the Republicans took the White House, Southern secession would surely follow. None of this stood out much from what most other Democratic editors were writing, or from the opinions of many of New York's business, civic, and religious leaders, including Archbishop Hughes. McMaster was a dissident but not disloyal. When Lincoln was elected, he wrote, "Whoever talks of resisting his inauguration is a traitor, and if he attempts resistance, ought to be hanged." As Southern states began seceding that December, many of the other editors in New York City—Greeley, Raymond, Bennett, Wood—wrote that they should be allowed to go in peace. McMaster argued that secession should not be countenanced. Putting the issue in terms he thought his Catholic readers would best understand, he wrote, "The Union is a solemn marriage of the states, and death—death political and social—alone can dissolve the Union."

The coming of war radicalized him. Now he charged that Lincoln and the Republicans had sacrificed Sumter in a conspiracy to force the Confederacy into war. Like Benjamin Wood, through the spring and summer of 1861 he would denounce every war action Lincoln took as unconstitutional and tyrannical. Both he and Wood would pay for their opinions.

The war created a different kind of factional split among Republicans. The moderate majority, like Henry Raymond, backed the Lincoln administration in most things, though many would have doubts about the wisdom of his Emancipation Proclamation and his suspending of habeas corpus and other civil rights. Extremists, known as Radical Republicans, came from the abolitionist movement and believed from the start—well before Lincoln or most anyone else in the Union did—that the chief purpose of the war was to end slavery, as well as to punish the South and destroy its culture. In their own way they were as critical of the administration as the Copperheads were. Radicals like Charles Sumner would hound Lincoln and his generals for not prosecuting the war fast or fiercely enough.

CHAPTER 19

New York to the Rescue

Now, there's our City Regiments,
Just see what they have done:
The first to offer to the State
To go to Washington,
To protect the Federal Capital
And the flag they love so dear!
And they've done their duty nobly,
Like New York Volunteers.
— "The New York Volunteer"

The start of hostilities put Washington City in a terribly vulnerable spot, wedged as it was between Virginia, which was about to secede, and Maryland, which almost did. It was very much a Southern city, and the Southerners who hadn't already left now considered the federal government a hostile foreign power. Some had stood in the long receiving line at Lincoln's inaugural reception in March only for the pleasure of refusing to shake his hand when their turn came. The city was effectively undefended against attack, with almost the entire U.S. Army out west.

Virtually all the rail lines connecting the city to the North ran through rebellious Baltimore. Lincoln commissioned John Dix a major general of volunteers for New York, then had him posted to Baltimore's Fort McHenry with the mandate of keeping the city from going into full-on revolt. Dix got quickly to work. "The condition of Baltimore was like that of a volcano intent on eruption," Morgan Dix later wrote, and "signs pointed distinctly to a terrible outbreak as imminent." Dix arrested prominent figures among the city's secessionists, shut down the city's more vociferously pro-South newspapers, and suppressed large public gatherings. It was well known that when the Maryland legislature returned to session in September it would most likely vote for secession. Dix prevented this by the simple expedient of jailing the legislators, along with Baltimore's mayor, George William Brown. For all Dix's efforts, Baltimore continued to seethe.

Southerners expected to seize Washington in short order. Because Congress was adjourned, and only Congress could increase the country's military size and budget, Lincoln called on the governors of the Union to raise seventy-five thousand militia volunteers and send them instantly to defend the capital and the Union. Lincoln would place the volunteers under General Winfield Scott, "Old Fuss and Feathers," who'd turn seventy-five in June. He had been in the service since Thomas Jefferson was president. Scott had come from New York to Washington late in 1860, anticipating conflict. He was mountainously overweight, rheumatic and gouty, "and his physical infirmities were such that he could scarcely leave his invalid-chair," Villard would later recall. "His mind, too, clearly showed the effect of old age." On Thursday, April 18, Scott met with the career officer he considered most qualified to command the Union army: Robert E. Lee. The legislature of their home state, Virginia, had voted for secession the day before, and after some soul-searching Lee resigned his commission. He would fight for Virginia.

To fund the start-up of the war effort, Secretary of the Treasury Chase went to the New York banks for loans. They were only too happy to comply, not least because they hoped that a swift and successful prosecution of the war would mean they could recoup some of the vast debt that Southerners were now defaulting on. They also hoped to go back to doing business with a chastened South as soon as possible. Of the $260 million Washington borrowed to pay for the war in 1861, New York banks put up $210 million.

Governors in the North had put their state militias, such as they were, on readiness alert back when South Carolina seceded; they now promised to have troops in Washington in forty-eight hours. The first troops to arrive, on the evening of April 18, were a contingent of Pennsylvania militia who were already bloodied: They'd been attacked by a mob of enraged secessionists as they changed trains in Baltimore.

New York's Republican governor, Edwin Morgan, convinced the

legislature to put $3 million toward raising thirty thousand volunteers. By the end of May, Morgan had already achieved that goal. New York State would provide more Union troops than any other during the war—an estimated 17 percent of the total—and have the most casualties, roughly fifty-three thousand. In New York City and Brooklyn, recruiting offices popped up "in almost every street," the *Tribune* said, and there was "no lack of persons desirous of joining the regiments being raised." Tent camps and ramshackle wooden barracks sprang up all over Manhattan—in Union Square and Central Park and City Hall Park—and on Staten Island and Long Island.

At first many recruits committed only to three months' service. In those heady first days of the war, optimists believed it would take no longer than that to crush the Rebels. In January, William Seward had told Judge Daly that there would be no war, and even if there were, it wouldn't last more than six weeks. Realists, including General Scott, considered the three-month volunteers an emergency stopgap to keep the Rebels out of Washington while the Union trained a better force. The majority of the three-month volunteers hastily shoved into uniform at the start of the war would come to the end of their contracted service without ever seeing combat. Some would immediately reenlist for longer terms of service; others had had their fling and went home. By the end of summer, volunteers would be signing up for two or three years.

Raising a company of volunteers (a hundred men), a regiment (a thousand), or a brigade (three to five thousand) was a way for ambitious men and organizations to show their patriotism, earn some glory, and maybe enhance their standing in the city's social, political, and business circles. Anybody could do it, and almost anybody did. No military expertise was required, and early on in the war little was demonstrated. Raising a company meant you got to call yourself a captain; raising a regiment made you a colonel; if you could pull together an entire brigade you were suddenly a brigadier general. Washington had to certify your commission, but in the desperate early period of the war that approval wasn't very hard to secure. The Union army's small cadre of trained and experienced officers would complain bitterly about having to fight alongside these overnight amateurs, whom they despised, usually with good reason, as "political officers." They'd also resent the amateur Lincoln's micromanaging their activities.

Tammany Hall put together a regiment, the Jackson Guard, officially designated the 42nd New York. It was mostly made up of Tammany's usual Irish street toughs from in and around the Five Points, but several of its officers were seasoned, and they drilled the men seriously at Camp Tammany in Great Neck, Long Island. The grand sachem himself, Colonel William Kennedy—Metropolitan superintendent John Kennedy's brother—led them at first. However, he would die of a "congestion of the brain" just a few days after they reached Washington.

William "Billy" Wilson, a lightweight boxer and Tammany stalwart, put together his own regiment, the 6th, another rowdy collection that was described at the time as "composed entirely of thieves, burglars, and pickpockets." That was a bit exaggerated; they also included volunteer firemen and grizzled veterans of the Mexican War. Maria Daly, who liked him, described Wilson in her diary as "very broad-shouldered, rather undersized, with a pair of black eyes which look as though they might blaze out like Drummond lights [i.e., limelight] when excited." Unlike many other overnight officers in the Union army, Billy affected no grand airs, preferring to wear a private's uniform. At the 6th's mustering-in ceremony at Tammany Hall he waved a sword and a pistol and whipped the men into a frenzy. They brandished knives and pistols, shouted, "Blood! Blood!" and vowed to build monuments of secessionists' bones. The frantic ceremony concluded with rousing renditions of "The Star-Spangled Banner" and "Dixie."

Not to be outdone, Mayor Wood recruited and funded "out of my purse" his own Mozart Regiment, the 40th New York Volunteer Infantry. New Yorkers wondered what to make of Wood's conversion to the cause of war. *The Sun* was not buying it. The mayor, it warned its readers, was still "a traitor down to the bottom of his heart." The Mozart Regiment signed up a father-son team, Frederick and Gustav "Gus" Schurmann. Frederick, an accomplished musician and music teacher, had left Prussia with his wife and one-year-old Gustav after the failed revolutions of 1848 and settled in New York City. He taught Gus several instruments. Gus was twelve and carrying a shoeshine kit around City Hall Park, three pennies a shine, when the war broke out. Frederick signed up with the Mozart Regiment's drum and bugle corps; it's likely he chose it, rather than one of the city's all-German regiments, for its musical name. When Gus begged to join as well, Frederick gave in. Eighteen was the official minimum age to serve with the Union army, but thousands of younger boys lied about their age to get in. Legend has it that a common trick was to write "18" on a slip of paper and stick it in your shoe, so that when the recruiter asked, you could say, "I'm over 18." Like Gus, the youngest of them served as "little drummer boys" or "little buglers." In addition they were officers' and hospital orderlies.

When Sumter fell, Dan Sickles was fresh out of Congress, back in the city, bored and unhappy at the prospect of practicing law with his father. His reconciliation with Teresa was proving hard. He went about his partying while she, still shunned by the whole city, hid at home with their pretty daughter, Laura. At Lincoln's call for volunteers, Sickles enlisted as a private in the National Guard. As a Tammany Democrat, Dan had always been sympathetic to the South, and when other states began to follow South Carolina out of the Union he had been among the New Yorkers who argued that they should be allowed to go if they did it peacefully. But for all his faults Dan was a patriot, and the taking of Fort Sumter pushed him over into the war camp.

He was about to embark with his battalion for Washington when he and a friend, drinking at the bar in Delmonico's, got to talking about putting together a regiment of their own, with Dan at the head of it. That sounded a lot better than serving as a private in someone else's unit, so Dan resigned from the National Guard and set to work. He had a major's rank from marching around parade grounds with the state militia but precisely no real military training or experience. He didn't let that stop him. With *rage militaire* at fever pitch, it didn't take long for Sickles and his friend to recruit not just a regiment but a full brigade of five thousand, attracting men not only from New York but from as far away as Michigan. They named it the Excelsior Brigade, after New York State's motto.

Raising a brigade was just the first step. Then you had to raise the funds to house, clothe, and feed them. The same men who had organized the Union Square rally formed the Union Defense Committee for that purpose. Officers and members included John Dix, president; Fernando Wood; Peter Cooper; John Jacob Astor; Moses Grinnell; George Opdyke; and the former governor Hamilton Fish. Twelve of them were Republicans, thirteen War Democrats. The city and state gave the UDC $3 million to spend on military and naval necessaries. Lincoln sent $2 million. In the first few months of the war the UDC equipped and armed an impressive thirty-six regiments.

Sickles secured his brigade a camp on Staten Island, then went asking for funds. But between his lurid reputation and his many political enemies, he found raising money very difficult. The quality of the volunteers he'd attracted didn't help. The Excelsior was yet another motley assortment of roughnecks and hard-drinking heathens, many of them Irish Catholic workingmen. A soldier in the brigade's 1st Regiment named James Stevenson wrote a pamphlet called *History of the Excelsior or Sickles' Brigade*, published in 1863. In it he recalled that "a person belonging to the Excelsior Brigade met with nothing but scorn and contempt" in the city and was "excluded from any society or company." "Such a collection of men was never before united in one body since the flood," wrote Irish-born Father Joseph O'Hagan, a Jesuit chaplain with the brigade. "Most of them were the scum of New York society, reeking with vice and spreading a moral malaria around them." Joseph Twichell, a young abolitionist and Congregationalist from Yale, was in New York studying at the progressive Union Theological Seminary in Chelsea when the war broke out. When he became a chaplain in the brigade, he wrote his father in Connecticut, "If you ask why I fixed upon this particular regiment, composed as it is of rough, wicked men, I answer, that was the very reason....I should expect to make some good impressions, by treating with kindness a class of men who are little used to it." He and Father O'Hagan became known as the Excelsior's Holy Joes.

For three months Sickles ran up bills everywhere from Delmonico's to the barbers who cut and shaved all the men to P. T. Barnum, who'd given him a large tent on credit. Seeing disaster loom, Sickles twice took a train to Washington and met personally with President Lincoln to ask his help. Although they were different in almost every way, he managed to charm Lincoln as he did so many others. The president promised federal assistance, and the two men would remain friendly for the rest of Lincoln's life.

The behavior of Colonel Billy Wilson's 6th was just as bad as the Excelsiors'. They also made camp on Staten Island, where they named their barracks Astor, Metropolitan, St. Nicholas, and Fifth Avenue. Surrounding Staten Islanders were soon complaining of an outbreak of thefts. Before they were to ship out in June, Wilson would rashly allow his men one last night on the town. Few showed up on the dock the next morning, the ones who did were worse for wear, and Colonel Wilson himself had somehow managed to fall down and crack his head. They shipped out a day late and several dozen men short. Although they would prove themselves fierce fighters during their two years of service, they'd be much better known for their hijinks off the battlefield. In 1863, while helping to secure the Mississippi for the Union, they'd reputedly confiscate any whiskey they could find, attempt to throw a reprimanding general off a steamboat, and burglarize plantation homes. One drunken soldier punched an officer, who shot him dead and had him buried on the spot in riverbank mud. "Colonel Wilson's men," a contemporary reported, "are to be quartered, rather appropriately, in the Baton Rouge penitentiary."

∼

Late on the afternoon of Friday, April 19, the same day that the *Baltic* arrived in New York harbor, massive crowds lined Broadway to cheer the first New York City regiment to head to Washington, the 7th Regiment of Volunteer Infantry, as they marched to the Cortlandt Street ferry terminal. There they "escaped the deafening noise, the struggling, jostling crowd, and the tears and caresses of friends and kindred" to cross the Hudson and board a southbound train in Jersey City. The 7th, also known as the Darling Seventh, the Silk Stocking Regiment, and the Kid Glove Regiment, represented the cream of New York City society, from old Knickerbocker families like the Verplancks and Schuylers and Lefferts (Colonel Marshall Lefferts, an engineer, was their commander) to the nouveau riche Vanderbilts and Tiffanys. Their chaplain was Reverend Weston of Morgan Dix's elite Trinity Church. Their headquarters above the butchers' stalls at the Tompkins Market and Armory on Third Avenue near Cooper Union was like a swanky gentlemen's club. Their gray uniforms were more smartly tailored than most men's Sunday suits. Marching among them were Herman Melville's cousin Henry Gansevoort and Whitman's well-born bohemian friend Private Fitz-James O'Brien. Another 7th volunteer, Private Robert Gould Shaw of Boston and Staten Island, is now famous as the officer who died leading the black 54th Massachusetts Infantry in battle in 1863. (He would write that he preferred fighting with black soldiers to Irish ones, whom he found impervious to discipline.) The 7th had never been to war, yet they were well experienced in combat of a sort: Whenever mob violence broke out on New York's streets, the 7th was called out to suppress it, as they had done in Astor Place in 1849 and when the Dead Rabbits ran amok in 1857.

By the time the 7th reached Philadelphia, rioters had burned railroad bridges and cut telegraph lines around Baltimore. The troops had to circumvent the area and sail to Annapolis. Along the way, Private O'Brien cheered his fellows with a little fake-Irish ditty he wrote in their honor, including the lines:

Like Jove above,
We're fond of love,
But fonder still of victuals,
Wid turtle steaks
An' codfish cakes
We always fills our kittles.
To dhrown sich dish,
We dhrinks like fish,
And Mumm's the word we utter,
An' thin we swill
Our Leoville [a type of very expensive claret],
That oils our throats like butter.

After repairing sabotaged rail lines outside of Annapolis, the 7th Regiment, dusty and unshaven, finally marched down Pennsylvania Avenue on Thursday, April 25, to "one of the wildest scenes of excitement ever witnessed here," a *New York World* correspondent wrote. "The fears, the hopes, the false alarms, the doubts, and the prayers of all for the past week were satisfied in an instant." The 7th turned smartly off Pennsylvania Avenue, onto the White House grounds, and past the front portico, where a relieved Lincoln, who just that morning had gloomily said he didn't believe the 7th would ever arrive, smiled and awkwardly doffed his hat as they passed. A *Tribune* reporter wrote that the president was now the "happiest-looking man in town."

As more regiments flowed into Washington over the coming days, the city scrambled to house and feed them. With Congress still adjourned, the 7th bedded down at first in the House of Representatives galleries, where, Private Shaw wrote his mother, "we each have a desk, and easychair to sleep in, but generally prefer the floor and our blankets, as the last eight days' experience has accustomed us to hard beds. The Capitol is a magnificent building, and the men all take the greatest pains not to harm anything. Jeff Davis shan't get it without trouble." When the 8th Massachusetts arrived, they lodged in the Capitol Rotunda, still open to the sky. Other units unfurled their bedrolls in the city's parks. The kitchens at Willard's and other hotels churned out meals for hundreds and gave them places to bathe. Eventually troops shifted to large tent camps around the city. The 7th set up Camp Cameron on a hill overlooking the Potomac. Lincoln, escorted by Fort Sumter's Major Anderson, visited them there.

So did the photographers George Barnard and C. O. Bostwick, working out of Mathew Brady's National Photographic Art Gallery on Pennsylvania Avenue. Many of the men and officers of the 7th had already stopped in there to have their pictures taken looking brave and dashing for *cartes de visite* to send to their families and loved ones back in New York. Now Barnard, a longtime associate of Brady's, took casual, jolly shots of the 7th in camp, some of the first field photography of the war. Like other early entrepreneurs of photography, Brady had quickly grasped what an enormous commercial opportunity the war presented. British and French photographers had begun documenting their wars about a decade earlier, and an unknown American had shot some carefully staged daguerreotypes of the Mexican War. But this was to be the first American war to be extensively photographed—more than a million photos would be taken—and Brady was determined to lead the pack.

The 7th tarried in Washington City only until June, when they returned to New York to a joyous reception and mustered out of federal service. The regiment would not fire a single shot in battle during the war. But many 7th men signed up with other units after mustering out; the 7th would in fact provide the Union army with more officers than any other militia regiment. Fitz-James O'Brien went on to help recruit another volunteer unit, the McLelland Rifles, in which he held the rank of captain. In November 1861 he'd make the news for shooting one of his own men. The *Times* reported that a Sergeant Davenport, "who is said to be the most desperate and unruly man in the regiment," attacked O'Brien, who was forced to shoot him in the abdomen.

Shortly after that O'Brien would leave the Rifles and join the regular army as a lieutenant, posted to West Virginia. In a clash with a Confederate patrol in February 1862 he and a Rebel officer would exchange fire; the Rebel died, and O'Brien's left arm was shattered. From his hospital bed he wrote an extraordinary letter to the *Times*, demonstrating that while his body was damaged his wit was not:

> For the first week of my wound, nothing but enormous doses of morphine kept me from going crazy with pain. I had to be kept all day in a lazy, half-slumberous condition, in which I felt like a kind of hot-house plant, dozing and living, and that's all....
> While highly morphinized, and in a semi-conscious state, I formed the idea that the aggravating limb did not belong to me,

but was a vagabond and malicious arm that had attached itself to me for the purpose of preventing my being Commander-in-Chief, which I was to be as soon as I had fought Beauregard in the Colisseum with a trident and a shrimp-net....

Jesting apart, the day is lovely. The sun shines on the distant hills. The singing of the birds comes through my window with a grateful sound as I lie sad, and silent, and suffering. Oh, liberty of motion, health and strength! I never knew what treasures you were till now.

As he wrote this O'Brien was dying a long and agonizing death, not from the wound itself but from lockjaw contracted when the doctors operated on it. His body was brought back to New York in April, where the 7th gave him a hero's funeral and interred him with full honors at Brooklyn's Green-Wood Cemetery. He was thirty-three.

Along with the scramble to defend Washington, there was a rush to build up the port of New York's harbor defenses against a feared assault by the Confederate navy. The harbor already bristled with fortresses from the War of Independence and War of 1812. Forts Lafayette and Hamilton (where both Robert E. Lee and Stonewall Jackson had served before the war) guarded the entrance from the Brooklyn side; Forts Richmond and Tompkins were on Staten Island; Castle Williams and Fort Columbus (originally called Fort Jay, and renamed that in 1904) stood on Governors Island, which was also a U.S. Army command headquarters; Fort Wood was a small garrison on Bedloe's Island (Liberty Island); and Fort Schuyler, up at the tip of the Bronx, guarded the northern entrance to the East River. They trained more than one thousand guns on the harbor from their various vantages, but it wasn't enough for the city's fretful civic leaders. With congressional funds, they saw to it that many more guns were added and the fortifications modernized. It was never enough for some New Yorkers, who worried throughout the war about a naval invasion that never came. Fort Lafayette and Governors Island would see the most action, not as defensive installations but as prisons and sites of military executions.

CHAPTER 20

Immigrants Join the Fight

Ye come from many a far off clime,
And speak in many a tongue
But Freedom's song will reach the heart
In whatever language sung.
—"Garibaldi War Song"

About one-fourth of the men who fought for the Union during the war were foreign-born immigrants. New York's immigrant communities responded to Lincoln's call for volunteers in such numbers that even Bennett's *Herald* was impressed. Many of them were used to marching around and firing muskets. Because the nativists had banned immigrants from most of the local militia, they had formed their own German, Irish, Italian, Scots, and French volunteer militias. Factories, shipyards, shops, and volunteer fire companies all had them. Determined to prove their superiority to the nativists' militia by actually learning how to shoot their rifles with accuracy, they were called "target companies." Their interest in riflery and marksmanship would help to inspire the founding of the National Rifle Association in New York City in 1871.

In 1861 there were more than a hundred target companies in the city, with names like the Washington Market Chowder Guard, the Peanut Guard, the Mustache Fusileers, Sweet's Epicurean Guard, Tompkins' Butcher Association Guard, and, perhaps inevitably, Nobody's Guard. On Sundays, the workingman's one day off, as well as on Christmas and Thanksgiving, they marched through the streets to the racket of fife and drum, rifles shouldered, wearing gaily colorful uniforms hand-stitched by

wives and girlfriends. A target bearer, preferably a black man of imposing size, led the column, holding the large wooden target aloft. This was
sometimes an impressive sight itself, carved as an eagle or stag, streaming ribbons. Some Sundays you'd see ten or more companies marching
up Broadway; on holidays it might be more than one hundred, comprising as many as ten thousand marchers. Citizens along the parade routes
considered them an awful nuisance. On his visit to the city Dickens noted,
"These incessant street processions allow no omnibus, van, or barouche
to break the ranks, leaving Broadway traffic benumbed." (A barouche
was an open, private carriage.) They'd proceed up to Jones's Wood on
the Upper East Side, a popular picnic spot that was once considered for
the site of what became Central Park, or take a ferry over to open land on
Staten Island or in New Jersey. There they'd spend the afternoon in target-
shooting competitions, called "schützenfests" by the Germans, with much
attendant drinking, picnicking, and bellowing of songs from the Old
Country. By the time they "marched" home on Sunday evening the day's
carousing had significantly loosened discipline, and citizens complained
of hooliganism, vandalism, and general loutishness.

New York City fielded more German units than any other city in the
Union. They grabbed the chance to show that they were just as good and
patriotic as any Know-Nothing. As it turned out, they would face as much
anti-Dutch prejudice in the military as they had in civilian life, but they
didn't know that yet. While German workers feared Negro competitors
as much as the Irish did, abolitionism ran high among the progressive
Forty-Eighters. They declared the end of slavery a goal of the war from
the start—almost two years before Lincoln did. A large percentage of the
white officers who commanded the United States Colored Troops would
be German immigrants.

One of the best known of the city's German regiments, and destined to
be the most ill-starred, was the 8th New York Infantry, a.k.a. the 1st German Rifles. A pair of Forty-Eighters, Louis (Ludwig) Blenker and Julius
Stahel, organized it. A German-speaking Hungarian who fled after the
failed revolt against Austria, Stahel arrived in New York City in 1859 and
was editing a weekly German-language newspaper when the war broke
out. Blenker, originally Hessian, also fled to New York after 1848, and
by 1861 he was a prosperous businessman living at the upscale Prescott
House, a hotel across Broadway from the St. Nicholas at Spring Street.
Blenker was the regiment's colonel, Stahel his lieutenant colonel. The

regiment camped at Terrace Garden, a German pleasure garden way uptown on East 58th Street. The German community funded them to the hilt: two sets of spiffy uniforms for Blenker's one thousand men and officers, artillery, and a fully equipped ambulance unit. Blenker rode at their head on a magnificent steed, wearing a crimson-lined cape and making regal gestures that some observers found grand and others ludicrous. When the 8th reached Washington, the lavish table he set made "an invitation to the camp of the 'First German Rifles' a top priority of wartime Washington's social elite." Three more regiments were added to the 8th, forming an all-German brigade.

Leopold von Gilsa, a Prussian army veteran, raised the all-German De Kalb Regiment, officially the 41st New York Volunteer Infantry. The UDC provided the funds to equip it. Von Gilsa had come to New York City in the early 1850s and made his living singing and playing piano in the German beer gardens on the Bowery. On the battlefield Colonel von Gilsa would be known for flying into rages at his men and fellow officers and screaming horrible curses at them in German. An American officer who bore the brunt of one of these inexplicable tirades reported that he believed von Gilsa had gone insane.

~

Meanwhile, New York's Irish leaders mulled over how to respond to Lincoln's call. Most of them were Democrats and had been pro-South, anti-abolition, and anti-Lincoln. Few Irishmen in the city had any interest in going to war on behalf of black slaves; beyond that, forcing the secessionist states back into the Union ran counter to their long-nurtured ideals of freedom. *The Irish-American* editorialized, "We deprecate the idea of Irish-Americans—who have themselves suffered so much for opinion's sake not only at home but *here even*—volunteering to coerce those with whom they have no direct connection."

But the firing on Fort Sumter got their blood up. Archbishop Hughes, no fan of Lincoln or blacks, decided that fighting for their adopted country presented his Irish Catholic flock an opportunity to silence their Know-Nothing detractors. The leaders of the Fenian Brotherhood were of two minds about the war. Combat would give their fighters experience they could later put to good use against the British, but inevitably it would also thin their ranks, even in the short and glorious war everyone expected.

New York Irishmen were also compelled to volunteer by a simple expedient. Employment, which was never high among poor Irish workers, plummeted with the economic downturn caused by secession. It was estimated at the time that unemployment among Irish males in 1861 was 25 percent higher even than in the wake of the Panic of 1857. Signing up for the army meant a job, even if it was only for three months, and a regular pay packet, even if the pay was low.

In all, nearly 150,000 Irishmen would fight for the Union, a third of them from in and around New York City. They largely volunteered in the early stages of the war; by the fall of 1862, after Irish troops had been massacred in several savage battles, convincing new ones to sign up would be much harder.

The first Irish regiment to leave New York City for the war was the 69th New York Volunteers, who would come to be revered as the Fighting 69th. At their head was Colonel Michael Corcoran. Born in Sligo in 1827, he'd been a private in the Crown's Revenue Police, a military unit that enforced the laws against the private distilling of liquor. Meanwhile he was also a member of the Ribbon Society, a secret independence organization and precursor to the IRA, identified by green ribbons in their lapels. Because of the latter he was compelled to flee to America in 1849. In New York he found work keeping the books for the Hibernian House, a tavern on Prince Street across from the original St. Patrick's Cathedral. In 1851 he joined the militia company that became the 69th. His time in the Revenue Police made him one of the few men with any military background, and he rose to the rank of colonel. He also joined Tammany, where he got out the vote in the Fourteenth Ward and was rewarded with a nice desk job in the post office. In 1859 he was reputedly the first naturalized Irish American citizen to sign up with O'Mahony's Fenian Brotherhood. When Lincoln put out his call for volunteers, Corcoran and his aide Lieutenant Colonel Robert Nugent, also a Fenian, headed up the 69th New York. It's believed that most of the men of the regiment were from the Brotherhood. At first, not all New Yorkers were convinced of the Irishmen's patriotism; a rumor flashed around the city that the 69th was heading south to join the Confederate army.

Thomas Francis Meagher heard the call as well. Like Sickles, he didn't let his complete lack of military experience hold him back. He ran an ad in the *Tribune* calling for one hundred Irish volunteers for a company of his own, which would join the 69th as soon as possible.

Father Thomas Mooney, pastor of the Catholic Church of St. Brigid on Avenue B in today's East Village (known as the Famine Church, as it was built in the late 1840s by Famine Irish workers), joined the 69th as its chaplain. John McSorley, a County Tyrone man who had opened his famous alehouse on East 7th Street in 1854, marched with the 69th. So did the journalist and satirist Charles G. Halpine, a Fenian who came to New York City in the early 1850s, got involved in Tammany, and was soon contributing to the major dailies. While serving as an officer through much of the war, Halpine continued to write. He created an alter ego, Private Miles O'Reilly, who would send many joking dispatches to the *Herald*.

In the *Sunday Mercury*, Orpheus C. Kerr signed up with a satirical version of the 69th, the "Mackerel Brigade." The fictitious brigade's name referred to the area around St. Brigid's and Tompkins Square Park that was called Mackerelville because its tenements were stuffed to bursting with Irish Catholics who ate fish on Fridays, and were thus "mackerel-snappers."

On April 23 the 69th Regiment, more than one thousand Irishmen strong, formed ranks on Great Jones Street just off Broadway in today's NoHo. The next day's *Times* reported that "the whole City turned out to bid them Godspeed." Corcoran cut a gallant figure. Tall, trim, his face youthfully smooth under a neat beard and mustache, he wore a uniform that dazzled with gold epaulettes and a large badge featuring the regimental insignia, an Irish harp. Maria Daly presented the regiment with a silk American flag, and the Judge Daly Guards marched with them. Captain D. P. Conyngham, a journalist, remembered, "The regiment moved into Broadway amid deafening cheers; flags and banners streamed from the windows and house-tops; ladies waved their handkerchiefs from the balconies, and flung bouquets on the marching column."

"About 5 o'clock the regiment reached Pier No. 4, North River," the *Times* reported. "Here a most interesting spectacle was exhibited. In every direction people had clambered into the rigging of the vessels; they covered the tops of the pier-sheds and houses, and every place where a view could be obtained." They also thronged the pier in such a crush that soldiers had to fight their way to the waiting steamboat, some losing their rifles and other equipment in the tumult.

The 69th reached Washington and was ordered to set up camp on Arlington Heights, across the river from Georgetown. The men named it Fort Corcoran. Maria Daly recorded with alarm that the judge went down to Washington to visit with them, and even stood guard one night with a pistol. "It seems as if my heart strings tighten whenever I hear him speak of the war. I know he would like the excitement of it. I thought him more of a philosopher."

Meanwhile it took only a week for Meagher to recruit his company. He hastily drilled them at the Ancient Order of Hibernians' ramshackle hall on Prince Street and at an Irish billiard saloon at Broadway and West 10th Street. Meagher's company reached Washington in late May. Henry Villard, who had a low opinion of the Irish in general and Meagher in particular, observed testily that Meagher "had devised a most extraordinary uniform for himself...literally covered with gold lace. It was a sight to see him strut along Pennsylvania Avenue in it, with the airs of a conquering hero." Meagher came to Washington a captain and was field-promoted to major as he folded his company into the 69th. Also joining the 69th at Fort Corcoran were the 5th New York Volunteers, organized by Colonel Abram Duryee, a Manhattan native and wealthy mahogany importer who'd previously marched with the 7th Regiment and been wounded during the Astor Place Riot.

The 69th was still at Fort Corcoran when Chaplain Mooney got in trouble with Archbishop Hughes. Catholic leaders had decided that it was fine for the Irish to fight for their country, but to act like bloodthirsty savages about it wouldn't do their image any good. That went double for their chaplains. Mooney went too far when he blessed one of the fort's cannons and reportedly preached that his troops should "flail" the enemy, and Hughes recalled him to New York.

⁓

Since the city's Italian population was still small, an initial attempt to raise an Italian regiment to be called the Garibaldi Guard—honoring the world-traveling revolutionary who had lived briefly on Staten Island in the 1850s—succeeded only in prompting the ever sensitive *Herald* to note that it would deprive the city of its organ grinders. Then a mysterious figure calling himself Count Frederick George D'Utassy popped up and pasted together a Garibaldi Guard that was a multinational crazy quilt of ten companies—three German, three Hungarian, plus an Italian, a French, a Swiss, and a Spanish company. General George McClellan later joked that he wouldn't have been surprised to find "Esquimaux or Chinese" among them. They became the 39th New York Infantry, with D'Utassy their colonel.

"Like the talking dog," William L. Burton wrote in *Melting Pot Soldiers*, "the remarkable thing about the regiment was not that it worked poorly, but that it worked at all." The officers spoke and wrote in six different languages. They marched behind three different regimental flags, to the tunes of "La Marseillaise" and "Yankee Doodle" played by a corps of forty buglers. Their comic-opera uniforms mixed Chasseur jackets, balloon pantaloons, and cocked hats with large feathers.

Everyone agreed that D'Utassy at least looked like a splendid commander. He was small of stature but made up for it with his fine military bearing and a Napoleonic flair for gesture. He claimed to be a Hungarian nobleman who had served in the Austrian army, then fought against Austria when Hungary revolted in 1848. Fleeing an Austrian death sentence, he said, he trained cavalry in Turkey, then went to England, whence he was sent to Canada as a secretary to the governor of Nova Scotia. From there he came to New York City in 1860. His romantic story and noble pedigree made it easy for him to raise funding for his regiment from the UDC.

The Garibaldi Guard reached Washington at the end of May. D'Utassy continued to put on airs, an aloof and lax commander more interested in living sumptuously in his tent and lobbying for a generalship than in training his mostly lowborn immigrant troops. There were problems with their pay and with their muskets. Bored, some of them wandered out of camp and got arrested in drunken brawls. Some others deserted. Ancient animosities among the various nationalities created feuds, and the officers had multilingual spats with one another. Some resigned. As morale plummeted, seven of the ten companies called for D'Utassy to resign. One Hungarian officer who quarreled with D'Utassy led his company in open mutiny. They marched from their camp near Alexandria into Washington, where the army rounded them up and imprisoned them.

To try to establish some order, the army folded D'Utassy's Garibaldis into Blenker's German brigade. Each man held himself in the highest regard and the other in the lowest, and both were prone to pomposity. Inevitably, they were soon engaged in their own private Austro-Hungarian war. Their problems were far from over.

CHAPTER 21

The First to Fall

*The Southern land shall rue the day
When he became the assassin's prey;
And traitors' wives shall weeping tell
Of that dark hour when Ellsworth fell.*
— *"In Memory of Col. Ellsworth"*

In an almost biblical turn of events, the first Union officer killed in the war was a young man whom Abraham Lincoln loved like a brother. He was also the commander of a New York City volunteer regiment. Already a celebrity, he became a martyr with his death.

Born poor in 1837 and raised in upstate New York, the handsome, small-statured Elmer Ellsworth was fascinated by military pageantry from boyhood, organizing other kids in his own drill teams and dreaming in vain of attending West Point. At seventeen he went to Chicago, where he studied law while rising up the ranks of the Illinois militia. When he was twenty he met a veteran of the French Zouaves, the dashing North African light infantry whose outfits featured baggy pantaloons, short jackets, wide sashes, and a turban or fez. Ellsworth transformed his militia unit into the United States Zouave Cadets, designing their exotic uniforms and developing elaborate precision drills that reportedly were more gymnastic than military.

In the summer of 1860, Colonel Ellsworth—*"le petit colonel,"* he was called—toured his troops around the North. When they came to New York and Brooklyn in July, they performed in parks and at the Academy of Music on 14th Street. Ladies swooned to see the gallant little colonel and his athletic men. The best hotel restaurants—including the Astor, Lafarge, and Everett Houses—wined and dined them; every politician and militiaman in the city turned out to honor them. "The name Zouave is just now a household word," the *Times* commented. Ellsworth's Zouaves "have daily, nay hourly, astonished, delighted, surprised" the crowds. The celebrity merchandising followed instantly. "We see in the shop windows Zouave hats, caps, coats, canes, umbrellas and shoes." Laura Keene added a dance number to *The Seven Sisters*, with chorus girls in tights doing a Zouave drill. The *Sunday Mercury* joked that a fellow "who can climb a greased pole feet first, carrying a barrel of pork in his teeth— that is a Zouave. A fellow who...can take a five-shooting revolver in each hand and knock the spots out of the ten of diamonds at 80 paces, turning somersaults all the time and firing every shot in the air—that is a Zouave." By the end of the summer dozens of militia units around the country had decided to be Zouaves too—or Zoo-Zoos, as they were popularly known—and many such units would fight on both sides in the war. Both Meagher's and Duryee's units, for example, dressed as Zouaves, as did Billy Wilson's, and the Garibaldis' outfits included Zouave elements. Many New York Zouaves bought their fanciful uniforms from R. H. Macy's Dry Goods on Sixth Avenue near 14th Street, the seed from which Macy's department store would eventually grow.

In the fall of 1860, at Lincoln's behest, Ellsworth went to Springfield to work for Lincoln's law firm and on his presidential campaign. He quickly distinguished himself by his diligence and enthusiasm. Lincoln called him "the greatest little man I ever met" and "loved him like a little brother," according to Lincoln's young secretary John Hay. Ellsworth accompanied Lincoln on his long train ride to Washington in 1861, and even the chilly Henry Villard took a liking to him.

When Sumter fell, Ellsworth rushed to New York City with Lincoln's blessings to raise a thousand men for a new Zouave regiment. Between his celebrity and the high level of war fever, it took only a few days. He set himself up at the Astor House and met with officials of the city's fire department, because he'd determined to recruit from among the brawny, brave fire laddies. He started enrolling on Friday, April 19, the day the 69th marched off to tumultuous cheers, and had a full regiment signed up by Sunday. Although they were officially the 11th New York Volunteers, everyone would know them as the Fire Zouaves. Like the Tammany and Excelsior volunteers, they were a tough, unruly lot. Notable among them were the celebrated prizefighters Harry and Johnny Lazarus, "the sporting sons of Izzy the 'Obese Man' Lazarus, a boxing instructor and owner of the Falstaff, a renowned Jones Street sporting saloon." Ellsworth hastily drilled them and issued them jaunty uniforms he designed: gray trousers, their red firemen's shirts, and French-style kepis. They could have marched off a week after he arrived, but they had to wait another week for their supply of Sharps rifles to be delivered. Each man also got a pistol and a bowie knife. On the morning of Monday, April 29, they formed ranks on Canal Street outside their makeshift headquarters in the basement of a dry goods store. One of their banners was inscribed "From Captain Laura Keene to her Brother Zouaves." They marched down Broadway to the Astor House and back, then across Canal to a dock where they boarded a waiting steamer—the *Baltic*—amid a roaring crowd and bands blaring.

When the Fire Zouaves reached Washington they slept for a week in the Capitol, the men bunking in the House of Representatives wing and the officers on the Senate side. For sightseeing they trudged up the long stairway to the top of the still incomplete dome, taking care not to slip on the tobacco juice previous visitors had spat out.

The rambunctious men of the 11th gave Ellsworth and his officers discipline headaches from the start. They were "a jolly, gay set of blackguards," Hay wrote, "in a pretty complete state of don't care a damn, modified by an affectionate and respectful deference to their Colonel." Few had ever tasted military discipline, and, let loose in a new city, some went wild. There were reports of their slipping out at night, breaking into shops, stealing food and cigars and "gentlemen's carriages," raiding brothels, and getting drunk in restaurants. None of this endeared them to the people of Washington, but they redeemed themselves on May 9, when the city's clanging fire bells woke them at 3 a.m. A fire, possibly set by secessionists, had broken out in a five-story building two doors down Pennsylvania Avenue from the much-loved Willard's Hotel, still stuffed to the rafters with job-seekers. Ellsworth and a few hundred Fire Zouaves poured out of the Capitol building and ran "for the various engine-houses to get the machines, which was done, in many instances, by breaking open the doors, as the Fire Department of the city were not particularly energetic in responding to the alarm," Henry J. Wisner, a *Times* writer attached to the regiment, reported. "How the boys astonished the natives when they rushed up the avenue to the scene of the fire, by the celerity of their movements and the confident manner in which measures were adopted for putting out the flames!" Clambering fearlessly all over the burning building, they got the fire out and saved Willard's. The next day, "all Washington" was "loud in praise of the gallant fellows for their heroism and public spirit, and the fact of its exhibition will be to retrieve the character of the regiment from the disgrace cast upon by the excesses of the few rogues who have been turned out of its ranks."

Virginia voters ratified secession on May 23. (The state would officially join the Confederacy in June.) A small force of Rebel troops was in Alexandria, a stone's throw down the Potomac. General Scott wanted to clear them out to give Washington a little breathing room. He ordered troops to move on May 24. Ellsworth begged to let the 11th be among them, and Lincoln couldn't deny his young friend. Wisner wrote a detailed account of what happened next. As the Union boats pulled up at the town in the early morning light, a few Rebel pickets fired at them and then ran away. Ellsworth was marching his men quick-time up a street to secure the telegraph office when he was outraged to see a large Confederate flag waving from the roof of the Marshall House, an inn. Ellsworth and some of his men impetuously rushed in. "He then went up stairs, and reaching the skylight, Col. E. ascended the ladder, myself after him," Wisner wrote. "Handing me his revolver, I handed him my knife, with which he cut the halliards, and hauled the flag down." They were coming down the stairs, Ellsworth triumphantly rolling up the flag, when James Jackson, the inn's pugnacious owner, appeared "at the foot of the stairs, with a double-barreled gun in his hands, and aimed at our party." Private Francis Brownell, from upstate New York, was descending ahead of Ellsworth and tried to knock the shotgun aside. "Jackson, however, discharged his gun, the contents lodging in the heart of the Colonel, who fell forward on his face, his life's blood perfectly saturating the secession flag."

Ellsworth had turned twenty-four a month earlier. After wishing all his life for a military career, he was dead at the very start of it. Brownell shot Jackson between the eyes. The ball went straight through Jackson's head and bored into the wall behind him.

Lincoln was devastated by Ellsworth's death. A *Tribune* reporter found him in the White House staring out a window; when the president turned, he shocked the correspondent by bursting into tears. Both the president and Mrs. Lincoln cried again at Ellsworth's funeral in the East Room. They and others at the service were struck by how lifelike the corpse looked in its open coffin. That's because Dr. Thomas Holmes, the Father of Embalming, had prepared it. He had been commissioned a captain in the Army Medical Corps and stationed in Washington. The Lincolns were so impressed that when their beloved son Willie died in 1862 they had him embalmed, and Mary did the same for the president when he was assassinated in 1865. Holmes did not carry out those two embalmings, but those who did used his techniques. He did train a cadre of "embalming surgeons" who traveled with the Union army and preserved, for a fee, thousands of fallen officers and soldiers.

Ellsworth's body was brought to New York City, residing for a night in the Astor House before being moved to City Hall, where thousands filed past the open coffin. "The faces of all were sad, and many eyes were suffused with tears as they gazed upon the rigid features of the noble young soldier," the *Times* reported. "At the head of the coffin there sat a modest young man in the Zouave uniform, who was no unmoved spectator of that touching scene. In his hands he held the musket that carried death to the murderer of his brave commander, and on his breast were pinned scraps of the flag through which the deadly ball had passed. He was recognized by many as the heroic avenger of Col. Ellsworth—young Brownell—and yet many passed hardly giving him a glance." Brownell would be promoted to sergeant in the regular army; in 1877 he'd get the Medal of Honor for his actions at Alexandria.

⌒

As Ellsworth lay in state, a small and hastily assembled flotilla of makeshift warships from the Brooklyn Navy Yard was engaging the enemy in Virginia. When the war broke out the tiny Union navy was either deployed off the coast of Africa interdicting slavers or in dry dock at the navy's largest and most modern shipyard, Gosport Navy Yard in Portsmouth, Virginia, now suddenly in enemy territory. Gosport was a rich prize for the Confederacy, filled with military stores and equipment, with a state-of-the-art dry dock and at least a dozen U.S. warships berthed there. Rather than let it all fall into Confederate hands, the officers set the whole shipyard ablaze and scuttled or burned as many ships as they could before they escaped into the night on April 20.

With so few available ships, the Union had nothing remotely like the navy it would need to carry out what General Scott called the Anaconda Plan—a total blockade of Southern shipping that would stretch from the Potomac down the coast to the Gulf of Mexico and up the Mississippi. Like a giant snake, the blockade would wrap itself around the Confederacy and choke off all supplies coming by water. The Union was particularly worried that Britain would use its immensely superior navy to support the South and keep the cotton trade open. (Although the Crown officially opted for neutrality, Britain would back the South in subtle ways, like allowing Confederate ships to be built and fitted out in British shipyards.)

Now that Gosport had been surrendered, the Brooklyn Navy Yard took over as the Union's main naval station for the duration of the war. By mid-April it was busy around the clock outfitting any ship it could get its hands on, not just hauling old navy vessels out of mothballs but procuring and bolting guns to private yachts, excursion steamers, even ferries. One of Herman Melville's cousins, Guert Gansevoort, a career navy man who had served in the Mexican War, oversaw the operation. As early as May 7 the *Times* was reporting that a Captain James Ward, a fifty-five-year-old career officer from Connecticut, was organizing a flotilla of three converted civilian steamships—the *Thomas Freeborn*, the *Resolute*, and the *Reliance*—and would sail it down to the Potomac, where he'd attempt first to neutralize Confederate batteries along the river, then to blockade Norfolk. Guert's crews outfitted and armed the ships in double-quick time. They steamed out of the navy yard on May 17 and shelled their first Rebel battery on the Potomac at the end of the month.

On June 29 the *Times* reported that while attempting to set up a Union battery on the river, Ward's flotilla was attacked by a superior force of some eight hundred Confederate soldiers. On the deck of the *Freeborn*, which was close to shore, one of Ward's gunners dropped. Ward took over manning the gun himself and was shot dead.

Ward's casket came back to the Brooklyn Navy Yard for a viewing on the deck of a ship he'd formerly captained. "The sides of the awning which inclosed [sic] the deck were draped with American flags," the *Times* reported. It continued:

> A cross of red bunting was hung at the head of the coffin, with colors covered with crape; wax tapers burned at the head and foot of the coffin, on which rested the sword, chapeau and coat of

deceased. A beautiful cross, formed of flowers rested upon the lid of the coffin.... The flags at the Navy-yard and upon the neighboring shipping were displayed at half-mast, and minute guns were fired for one hour during the moving of the procession.

Herman Melville happened to be in the city visiting family. He went to the navy yard to see Guert, and viewed Ward's casket. The incident must have left an indelible mark on his memory. The man who planned the flotilla with Ward and captained the *Resolute* was a tough, pugnacious salt named William Budd. In the late 1880s Melville would return to writing fiction for the first time in thirty years. He was working on a novella when he died in 1891. It was based on a story Guert had told him about some mutineers who were hanged at sea when Guert was a midshipman. The unfinished manuscript would be found among Melville's papers in 1919 and published for the first time in 1924. It was *Billy Budd, Sailor.*

CHAPTER 22

Seeing the Elephant; or, The Great Skedaddle

It was one of the best-planned battles of the war, but one of the worst-fought.

—*William Tecumseh Sherman*

Through June the whole Union screamed for Colonel Ellsworth's death to be avenged. (Or almost the whole Union. Characteristically, the *Daily News* was more reserved, noting that Ellsworth's death was sad, but so was the innkeeper Jackson's.) He was mourned and commemorated in poems, engravings, on patriotic stationery, and in funeral marches.

The *Tribune*, *Times*, and *Post* all criticized Lincoln for taking too long to send a punitive expedition into Virginia. The "newspaper generals," as Lincoln grumbled, had decided that a swift, powerful stroke could kill the rebellion in its cradle. In the *Post*, Bryant complained that the Union was being "sluggish in our preparation and timid in our execution." Raymond accused the administration of "a blindness and a stolidity without parallel in the history of intelligent statesmanship." The *Tribune*, true to form, shouted the loudest. In May, while chopping wood on his farm in Chappaqua, Greeley had gashed his knee with an ax. While he was recuperating, Charles Dana ran a series of editorials under the banner "The Nation's War-Cry," screaming, "Forward to Richmond! Forward to Richmond! The Rebels Must Fight or Run. The Rope to Hang Jeff. Davis

Is Made." Dana and a *Tribune* Washington correspondent wrote most of it, but it was Greeley's paper and his responsibility.

Goaded by the public outcry, Lincoln held a war council on June 29. Intelligence put General Beauregard, the same man who'd taken Sumter, with some twenty to twenty-five thousand Rebel troops in Manassas Junction, a railroad hub just twenty-five miles south of Washington. General Scott advised waiting until the Union volunteers were better trained, but Lincoln wanted to act before their three-month contracts expired. He ordered General Irvin McDowell to march on Manassas. McDowell was a career soldier who'd fought with distinction in Mexico, but he'd been behind a desk ever since and was surprised to be abruptly promoted from major and handed an army. Interviewing him in his headquarters at Arlington House—Robert E. Lee's confiscated home, and later the site of the Arlington National Cemetery—Villard found McDowell just as doubtful and reluctant as Scott.

On Tuesday, July 16, the weather soupy with midsummer heat, McDowell began to shift a motley army of some thirty thousand across the Potomac. Fewer than a thousand were regular troops and officers, the rest green volunteers. Representing New York City along with Corcoran's 69th, the martyred Ellsworth's 11th, and Blenker's brigade were the 79th New York Highlanders, who had started as a small Scottish target company and mobilized in June. By the time they had recruited up to regimental strength, many of the Highlanders were in fact of Irish descent, but the proud Scots among them still wore their kilts. Their lieutenant colonel, Samuel Mackenzie Elliott, was a pioneering ophthalmologist who'd emigrated from Scotland and settled in New York City by the early 1850s. On Staten Island farmland he had built a cluster of cottages that came to be known as Elliottville, where he mixed eye treatment with abolitionism and possibly maintained a stop on the Underground Railroad. This was where Robert Gould Shaw's family moved from Boston, so that Shaw's abolitionist mother could be in Elliott's care.

From Brooklyn came the 14th Regiment of New York State Militia, mostly made up of abolitionists. After seeing Ellsworth and his Cadets in 1860 they'd turned themselves into Zouaves, sporting bright red pantaloons, navy blue jackets, and kepis. Lincoln was especially fond of the 14th, whom other units grumblingly took to calling "Lincoln's Pets" and "Lincoln's Pups."

If McDowell's mood was dark, most everyone else treated the march like a lark. The volunteers sauntered down the Virginia roads, singing "Dixie" and other popular songs. They scampered out of formation to fill their canteens in roadside creeks, wander into fields and orchards to pick cherries and berries, and raid the barnyards they passed for chickens. One Highlander chased a pig across a barnyard, waving his sword, his kilt flapping, while soldiers from other units shouted, "Take off that petticoat!" and "Put on your drawers!" Officers fumed but could keep little order among the volunteers, many of whom were due to muster out when their contracts ended in just a few days.

Mathew Brady and a crew rolled along in a mysterious black-draped wagon the soldiers called the What-Is-It?, echoing the Barnum exhibit. It was loaded up with field equipment. Riding horseback alongside Brady was the thirty-two-year-old Alfred "Alf" Waud (pronounced Wode), who would go on to be one of the most prolific battlefield illustrators of the war. The Civil War was America's first modern media war. Illustrators and reporters—known as special correspondents, or specials—would travel with the armies everywhere they went. Born and educated in England, Waud had come to New York City in 1850 to paint scenery for Brougham's Lyceum on Broadway. When that fell through he picked up work at Barnum's *Illustrated News*. Late in 1861 he'd join the staff at *Harper's Weekly* and contribute both drawings and written dispatches throughout the war. Waud would see more combat than most soldiers, and get much closer to it than most other specials. He carried everything he needed on his person: sketchbooks and pencils, pistol and bowie knife, bedroll and hip flask. Companionable in camp and cool under fire, he was widely liked and admired in an army that tended to regard specials as a species of pest akin to the lice and fleas that bedeviled them. In Gardner's iconic photo of him at Gettysburg, Waud is "the very picture of a nineteenth-century cavalier," one biographer wrote, with his sketchbook on his knee and his pistol on his hip, wearing a bushy beard, a slouch hat, jackboots, and a seriously alert expression. His younger brother William, who had trained as an architect in England and then joined him in New York in the mid-1850s, also covered the war, for *Frank Leslie's* and *Harper's*.

Henry Raymond was the only Northern editor who decided to be there personally, and the others mocked him for grandstanding. He and his correspondent shared a carriage. Trailing them came William Howard Russell, the London *Times'* most famous war correspondent, who had been traveling around the country since March.

Henry Villard rode up to Colonel William Tecumseh Sherman, who had reluctantly folded Corcoran's 69th into his brigade. According to Villard, he "was not very proud of his command, which hardly contained a single competent officer, and both the rank and file of which it was especially difficult to discipline properly." Born into a prominent Ohio family and orphaned early, Sherman had graduated West Point sixth in his class in 1840, but then, after a disappointingly undistinguished military career, resigned in 1853 and became a managing partner in a San Francisco bank, which in those gold rush years "was on the top wave of speculation and prosperity," he wrote in his memoirs. On the Fourth of July 1857 he had moved to New York to take a room in the Metropolitan Hotel and set about helping to establish a Wall Street branch of his bank. His timing was dreadful. Soon the Panic of 1857 hit, and by January 1858 his bank had dissolved. The following year he was serving as the headmaster of a military academy in Louisiana. When Louisiana moved toward secession, he left.

Like his friend Ulysses S. Grant, Sherman saw the war as a chance to prove himself. He had a low opinion of the Irish and absolutely no patience for political officers and untrained volunteers. After the Battle of Bull Run he would say, "Our men are not good soldiers. They brag, but don't perform, complain sadly if they don't get everything they want, and a march of a few miles used them up....For us to say we commanded that army is no such thing. They did as they pleased." For their part, the men of the 69th complained of Sherman's contemptuous treatment.

Villard spied Meagher with the 69th. "As I approached him, I noticed that he was resting his right hand with a cocked revolver on his hip. 'Well, Captain,' I sang out to him, 'you are all ready for the fray?' 'Yes,' he replied, 'there is nothing like being always ready for the damned rebs.' The leer from his eyes and a certain unsteadiness in the saddle indicated plainly that he had braced himself up internally for the fight."

Sutlers, merchants who followed the armies, also joined the column, their wagons loaded with sundries to peddle to the troops—cigars and tobacco plugs, cakes and pies, boots and socks. Because the intended place of battle was so near, on the weekend of the actual fighting several hundred civilians also came out of Washington in private carriages, dressed gaily for a summer outing, with picnic baskets, to watch the show through opera glasses. They fully expected to see their gallant Union forces trounce the Rebels and be home in time for a late supper.

After some skirmishing on Saturday, the First Battle of Bull Run—First Manassas to Southerners—turned heavy on Sunday morning, with the civilians watching from hilltops. At first the Federals seemed to be getting the advantage of the outnumbered Rebels, such that by noon McDowell's victory seemed almost secure. In fact a few Northern specials rushed off at that point to telegraph reports of a great Union victory, which the *Herald* and others ran on Monday. The *Herald* would print a late edition quietly correcting that report with a short, more accurate piece by Villard. Raymond also telegraphed his office that a Union victory appeared likely. His corrected report wouldn't see print until Wednesday, trailing his competitors, who reveled in schadenfreude. Throughout the war, the temptation to beat the competition by firing off half-cocked reports on "the lightning" would lead to embarrassing gaffes.

Experiencing battle for the first time was called "seeing the elephant." A *Times* article in 1861 explained that it came from an old joke about a farmer whose "life's desire was to behold this largest of quadrupeds, until the yearning became well nigh a mania. He finally met one of the largest size traveling in the van of a menagerie. His horse was frightened, his wagon smashed, his eggs and poultry ruined. But he rose from the wreck radiant and in triumph. 'A fig for the damage,' quoth he, 'for I have seen the elephant!' "

The green volunteers on both sides saw the elephant this Sunday. On the Union side, some performed well enough, at least at first, that even Sherman would grudgingly concede they'd done adequately. One of Corcoran's officers, Lieutenant Colonel James Haggerty, displayed a reckless courage and died for it, the first man in the regiment killed. A Donegal man, he'd come to America in the famine years. When the war started he was forty, a member of the Fenian Brotherhood, a carpenter with a small family on Bleecker Street. On Sunday morning the 69th came on a column of retreating Confederates. Haggerty rashly rode out alone ahead of his foot soldiers and tried to turn the Rebels back. One of them shot him off his horse at close range. The Rebels were Irishmen themselves, a Zouave unit of longshoremen from Louisiana. The Highlanders' Colonel

James Cameron (the secretary of war Simon Cameron's brother) led his kilted men bravely until he also was shot and killed. One in four Highlanders fell with him. The Brooklyners of the 14th performed gallantly, hurling themselves at Rebel lines so relentlessly that Stonewall Jackson was said to have shouted at one point, "Hold on, boys! Here come those red-legged devils again!" It became the regiment's nickname.

The Fire Zouaves earned a reputation that afternoon, but it was not one they wanted. They had the terrible luck to charge across a field into their first battle only to be sandwiched between Jackson's infantry and Jeb Stuart's cavalry. They were cut to ribbons, losing two hundred men in minutes. The remaining men, shocked and demoralized, bolted for the rear. The *Times* and other papers would denounce them as cowards. The *Herald* jabbed that maybe Laura Keene's Zouave dancers should replace them. Orpheus C. Kerr claimed that the Mackerel Brigade ran right alongside the Fire Zouaves and "was about the worst demoralized of all the brigades that covered themselves with glory and perspiration," though he noted that "it never had much morals" to begin with.

Other Yankee units, similarly mangled, also began to retreat. Then panic set in, and retreat deteriorated into a humiliating rout that came to be known as the Great Skedaddle. Villard watched "a wild, senseless rabble" racing through fields and woods, throwing away their muskets and gear. Officers ran right alongside their men. The hilltop picnic crowd saw the scampering Yankees chased by yowling Rebs and panicked as well, adding to the chaos. Abandoned sutlers' wagons and private carriages caused massive traffic jams at bridges and other narrow places as their owners scurried off on foot. Men unyoked horses from ambulances and galloped off on them, leaving the wounded behind. Alf Waud had to point his pistol at a soldier trying to commandeer his ride.

"There was a regular mingling and confusion of soldiers without arms," Conyngham of the 69th recorded, "members of Congress and editors without hats or coats, ladies in buggies, wagons, and on horseback; special correspondents...almost scared to death, while behind all came the rebel cavalry, cutting and slashing." They kept running until they reached Washington. The Union had lost about three thousand men, or one in ten.

Caught up in the pell-mell race to the rear, Mathew Brady had to abandon his overturned wagon, and many of his glass plates were smashed. He collected some in a wooden box and ran into the woods with everyone else. At one point, fleeing Fire Zouaves gave him a sword with which to defend himself from pursuing Rebs. It took him three days to straggle back to Washington, without a single usable image. Determined not to let that happen again, he would spend the rest of the summer raising the large sum of $100,000 to hire and equip a small army of photographers and assistants he would deploy far more successfully throughout the theater of war over the next four years.

Blenker's brigade, including the Garibaldis, surprised some of their Anglo comrades by standing firm and helping to cover the other troops' headlong retreat. They did well enough that Blenker would be promoted to brigadier general and given a second German brigade, putting him in command of the only fully ethnic division in the war. It inflated his already vaulting ego. He sat in imperial splendor inside his royal-blue tent, surrounded by foreign officers of mysterious and dubious provenance, and other generals vied for invitations to his increasingly lavish dinners. D'Utassy found himself losing the battle of egos with Blenker, and it made him testy. More Garibaldis deserted and more officers resigned. Questions of how Blenker was paying for all the opulence led to accusations of fraud and extortion that would dog him for the rest of his federal service.

Gus and Frederick Schurmann's Mozart Regiment was also stationed in the rear at Bull Run, but saw no action. Frederick was stricken with malaria and sent back to New York, leaving his twelve-year-old son facing a three-year stint alone. He gave Gus his horn, and the boy was soon his company's bugler.

At least one New York unit didn't even stay around long enough to see the elephant. The 8th New York State Militia's three-month term of service ended the day before the big battle. James "Jimmy" Lynch, a Tammany and then Mozart man, was in the 8th's battery. He loudly demanded that they be allowed to go home. After a protracted argument with commanding officers, Lynch and the battery walked to the rear and never fired a shot.

When all others were walking off or running in terror, Corcoran, Nugent, and the core of the 69th stood their ground "like a rock in the whirlpool rushing past them," a Southern officer later said. The Rebels surrounded them, Corcoran's horse was shot out from under him, and he was captured with some six hundred of his men. Most of the men captured with him were soon released in a prisoner exchange, but Corcoran would remain in custody for more than a year. He was one of the scant handful of officers the North could claim as heroes of Bull Run. An engraving made from a Waud sketch of the 69th bravely charging with bayonets into Rebel cavalry ran on the cover of the August 3 *Illustrated News*. *Harper's Weekly* ran its own version two weeks later. It took up to a month for a battlefield sketch or photo to appear in print. First it had to get back to the New York office. There a team of artists copied it faithfully as they could as a wood engraving. This was transferred to a metal plate for the printing press.

There were highly conflicting reports of Meagher's conduct at the battle. One member of the 69th was quoted in the *Brooklyn Daily Eagle* praising him as "the most conspicuous man in the field, riding on a white horse, with his hat off, and going into the battle most enthusiastically. At one time our regimental color was taken, and Meagher seized the green flag of Ireland, went to the front, leading the men to the charge." Yet in a long report to the London *Times* damning the Union army's "disgraceful" performance, William Russell claimed that after Meagher's white charger was shot out from under him he raced terrified for the rear with everyone else. It was hearsay. Because of delays on the crowded roads, Russell never actually saw the battlefield, just the chaos in the rear late on Sunday afternoon. And Russell was as pro-South and anti-Irish as any Englishman. Still, his version was widely read, and, coupled with Villard's suggestion that Meagher was drunk before the fight, it put a dent in Meagher's prestige.

In her diary, Maria Daly called the news from Bull Run "exasperating.... My flag, which I gave to the 69th, was lost. The ensign dropped it in his retreat, and as he escaped unhurt, has not dared to show his face. The Regiment declared that he shall be shot if he does. He is skulking somewhere about in Washington."

~~~

Fully a third of the Union casualties at Bull Run were from New York State. Many died lingering deaths lying unattended on the battlefield, some drowning in rain-filled ditches, others burned in brush fires. The carnage shocked and horrified the Irish community in the city. Sixty thousand New Yorkers paid twenty-five cents each to attend a "festival" in Jones's Wood to raise funds for all the new widows, orphans, and cripples the battle created. The enthusiasm for war that had so lit up the community just a few months earlier dimmed. When Meagher set out to recruit a new unit in the city, a full Irish Brigade this time, Archbishop Hughes warned him of a rumor in the city that Lincoln was really prosecuting the war to free the slaves; if it was true, he said, Irishmen "will turn away in disgust from the discharge of what would otherwise be a patriotic duty." But that day didn't come for another year yet. Meagher raised his Irish Brigade, formed around Robert Nugent and the nucleus of the returning 69th, who were mustered out of service at the end of their three months. Because the Irish Brigade was overwhelmingly Catholic, several priests signed up as chaplains. They included Father William Corby, who'd later write the engaging *Memoirs of Chaplain Life* about his three years' service.

Given Meagher's tarnished reputation after Bull Run, there was some opposition in the city's Irish community to his commanding the brigade. Maria Daly, for one, had gone from being his fan and sponsor to thinking he was a drunk and a schemer—"the fox all over, as anyone might see by watching his small bright eye." Apparently she was also jealous of Elizabeth Townsend Meagher, who was younger and prettier than she was— Maria had low opinions of all women younger and prettier than she was. Lincoln promoted Meagher to brigadier general anyway.

Lincoln called for another half million volunteers, who would sign up for three years. Cameron sent for Dan Sickles's Excelsior Brigade to join other units heading to Washington. "This order was received by the men with loud and repeated cheers," James Stevenson recorded, "and the greatest enthusiasm prevailed from the General to the private—all were anxious to get to the field in order to bring the war to a speedy end, and to show their worth to those who had hitherto heaped such censure upon them." Sickles marched them to the train station and they embarked. As usual, he left a pack of angry creditors behind.

Stevenson recalled the brigade marching down Pennsylvania Avenue past the White House, where Sickles stood with Lincoln watching them pass. The men looked smart going by, but Stevenson noted that they hadn't gone much farther when, in their wool uniforms and carrying heavy knapsacks, they started fainting from the cruel heat and humidity of Washington in midsummer.

CHAPTER 23

The Hyenas of War

In the inevitable finger-pointing that followed the fiasco at Bull Run, Raymond and Weed ganged up and blamed Horace Greeley. Raymond charged, rather hypocritically, that the "insane clamor" in the *Tribune* had forced Lincoln and his generals to move too soon. Weed's *Evening Register* accused Greeley of adding a year and thousands of casualties to the war. Dana fought back in a *Tribune* editorial blaming everything on Lincoln's cabinet and calling for them all to resign in disgrace. But Greeley published an apology, explaining, "The precise phrase 'Forward to Richmond!' is not mine, and I would have preferred not to iterate it." He added, "If I am needed as a scapegoat for all the military blunders of the last month, so be it. Individuals must die that the nation may live. If I can serve her best in that capacity, I do not shrink from the ordeal."

If this sounds a little unhinged, it was because Greeley actually was feeling crushing guilt and shame, and the stress pushed him into another bout of brain fever. On July 29 he scrawled an astounding letter to Lincoln, reproaching himself for his role in the debacle. "This is my seventh sleepless night—yours, too, doubtless—yet I think I shall not die, because I have no right to die. I must struggle to live, however bitterly," it began. Calling himself a "hopelessly broken" man, he asked Lincoln, "Can the Rebels be beaten after all that has occurred, and in view of the actual state of feeling caused by our late awful disaster? If they can—and it is your business to ascertain and decide—write me that such is your judgment, so that I may know and do my duty. And if they cannot be beaten—if our recent disaster is fatal—do not fear to sacrifice yourself to your country....If the Union is irrevocably gone," he argued, then war was pointless and "every drop of blood henceforth shed in this quarrel will be wantonly, wickedly shed, and the guilt will rest heavily on the soul of every promoter of the crime." He signed it, "Yours, in the depth of bitterness."

Lincoln, who was no stranger to bleak depression himself, kept the letter hidden for three years. When John Hay finally saw it, he called it "the most insane specimen of pusillanimity that I have ever read." Lincoln was told that Bennett would pay him $10,000 for the right to print Greeley's letter in the *Herald*. Lincoln replied, "I need ten thousand dollars very much but he could not have it for many times that." He wrapped it in red tape and kept it in a desk drawer. It can now be viewed among his papers at the Library of Congress.

In April 1862, Greeley would ask Dana to leave the *Tribune*. Dana had been Greeley's right-hand man, and often his surrogate, for fifteen years. "Mr. Greeley never gave a reason for dismissing me, nor did I ever ask for one," Dana would write in his 1897 *Recollections of the Civil War.* "I know, though, that the real explanation was that while he was for peace I was for war, and that as long as I stayed on the *Tribune* there was a spirit there which was not his spirit that he did not like." Dana accepted an invitation to work for the War Department and would become an assistant secretary of war.

The shock and ignominy of Bull Run pushed Bennett all the way into the war camp. "The war now ceases to be an uninterrupted onward march of our forces southward," he editorialized. "The government in a single day and at the Capitol of the Nation, is thrown upon the defensive, and under circumstances demanding the most prompt and generous efforts to strengthen our forces at that point. Every other question, all other issues, and all other business, among all parties and all classes of our loyal people, should now be made subordinate to the paramount office of securing Washington.... Action, Action, Action!"

The city's more doctrinaire Copperhead editors took exactly the opposite lesson from the debacle. The *Daily News, Freeman's Journal, Journal of Commerce*, and *Day-Book* all ratcheted up their attacks against Lincoln, his war, the abolitionists, and Negroes. Benjamin Wood was now openly calling for revolt: "It is time! Wait no longer! Democrats, arise in your might. Throw off your allegiance to the vampires of your party and declare yourselves free men!...Thus will you tame the hyenas of war."

After the disaster of Bull Run the Republicans had no more tolerance for this type of speech. In August a New York circuit court grand jury charged all these papers with printing seditious opinions. A week later, Lincoln's postmaster general, Montgomery Blair, ordered the postmaster in New York to suspend the papers' mailing privileges. In effect this shut them down, since they depended on mail subscribers.

Some editors took the hit stoically. The *Day-Book* closed its daily edition but continued as a weekly paper, with its name changed to the *Caucasian*. McMaster, on the other hand, was outraged. In the August 24 issue he promised that the *Freeman's Journal* would "live and be published when the tools of the slaves of the present despotism will be buried in an ignominious oblivion." That was the last issue. For the following three weeks he put out a new *Freeman's Appeal* that was even more critical than the *Journal*. On September 13 the U.S. marshal for New York, Robert Murray, wrote Seward asking what he should do. Seward fired back the next day, "You will arrest him and send him to Fort Lafayette."

Murray and five deputies showed up at McMaster's office on the sixteenth to arrest him for sedition. McMaster flew into a rage. He threatened to shoot Murray, his deputies, and Seward as well, though he was found to be unarmed. Handcuffed with manacles taken off a slave ship, he was led out to a waiting carriage. As it rolled, he thrust his manacled hands out the window and shouted to pedestrians, "There! There's Seward's work!" He was in a cell at Fort Lafayette an hour later.

Originally called Fort Diamond, Fort Lafayette was built during and after the War of 1812 on a tiny island just offshore of Fort Hamilton in Brooklyn. An 1865 piece for the *Times* would describe it as "a low, diamond-shaped structure, sitting squat upon a little pile of rocks, a few hundred feet from the shore, unattractive, dismal and gloomy with no redemptive sign, save the beautiful flag which floats ever, from sunrise to sunset." It would disappear under pilings for the Verrazano-Narrows Bridge in the early 1960s.

Through the war, when it was nicknamed the American Bastille, Fort Lafayette housed Confederate POWs and Northern political prisoners accused of all sorts of seditious acts, such as McMaster's printing of antiwar screeds; resisting or evading the draft; serving on blockade runners; desertion; profiteering; and spying or otherwise actively conspiring against the Union. The war had barely gotten under way when George William Brown, mayor of seditious Baltimore, was imprisoned there as part of General Dix's effort to keep Maryland from seceding. He wouldn't be released until November 1862. Because Lincoln suspended habeas corpus, many of Fort Lafayette's prisoners languished there for long periods without trial.

As wartime prisons went it was very far from the worst. The battlements surrounding the central courtyard held the prisoners' cells and the offices and living quarters of the commandant, his small staff, and their wives. "Everything is as clean and bright as whitewash and black paint can make it," the *Times* reported. "The walls glisten in the sun, the cannon-balls, black as Erebus, shine like the contraband heel [i.e., a Negro's heel], and the level parade-ground is divested of all irregularities, robbed of every pebble, swept of every surplus particle of dust."

As long as they caused no trouble, prisoners were treated strictly but kindly by their guards and the commandant, Colonel Martin Burke, a Mexican War veteran and close favorite of General Scott. He earned wide respect "watching over the safety of Uncle Sam's naughty boys, and obeying to the very letter the orders of his superiors," the *Times* said. Burke never set foot off the island during the second two years of the war. This was to avoid being handed summonses to appear in any of the New York civil courts where Tammany judges wanted to grill him for not producing prisoners he was holding without due process. Process-servers from civil courts were prohibited from delivering these summonses to the military island.

After a month in a Fort Lafayette cell, McMaster agreed to sign a loyalty oath—though, characteristically, he insisted it include an addendum protesting the whole affair. He was out by the end of October. He resumed publishing the *Freeman's Journal* the following April and went right back to condemning the war as a Republican and abolitionist conspiracy. He would call the Emancipation Proclamation "a palpable and perilous infraction of the Constitution" and Lincoln "as absolute a monarch as the autocrat of all the Russias."

Revoking the *Daily News'* mail rights cut it off from its large subscriber base outside of New York City—a full third of them in the Confederacy, where it had reached them through Louisville. Benjamin Wood had no choice but to suspend publication in September.

He did not stop writing against the war, however; he just did it in another format. He wrote what's believed to be the only antiwar novel published in the Union during the conflict: *Fort Lafayette; or, Love and Secession*, published in New York City early in 1862. The story combined antiwar propaganda with a melodramatic potboiler about four young friends, two Southern and two Northern, and the war's tragic consequences to their lives. After assorted deaths, betrayals, battle scenes, and broken hearts, one of the Northerners is unfairly accused of sedition and confined at Fort Lafayette. *Fort Lafayette* attracted little attention at the time and soon vanished, not to be seen again until it was republished with a scholar's introduction as *Copperhead Gore* in 2006.

As a congressman representing New York Democrats, Wood voted against every war measure that came up. In calmer tones than he had used in his paper, he delivered carefully worded and closely reasoned speeches detailing his objections to the conflict. He predicted, accurately, a protracted and devastating struggle that would inevitably fail to reunify the nation, because the Union could win it only by brutally conquering the South, occupying it, and subjugating its resentful citizens.

Covered by papers throughout the North and South, this new Benjamin Wood, a principled and one might even say conscientious objector to the war, reached a far wider audience than either the novelist or the fire-breathing newspaperman. House Republicans looked for new excuses to silence him. The chairman of the House Judiciary Committee initiated hearings to investigate charges that early in the war Wood had sent a *Daily News* correspondent into the South ferrying secret information to the leaders of the Confederacy. If convicted, Wood would be impeached and imprisoned—most likely in Fort Lafayette. More than two dozen witnesses, many of them taken from their homes and dragged to Washington under guard, offered various species of rumor and hearsay. When it turned out that the star witness against Wood was a fraud and hoaxer, the chairman quietly ended the hearings and had the records locked away, so Wood was never officially exonerated. And he never stopped criticizing.

CHAPTER 24

The Shoddy Aristocracy

As the businessmen had all feared, the start of the war cast New York City into a quick, steep depression. The transatlantic cotton trade on which so many of its merchants, bankers, and others had thrived for so long nearly vanished. Coastal shipping in the port abruptly fell by half, and as skittish maritime insurers hiked the rates on international shipping under the American flag, many of the city's ship owners had to sell to foreigners at bargain prices. The East River shipyards, ironworks, and machine shops went quiet, the merchant marine idle. The Southern markets that had always been so hungry for New York goods from clothing to carriages to hardware to edibles were now shut off. Overstocked merchants slashed prices: "Dry goods at marvelous sacrifices," the *Tribune* reported. "Clothing at next to no price. Beef, pork and mutton at almost nothing. Everything that you have to sell going for next to nothing." Southern creditors made good on their threat to default on their more than $150 million in debts, causing almost one hundred of the city's dry goods firms to fail in the first six months of 1861. The Southern buyers and vacationers who had always helped keep the hotels, boardinghouses, and theaters filled disappeared. "Even the ice industry was crippled by lack of orders from the South," Edwin Burrows and Mike Wallace noted in *Gotham*. It wasn't just owners and bosses who suffered, of course; by midsummer some thirty thousand workers had lost their jobs, one reason why so many New York workingmen signed up with the army so eagerly in 1861. (McMaster, who had his biases, claimed that four of five New Yorkers who enlisted did so out of economic need.)

And yet by the fall of 1861, New York's economy was booming again, and Brooklyn rode the rising tide with it. After all the prophecies of doom, it turned out to be rather easy to find replacements for Southern cotton and Southern customers.

Government war spending provided an early boost. The Wall Street banks gave Washington a first, crucial $150 million loan after Bull Run. Washington immediately started spending much of it in New York and Brooklyn. The first windfall went to the city's ready-made clothiers like the Brooks brothers and George Opdyke, who took huge orders from the military for uniforms, boots, shoes, belts, caps, and backpacks. The wool they imported went some way to replacing the lost cotton trade. The East River bustled again, refitting wooden warships and building ironclads and steam engines for the navy. Opdyke branched out to arms manufacturing and took an order to produce ten thousand carbines for the army. He set up a factory at 21st Street and Second Avenue but would complete only about a tenth of the order when the operation met a violent end in 1863. Other contractors in the city and Brooklyn produced gun barrels, gun cotton, shot, and shell. Carriage-makers got back to work building army ambulances and wagons. New York City had always been a great importer of horses to pull all its trucks, omnibuses, streetcars, and carriages. Now the military came to shop at the large horse market on East 24th Street, where it bought more than one hundred thousand horses in the first eighteen months of the war. Many tons of hay for those horses also passed through the city. Bakers fired up their ovens around the clock to produce bread and crackers for the soldiers and sailors; Brooklyn's Enterprise Rubber works made rubber buttons and flasks; Brooklyn's Charles Pfizer and Edward Squibb mass-produced pharmaceuticals and bandages.

The continuing and expanding war effort would push annual federal spending to a billion dollars by 1864, and much of that money came to New York. All the federal money being thrown at the city was an open invitation to graft, inflated bills, cut corners, and other types of war profiteering. Opdyke and Brooks Brothers were both accused of selling woefully inferior uniforms, blankets, and other dry goods to the army. Instead of wool, Brooks Brothers used a cheap cloth of pressed rags called shoddy, which actually melted back into rags on soldiers' backs in the rain. Opdyke had approved the use of shoddy as the state clothing inspector. The noun "shoddy" became an adjective during the war. Other city contractors sold the government tins of rotten meat, boots with soles made from glued-together wood chips that fell apart on the first march, glued-together backpacks that also melted into their constituent parts in the rain, and half-blind, spavined old horses that could hardly pull a wagon or carry a cavalryman into battle. A young Wall Street financier named J. Pierpont Morgan, with a couple of partners, bought a cache of five thousand obsolete and unserviceable rifles for $3.50 each and sold them to the army for $22 apiece.

City and state politicos arranged for wartime contracts to go to the highest bidders and took a portion of the overage in kickbacks. Many Tammany Democrats fed at the wartime trough, of course, but Opdyke was far from the only Republican to elbow his way in. Henry Bowen and Thurlow Weed, already prosperous, both grew richer on war profits. As collector for the port of New York, Bowen wielded the authority to seize illegal vessels and confiscate their cargoes, which found their way into his warehouses for resale. In one year of the war his income increased sixfold.

Weed may have been the most egregious profiteer of them all. He arranged contracts for gunpowder, blankets, shoes, and ships, customarily taking a 5 percent commission for each deal. Most unseemly and strange, though perfectly legal, were his profits from trade with the South. In July 1861, as shoddy uniforms melted off soldiers' backs, Congress passed a law allowing the purchase of cotton from the Confederacy. Although Union military men protested, unimpeachably, that this trade directly supported the Confederate war effort, Lincoln and Congress deemed it a necessary evil, and millions of bales crossed the battle lines during the war. Weed the antislavery Republican collaborated with cotton merchants in New York City, Memphis, and elsewhere on numerous deals. The profits were staggering: Cotton bought in the South at twenty cents a pound sold for nearly two dollars in the North.

The war was beneficial to the city's economy in other ways. Goods that used to float down the Mississippi to New Orleans—cattle, hogs, corn, wheat, lumber—now came through New York by rail and the Erie Canal. The same New York businessmen who had abandoned the West in 1857 now saw it as a replacement for the South. Stockyards in the city would soon be butchering and rendering more livestock than Chicago's, filling the city's already noxious air with the shrieks and stinks of millions of dying pigs and cows. Merchants built new floating grain elevators on the East River to handle the hugely increased volume of wheat. Some of the foodstuffs went to feed the military; the rest went to Europe and England, which were racked by crop failures in the early 1860s.

New York also became the major exporter of a new commodity, petroleum. The country's first commercial oil well had begun gushing in western Pennsylvania only two years earlier, and already it was the wonder of the age. Kerosene refined in Brooklyn plants was soon lighting lamps throughout the country and Europe. The rise in oil exports was spectacular, and almost all of it flowed through the port of New York, from around seven million gallons in 1862 to twenty-one million by 1864.

Wall Street not only recovered but soared to previously unthinkable heights during the war. The boom was initially powered by the surging stock prices of New York's railroad companies, whose value skyrocketed as they carried all those goods from the West to the port. Even the perpetually struggling Erie Railway's common stock shot up from below 8 to 122 points. The market would have its usual flighty moments, but for the most part it was exuberantly bullish. Everyone wanted to invest. By late 1862 the *Herald* was crowing that "Wall Street is giddy with excitement," and "every man you meet is rich, and will be richer tomorrow." Stockbrokers' commissions could amount to $3,000 a week—ten times the average worker's *annual* salary. The New York Stock Exchange, which had floated around the financial district since the early days of the republic, built itself a permanent home at Broad and Wall Streets.

The war also stimulated Wall Street speculating on the price of gold. The banks' big loan to the federal government in the summer of 1861 was in gold, which almost depleted their holdings. As the banks stopped paying out in specie, anxious people hoarded. The threat of Confederate privateers seizing bullion-laden ships coming from the California gold fields heightened the sense of insecurity. By the end of the year the federal treasury had spent the millions loaned it by the banks, and the war debt kept deepening. Treasury Secretary Chase authorized the printing of the first national paper money, nicknamed the greenback, rather than continuing to mint the dwindling reserves of gold and silver for coins. The idea came from a New York banker, John Thompson, founder of the First National Bank of New York City. When coins vanished, even stores began handing unhappy customers their own paper, nicknamed "shinplasters." As the Union's fortunes on the battlefield fluctuated, so did investors' confidence that the government would ever buy back its greenbacks with gold. Thus the price of gold shot up with every Union victory, and plummeted with every loss. Gambling on which direction gold would take made some speculators quick fortunes and wiped others out. Meanwhile, when gold went up, the value of the unsecured greenback dropped, causing widespread inflation. The federal government tried unsuccessfully to ban gold speculating, and Lincoln growled that he wished every speculator "had his devilish head shot off!"

Between the speculators making killings on Wall Street and the contractors reaping the windfall of government spending, the war quickly created a class of nouveau riche New Yorkers that old money, like Maria Daly, sneered at as "the shoddy aristocracy." From a handful of millionaires in New York at the start of the war there were hundreds, many of them multimillionaires, by the end. Like parvenus in any era, they enjoyed showing off their money and consuming luxuries as conspicuously as possible. They "outdress and outshine the old families," Junius Browne wrote, "in whatever money can purchase and bad taste can suggest." Gents encrusted their vests with diamond pins and closed them with gold buttons. Their wives sported mink, velvet, silks, and their own diamonds. The new rich bought brand-new carriages and winter sleighs and paraded in them up Fifth Avenue and inside Central Park, wearing thousand-dollar camelhair shawls.

To get away from the hurly-burly of the city, the top families had begun building new mansions up Fifth Avenue north of 14th Street in the 1850s. Now they were dismayed to have the new crowd throwing up their own grand manors next door, and staffing them with liveried servants. The fanciest shops and priciest restaurants followed the wealth uptown. Late in 1862, A. T. Stewart opened his new "Iron Palace," a five-story white cast-iron department store that took up a block of Broadway between 9th and 10th Streets. He filled it with luxury goods. Five hundred male clerks (known derisively as "counter-jumpers," code for gay or girly men) bustled around. Delmonico's opened a new location uptown at 14th Street. All the finest and most expensive restaurants were packed with newly minted swells gorging on pheasant and oysters, then retiring to the bar for brandies and footlong cigars. The theaters, concert halls, minstrel halls, gambling dens, bordellos, and other places of entertainment thrived again. Long Branch, Saratoga, and Newport, New York toffs' favorite summer resorts, flourished. For New Yorkers who could afford it, the war tended to be a distant rumble, only occasionally intruding on their high-rolling lives.

The wartime boom had more equivocal results for the city's poor and workers. There were certainly more jobs, from the shipyards to the stockyards to rich men's pantries and stables. As the military siphoned off able-bodied volunteers, and immigration slowed to a trickle in the war's first two years, competition for those jobs eased. There was more work for women as well. With all the money flowing into the city, charity for the city's most wretchedly poor and relief for the families of killed and wounded soldiers increased.

But as wartime inflation ran amok, doubling the cost of almost everything, workers' real wages stagnated or declined. It didn't take long for workers to see that the war was treating their bosses a lot better than it was them. As the war dragged on, the city would see a great upturn in workers' organizations, strikes, and a growing sense that they were being had.

Running for reelection in the fall of 1861, Mayor Fernando Wood once again found himself surrounded by enemies. The Republicans, of course, denounced him as a secessionist traitor. They nominated George Opdyke again. Tweed and the Tammany War Democrats nominated Charles Godfrey Gunther, a longtime Tammany functionary. Even many of Wood's Mozart men mistrusted him now after his fling as a flag-draped war supporter. New corruption scandals battered him as well. In one instance he awarded a contract for cleaning the city's streets to a firm that had been underbid by two dozen other applicants. Of the $280,000 a year the city paid, the contractor allegedly kicked back some $70,000 to Fernando and Benjamin Wood. And the streets remained as filthy as ever.

In his campaign Wood tried to steer a course between Opdyke and Gunther. He played to both the war and peace camps by arguing that the best way to bring the Rebel states back to the Union was to carry "a sword in one hand and an olive branch in the other." He warned workers that unless he continued to be their mayor, the rich Republicans would soon be conscripting them to go fight for them. Election day was the city's usual tumultuous affair, a day of stuffing ballot boxes and marching repeaters from poll to poll. The votes were almost equally split among the three candidates. Opdyke won by fewer than a thousand votes. Fernando Wood was out as mayor, yet his political career was still far from over.

In the midst of war, New York City had elected, by the slimmest margin, an antislavery Republican mayor who had made a fortune clothing slaves. Opdyke would not find many opportunities to enjoy the office. The anti-Fernando Republicans in Albany had stripped the mayor of much of his power. Opdyke nominally led a municipal government that was really run by Democrats, from the Tweed-dominated Board of Supervisors who controlled the budget to a Common Council full of Copperheads. The city was sitting on a volcano, rumbling with antiwar, anti-Negro, and anti-Republican sentiments, with a Republican mayor precariously perched on top.

That fall, the slave ship captain Nathaniel Gordon was tried and convicted, in what was actually his second trial. The first, back in June, with judges Samuel Nelson and William Shipman sharing the bench, had ended in a hung jury. Just a year or two earlier Gordon would have walked, but the Republican prosecutor E. Delafield Smith immediately won a new trial. Gordon, who was literally wasting away in the Tombs, now understood the gravity of his situation. He gratefully accepted the pro bono representation of Beebe, Dean & Donahoe of Wall Street, long known as the city's premier law firm for getting slavers off the hook.

Despite their help, it took the jury at this second trial just thirty minutes to find Gordon guilty. Unlike Minthorne Westervelt, Gordon was just a sailor from Maine, with no important family connections to influence the judges. Shipman signed his death sentence, to be carried out in early February 1862.

The defense appealed to President Lincoln for a pardon. So did eighteen thousand citizens of Portland, Maine, Gordon's hometown. Lincoln was known to be a soft touch when it came to commuting heavy sentences. He would pardon fifty-five deserters from the Union army in a single stroke, and throughout the war there would be a line of tearful mothers and wives snaking into the White House to beg clemency for sons or husbands who had been caught going AWOL, jumping ship, or, later, dodging the draft. He didn't always comply, but he did often enough to make it worth a try. Lincoln issued Gordon a two-week stay, but no pardon. Gordon's execution was to be a sign of the administration's resolve to end American involvement in the transatlantic slave trade (the agreement to cooperate with the British navy came soon after); it can also be seen as a prelude to the actions Lincoln would soon take to end domestic slavery as well. Most New York papers, even the *Herald*, agreed with his decision.

Around 3 a.m. on the appointed day, February 21, 1862, on his cot in his fetid cell at the Tombs, Gordon would try to cheat the gallows by swallowing strychnine powder. Three doctors rushed to his cell and revived him. At 11 a.m. he was brought to the Tombs' inner courtyard, where a company of armed marines and three hundred invited spectators, all gentlemen in silk top hats, surrounded the gallows. The device was a relatively new design known as an upright jerker. Instead of falling through a trapdoor, the condemned was yanked straight up into the air by a long weighted armature. It was thought to be a speedier and more humane death than twisting at the end of the rope. Gordon did in fact die quickly, a little past noon.

The last slave ship captain tried in New York City would stand before Judge Shipman that same month. Smith's case against him was weak and the jury would acquit. Still, the city's large network of men and businesses involved in the trade got the message of Gordon's hanging. They quietly dismantled their operations. New York's long participation in the international slave trade was over.

CHAPTER 25

We Are Coming, Father Abraham

When the war started, neither Union nor Confederate leaders had the slightest idea of the enormous loss of life they were about to unleash. But in New York City, Elizabeth Blackwell and her sister Emily foresaw the coming holocaust right away. Elizabeth was a friend and student of Florence Nightingale, and she had learned from Nightingale's experiences in the Crimean War. Elizabeth knew what she was doing better than many men in the medical establishment. The problem was convincing them of that. This was a battle she had been fighting for a decade by then, as the first woman M.D. in America.

Within a week of Lincoln's call for volunteers in April 1861, the Blackwells began organizing the Women's Central Association of Relief (WCAR). They held a meeting at Cooper Union where some three thousand New York women volunteered to be trained as nurses and hospital workers.

Elizabeth Blackwell had grown up one of nine children in a loving Congregationalist household in Bristol, England, where her father ran a successful sugar refinery. Despite—or maybe because of—sugar's direct link to the African slave trade, he became involved in England's abolition movement. In the summer of 1832, when Elizabeth was eleven, he packed his whole brood aboard a merchant steamer for the twelve-day passage to New York City. They found the city almost deserted, as everyone who could afford it had fled the same dreadful cholera epidemic that twenty-one-year-old Horace Greeley witnessed in his second year as a New Yorker. Mr. Blackwell started the Congress Sugar Refinery, joined Samuel Cox's congregation, and welcomed American abolitionists like Garrison into his home. Meanwhile, his children stopped eating sugar as their own antislavery gesture.

With his business failing in New York, Blackwell moved the family to Cincinnati, then died of a fever when Elizabeth was seventeen. By the mid-1840s she was saving up to apply to medical school, despite universal advice against it (including from Harriet Beecher Stowe, still living in Cincinnati), since no woman had ever been admitted before. At the time, "female physician" was a euphemism for abortionist. "The gross perversion and destruction of motherhood by the abortionist filled me with indignation, and awakened active antagonism," Elizabeth later wrote. "That the honorable term 'female physician' should be exclusively applied to those women who carried on this shocking trade seemed to me a horror. It was an utter degradation of what might and should become a noble position for women." One school after another rejected her out of hand until she was admitted, almost on a lark, by the Geneva Medical College in upstate New York. She earned her M.D. in 1849. By the start of the war around two hundred American women, including her sister Emily, had been inspired by her example to get their own degrees.

In the early 1850s Elizabeth returned to New York City to start a practice. "I took good rooms in University Place, but patients came very slowly to consult me. I had no medical companionship, the profession stood aloof, and society was distrustful of the innovation. Insolent letters occasionally came by post, and my pecuniary position was a source of constant anxiety." She and most of the women doctors she'd inspired found themselves restricted to working only with female patients. In 1857 she and Emily opened the New York Infirmary for Women and Children on Bleecker Street, with Henry Ward Beecher and a few other pillars lending moral support. Although the sisters and their female staff did all the medical and surgical work, they wisely set up an all-male board of "consulting physicians" to help disarm the skeptical and the scandalized.

They used the same approach in 1861, recruiting the Reverend Henry Whitney Bellows, the popular pastor of the Unitarian All Souls Church at Fourth Avenue and East 20th Street, as the male figurehead of the WCAR. Over the summer this developed into the United States Sanitary Commission (USSC), a civilian-run quasi-federal agency. Frederick Law Olmsted signed on as its secretary-general. Julia Ward Howe's husband, Samuel, also joined.

Initially the men of Washington's military and medical establishments rebuffed the group. Lincoln himself fretted that they would become "a fifth wheel to the coach." The Union Army Medical Bureau was a small fiefdom completely unprepared for the coming Armageddon. In April 1861 it included 114 surgeons, 24 of whom left to join the Confederacy. The surgeon general died of old age that May, to be replaced by another old incompetent. The thousands of physicians who soon joined up had little to no military experience; many also lacked basic knowledge of how to deal with the diseases—malaria, smallpox, measles, typhoid, dysentery—that would kill two Union soldiers for every one who died in battle.

That ratio was a significant improvement over former wars. In the Mexican War seven men had died from disease for every one killed on the battlefield; in the Crimean War, Nightingale's practices had reduced it to four to one. Medical historian Margaret Humphries attributes the improvement to the more than twenty thousand Civil War women who mobilized to make military hospitals—both the field hospitals near the battle lines and the "general hospitals" far behind the lines—as clean and conducive to health as was possible in the 1860s. They served as nurses, cooks, laundresses, and administrators.

Those women did not include the Blackwell sisters. Because they had dared to invade the male realm of the physician, men froze them out of any significant role in the USSC. To recruit nurses the men brought in Dorothea Dix, the crusading New England reformer of asylums for the poor and insane. Dix (no relation to New York's General Dix) was the very model of the starched Victorian spinster, and she had no medical training to threaten the males' egos. The "jealousies were too intense for us to assume our true place," Elizabeth wrote. She and Emily returned to their infirmary. Elizabeth would go back to England after the war. She would actively campaign for social and health reform on a wide array of fronts, usually to the same cold reception that had frustrated her in America. When she died in 1910 her pioneering efforts had largely been forgotten.

Although the Blackwells were ostracized from the movement they'd started, at least Olmsted was in place to carry on. He was appalled to learn that men wounded at Bull Run lay on the battlefield for up to four days before help arrived. He was in Washington when the defeated rabble filled the city. "Human nature has seldom showed itself so degraded," he wrote. He described the demoralized soldiers as "pale, grimy, with bloodshot eyes, unshaven, unkempt, sullen, fierce, feverish, weak, and ravenous.... They were wearing parts of different uniforms, soiled and dank with dew." Some huddled like crows "in rows along the curb; others went from house to house begging for food." Sanitary Commission volunteers fanned out among them, interviewing them about their experiences; Olmsted prepared the resulting *Report on the Demoralization of the Volunteers*, a blistering denunciation of the political and military leaders—blackguards, knaves, and tyrants, he labeled them—who had flung the men into this disaster and made virtually no plans to treat the wounded. He successfully lobbied to have the aged surgeon general—"a self-satisfied, supercilious, bigoted block-head"—replaced. The army's medical and sanitation procedures improved immeasurably as the war went on, largely through the constant and fierce criticisms of Olmsted and the USSC.

To whip the post–Bull Run mob into a functioning army, Lincoln called on General George McClellan. Lincoln and McClellan were different in almost every way possible. In photographs the tall, swarthy president towers ludicrously over the stout and fair "Little Mac," who was of average height for the time, five foot eight, but something about his gamecock demeanor gave the impression he was smaller. Where Lincoln generally looked like his clothes had been thrown on him from a distance, Mac was always impeccably turned out, from his jaunty kepi to his precise little goatee to his gold buttons.

Born into Philadelphia high society, McClellan had entered West Point at fifteen. Among his classmates he associated only with other young gentlemen of breeding, mostly Southerners. He graduated second in his class just in time to go off to the Mexican War in 1846. As a second lieutenant he served under Generals Zachary Taylor and Winfield Scott, and Captains Robert E. Lee and Ulysses S. Grant. He developed a reputation as a haughty and argumentative popinjay, often contemptuous of his superiors.

After that he became something of a pet of President Pierce's secretary of war, Jefferson Davis. Bored in the peacetime army, he resigned his commission in 1856, at the age of thirty, and took an executive job with the Illinois Central Railroad, rising rapidly to chairman. (West Point stressed engineering, and many graduates went on to civil engineering and rail-roading in their civilian careers.) He met Lincoln, did not think highly of him, and put the Illinois Central at the disposal of Stephen Douglas's campaign in their 1858 senatorial contest. Because the railroad's financial offices were in New York, McClellan spent much time in the city develop-ing important business and social connections, and he was married there.

After McClellan's forces successfully routed Confederate troops from western Virginia in the spring of 1861, the *Herald* and other papers cheered him as the Union's "Young Napoleon." Visiting his friends in New York, he had Brady take his portrait with one hand thrust into his jacket; this Napoleonic pose was reproduced as a *carte de visite* distrib-uted throughout the North.

When Lincoln called him to Washington in July, Little Mac entered the city a conquering hero. Already vainglorious to a fault, he let the huz-zahs go to his head. "I find myself in a new & strange position here," he exulted in a letter to his wife, Ellen. "Presdt, Cabinet, Genl Scott & all deferring to me—by some strange operation of magic I seem to have become *the* power of the land." If he wanted to, he playfully wrote her, he could become "Dictator."

At first he lived up to the great expectations. His initial act was to sweep all the men in uniform out of Washington's bars and brothels and put them back on the parade ground. He also put down a mutiny by the Highlanders, who wanted to go home to New York and recruit new men to replace the ones who'd fallen. McClellan trained artillery on them, clapped the ringleaders in irons, and as the final humiliation took away their regimental flags. He returned them a month later when the High-landers showed better discipline. Unlike other military leaders at the start of the war, McClellan approved of the Sanitary Commission's work and ensured that his army cooperated.

Through that summer and into the fall, McClellan transformed the rabble into a spit-and-polish army that impressed and heartened all who watched it march and drill. He gave the men back their pride and they loved him for it. He seemed to be everywhere at once, trailing a large staff of aides that included one of New York City's wealthiest men, John Jacob Astor III. Astor retained his civilian status but held the honorary rank of colonel. With him came his valet, his chef, and his steward.

Watching McClellan's increasingly grand army march around that autumn, banners snapping and fifes tootling, was some of the best entertainment civilians could find in Washington. It helped inspire one visitor, Julia Ward Howe, to pen the lyrics for one of the most popular Civil War anthems. She was on her first visit to Washington in the fall of 1861. She and Samuel stayed at Willard's and were in a small group who met with Lincoln in one of the White House drawing rooms. As she recalls it, the men did all the talking as usual, while she observed "the sad expression of Mr. Lincoln's deep blue eyes, the only feature of his face which could be called other than plain."

In a carriage on a street choked with soldiers, her party began to sing the new song "John Brown's Body," which had a curious background. The tune was from an old camp meeting spiritual. Volunteers of a Massachusetts regiment are credited with first singing it as a marching song at the start of the war, with lyrics that referred at first not to the abolitionist martyr but to a Sergeant John Brown among them. Thus the odd lines about John Brown's knapsack and hanging "Jeff Davis to a tree" and such. As it spread to other units it became associated with Brown the abolitionist and the lyrics morphed into many variations. Now, as Howe's group sang it, the soldiers cheered, and a member of her party urged her to write new lyrics for the tune.

"I went to bed that night as usual, and slept, according to my wont, quite soundly," she wrote. "I awoke in the gray of the morning twilight; and as I lay waiting for the dawn, the long lines of the desired poem began to twine themselves in my mind."

It was "The Battle Hymn of the Republic." First published in the *Atlantic Monthly* in 1862, it would be sung ubiquitously in the North throughout the war.

⁓

Based on intelligence fed him by Allan Pinkerton, McClellan told General Scott and Secretary of War Cameron that a Rebel force of 150,000 was massing around Manassas Junction, and that he must match them with more troops, more guns, more everything. But Pinkerton's information was very faulty: The Confederates had maybe a third of the force he reported. Scott and Cameron brushed McClellan off. He publicly feuded with Scott, whom he called "a perfect imbecile"; in November, truly sick and tired, Old Fuss and Feathers resigned. He took a train back to New York City, where he lived the rest of the war, dying at West Point in 1866. Cameron would resign in January, to be replaced by Dan

Sickles's friend Edwin Stanton. Bearded like a billy goat and notoriously pigheaded, Stanton would argue often with Lincoln and fellow cabinet members, especially the prickly secretary of the navy, Gideon Welles. But Stanton was a loyal unionist and Lincoln came to depend on him heavily. A Democrat, Stanton would switch to the Republican Party and then gravitate toward the Radical wing. McClellan feuded with him as well, telling Ellen he was "the most depraved hypocrite & villain."

From the fall of 1861 into the spring of 1862, McClellan expanded his grand Army of the Potomac into the largest and best-equipped fighting force in the Western Hemisphere, but he always found some fresh excuse not to march it south. The longer he delayed, the more frustrated Lincoln, Stanton, and Seward ("a meddlesome, officious, incompetent little puppy") became with him. McClellan also picked fights with Sumner, whom he detested, and the Radical Republicans, going out of his way to tell them that he would fight to save the Union but never to free the "niggers." He decided the politicians were his real enemies, not the Confederates. He called Lincoln "an idiot" and "nothing more than a well meaning baboon" and reported to his wife, "I went to the White House shortly after tea where I found 'the original gorilla,' about as intelligent as ever. What a specimen to be at the head of our affairs now!"

Finally, responding with greatest reluctance to an ultimatum from the president, McClellan did shift his enormous force of 120,000 men (not the 300,000 he wanted), with forty-four artillery batteries and more than 14,000 draft animals, off the parade ground in March 1862. But rather than hit the Rebels at Manassas and proceed south to Richmond, he devised a flanking maneuver. He would sail his troops in a vast armada, the largest amphibious assault ever assembled, down to the lower Chesapeake Bay, to commence a westward advance up the Virginia Peninsula twenty-five miles to Richmond. The fleet took three weeks to ferry Mac's massive force the short distance.

Among the units were Sickles's Excelsior Brigade, the Mozart Regiment, and Meagher's Irish Brigade. The 61st New York Volunteer Regiment was also in McClellan's army, led by the boyish-looking Colonel Francis (Frank) Channing Barlow. He was born in 1834 in Brooklyn, to which his Yankee father had just come to be pastor of the First Unitarian Church. Two years later, Pastor Barlow was removed from the pulpit for displays of "mental stress" and abandoned his family. Frank's mother returned to her home state of Massachusetts and raised her boys at Brook Farm and in Concord. Emerson, Charles Dana, and Margaret Fuller were among Frank's early mentors. He graduated from Harvard the class valedictorian in 1855 and moved straight to New York, where he tutored college-bound students, including Robert Gould Shaw. After passing the bar he founded his own law firm, while writing occasional legal articles for Greeley and Dana at the *Tribune*. He socialized in Charles and Maria Daly's circle, and with the writers and artists they patronized. The latter included Winslow Homer, who happened to be a distant cousin of Frank's. It was probably through the Dalys that Frank met Arabella Griffith, called Belle. Like Maria Lydig when she met Daly, Belle was an unmarried "spinster" in her midthirties, ten years older than the youthful-looking Barlow. In her diary, Maria calls Frank "Arabella's boy-husband" and snipes that when they came calling, her maid thought Belle was Frank's mother.

Frank and Belle were married at St. Paul's Chapel on April 20, 1861, the evening of the day he enlisted for three months with the 12th New York Volunteer Regiment. He was commissioned a lieutenant despite never having held a gun. Then again, his commanding officer, Colonel Dan Butterfield, had done little more than march around a few parade grounds himself. Butterfield's father was one of the founders of American Express in 1850. Dan had come to New York City from upstate to run the company's offices at Hudson and Jay Streets in today's Tribeca. He was a playboy, a drinking and womanizing buddy of Dan Sickles, and Barlow disliked him.

To compensate for his boyish affect and lack of experience (a fellow officer remarked that Barlow looked like "a highly independent mounted newsboy"), Barlow drilled his men relentlessly. One of his men, Private Charles Fuller, who had rushed from upstate to New York City to sign up, later wrote, "At first, from his exacting requirements and severity he was quite disliked, if not well hated." When the 61st sailed with McClellan for the Peninsula, the twenty-five-year-old Barlow had been promoted to colonel.

Winslow Homer met up with him on the Peninsula. Born in Boston, Homer had moved to New York City in 1859. He studied at the National Academy of Design a few doors up from Pfaff's on Broadway, fell in with the artists and bohemians, and began freelancing for *Harper's Weekly*. Twenty-five when the war broke out, Homer went to the front as a special artist. He would spend two months on the Peninsula, mostly with

New York units, creating dozens of sketches that *Harper's* reproduced as engravings. He would dine out for years on his brief time at the front, using his sketches as studies for celebrated paintings like *Prisoners from the Front*, in which he used Barlow as the model for the haughty young Union officer, and *The Briarwood Pipe* and *Pitching Horseshoes*, which immortalized Duryee's Zouaves.

Olmsted and the Sanitary Commission sailed with McClellan as well. They had converted a handful of steamboats and ferries into hospital ships, staffed with surgeons, wound-dressers, and both male and female nurses. Their main role was to carry the sick and wounded to general hospitals in the North, away from the battlefront. They met stiff resistance from many officers, who feared—not without reason—that if the men were taken too far away from the fighting, they wouldn't return when they were fit again.

Maria Daly's friend Harriet Whetten from Staten Island was among the nurses. Daly treated Whetten, who was also still unmarried in her thirties, with condescending fondness. She thought Whetten too "impractical" and flighty to be of any use in the hospitals. "I don't believe in dilettante nursing," Daly commented in her diary. "If I were [one of] the boys, I would not want a lady about my sickbed unless she were some motherly person with a snowy-white cap and ample shape. Harriet will never be a motherly-looking person." As time went on and Whetten continued to serve, Daly would relent somewhat.

Low in the pecking order, volunteers like Whetten mostly did housecleaning, served meals, and offered "motherly" tenderness to the boys. The Peninsula Campaign kept them busy. The men came from the battlefield stuffed into boxcars. In her Peninsula diary, Whetten described one group as "in a wretched condition, their wounds full of maggots, their clothes of vermin & nearly starved."

⁓

Convinced he was facing an army twice the size of his, when in fact the reverse was true, McClellan moved his great force toward Richmond so slowly and gingerly that he earned the nickname "the Virginia Creeper." As April flowed into May, he kept preparing for an apocalyptic battle that never came, while all of Washington howled. Lincoln complained that "Tardy George" had a bad case of "the slows." While Lincoln and

Stanton grumbled, many of Little Mac's officers and common soldiers loved him for his caution: Every day he avoided a fight was a good day for them. Halpine had Private Miles O'Reilly sing:

Wid patient toil an' pityin' breast
You sought your soldiers' blood to threasure,
Nor ever tried the cruel test
How much we could endure to measure.

All the New York papers had sent specials to the front; Bennett sent the most—fourteen. Despite the ribbing he'd taken after Bull Run, Raymond was on hand through most of the campaign to boss his *Times* specials around. That sort of up-close meddling by an editor came to be known among journalists as "bigfooting," and still is. The army reviewed all dispatches to censor any information, such as troop strengths or movements, that might aid the Confederacy. And it banned one correspondent outright: the London *Times*' Russell, whose reports on the debacle at Bull Run had been so negative and embarrassing. He returned to England.

Except for the *Tribune*, the New York papers tended to take Mac's side. They dutifully reported his grossly inflated estimates of enemy strength and wrote up every skirmish as a grand victory. In the *Herald*, Bennett warned McClellan's enemies in Washington to "draw in their horns." The *World* and *Journal of Commerce* suspected Lincoln and Stanton of conspiring with radical abolitionists to engineer McClellan's downfall.

Fighting fierce battles, fever, and torrential rains, the Army of the Potomac lumbered toward Richmond. Meagher's Irish Brigade fought with honor. One Union general remarked that if he ever saw the Irish running to the rear he'd run too, because he'd know the cause was lost. A Currier & Ives lithograph of Meagher heroically leading his men in a charge at Fair Oaks (Seven Pines) hung in many New York Irish homes and bars.

The Excelsior Brigade fought its first battle that May and lost almost eight hundred killed or wounded. The unburied dead "lay in heaps," Chaplain Twichell wrote his father. "I shall remember it long." Sickles was not with them that day. He'd gone off to Washington to politick and then to New York to recruit more troops. He first led the Excelsiors into battle at Fair Oaks later that month and was in the thick of it throughout, proving himself a plucky and even reckless commander, if not a trained one. Waud sketched the brigade in a bayonet charge across open ground toward Rebels firing at them from a stand of trees.

At Sherwood Forest, midway up the Peninsula, Julia Tyler put on a brave front as McClellan's army surrounded her that May. She ran the plantation on her own now—John Tyler had sickened and died at the age of seventy that January. McClellan ordered his troops to respect the plantation and everyone on it. Except for pulling down Julia's wooden fences for their campfires, the Union troops left it untouched. The presence of the Union army made Julia's slaves "restless." One by one, they began to walk off the plantation. In the fall she would send most of her children north to stay with her mother, who now lived on Staten Island in a large house and property called Castleton Hill.

By the start of June the Union army had ground its way to within a few miles of Richmond, close enough that its pickets could hear the church bells. There McClellan halted and hesitated to deliver the coup de grâce, while the city's terrified citizens, including Varina Davis and her children, fled the expected invasion. It never came. For weeks McClellan sat and stewed and bickered with those meddling ignoramuses in Washington. The Confederates—led first by Joseph Johnston, then Robert E. Lee— saw their opening and came out fighting. McClellan, claiming wrongly as always that he'd been attacked by a vastly superior force, ordered his army to begin withdrawing back down the Peninsula.

The man who reputedly coined the nickname Virginia Creeper was outraged. Brigadier General Philip Kearny of New York City lived to do battle. He was a figure so heroic, fearless, and romantic that he almost seemed fictional. He was one of the most battle-tested officers in the Federal army. He was also probably the wealthiest (except for Astor, who wasn't officially an officer).

He was born in 1815 in a grand house at the foot of Broadway, into a family of Scots-Irish-Huguenot heritage that had built an enormous fortune in shipping and on Wall Street. After his parents died when he was a boy his grandfather raised him and sent him to Columbia to study law, which bored him. When the grandfather died in 1836 he left Philip more than a million dollars. Of all the avenues open to a twenty-one-year-old with such unspeakable wealth, Philip chose a life of military adventure, following a history of fighting men on both sides of the family. He joined the U.S. cavalry and chased Indians out west. One of his superior officers was Jefferson Davis. A few years later he went to France, where he trained at the illustrious Ecole Royale de Cavalerie at Saumur. He rode into battle with the French Chasseurs in North Africa, fighting as they did with a sword in the right hand, a pistol in his left, and the reins in his teeth. From then on he sported French touches to his uniform—a kepi jauntily tilted on his head, a short cape, and a wide sash.

When the war with Mexico commenced he handpicked his own company of 120 dragoons and equipped them like no other unit in the army. Riding matching dappled gray horses, they served as Old Fuss and Feathers's personal bodyguard. Leading his dragoons on a reckless and failed assault on Mexico City, Kearny lost his left arm. It only made him that much more a storybook hero. He was back in the saddle in days, reins in his teeth, and was reputedly the first man to storm into Mexico City when it was finally taken. General Scott would call him "the bravest man I ever knew."

In Paris in the 1850s he met and began openly living with Agnes Maxwell, the daughter of Hugh Maxwell, Zachary Taylor's collector for the port of New York. Kearny abandoned his wife and four children, Agnes dropped her fiancé, and all of New York society was scandalized. It was a few years before his enraged wife would grant him a divorce. He built a mansion called Bellegrove for himself and Agnes across the Hudson in New Jersey. In 1859 he went back to France to ride as an officer in Emperor Louis Napoleon III's Imperial Guard. For his courage at the Battle of Solferino he was the first American to be awarded the Légion d'honneur.

At the start of the Civil War he raised the first volunteer unit from New Jersey. McClellan gave him command of his Third Corps, which included the Mozart Brigade. They participated in the bloodiest battles of the Peninsula Campaign, Kearny leading as always from the front, looking magically impervious to Rebel shot and shell, shouting encouragements like "Don't flinch, boys! They're shooting at me, not you!" Lieutenant George Custer, who served as an aide to Kearny and then McClellan, said that Kearny "was always where the danger was greatest." Confederates dubbed him "the One-Armed Devil." In several battles his men charged ahead when all others were falling back. They took heavy casualties but adored their courageous commander.

When McClellan lost his nerve within sight of Richmond and began to fall back, Kearny fumed that he was "feeble" and judged that the order to retreat could only be "prompted by cowardice or treason." Lee proceeded to humiliate McClellan in a bold series of harassments that came to be known as the Seven Days. By the first days of July, Lee had whipped Little Mac all the way back down the Peninsula to where he'd started. The hospital ships and field hospitals overflowed with the twelve thousand casualties McClellan's army had sustained in just the one week.

Lincoln sailed down to the Peninsula again to ask McClellan what had gone wrong, and to review the troops on July 4. He promoted Kearny to major general that day. Kearny asked for the best bugler in his division to be by his side for the occasion. They sent him Gus Schurmann. Taking a shine to the thirteen-year-old, Kearny made Gus his orderly and gave him a new bugle to replace his battle-dented one.

After a full year of great expectations, after all the delays and buildup and brouhaha, McClellan had failed miserably. The North reeled from a defeat far grander and more dispiriting than Bull Run had been. One Republican fumed, "McClellan is an imbecile if not a traitor. He has virtually lost the army of the Potomac" and "deserves to be shot." Lincoln took the Army of the Potomac away from him and gave it to John Pope, who'd done well fighting out west. The Peninsula Campaign was abandoned.

Instead of celebrating an end to the war, Lincoln was forced to issue a call for three hundred thousand more volunteers to sign up for three years. In the *Tribune*, Greeley approved, declaring that "a 'speedy conclusion' of the war is what the nation demands." The *Evening Post* published a poem that Stephen Foster set to a spritely march to create a new recruiting song:

We are coming, Father Abraham, 300,000 more,
From Mississippi's winding stream and from New England's shore.
We leave our plows and workshops, our wives and children dear,
With hearts too full for utterance, with but a silent tear.

But the gung-ho sentiment was far from universal. Enlistment did not pick up. In July, Congress passed the Militia Act, allowing a state to draft militiamen if it did not reach its quota of volunteers. It was the first step toward a national draft, requiring all males between eighteen and forty-five to register. The Union's first draft dodgers began heading for Canada shortly thereafter. New York City Republicans and War Democrats organized a National War Committee and threw another big rally in Union

Square to drum up volunteers. Judge Daly told the crowd, "If a man is unwilling to defend this free government when the lot falls upon him, he is unworthy to live in it and to enjoy its blessings." He explained that if not enough men volunteered, "we must draft." In the *Times*, Raymond called on Lincoln to begin conscription immediately, and many political heavyweights in the city agreed. McClellan's failure on the Peninsula had convinced them that the war could drag on for a very long time unless the Union took extraordinary measures, and quickly. Even Archbishop Hughes preached a sermon in which he declared, "The people should insist on being drafted, and so bring this unnatural strife to a close." The people would show they had very different thoughts about that.

CHAPTER 26

Three Cheers for Ericsson

In September 1861, while McClellan was still drilling his army in Washington, a representative of the Navy Department had traveled to New York and knocked on the door of the three-story brick house at 36 Beach Street, facing the handsome St. John's Park in the lower Manhattan area now called Tribeca. Some of Beach Street has vanished since; the length of it where the house once stood has long been called Ericsson Place for the man who lived at 36.

John Ericsson was a brilliant but quarrelsome inventor. Born in Sweden in 1803, he had moved to New York at the end of the 1830s and would remain there until he died in 1888, taking U.S. citizenship along the way. By 1861 he'd had a long and stormy relationship with the U.S. Navy. In 1844 he designed the USS *Princeton*, a revolutionary new warship with a coal-fired steam engine, a rotary screw propeller (as opposed to the paddlewheels that had been in use until then), and a gun that could launch a 225-pound shell five miles with deadly accuracy. The navy was showing off the *Princeton* to President John Tyler, his future wife, Julia Gardiner, and some four hundred dignitaries when an innovative new cannon—not of Ericsson's design—exploded, killing the secretaries of state and the navy, a couple of sailors, one of Tyler's slaves, and Julia Gardiner's father. The navy had unfairly blamed Ericsson, and he'd spent the next several years in courtrooms trying to clear his name, while also suing infringers of his propeller patent. It all turned him into an infamously ornery cuss. In 1851 he had unveiled another stunning new design, a "caloric" engine that ran on hot air rather than steam. In the *Tribune*, Greeley, always ready to cheer the new, wrote that "the age of steam is closed, the age of caloric opens. Fulton and Watt belong to the past. Ericsson is the great mechanical genius of the present and future."

Ericsson's visitor was on a mission from Navy Secretary Gideon Welles. Among the wrecks the fleeing Union officers had scuttled in Gosport Navy Yard when the war started was the *Merrimac*. Once a big, sleek steam-and-sail frigate bristling with forty guns, it was turned overnight into a charred and sunken wreck. Originally its name was spelled "Merrimack" for the New England river, but it somehow lost the "k." The Confederates conceived a bold plan to refloat her, repair her, and sheath her hull in iron, with a massive battering ram fitted to the prow, to create a "floating battery," "a warship of unparalleled power and terror." The concept was not new. In the early 1840s the brothers Edwin and John Stevens of Hoboken had designed and partially built the giant "Stevens Battery," an iron warship meant to augment the defense of New York's harbor against a possible British invasion. They never completed it. The French launched the first ironclad in 1859. But the U.S. Navy had not caught up, and the *Merrimac* could make everything in the Union fleet obsolete.

The Confederacy was not rich in the sort of ironworks and workers who could pull this off, however. The South had always depended on the industrialized North for such projects. It would be almost a year before the dreadnought was ready to fight. Mary Touvestre, a free black woman working as a domestic for one of the engineers, stole a copy of the plans and sneaked them to Washington. The Union had ample time to come up with a response.

Ericsson was confident he had just the thing. He showed his visitor plans and a cardboard model of a "sub-aquatic system of naval warfare," an entirely new type of warship he claimed could be built in ninety days. It was an iron lozenge that would lie mostly underwater, just a flat deck breaking the surface, with a rotating pillbox gun turret in the middle. The visitor returned to Washington and in a few days was showing the radical design to Lincoln. During the war, New Yorkers would write Lincoln proposing all sorts of exotic weapons, from a steam-driven cannon to an electrically charged artillery shell that would produce an explosion "equal to any shock of electricity in the heaviest thunder storm." This one he liked. He said it reminded him of the Mississippi flatboats he worked on as a young man in the late 1820s (which, not coincidentally, gave him his first close encounters with plantation slavery). A panel of naval officers, recalling the navy's prickly relationship with Ericsson, urged Lincoln to reject the plan. Resorting to one of his rustic witticisms, he declared, "All I have to say is what the girl said when she put her foot into the stocking. 'It strikes me there's something in it.'"

Several sites got to work. In Manhattan, the Delamater and Novelty ironworks built the engine, propeller, and turret. Erastus Corning's ironworks supplied hull plates. Continental Iron Works in Brooklyn's Greenpoint area put it all together in 101 days, then it was shifted down to the Brooklyn Navy Yard for final fittings. Ericsson shuttled from one spot to the other, hectoring the workers. In mid-February the *Monitor*—so named because Ericsson said it would "monitor" any attempts by the Confederates or their allies to break the Anaconda blockade—headed out gingerly on her first test run. She immediately developed serious steering problems and had to be towed back up the river. On her next test the two massive guns in the turret recoiled clean off their carriages. It was not an auspicious start.

Finally, with a crew of fifty-eight understandably nervous volunteers, she made for the open sea on March 6, 1862. Lieutenant John Worden, a New Yorker, was commanding, but he wasn't happy about it. Like many navy men, he distrusted Ericsson and his inventions. He was a slight man, not the picture of machismo despite a bushy beard—other officers, for instance, noted his soft, ladylike hands—but he was tough in a fight. The journey southward almost ended the *Monitor*'s career before it had a chance to fire a shot. It foundered in stormy seas its second day out. Then the engines quit, filling the ship with deadly carbon monoxide. The crew kept passing out but managed to make repairs.

On Saturday, March 8, the massive, barely maneuverable *Merrimac* finally lumbered out of Gosport. She was officially rechristened the *Virginia*, but everyone in the Union and even some in the Confederate navy continued to use her original name, which is how she's gone down in history—not least because "the *Monitor* and the *Merrimac*" has a more felicitous and memorable ring than "the *Monitor* and the *Virginia*." At Hampton Roads just outside Norfolk, three wooden Union ships had set up a blockade. The *Merrimac* engaged them. As cannonballs bounced off her plating, "having no more effect than peas from a pop-gun," as a *Times* correspondent would report, she rammed and sank the Union's *Cumberland* while her guns bludgeoned the *Congress*. The third Federal ship, the *Minnesota*, ran aground in the fight. The triumphant yet battered and dented *Merrimac*, its ram broken off, quit the fight and returned to Gosport for overnight repairs.

The *Monitor* and the *Merrimac* met at Hampton Roads the next morning for their much-storied battle. The *Monitor* had only two guns to the *Merrimac*'s twelve, and looked tiny going up against the massive foe—Confederate sailors jeered that she looked like a cheesebox on a raft—but she was more maneuverable, and Worden sailed rings around the behemoth, their shells clanging off each other's sides. Worden was the only casualty in the battle, blinded by a bursting shell. After four hours both ships backed away, damaged but still more or less seaworthy.

Though they had fought to a draw, both sides claimed victory. All New York cheered Ericsson and his invention. Tony Pastor debuted a new song, "The Monitor and the Merrimac." Since the start of the war he'd specialized in songs on ripped-from-the-headlines topics like "The Irish Volunteers" ("Long life to Colonel Meagher, he is a man of birth and fame / And, while our Union does exist, applauded be his name!"). The chorus of "The Monitor and the Merrimac" went:

> *Raise your voices everyone—*
> *Give three cheers for Ericsson,*
> *Who gave us such a vessel, neat and handy, oh—*
> *And now we'll give three more*
> *For the gallant Monitor;*
> *And three we'll give for Yankee Doodle Dandy, oh.*

Lincoln visited Worden in his hospital bed in Washington. "You do me a great honor, Mr. President, and I am only sorry that I can't see you," the lieutenant said.

"You have done me more honor, sir, than I can ever do to you," Lincoln replied. Worden still held a relatively low opinion of Ericsson's ship and warned Lincoln, as the president paraphrased it, that "she should not go sky-larking up to Norfolk" to seek another clash with the *Merrimac*.

~

Worden wasn't the only one who still felt a healthy fear of the Rebel beast. Rumors flew around the North that "the marine monster" was steaming toward Washington to "smash Congress as badly as it did the vessel of that name at Hampton Roads." After that, it was feared, she would do the same to New York. In fact she was undergoing repairs in Gosport, but New York and Washington trembled anyway. In Washington, to Secretary Welles's great indignation, Stanton convinced Lincoln that Welles's navy could not stop the monster. With the president's permission, he called on another New Yorker for help.

Thus a week after the *Monitor* and *Merrimac* clashed, Cornelius Vanderbilt answered Stanton's urgent request to come to the White House and consult with him and the president. Welles fumed. He considered Stanton a hopeless ninny, and had already had flinty relations with Vanderbilt as well.

At sixty-seven, Vanderbilt had come a very long way from his humble origins among the Knickerbocker farmers of Staten Island. He'd started out as a teenager with a small sailboat ferrying passengers between there and Manhattan for a shilling each way. In the 1820s he'd jumped into the free-for-all among competitors for control of Hudson River steamboat traffic. Now the commodore was the multimillionaire master of a steamship empire linking the Atlantic and Pacific, and expanding into railroads as well. Along with oceanic passengers, his ships had hauled cotton from the South to the mills of the Northeast, taken many of the miners to the California gold rush, and carried tens of millions of dollars in gold bullion back to the Wall Street banks. The commodore was an imposing presence, tall, stony-jawed, strong, and fearless. He was also irrepressibly virile—he wore his wife out siring more than a dozen children with her, and always had pretty young women on the side. He was just as driven by a lust for competing and dominating in business. In an 1859 critique that compared him to the highwaymen of old, the *Times* said he displayed a "sordid audacity" for winning at any cost. He was one of the first of a new breed of monopolists, tycoons, and robber barons who would radically alter American business and high finance after the war.

But fiercely focused on his own empire as he was, Vanderbilt was still a patriot. When Sumter fell he'd written to Welles, offering the navy the use of his flagship, modestly named the *Vanderbilt*. When he launched it at a Greenpoint shipyard in 1855 it was the largest, fastest steamship in the world. With two giant paddlewheels, two colossal engines, and five decks of opulent cabins, it made travel to Liverpool luxurious and quick, slashing the time to nine days. Vanderbilt proposed that Welles arm it and use it to crush the Confederate navy.

The infamously tetchy Welles didn't even reply to what the *Herald* called this "princely and munificent" offer. Washington did then lease the *Vanderbilt* and several other of the commodore's Atlantic and Pacific

Steamship Company vessels for use as transport ships, operating through New York middlemen who drove the price up as they took their cuts. Because of this, and the fact that a couple of the ships were leaky old tubs, Vanderbilt developed a not altogether undeserved reputation as a war profiteer.

Nevertheless, Lincoln and Stanton now eagerly accepted the commodore's offer to pit the *Vanderbilt* against the *Merrimac*. Vanderbilt rushed home and had the huge steamship refitted in Greenpoint with a ramming prow of timbers and iron. Toward the end of March he personally sailed it down to Virginia and up the Potomac to join the *Monitor* and other Union warships in the blockade. But the *Vanderbilt* and the *Merrimac* never clashed in battle. The *Merrimac* steamed out of Gosport a few times, but kept a respectfully wary distance. That May, when Confederate troops abandoned Portsmouth to protect Richmond against McClellan's advance, the captain of the *Merrimac* ran her aground and set her alight rather than let her fall into Yankee hands.

On New Year's Eve 1862 the *Monitor* would sink in a storm off Cape Hatteras, but it had done its job. Lincoln ordered more *Monitor*-type ships built; during the course of the war almost seventy of them, several built on the East River, would prove that the age of the wooden warship was over. The Royal Navy had already canceled all construction of wooden warships just two days after the Hampton Roads battle. The Confederacy, with its limited means, also built a few more ironclads, as well as the *H. L. Hunley*, the first submarine to sink a warship (the *Hunley* also sank in the process).

Ericsson, finally vindicated, oversaw constant improvements and additions to ironclads' designs. After the war he would continue to experiment with his caloric engine, with "hydrostatic javelins" (torpedoes), even with solar power. When he died in 1889 he was buried first in New York; later his remains were moved to Sweden with all honors. Worden was at his funeral. He'd regained his sight, though the side of his face was permanently darkened from the gunpowder burn that had temporarily blinded him. He reached the rank of admiral, served as superintendent of the Naval Academy, and died in 1897.

⌒

Another sea battle that spring pitted a Southerner who had moved to New York against a New Yorker who had defected to the South. David

Farragut was born in Tennessee in 1801 and spent most of his life on land in Norfolk. When the war broke out he'd served half a century in the U.S. Navy. Commissioned as a midshipman when he was only nine, he'd been through some of the fiercest sea battles of the War of 1812 before his thirteenth birthday. Over the ensuing decades he'd persevered through the painfully slow process of advancement in the small and antiquated navy. When the firing on Sumter began he was a captain approaching his sixtieth birthday. Confederate leaders wooed him for their new navy, but he and his family slipped out of Norfolk a few days after Fort Sumter fell and made their way to the hamlet of Hastings-on-Hudson just north of New York City, where they'd live for the duration.

He was posted to the Brooklyn Navy Yard while the wary War Department grilled him on his willingness to lead combat missions against the South. (Some Southern officers who'd chosen the Union side had asked for noncombat postings.) After some soul-searching, Farragut answered in the affirmative, and was appointed to lead a daring naval invasion of New Orleans. In April 1862 he led a squadron of seventeen Union warships from the Gulf of Mexico into the mouth of the Mississippi River, running the gauntlet of two river fortresses and a Confederate naval force that included the *Manassas*, a low-lying 143-foot ironclad designed solely to sink ships with its twenty-foot ram. William Waud, drawing from one of Farragut's ships, said the *Manassas* looked like "an enormous turtle" as it scudded through the water toward its prey. Farragut's fleet sank it in a maelstrom of cannon fire and steamed on to New Orleans.

Confederate general Mansfield Lovell, who was tasked with defending New Orleans, was a West Point graduate and Mexican War vet who settled in New York City in 1854 and went into business as a civil engineer. He commanded the Old Guard of the City of New York, a ceremonial unit that turned out for parades. As a faithful Tammany Democrat, he secured a ripe appointment as deputy street commissioner, serving under another engineer and retired West Point man, Gustavus W. Smith. When the war started, Smith and Lovell, both pro-South conservatives, left the city to go fight for Jefferson Davis. General Smith led Rebel troops against McClellan on the Peninsula, while Lovell was sent to New Orleans.

Lovell commanded a ragtag lot of three thousand volunteers carrying their own muskets and shotguns. Expecting that Farragut's flotilla would flatten the city with its guns if he tried to mount a defense, he withdrew his force by rail. The entire Confederacy denounced him as a coward and he was relieved of his command. Tony Pastor mocked him in "The New Ballad of Lord Lovell," a parody of the traditional song:

> *Sir Farragut came with a mighty fleet,*
> *With a mighty fleet came he,*
> *And Lord Lovell instanter began to retreat*
> *Before the first boat he could see.*

Lovell would return to New York City after the war.

When Farragut's armada steamed up to New Orleans' undefended wharves, the city was in a wild panic. Mobs looted warehouses and stores and had set so many fires that the city lay under dense clouds of black smoke. An enraged crowd at the waterfront shouted and jeered at Farragut's ships, but the city managed little more in the way of resistance. Farragut continued up the river, leaving the occupation of New Orleans to General Benjamin Butler. Butler was a political officer. A Massachusetts Democrat who had cast his ballot fifty-seven times for Jefferson Davis at the fractious 1860 convention, he became one of the harshest of War Democrats with the firing on Sumter. Like Stanton, he would switch to the Republican Party and become one of the Radicals. He made himself hated in New Orleans right away by hanging a man who had tried to haul down one of the American flags that had replaced the stars and bars on flagpoles all over the fallen city. He ordered the arrest of local women who insulted Union officers in public. Butler had already angered Southerners a year earlier, when slaves from nearby plantations escaped to his camp in Virginia and he refused to return them, declaring them "contraband of war." Lincoln soon signed a law authorizing confiscation of Rebel property, implicitly including slaves. "Contrabands" became the common term for the many thousands of slaves who ran away to Union-held territory during the war. Butler earned a death sentence from Jefferson Davis, and the nickname "Beast." He looked the part, a squat, bandy-legged troll with a large pumpkin of a head. Later in the war he'd bring what he learned about urban pacification in New Orleans to the unruly streets of New York City.

CHAPTER 27

I Goes to Fight mit Sigel

Mine heart ish proken into little pits,
I tells you, friend, what for;
Mine schweetheart, von coot patriotic kirl,
She trives me off mit der war.
I fights for her, der pattles of the flag.
I schtrikes to prove as I can;
Put now long time she nix rempers me,
And coes mit another man.

—Henry Clay Work

Blenker's German division had been sent west rather than invade the Peninsula with McClellan. Stonewall Jackson was prowling the Shenandoah Valley, menacing Washington, and Blenker was to help General John C. Frémont, the former Republican presidential candidate, remove the threat. Blenker's division set out March 10, 1862, on "one of the most miserable, ill-timed, and ultimately useless forced marches in the Civil War," according to historian Christian B. Keller. They slogged through mud, drowned in the swollen Shenandoah River, and clambered over three mountain ranges, sleeping without tents in rain and snow. As food ran out they were reduced to butchering their dogs and tossing empty coffee sacks into boiling water. When Blenker let the men out in foraging parties, they treated the Virginia locals so roughly, looting their homes and pillaging their farms for anything edible, that "to blenker" became slang for "to plunder" or "to pilfer." Southern papers denounced the "bloodthirsty Dutch," and some in the North, including the *Herald*, chastised them as well. By the time the ragged and starving division met up with Frémont two months later, Blenker had lost an appalling two thousand of his ten thousand men to drowning, frostbite, malnutrition, and Rebel bushwhackers.

On June 8, Frémont sent them crashing into Jackson's forces at Cross Keys. The Garibaldi Guard took heavy losses but held the center of Frémont's line against repeated Rebel attacks. The battle was disastrous for Blenker's original regiment, the 8th New York. Somehow they found themselves marching alone across an open field of clover, lined up perfectly, their muskets on their shoulders as though they were crossing a parade ground, when more than a thousand Confederates fired on them from the trees. Almost two hundred of the regiment's men were cut down in a single thundering volley; the rest broke and ran. "In their very first battle and in one brief moment," Keller writes, "the 8th New York suffered one of the worst regimental casualty rates of the Civil War."

For all his earlier showing off, Blenker fought the battle from the rear. In disgrace he yielded to his critics, resigned, and would die a dejected man on a farm in New York's Rockland County in October 1863.

The two preeminent Forty-Eighters in America, Franz Sigel and Carl Schurz, now joined the division. Sigel, a newly minted major general, assumed Blenker's command. He was a legend among Forty-Eighters for commanding an army of volunteers in Baden's failed revolution and successfully leading them on a storied flight into Switzerland afterward. He'd immigrated to New York City in 1852, taught school there, then in 1857 moved out to St. Louis, where he ran the public schools. At the start of the war he joined the Union fight and quickly made brigadier general. In December 1861, feeling he'd been slighted by English-speaking officers— which he most likely had, given the high levels of anti-Dutch prejudice among them—Sigel resigned. Seemingly every German in Kleindeutschland turned out for a pro-Sigel rally at Cooper Union in January 1862. Not wanting to lose German support, Lincoln not only reinstated Sigel but bumped him to major general. This only increased the resentment of him among Anglo officers, especially the West Pointers. Sigel even had a popular song written about him, "I Fights mit Sigel," also known as "I Goes to Fight mit Sigel":

> *I've come shust now to tells you how,*
> *I goes mit regimentals,*
> *To schlauch dem voes of Liberty,*

Like dem old Continentals,
Vot fights mit England long ago,
To save der Yankee Eagle;
Und now I gets my sojer clothes;
I'm going to fight mit Sigel.

More politician than soldier, Carl Schurz had fled Germany after the unsuccessful revolution and sailed into New York harbor in 1852. He moved on and settled among the large German population in Wisconsin, learning to speak and write excellent English along the way. Toward the end of the decade he joined the Republican Party and stumped for Lincoln. When the war broke out, Schurz was in New York City and recruited the 1st New York Volunteer Cavalry Regiment, nicknamed the Lincoln Cavalry, combining Anglo recruits with companies of German, Hungarian, and Polish New Yorkers. Lincoln rewarded him by making him ambassador to Spain, and the regiment went to war without him. Reading about the furor over Sigel's resignation the following winter, Schurz begged Lincoln to bring him home and let him fight. Lincoln did, and made him a brigadier general. The Germans of the division were ecstatic to have men they considered real heroes leading them now rather than the opéra bouffe Blenker. Despite the mocking stereotype, they adopted "I fights mit Sigel" as their motto.

The German troops rejoined the army in the east, which was now under General Pope. Sigel took command of the largely German First Corps, with Schurz leading one of its three divisions. All through August 1862, Pope skirmished and maneuvered around the Rappahannock River with Lee and Jackson, who'd escaped Frémont's grasp. They finally clashed at the Second Battle of Bull Run (Second Manassas). Lee sent Jackson around behind Pope to cut his lines of supply. On August 29, Pope detailed Sigel's First Corps to root out Jackson's well-entrenched forces. The fighting was vicious, and the Germans might have broken Jackson's line had Philip Kearny shown up with his division to assist as ordered. He did not. Kearny was one of the Anglo officers who resented Sigel, and historians believe he simply ignored his orders and let the Dutch be mauled. Alfred Waud was on hand to draw the Germans scattering in full retreat.

Kearny might have faced a court of inquiry, but his actions three days later rendered that unnecessary. The morning of September 1, in fog and rain, he found some soldiers cowering behind a fence at the edge of a cornfield. When he tried to spur them on, they told him there were Rebels hiding in the fog out there. He flew into "an ungovernable rage" and charged out into the field to prove it was safe. Rebels surrounded him and shot him dead. Lee, who had admired Kearny since Mexico, had his body carried over to the Union side. The whole North—except in German communities—mourned for the man the *Times* called "the best general in the army." He was interred in the family crypt in Trinity churchyard, and moved to Arlington National Cemetery in 1912. The township around Bellegrove named itself Kearny, New Jersey, in 1867.

⁓

Michael Corcoran was back in New York City to mourn for Kearny. For thirteen months, as he'd been shifted from one prison to another, his legend had grown in the North. The *Times* printed his letters home, balladeers like Tony Pastor wrote odes to his courage, and the entire Union kept track as he was threatened with hanging, stricken with typhoid, and caught in an escape attempt. Finally released in an exchange of officers in August 1862, Corcoran went first to Washington, where he dined with Lincoln, who promoted him to brigadier general, and a large crowd greeted him with "an outburst of irrepressible and vociferous enthusiasm," the *Times* said.

When he reached New York a few days later, normal business was suspended and a crowd the *Times* estimated at one hundred thousand massed in the streets to cheer him. In an editorial headlined "Corcoran, the Patriot," Raymond thought he saw an important turning point in the relations of the city's Irish and nativist populations. "If any class of our population who yesterday so grandly received and honored Col. [*sic*] Corcoran had a special appreciation of the occasion, we hold that it was the native-born Americans. And the reason is this; that Col. Corcoran, in all his military career, marked as it has been by vicissitudes unequaled in the war, has on all occasions exhibited a devotion to the American Government and to republican principles that proves him a patriot of faultless intelligence and perfect mold....Never were nationalities more entirely forgotten than in New-York's reception of Col. Corcoran." It was the peak of Corcoran's fame. Soon enough he would sully his dazzling image.

⁓

That September, D'Utassy and the Garibaldi Guard were attached to the Federal garrison guarding the Harpers Ferry armory. Flush with victory after Second Bull Run, Lee sent Stonewall Jackson to encircle and take the armory. D'Utassy got to command not only the Garibaldis but a whole brigade. As Jackson laid siege, brutally shelling the garrison from the surrounding hills, D'Utassy and his men distinguished themselves for their tenacious and sometimes reckless courage. With hope fading and ammunition low, the commander of the garrison, a Colonel Miles, ran up the white flag. D'Utassy was outraged and begged leave to lead his men on a breakout charge through the enemy lines. Miles denied him. Civil War historians tend to agree with D'Utassy that Miles gave up too soon and might have faced a court-martial had not one of the last Confederate shells fired at the garrison landed on him. Released in a prisoner exchange, D'Utassy and the Guards were back in the Washington area by November.

CHAPTER 28

The Dead of Antietam

For Pope's bungling at Second Bull Run, Lincoln sacked him. The president and all of Washington were frantic: Pope's failure left Lee with a clear path to the city. At wit's end, gritting his teeth, Lincoln asked George McClellan to take over Pope's battered forces and save the city.

On September 17, 1862, Lee and McClellan clashed at Antietam, still the single bloodiest day in the history of American warfare—a ghastly twenty-three thousand men killed, wounded, or missing. (There have been greater casualties in other battles, but never more in a single day.) As usual, McClellan overestimated the size of the enemy army, which was only half as large as his, and directed a cautious engagement. Meagher's Irish Brigade saw one of its finest hours at Antietam, stoutly holding the center of the Union line at fearsome cost, some of its units losing more than half their men—cut down, it was said, like "corn before the sickle." "As soon as my men began to fall," Father Corby recalled, "I dismounted and began to hear their confessions on the spot," bullets whizzing past his head. He saw "one poor man with a bullet in his forehead, and his brains protruding from the hole made by the ball. Strange to say, he lived three days, but was speechless and deaf, and had lost his senses entirely."

Barlow's 61st, reduced to around a hundred men by the end of the Peninsula Campaign, still fought bravely. Lieutenant Ezra Ripley, who knew Barlow from Concord and Harvard, described him in a letter as "looking so handsome, facing his men to cheer them, moving with such grace and elasticity, that it seemed as if he were dancing with delight. I have seen brave men and brave officers...but I never saw such a sight as Barlow's advance."

Barlow and his depleted regiment killed many Rebels and routed the rest. Later that day, shrapnel ripped into Barlow's groin and he was carried off the field. Arabella had followed him to the front, a not uncommon practice for officers' wives. She rushed to the hospital tent to nurse him. Maria Daly, who seems to have conceived a thorough dislike of Arabella by this time, refused to believe that Arabella did anything in the hospital but "lounge on a sofa." Barlow wrote his mother reassuringly that it was "an ugly looking wound but not a serious one. It will be painful and a long time in healing but does not endanger life or limb." Yet it was grievous enough that he was brought back to New York for several months' convalescence. His promotion to brigadier general came through a few weeks before his twenty-eighth birthday. Judge Daly had been on the list of distinguished figures who had lobbied for him, along with Emerson, Sumner, Nathaniel Hawthorne, Oliver Wendell Holmes, and Samuel Gridley Howe.

Meagher's conduct was again questioned when he was thrown from his horse at Antietam and the rumor flashed around that he'd simply fallen off it, drunk. Colonel "Porte Crayon" Strother was one of the rumormongers. Father Corby, who was certainly closer to Meagher, conceded that "when no fighting was going on, and time grew heavy on his hands, his convivial spirit would lead him too far," but insisted Meagher was never drunk in battle.

Although the fighting was brutal, McClellan managed only to damage Lee's forces. As Lee withdrew, Lincoln wired McClellan, "Destroy the rebel army, if possible." He was convinced that if McClellan acted decisively the war could be brought to a swift end. McClellan exchanged flinty telegrams with his president and did not budge. Lincoln traveled to the battlefront to urge him to pursue. McClellan would finally stir himself in late October, by which time Lee had fully escaped. Private Charles Fuller spoke for many Northerners when he wrote, "If the commander of the Army of the Potomac had been a brave and competent general, he would have disposed of Lee at this time."

∼

Mangled, putrefying corpses of men and animals still littered the Antietam battlefield when Alexander Gardner and an assistant arrived two days later. Over four days they took some seventy grisly photos. Gardner sent the glass plates to New York, where Brady had albumen prints made from them. Early in October, Brady displayed them in a new exhibition in his space on Broadway at 10th Street, "The Dead of Antietam."

Brady had been doing a good business in war-related images for a year by then. His galleries in New York and Washington churned out portraits, camp scenes, and battlefield landscapes in various formats: small *cartes de visite*; prints sized to slip into the photo albums that were in every household that could afford them; a series of large-format prints bound in leather as *Brady's Incidents of the War*, an expensive edition for wealthy customers said to be the first intentionally collectible photographic series in America.

But "The Dead of Antietam" was something entirely new. No glory or gallantry, no jaunty bravado was evident. These images presented the horrifying, grotesque reality of war. Some New York volunteers had experienced these horrors firsthand, and some had come home wounded and maimed. But for many New Yorkers, especially the middle and upper classes, the war had been hundreds of miles away and known to them only through newspaper articles they chose to read or not. The exhibition was a shock and an immediate sensation. The line of viewers wrapped around the block. In the *Atlantic Monthly*, Oliver Wendell Holmes wrote, "Let him who wishes to know what war is, look at these series of illustrations." An unnamed *Times* correspondent well understood the images' impact, writing that "the dead of the battle-field come up to us very rarely, even in dreams. We see the list in the morning paper at breakfast, but dismiss its recollection with the coffee." He went on:

Mr. Brady has done something to bring home to us the terrible reality and earnestness of war. If he has not brought bodies and laid them in our dooryards and along the streets, he has done something very like it. At the door of his gallery hangs a little placard, "The Dead of Antietam." Crowds of people are constantly going up the stairs; follow them, and you find them bending over photographic views of that fearful battle-field, taken immediately after the action. Of all objects of horror one would think the battle-field should stand preeminent, that it should bear away the palm of repulsiveness. But, on the contrary, there is a terrible fascination about it that draws one near these pictures, and makes him loth to leave them. You will see hushed, reverend groups standing around these weird copies of carnage, bending down to look in the pale faces of the dead, chained by the strange spell that dwells in dead men's eyes.

Despite the gruesomeness of the images, Brady did a brisk business selling the prints—and the handsome albums in which to display them. Without doubt "The Dead of Antietam" played a role in the sharply diminishing enthusiasm New Yorkers were showing by the fall of 1862 for "Mr. Lincoln's war." It was an interesting turn of events for Brady, whose portrait had played such a hand in getting Lincoln elected two years earlier.

Brady's name was all over the exhibition, the prints themselves, and the press they earned; Gardner's was nowhere mentioned. Even as the exhibition was enjoying its stunning success, Gardner was redressing that situation. He left Brady's employ, opened his own studio and gallery in Washington very near Brady's, and would be his competitor from then on. In 1866 he'd publish his own landmark in photography, the two-volume *Gardner's Photographic Sketch Book of the War.*

CHAPTER 29

Sambo's Right to Be Kilt

As frustrating as Lincoln found McClellan's incomplete victory, it did give him the pretext for an epochal act. He had been waiting since midsummer for a Union triumph so he could issue his Emancipation Proclamation. Historian Stephen B. Oates called it "one of the great ironies of the war" that it was McClellan, Lincoln's most outspoken foe in the army, a racist and pro-South Democrat, who gave him that opportunity.

Lincoln had come to this watershed in tentative stages. He had said repeatedly since before the war began that abolishing slavery was never his goal. After Horace Greeley got over his post-Manassas fit of brain fever in 1861, he had gone back to hectoring the president about it. On January 3, 1862, Lincoln had attended a Greeley lecture at the Smithsonian Institution. Blinking through his spectacles directly at the president, Greeley had insisted that the abolition of slavery was the "one sole purpose of the war." Exasperated, Lincoln asked a *Tribune* Washington correspondent, "What in the world is the matter with Uncle Horace? Why can't he restrain himself and wait a little while?"

Knowing how widely unpopular abolition still was in the North, Lincoln assayed some half-measures before committing to it. That March he tried to convince the four border states of the Union that still allowed slavery—Maryland, Delaware, Missouri, and Kentucky—to begin programs of gradual manumission. He failed. He also tried to keep the colonization idea vital, bringing a group of "Free Negroes" to the White House to try to enlist their support for creating a Liberia-type colony in Panama. He failed at that too. At the same time, one of his generals was pushing him from another direction. General David Hunter, a cousin of David Hunter Strother, was commander of the army's Department of the South (South Carolina, Georgia, and Florida). He unilaterally declared all slaves under his jurisdiction free, and issued an order to recruit two regiments of Negro soldiers from among them.

Charles Halpine, a.k.a. Miles O'Reilly, had left Corcoran's 69th by then and was a staff officer to Hunter. As an Irishman and Tammany Democrat, Halpine had no great love for Negroes. He once wrote his wife that he thought contrabands "ought all to be drowned." But he believed that the Union should prosecute the war by any means available, so at Hunter's direction he drafted the order to recruit black regiments, and even organized the first one, called the 1st South Carolina Volunteers (African Descent). Meanwhile, as Miles he wrote a little ditty for the *Herald*, "Sambo's Right to be Kilt," which began:

> *Some tell us 'tis a burnin' shame*
> *To make the naygers fight;*
> *And that the thrade [trade] of bein' kilt*
> *Belongs but to the white:*
> *But as for me, upon my sowl [soul]!*
> *So liberal are we here,*
> *I'll let Sambo be murthered instead of myself,*
> *On every day in the year.*

In New York, the Democracy staged a giant anti-Hunter rally at Cooper Union. Fernando Wood was the star speaker, denouncing "Black Dave" and all abolitionists, who he said had started the war in the first place and were now doing everything they could to drag it out. The packed crowd of several thousand huzzahed.

Lincoln liked and admired Hunter; Hunter had been in the retinue who trained with him from Springfield to Washington for his inauguration. But the president didn't want to be rushed by him any more than by Horace Greeley. He immediately nullified his friend's rash acts. Then a few more months of pondering, and more lectures from Greeley and from Radicals like Sumner, finally brought him to the justification that declaring Southern slaves free could strike a serious economic, psychological, and political blow against the Confederacy. He discussed it with his cabinet in July.

Seward advised him to wait until the army achieved some significant victory in the East, lest it look like a desperate attempt to distract the world from the army's ongoing failures.

They were still waiting for that Union victory when Greeley ran an open letter to the president in the August 19 *Tribune*. Under the headline "The Prayer of Twenty Millions," Greeley cried that "a great proportion of those who triumphed in your election…are sorely disappointed and deeply pained" by how "strangely and disastrously remiss" Lincoln was in not immediately emancipating Southern slaves. Lincoln responded with an open letter of his own. He didn't send it to the *Tribune*, however, but to his more dependable friend Raymond, who published it in the *Times*. It included the often-cited passage:

> My paramount object in this struggle is to save the Union, and is not either to save or to destroy slavery. If I could save the Union without freeing any slave I would do it, and if I could save it by freeing all the slaves, I would do it; and if I could save it by freeing some, and leaving others alone I would also do that. What I do about slavery, and the colored race, I do because I believe it helps to save the Union; and what I forbear, I forbear because I do not believe it would help to save the Union.

That September, McClellan's victory gave Lincoln his opening. Within a few days of the battle he called his cabinet together to announce his intentions. Yet even then he marked time. He flabbergasted cabinet members when he began the momentous meeting by reading aloud two chapters of *The Complete Works of Artemus Ward*, which had been published the previous spring, and cackling at all his favorite lines. Artemus Ward was the pen name of Charles Farrar Browne, a New Englander who had created his frontier alter ego Ward and his fictitious town of Baldinsville, Ohio, while writing for the *Cleveland Plain Dealer* in 1858. In 1860, Browne moved to New York City to take over the editorship of *Vanity Fair* from Whitman's friends at Pfaff's. When the war started, he made Ward "Captin of the Baldinsville Company," and "havin notist a gineral desire on the part of young men who are into the crisis to wear eppylits, I determined to have my company composed excloosively of offissers, everybody to rank as Brigadeer-Ginral." He "recroots" new men with questions like, "If I trust you with a real gun, how many men of your own company do you speck you can manage to kill durin the war?"

Lincoln found Ward's exploits hilarious. His cabinet members were unmoved. "Not a member of the Cabinet smiled; as for myself, I was angry," Stanton later recalled. "It seemed to me like buffoonery....I was considering whether I should rise and leave the meeting abruptly, when he threw his book down, heaved a sigh, and said: 'Gentlemen, why don't you laugh? With the fearful strain that is upon me night and day, if I did not laugh I should die, and you need this medicine as much as I do.'"

Privately, the cabinet was not unanimous in approving the proclamation. Blair worried, correctly as it turned out, that it would cost many Republicans votes in the upcoming midterm elections. Bates thought that the Supreme Court, still very conservative and with Taney still its chief, might declare it unconstitutional. Secretary of the interior Caleb Smith, one of the more conservative cabinet members, was against it on general principles and would soon resign.

Lincoln issued his Preliminary Emancipation Proclamation on September 22, five days after Antietam. He would sign it into effect on January 1, 1863. He worded it with lawyerly care to try to avoid conflict with the Supreme Court, and expressly defined it not as a humanitarian gesture but a strategic tool, "a fit and necessary war measure for suppressing rebellion." He exempted those four border states, and any Southern territory that had been taken by Union forces. Emancipation was strictly a blow against the Confederacy.

Even with these limitations, blacks and abolitionists cheered. At a big "Jubilee Meeting" a few nights after the announcement, in the Shiloh Church on Prince Street, black New Yorkers heard the Reverend Henry Highland Garnet, a former slave who'd become one of the city's leading abolitionists, thank God and sing the president's praises. At Plymouth Church, Beecher conceded that the proclamation "may not free a single slave, but it gives liberty a moral recognition." In the *Tribune*, Greeley enthused that the proclamation "is one of those stupendous facts in human history which marks not only an era in the progress of the nation, but an epoch in the history of the world. Shall we recognize and use it wisely, or shall we, blindly and foolishly, refuse to see that he have now our future in our own hands, and enter upon that downward career which leads eventually to ruin and oblivion?" With a little more reserve, Raymond declared that "looking at its possible economical and moral results in the future," the proclamation "is undoubtedly one of the great events of the century."

Many Northern whites, however, reacted negatively. White workers, still fearing that freed blacks would compete for their jobs, hit the streets in angry protest rallies in the major cities. The majority of Northerners, including those in uniform, had believed that the point of the conflict was to put North and South back together and restore the nation, even if that meant allowing slavery to continue in the South. The president himself had said it over and over, and reiterated it in that letter in the *Times* just a few weeks earlier. To learn that they were now supposed to sacrifice and die to free the slaves and create an entirely different nation enraged and disgusted a good number of them. Soldiers deserted in record numbers in the months after the Preliminary Proclamation. Some New York City and State regiments were decimated. A soldier in the city's 51st Regiment wrote in a letter home, "Soldiers are constantly deserting & say that they will not fight to put niggers on a par with white men—that they had been duped & that they only enlisted for the preservation of the Union & nothing else." Officers' resignations also rose sharply. "I did not come out to fight for the nigger or abolition of slavery," Lieutenant Colonel Henry Hubbell of the 3rd New York Infantry wrote his brother. "I would sooner see every nigger now free *in* slavery, than see slavery abolished." A lieutenant in the city's 99th Infantry, formerly a loyal and dedicated young officer, wrote his wife, "I am sick and tired of this Nigger War. A soldier has nothing to encourage him to fight for a lot of Nigger lovers at home." He resigned.

Halpine's Miles O'Reilly versified, "To the flag we are pledged, all its foes we abhor, / And we ain't for the nigger, but are for the war." The Pittsfield *Sun*, Herman Melville's local paper in the Berkshires, addressed a poem to the president with the lines:

> *Our mothers love their absent sons,*
> *Our wives their husbands true,*
> *But no one cares a mouldy fig*
> *For Cuffy or for you*

(Cuffy was a stereotypical name for a male slave, often heard in minstrel songs.)

Melville and the Democrats in his family agreed with the poem's sentiment. Melville was neither pro-slavery nor anti-Negro, but, like Whitman, he considered emancipation a dangerous distraction from the war's real goal of saving the union.

Fearing a general collapse of military discipline, Lincoln and Stanton cracked down. A few captured deserters were swiftly executed before assembled troops as grim examples. Officers who expressed their disgruntlement aloud—nicknamed Grunters—were summarily dismissed and court-martialed.

Michael Corcoran was putting together four regiments to form a new brigade, Corcoran's Irish Legion, that fall. He found that recruiting Irishmen in New York wasn't anywhere near as easy as it had been in the heady spring of 1861. When news of the terrible losses the Irish Brigade sustained at Antietam had reached the city, Irish volunteering plummeted. The added onus of fighting for Cuffy made recruitment even harder. Corcoran had to scrape the bottom of the barrel to fill the ranks. One of his new regiments, the 155th New York Infantry, or "Wild Irish Regiment," was actually led mostly by non-Irish officers like Lieutenant John Winterbotham, who had "toured New York's jails and prisons, offering bribes to criminals to entice them into his company." Winterbotham disparaged his Irish troops as "childlike, drunken, and poorly educated." An Irish officer under Corcoran tried to ban whiskey because so many of his fellow officers were drinking all the time. Some of the men even belonged to drinking associations called the Rum Rackers' Club and the Monks of the Screw.

Lincoln had of course been prepared for much protest in response to the September 22 proclamation, but he wasn't going to allow protest to tip over into sedition. Just three days later, on September 25, he issued another edict. He declared that "all Rebels and Insurgents, their aiders and abettors within the United States, and all persons discouraging volunteer enlistments, resisting militia drafts, or guilty of any disloyal practice, affording aid and comfort to Rebels against the authority of United States, shall be subject to martial law and liable to trial and punishment by Courts Martial or Military Commission." For good measure, he added that "the Writ of Habeas Corpus is suspended in respect to all persons arrested."

Lincoln had suspended habeas corpus in seditious Maryland back at the very start of the war, but this blanket, Union-wide edict startled many. Congress wouldn't pass a bill authorizing it until the following March. Still, in the space of three days Lincoln had twice rocked the North. He had radically altered the meaning of the war, for everybody. Now they were fighting to save the Union *and* free the slaves, and everyone in the North was going to do their part, *or else.*

This was a golden opportunity for New York's Democrats, and they took full advantage. Denouncing abolitionists and "the evils which a visionary and wild radicalism has brought upon our Government, our army and our people," they swept the midterm elections that November. Horatio Seymour, who blamed the war on Radicals suffering from "Nigger on the Brain," went to the governor's mansion, taking *70 percent* of the vote in New York City. (It was his second time in the governor's mansion. He'd served one term back in 1853–54.) All six of the city's congressional seats went to Democrats. Benjamin Wood was reelected, and Fernando surfed the Lincoln backlash to a congressional seat of his own. "There has never been so great a revolution of public feeling," Maria Daly exulted. "Everything two years ago was carried by the Republicans, but now radicals have ruined themselves and abolitionism." However, she did not approve of the election of "those two scamps, Fernando Wood and his *foolish*, unprincipled brother....It is a blot upon the party."

Benjamin Wood resumed publishing the *Daily News* the following May and was shortly annoying Republicans with a new, lucrative, and probably subversive feature. Readers in the North who wished to communicate with friends or loved ones in the South took out personal ads in the *News*, which the *Richmond Enquirer* reprinted. Personal ads by Southerners in the *Enquirer* were reprinted in the *News*. By the middle of 1864 the *News* would be running two or three hundred such personals a day. At that point the government would order Wood to cease and desist, worried that spies were using the ads to send coded messages, which they almost surely were.

∼

> Give us back our old Commander,
> Little Mac, the people's pride;
> Let the army and the nation
> In their choice be satisfied.
>
> —*Septimus Winner*

That November, after weeks of arguing with McClellan, Lincoln fired him, this time permanently. He gave the army to Ambrose Burnside, whose sweeping whiskers gave rise to the term "sideburns." While he was at it, the president used the occasion to purge the army of several other Democrat officers accused of "disloyalty and insubordination." He replaced them with loyal Republicans.

The Army of the Potomac, soldiers and officers alike, came close to mutinying over the removal of their beloved Little Mac. His aide Custer, whom he promoted to a captaincy, complained about the "dastardly attacks" of the general's cowardly and unpatriotic enemies, and wrote his parents, "I have more confidence in General McClellan than in any man living. I would forsake everything and follow him to the ends of the earth. I would lay down my life for him." Democrats throughout the North decried what they saw as the president's blatantly political vendetta against the man Melville would call the "Hero of Antietam."

In the *Times*, however, Raymond rallied behind his president. "We have no theory on which to explain this most extraordinary failure of Gen. McClellan as a commander, or the still more extraordinary persistence of the President in committing the fortunes of the war to his hands," he editorialized. "Gen. McClellan has shown too many of the qualities of an accomplished soldier to attribute his failure to simple incapacity. That he is absolutely disloyal to the Government we have never permitted ourselves to believe. Yet we think it quite probable that his heart has never been in the war,—that through it all he has had hopes of a compromise which should end it, and that he has feared the effect upon such a compromise of a stern and relentless prosecution of hostilities."

As McClellan's train took him north to New Jersey, large crowds cheered him at every stop. New York City's newly triumphant Democrats welcomed him as a conquering hero. He took rooms in the Fifth Avenue Hotel facing Madison Square. His reception by the city's Copperheads was, his biographer Stephen Sears wrote, "tumultuous." A crowd filled the street outside the hotel. When he stepped out onto his balcony, the crowd roared, a band played, and a local militia's small field piece banged. He was soon making the rounds of balls and gala feasts. While he was careful to keep his distance from Copperhead extremists like the Wood brothers, he happily basked in the attentions of more respectably conservative Democrats including Belmont, Melville's friend Lathers, Governor Seymour, John Van Buren, and John Jacob Astor. They made him a gift of a spacious new town house on West 31st Street off Fifth Avenue and began to groom him to run against Lincoln in 1864.

Over steaks at Delmonico's one night a month after emancipation went into effect, Belmont, Seymour, McClellan, and other top Democrats founded the Society for the Diffusion of Political Knowledge to publish and distribute pamphlets and scholarly papers mostly presenting their views that slavery was divinely ordained and emancipation was the folly of fanatics. They installed Samuel F. B. Morse as the society's president and figurehead, and he obliged with language such as his description of abolitionists as "that dark conclave of conspirators, freedom-shriekers, Bible-spurners, fierce, implacable, headstrong, denunciatory Constitution-and-Union-haters, noisy, factious, breathing forth threatenings and slaughter against all who venture a difference of opinion from them."

In the meantime, McClellan set to work organizing and writing his voluminous official reports on his tenure as commander of the Army of the Potomac—his defense against all his critics in Congress and the Republican press. His former aide and devoted fan Custer would spend the month of April 1863 in Manhattan assisting him. Custer took a room at the Metropolitan Hotel, his favorite in the city, and went each day to McClellan's town house to work. In the evenings he made the rounds of balls, theaters, and gambling establishments. Custer loved the bustle and whirl of New York City and would often return.

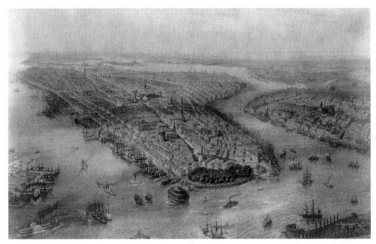

An artist's rendition of New York City and Brooklyn in the 1850s, looking north. Trinity Church rears its spire at Broadway and Wall Street. Farther up Broadway is the spire of St. Paul's Chapel. Governors Island, with the semicircular Castle Williams and star-shaped Fort Columbus (Fort Jay), is at lower right. The indentation in the Brooklyn waterfront is Wallabout Bay, site of the Brooklyn Navy Yard. Below that is Brooklyn Heights. *(1)*

Another view, from the steeple of St. Paul's Chapel at Broadway and Vesey Street down to the Trinity spire. Barnum's American Museum is directly across Broadway; Mathew Brady's first studio is to the right of the church, past the trees, and the Astor House is just out of the picture to the left. *(2)*

A Mathew Brady portrait of *Tribune* editors in the late 1840s. Horace Greeley is seated third from left. Charles Dana stands behind Greeley's right shoulder and Henry Raymond behind his left. *(3)*

James Gordon Bennett of the *Herald*. *(4)*

The phrenologist Orson Fowler reading the bumps on Zachary Taylor's head in 1848, trying to determine the presidential candidate's politics, while Greeley takes notes. *(5)*

Fernando Wood. (6)

Reverend Henry Ward Beecher, "a remarkably handsome man when in the full tide of sermonizing," according to Mark Twain, but "homely as a singed cat when he isn't doing anything." (7)

James Redpath, posing with a gun and a copy of the *Tribune*, in "Bleeding Kansas." (8)

Walt Whitman. *(9)*

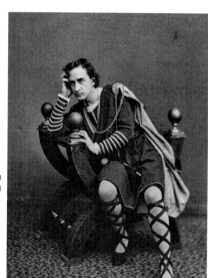

Edwin Booth in an
iconic pose. *(10)*

Laura Keene. *(11)*

New York congressman Dan
Sickles murdering his wife's
lover in 1859. *(12)*

David Hunter Strother's depictions of rebellious Negroes after John Brown's raid on Harpers Ferry. *(13)*

On February 27, 1860, Mathew Brady had Abraham Lincoln assume the same pose he'd previously used for another future president, Jefferson Davis. Note the wrinkles in Lincoln's frock coat. *(14, 15)*

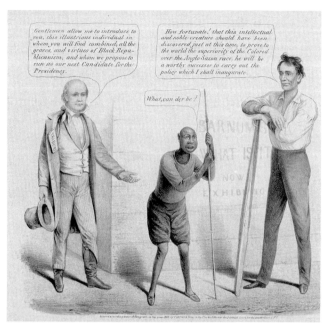

A Currier & Ives cartoon of 1860 lampooning Lincoln, Greeley, and their "Black Republican" agenda. (16)

A procession of Wide-Awakes in Printing House Square. The offices of the *Times*, *Tribune*, and *Day-Book* are all visible. City Hall Park is at the right edge of the image. (17)

The Seventh Regiment marches down Broadway, off to save Washington City. *(18)*

Louis (Ludwig) Blenker. *(19)*

Michael Corcoran. *(20)*

Charles Halpine, aka Private Miles O'Reilly. *(21)*

A soldier in the Garibaldi Guard. *(22)*

Elmer Ellsworth, the first Union officer killed. *(23)*

Alfred Waud, photographed by Alexander Gardner. *(24)*

Mathew Brady, on returning from the "Great Skedaddle." *(25)*

The hanging of the slaver Nathaniel Gordon at the Tombs. *(26)*

George and Ellen McClellan posing for a portrait at Brady's studio. *(27)*

A heroic Currier & Ives image of Meagher of the Sword during the Peninsula Campaign. *(28)*

Frank Barlow. *(29)*

Philip Kearny, the "One-Armed Devil," leading from the front as always. *(30)*

John Ericsson's *Monitor* (left) in its battle with the *Merrimac. (31)*

The "Commodore," Cornelius Vanderbilt. *(32)*

Admiral David Farragut. *(33)*

A cartoonist depicts Lincoln thanking General Benjamin "Beast" Butler for "scrubbing" New Orleans. *(34)*

Franz Sigel. *(35)*

Carl Schurz. *(36)*

One of Alexander Gardner's photographs of the dead at Antietam. These were men of the Irish Brigade. *(37)*

Dan Butterfield. *(38)*

Sickles (center) after Gettysburg. *(39)*

Governor Seymour's notorious "My Friends Speech" to the draft rioters. *(40)*

Thomas Nast's drawing of draft rioters in Printing House Square. *(41)*

William "Boss" Tweed. *(42)*

Thomas Nast's highly influential illustration decrying a negotiated peace helped Lincoln get re-elected in 1864. *(43)*

A *Harper's Weekly* illustration of the "Hippodrome of Sorrow." *(44)*

Boston Corbett, the mad assassin's mad assassin. *(45)*

CHAPTER 30

Burnside Falls, Sickles Rises

Lincoln's bad luck with his generals in the East persisted through the rest of 1862. That December, Burnside, reluctantly leading an army filled with soldiers and officers who resented him, blundered into Lee's hands at Fredericksburg on the Rappahannock River. Fighting in mud and snow, the Federals took an awful punishment, with more than thirteen thousand killed or wounded. Meagher's Irish Brigade charged the enemy lines so fearlessly that the Rebels, some of them Irish themselves, cheered them even as they cut them down in great numbers. "As we advanced, our men simply melted away before the grape and canister, and the tens of thousands of muskets," Father Corby wrote. It was, he said, "simply a slaughter-pen." Robert Nugent called it "a living hell." Shot in the groin, he would resign his command and return to New York City. The brigade sustained shattering losses and earned undying glory, but once again Meagher's leadership was questioned. For eventually ordering what remained of his unit to retreat he was accused of "arrant cowardice," this time by Villard. As darkness fell, the whipped Yankees backed off from battlefields strewn with carnage and gore. That night many wounded Federals froze to death where they had fallen.

Northern newspapers ran tragically long lists of men killed, wounded, or missing. Reading one of these in the December 13, 1862, *Herald*, Walt Whitman saw the name of his younger brother George. George was a lieutenant with the 51st New York Volunteers. Walt rushed out of the family home in Brooklyn and went to Washington, where he spent several days searching for George in vain in the overcrowded military hospitals. He then secured a pass to visit the army's encampment at Falmouth, just across the Rappahannock from Fredericksburg, where he was relieved to find that George had only been grazed on the jaw by a piece of shrapnel. He began visiting with the wounded. At Falmouth he spent time in "a large brick mansion on the banks of the Rappahannock, used as a hospital since the battle—seems to have receiv'd only the worst cases." He recorded the horrific scenes he witnessed there:

> Out doors, at the foot of a tree, within ten yards of the front of the house, I notice a heap of amputated feet, legs, arms, hands, &c., a full load for a one-horse cart. Several dead bodies lie near, each cover'd with its brown woolen blanket. In the dooryard, towards the river, are fresh graves, mostly of officers, their names on pieces of barrel-staves or broken boards, stuck in the dirt....The results of the late battle are exhibited everywhere about here in thousands of cases, (hundreds die every day,) in the camp, brigade, and division hospitals. These are merely tents, and sometimes very poor ones, the wounded lying on the ground, lucky if their blankets are spread on layers of pine or hemlock twigs, or small leaves. No cots; seldom even a mattress. It is pretty cold. The ground is frozen hard, and there is occasional snow. I go around from one case to another. I do not see that I do much good to these wounded and dying; but I cannot leave them. Once in a while some youngster holds on to me convulsively, and I do what I can for him; at any rate, stop with him and sit near him for hours, if he wishes it.

Whitman had previously spent some time visiting hospitalized soldiers in New York, and he now decided to stay in Washington and do the same. During the course of the war he would make many visits to the hospitals, serving as an amateur nurse's aide and a kind of one-man, unofficial USO. He wrote and read letters for the men; handed out fruit, tobacco, and such money as he could; read from the Bible when they asked; or just sat, talking or not. Occasionally, he wrote, he "took a fancy" to one of the young men:

> In one of the hospitals I find Thomas Haley, company M, 4th New York cavalry—a regular Irish boy, a fine specimen of youthful physical manliness—shot through the lungs—inevitably

dying—came over to this country from Ireland to enlist—has not a single friend or acquaintance here—is sleeping soundly at this moment, (but it is the sleep of death)—has a bullet-hole straight through the lung....He lies there with his frame exposed above the waist, all naked, for coolness, a fine built man, the tan not yet bleach'd from his cheeks and neck....Poor youth, so handsome, athletic, with profuse beautiful shining hair. One time as I sat looking at him while he lay asleep, he suddenly, without the least start, awaken'd, open'd his eyes, gave me a long steady look, turning his face very slightly to gaze easier—one long, clear, silent look—a slight sigh—then turn'd back and went into his doze again. Little he knew, poor death-stricken boy, the heart of the stranger that hover'd near.

Walt received no pay for his visits, and wrote to friends and fans for donations. James Redpath asked the help of Emerson, Thoreau, and other literati in and around Boston. He found them squeamish; they were aware of Whitman's sexuality and doubtful that his motives were entirely altruistic. Redpath wrote Walt, "It is believed that you are not ashamed of your reproductive organs, and, somehow, it would seem to be the result of their logic that eunuchs only are fit for nurses."

Whitman had made a few friends and fans in Lincoln's administration, and he lobbied them for some kind of government job. It wouldn't come until the war was nearly over. His steadiest benefactor was another younger brother, Jeff, a civil engineer at the Brooklyn Water Works, who often enclosed five or ten dollars, from his own pocket or solicited from coworkers, in his affectionate letters to Walt in Washington. "Walt, how I should like to see you, do you look the same as ever or has the number of unfortunate and heart-working cases given you an sobre [sic] and melancholy look," he wrote after Walt had been at work for some months. "But then the cases that you releive [sic] and those dear lives that you save must bring back the old look again."

Lincoln removed Burnside from command for his terrible performance at Fredericksburg and packed him off to the army's Department of the West in Ohio. McClellan's fans in New York called on Lincoln to bring Little Mac back. "We can tell the imps of faction who are shrieking for the restoration of McClellan that their wind is wasted," the *Times* scoffed. "The people have bidden a grim good-night to all imbeciles."

Lincoln gave Burnside's command to General Joseph "Fighting Joe" Hooker. Hooker was a swaggering, big-talking, and hard-drinking womanizer. He was also an aggressive and hard-charging leader under fire. He reorganized the Army of the Potomac, giving Dan Sickles—now a major general and the highest-ranking non–West Pointer in the army—command of Kearny's old Third Corps. With that, Gus Schurmann became Sickles's bugler and orderly.

Hooker was a man after Sickles's heart. The two of them and Hooker's chief of staff, Dan Butterfield, became drinking buddies. Butterfield was now a general. During the Peninsula Campaign he had adapted a cavalry bugle call to create "Taps." According to lore, buglers remembered the now universally recognized first six notes by the mnemonic "Dan Dan Dan…Butt-er-field…" Gus Schurmann may have been one of the first to learn it. Butterfield liked his women and liquor as much as Sickles did. The upstanding, happily married, and professional General George Meade, then commanding the Fifth Corps, considered them "bad influences" on Hooker. They quickly proved him right.

Because nineteenth-century armies couldn't move and fight well in the winter, after the Battle of Fredericksburg the two sides settled down on either side of the Rappahannock, so close that opposing pickets yelled jokes and wisecracks at each other across the icy water. With little else to do during that long winter encampment of 1862–63, Sickles and Butterfield threw gala parties to keep their fellow officers' morale up. Washington was just a day to the northeast, and the two ordered up loads of fine food, champagne, and cigars to stock the affairs. Civilians came too—politicians, bureaucrats, their wives, newspapermen, and the clouds of single young women whom men in uniform always attract. Hooker happily joined in. Uninvited, the straitlaced Meade sat in his quarters and grumbled that the trio were dissipated embarrassments to the service. The prudish cavalry captain Charles Francis Adams Jr., President John Adams's great-grandson, was also scandalized by the goings-on. He wrote that the festive winter camp of 1863 was "a place to which no self-respecting man liked to go, and no decent woman would go. It was a combination of bar-room and brothel."

The belle of the winter revels was the young Princess Salm-Salm, recently married to one of the more exotic officers in Louis Blenker's

German brigade, Felix Constantin Alexander Johann Nepomuk zu Salm-Salm. A monocled, mustachioed swashbuckler from a small principality on the Rhine, Prince Salm-Salm had ridden with the Prussian cavalry, squandered a princely fortune on youthful excesses, and come to Washington seeking adventure in the war. Because he spoke no English, the army made him a colonel under Blenker. His wife, Agnes Elisabeth Winona Leclerq Joy, was rumored to be an Indian princess, a former circus rider, and an actor in Havana. She was actually the daughter of Puritan farmers in Vermont, just one of the many girls whom the army attracted. She and the prince quickly got over their language barrier and married. They made a good pair. She used her considerable charms to get him appointed to the command of New York's 8th Regiment, and when the 8th came to the end of its contracted service in the spring of 1863, she got him a new command, the 68th New York Infantry.

During the winter encampment, Philip Kearny's widow, Agnes, wrote the army asking if she could meet the little bugler of whom her husband had become so fond at the end of his life. Sickles gave Gus a week's furlough. Gus called on the widow at Bellegrove, then went into Manhattan to visit his family, whom he hadn't seen in almost two years. He learned that his father had died a week earlier; the news hadn't reached camp until after he'd left.

In April, a few weeks before the spring campaign was to begin, President Lincoln came out from Washington with Mary and their youngest son, ten-year-old Tad, to visit the camp. The troops lined up on a wide plain for a grand presidential review. Regimental bands played "We Are Coming, Father Abraham" and "Hail to the Chief" as Lincoln, on a black horse, slowly passed down the line. Tad spotted Gus Schurmann mounted beside Sickles. They were about the same size and age, but where Tad had only played with toy soldiers, Gus actually was one. With his father's permission, Tad borrowed a mount from a cavalryman and rode beside Gus. A correspondent from the *Herald* noted that Gus "accompanied Master Lincoln as inseparably as his shadow....The boys are fast friends, and ramble around together like brothers." At the end of the afternoon Tad asked his father to let Gus come back to Washington with him. Sickles gave the bugler another furlough.

Sickles organized a reception for that evening. At his urging, the flirtatious Princess Agnes stood on tiptoe and gave the president a peck on the cheek. Reputedly, when he joined the Lincolns for dinner later, a jealous

Mrs. Lincoln stared daggers at both men. To break the silence, the president cleared his throat and said, "Sickles, I never knew you were such a pious man until I came down this week to see the army."

"I am quite sure, Mr. President," Sickles replied, "I do not merit the reputation, if I have gained it."

"Oh, yes," the president said. "They tell me you are the greatest Psalmist in the army. They say you are more than a Psalmist—they say you are a Salm-Salmist."

Even Mrs. Lincoln couldn't resist a chuckle. From then on she would be as much a friend to Sickles as her husband was.

Gus Schurmann spent two weeks in Washington playing with Tad. He slept in a guest room at the White House. They rode horses, barged in on cabinet meetings. On April 18 they went to Grover's Theatre to see a drama called *The Marble Heart*. They were very taken with the intense young star and went backstage at intermission to meet him. John Wilkes Booth greeted them courteously as he made up for the next act. Tad's father would see Booth reprise the role the following November and be impressed by him as well. Gus was back at Sickles's side by April 23.

❧

Another New York general offered some diverting entertainment during that long winter. In 1842, Barnum had met Charles Sherwood Stratton, a four-year-old midget whom he christened General Tom Thumb. For four decades the general would star at the American Museum and on international tours, charming Queen Victoria and trading witticisms with the Duke of Wellington.

In February 1863, Tom Thumb, twenty-four years old and thirty-two inches tall, married the equally diminutive Lavinia Warren Bump. The "Loving Lilliputians," as Barnum ballyhooed them, were wed at Grace Episcopal Church, the Gothic Revival masterpiece at Broadway and East 10th Street. Barnum had wanted it to be in the city's most prestigious church, Trinity, but Pastor Morgan Dix refused. The *Times* reported that a crowd of many thousands thronged Broadway and almost crushed the tiny pair as gawkers pushed forward to glimpse them entering the church.

The "Fairy Wedding" was the social event of the season. The cream of New York society, including the Vanderbilts and Astors, as well as General Ambrose Burnside, were among the invited guests who packed the church. Brady took the wedding photos. The tiny couple stood on a platform so that they could be seen during the ceremony. Commodore Nutt, another of Barnum's little people who had been a rival for Lavinia's hand, graciously served as best man. Afterward the newlyweds climbed onto a grand piano at the Metropolitan Hotel to greet two thousand well-wishers. The mountain of wedding presents displayed in the hotel's lobby included gifts from August Belmont, Edwin Booth, James Gordon Bennett, and the Tammany pol Charles Godfrey Gunther. The front page of the next day's *Herald* led with the story. War news—including a Battle of ironclads in Georgia's Ogeechee River—got less play.

The Strattons' honeymoon trip included a stop in Washington, where Mary, Tad, and Abraham Lincoln received them in two receptions at the White House. At the first, on a Friday, the president took Lavinia's tiny hand in his huge paw and held it gently, "as though it were a robin's egg, and he were afraid of breaking it." Mrs. Lincoln's regular Saturday levee the next day was unusually packed, as visitors crammed in to see the famous newlyweds.

⌒

Posted near Newport News, Michael Corcoran and his bottom-of-the-barrel Legion drank and partied through that winter as well. For Christmas of 1862 they transformed their camp into a festive holiday village, with horse races, wheelbarrow races, the chasing of a shaved pig, and a feast for Corcoran and his officers followed by many rounds of toasts. The following St. Patrick's Day, Corcoran personally led the whole Legion in a day and night of drunken revels, including a wild cavalry ride round and round the camp with bugles blowing, brass bands blaring, and howitzers banging off salutes. They descended on the town of Suffolk for raucous processions, a gala dinner, and many toasts, not straggling back to camp until 4 a.m.

Riding the line one dark night about a month later, Corcoran came upon a drunken officer who drew his sword and would not let him pass. Harsh words flew, then Corcoran drew his pistol and shot his fellow officer dead. Corcoran's version, and that of John O'Mahony of the Fenian Brotherhood, serving under Corcoran as a colonel, were printed in the *Times*. Corcoran contested the rumor that he had been drinking himself. O'Mahony claimed that Corcoran had been "patient, mild and

conciliatory in the extreme, while his opponent appeared to act the part
of an insensate brawler, anxious for a row at any cost, or else of an enemy
in disguise."

~

When the spring campaign commenced at the end of April 1863, Hooker
intended for his 120,000 troops to squeeze Lee's army, roughly half its
size, in a pincers movement around the hamlet of Chancellorsville, about
ten miles west of Fredericksburg. The plan depended on Lee and Stonewall Jackson sitting still—something they'd displayed no inclination to do
so far in the war—while the ponderous Federal force surrounded them.
With the trap set, Hooker suffered a McClellanish bout of timidity and
failed to spring it. Lee pounced. All day of May 2, Union pickets reported
that the Rebels were moving to attack Hooker's right flank, occupied by
the Eleventh Corps, which now was comprised about equally of American
units and Sigel's German veterans. Sigel no longer led the Germans. He
had worked himself into a high dudgeon again, and this time Lincoln and
Stanton let him go, at least for a while. Brigadier General Barlow was the
new commander of one of the corps' American brigades. A few weeks
earlier, despite looking "very frail" to Maria Daly, he'd ended his long
convalescence and returned to active duty.

Sickles, commanding the Third Corps, convinced himself and Hooker
that the Rebels weren't flanking, but in fact withdrawing. It was a terrible mistake. The men of the Eleventh Corps were cooking their dinners
around campfires when frightened deer, foxes, and rabbits burst out of
some nearby woods, followed closely by Jackson's twenty-six thousand
Confederates shrieking their Rebel yells. The terrified Germans threw
down their pots and pans and bolted for the rear. A third of them were
taken prisoner. The rest managed to re-form and the Union line eventually
held.

The battle raged on for the next few days, with fearsome losses on both
sides. The tattered remains of Meagher's Irish Brigade barely survived it.
Of the five thousand Irishmen he had originally recruited, only about five
hundred were still standing at the end of the battle. Meagher asked for a
new command. Given his checkered reputation, the army chose not to give
him another battlefield posting. Bitter, he returned to New York City.

The North was shocked and outraged that the Army of the Potomac had
once again snatched defeat from the jaws of sure victory. Recriminations

flew in all directions. For having crumbled first, the "flying Dutchmen" of the Eleventh Corps and their "scandalous poltroonery" took the most abuse. The *Times* declared them cowards. The *Herald* said they "fled like so many sheep before a pack of wolves." Never to be outdone in the heat of the moment, Greeley cried that "if it be deemed too rigid to shoot them all, they may at least be decimated and then dissolved." In June thousands of Germans from throughout the East, the largest gathering of Germans in American history, converged on Cooper Union to protest what they described as the Know-Nothing slanders in the press. They also called for Sigel to be reinstated. The *Times* called it "the German Indignation Meeting." Greeley, being Greeley, had a change of heart and apologized to the German people for his rash language.

In the ranks of the army, the Eleventh Corps remained the scapegoats for Hooker's poor performance. A little ditty passed among the troops: "O, I'd better stayed at home with the gal I love so much / Than be traveling round the Country with these damn Dutch." Barlow wrote his family, "You can imagine my indignation & disgust at the miserable behavior of the 11th Corps.... You know I have always been down on the 'Dutch' & I do not abate my contempt now, but it is not fair to charge it all on them. Some of the Yankee [regiments] behaved just as badly."

To help whip the corps into shape, Barlow was bumped up from command of a brigade to one of its three divisions. He was even more of a strict disciplinarian than before. He took to wearing an oversize comic-opera sword that he used to whack stragglers back into the line on the march. "As a taskmaster he had no equal," one of his American troops later wrote. "The prospect of a speedy deliverance from the odious yoke of Billy Barlow filled every heart with joy." The German soldiers, already "in a most disgusting condition as to discipline and morale," as Barlow put it, hated him when he arrested Colonel Leopold von Gilsa on a very minor infraction. "I expect to have to arrest them all the way down until I find some private soldier who will make them do things properly," Barlow reflected. Meanwhile, he was actively lobbying to get out of the Eleventh Corps: He wanted to be what he called the "Darkey Superintendent," the commander over all the new black regiments the army was drilling. His former student Robert Gould Shaw, training the 54th Massachusetts, hoped Barlow got the job.

When they were called to testify before Congress about the fiasco at Chancellorsville, Hooker, Sickles, and other officers passed blame around among themselves. Privately, Captain Francis Adams, who had been so scandalized back in winter camp, blamed the Hooker-Butterfield-Sickles triumvirate, railing that they were "the disgrace and bane of this army; they are our three humbugs, intriguers and demagogues."

To buck up the Army of the Potomac's battered morale, the army issued five hundred soldiers who had fought admirably a new medal of valor, the Kearny Cross of Honor. Dan Sickles personally awarded one to Gus Schurmann.

~

Meanwhile, Grant and Sherman had gotten bogged down in the Union effort to take the Mississippi away from the Confederates. Specials sent by the *Tribune*, the *Herald*, and other New York papers wrote long, depressing reports on the lack of progress, criticizing the two generals' competence, even their sanity.

Albert Richardson was there. When he returned from the South in 1861, Greeley and Dana had sent him to organize a news bureau to cover the western theater. One of the first writers he hired was Junius Browne. They were a Mutt 'n' Jeff pair, the burly Richardson and the balding, bookish Browne. Born Junius Brown in Cincinnati the same year as Richardson, he'd added the "e" for class. They were the nucleus of what Browne dubbed the Bohemian Brigade, a little corps of New York writers and artists who included Richard Colburn of the *World*, a *Times* special, and illustrators for *Harper's Weekly* and *Frank Leslie's*. They reported on gunboat battles on the Mississippi and the fall of Memphis. Browne described his battles with fleas, mosquitoes, and gnats in the same tones of desperate heroics as he did the fighting between the armies. He also never failed to note the qualities of the womenfolk in every locale, from the mannish "viragoes" of Arkansas to the dainty Southern belles of Memphis.

Most general officers disliked the specials, but none hated them so passionately and openly as William Tecumseh Sherman. He considered them at best meddlesome outsiders who got in the way and wrote lies, and at worst traitors and spies who fed information to the enemy. He did everything in his power to make their jobs impossible, finally issuing General Order No. 8, banning journalists from his camp and threatening to arrest and prosecute any he caught snooping around.

The specials hated him back, and when his assault on the fortified Mississippi river town of Vicksburg failed in December 1862 they pounced. "Another national humiliation! Defeated, baffled, repulsed, disheartened!" the *Times*' F. C. Foster wailed. The *Herald*'s Thomas Knox blamed Sherman's "insanity and inefficiency," and called for "another brain" to replace him. Sherman arrested Knox and brought him before a court-martial on charges of spying for the enemy and disobeying a direct order.

During a war when the president was shutting down whole newspapers and suspending habeas corpus, no one seems to have questioned a general's right to arrest and try a lone journalist. Through the two weeks of trial not a solitary newspaper in the country, not even Knox's own *Herald*, uttered one word of protest. A panel of Sherman's officers acquitted Knox on the more serious charges but found him guilty of disobedience and banned him from writing any more war coverage.

Now finally some of Knox's fellow specials spoke up; a committee led by Albert Richardson appealed to the president. Lincoln's response was Solomonic: He would order Sherman to let Knox come back, but only if Sherman's commanding officer General Grant agreed. Grant, who banished a few specials himself, backed Sherman. Lincoln washed his hands of the matter. When Knox wrote a contrite appeal directly to Sherman, Sherman's terse reply ended with the word "Never."

In May 1863, Grant's army was still below Vicksburg, preparing another assault. If the city could be taken, the Union would own the Mississippi, cleaving the Confederacy in two. The Bohemians were upriver. One night Richardson, Browne, and Colburn climbed onto a tugboat-drawn barge of hay bales that tried to sneak past the Confederate batteries surrounding the city. A rain of cannon fire struck and sank the tug, the bales of hay in the barge caught fire, and the Bohemians jumped overboard. Clinging to floating bales, they were easily scooped out of the water by the Rebels.

They spent the night in a Vicksburg prison yard. The next day a Confederate lieutenant paroled them, the first step in a prisoner exchange. But there was no exchange for Browne and Richardson, and they would spend the next twenty months being shifted around the South, sometimes shoved into jail cells, sometimes staying in hotel rooms with guards outside. Because they were journalists who might write about it someday, they were generally handled more gently than other prisoners, whose treatment could be cruel and often deadly. Richardson's wife sickened and died during his captivity.

In December 1864 a secret society of Southern Quakers and unionists called the Heroes of America would help Browne and Richardson escape from the horrific prison at Salisbury, North Carolina. They lit out on foot through the wilds of western North Carolina, heading west across the wintry Blue Ridge Mountains, trekking by night through woods thick with Confederate and unionist bushwhackers, aided by slaves and by Heroes identified through secret signs. On January 13, 1865, Richardson would telegraph the *Tribune* that they'd reached Union lines near Knoxville. The following month the paper ran their long accounts of their captivity, as well as a list Richardson had brought out of Salisbury of some twelve hundred Union men known to have died there.

Both Browne and Richardson would churn out books on their experiences: Browne's *Four Years in Secessia* and Richardson's *The Secret Service, the Field, the Dungeon, and the Escape*. Both were bestsellers. Browne would thoroughly enjoy a long, comfortable postwar career as a *Tribune* editor and popular man-about-town in New York. Richardson would not be so lucky. In 1867 he would start an affair with the beautiful poet and actress Abby Sage McFarland, who was trapped in an abusive marriage. After one of her performances at the Winter Garden, Albert and Abby were walking down the street when her husband popped up, cried, "Libertine!" and fired a pistol three times, striking Albert once in the thigh. Even after Abby won a divorce, her ex-husband would not let it rest. In 1869 he would walk into the *Tribune* offices and shoot Richardson again, this time with deadly accuracy. Friends carried Richardson in a chair the short distance to a room in the Astor House. Junius Browne watched over him until Abby arrived. Richardson asked Abby to marry him and they sent for a preacher—Henry Ward Beecher, who was among the many admirers of Richardson's writing. He performed the ceremony in the hotel room, with Browne and a few others as witnesses. Richardson died within hours, at the age of thirty-six.

CHAPTER 31

Grafted into the Army

Our Jimmy has gone for to live in a tent,
They have grafted him into the army;
He finally pucker'd up courage and went,
When they grafted him into the army.
I told them the child was too young, alas!
At the captain's forequarters, they said he would pass—
They'd train him up well in the infantry class—
So they grafted him into the army.

—*Henry Clay Work*

Lincoln and Stanton faced a potentially disastrous manpower shortage in the spring of 1863. More than one hundred regiments of two-year and nine-month enlisted men were demobilizing all at the same time. Death, desertion, and illness had already depleted the army's ranks at a disturbing rate, while bloody debacles like the defeats at Fredericksburg and Chancellorsville had reduced volunteerism to a trickle. Even the generous signing bonuses, or bounties, that enlistment offices had begun tacking on in the fall of 1862 as added enticement weren't working.

One of the bestselling songs of the war came out in 1863 and expressed the general sentiment: "Weeping, Sad and Lonely," also known as "When This Cruel War Is Over." Composer Henry Tucker of Brooklyn and lyricist Charles Carroll Sawyer, a Yankee émigré to New York, wrote it; Wood's Minstrels (as in Henry Wood, Fernando and Benjamin's brother) introduced it in their hall on lower Broadway, and the Fulton Street firm of Sawyer & Thompson published the sheet music. Its doleful melody and extraordinarily sad lyrics ("Oft in dreams I see thee lying on the battle plain / Lonely, wounded, even dying, calling but in vain") struck a deep chord. Reputedly a million copies of the sheet music sold, in the South as well as the North. It's said that one Union general forbade his men from singing it in camp because it took all the fight out of them.

Regardless, the Union needed another three hundred thousand men in uniform, and there seemed only one way to get them. In March, Lincoln finally signed the Enrollment Act, making able-bodied men between twenty-five and forty eligible for conscription. The Confederacy, with its much smaller pool of men, had already resorted to conscription; Union states had drafted militiamen since 1862, and many Northern politicians had been calling on Lincoln to begin federal conscription since then.

Nevertheless, the men who were most likely to be drafted, and their families, reacted with widespread disobedience and localized eruptions of murderous rage. Two aspects of the law particularly rankled. For one, at Lincoln's insistence, the law was worded vaguely enough to make black men as well as white men eligible. Democrats complained that Lincoln was using the war as an excuse to advance his Black Republican agenda. For another, a draftee could buy his way out of service, either by paying a three-hundred-dollar commutation fee or by hiring a replacement. Three hundred dollars was equal to the average workingman's annual salary. "The laboring classes," Maria Daly noted, "say that they are sold for three hundred dollars, whilst they pay one thousand dollars for Negroes." For many workers, this blatantly class-based exemption was proof that it was "a rich man's war but a poor man's fight." A parody of "We Are Coming, Father Abraham" made the rounds:

> We are coming, ancient Abraham, several hundred strong
> We hadn't no 300 dollars and so we come along
> We hadn't no rich parents to pony up the tin
> So we went unto the provost and there were mustered in

Adding a final insult, at the same time that Congress passed the Enrollment Act it ratified the blanket suspension of habeas corpus that Lincoln had proposed back in the fall.

Up to this point, states had been responsible for recruitment. A national draft meant constructing a large new federal bureaucracy: investigators to fan out through the North and compile lists of potential draftees, new enrollment offices in every locale, provost officers to man them, enforcement agents to track down draft dodgers. In the end it entailed some 75,000 new jobs. The *Chicago Tribune* wondered if it wouldn't have been more efficient simply to put all those employees in uniform and send them to the front.

Although New York City would be the site of the most infamous antidraft rebellion, there was resistance throughout the Union. Draft dodging was rampant. Of the roughly 292,000 names pulled in the first draft in 1863, almost 40,000 men never showed up. By war's end, some 160,000 males would have turned draft dodgers. Just as during the Vietnam War, many would flee to Canada for the duration. Many others went to New York City and melted into the milling crowds there. The mood in the city was such that most citizens were more likely to buy a deserter a drink than to turn him in. From the start, investigators who went door-to-door gathering the information for eligibility lists met with hostile and sometimes deadly response. By war's end thirty-eight of them had been murdered and another sixty wounded. Besides New York, antidraft riots would break out in cities all along the East Coast and as far west as Chicago and Detroit, as well as in coal-mining regions.

From the moment the draft and the suspension of habeas corpus became law, New York's Copperheads and Catholic newspapermen howled at these outrageous new signs of Lincoln's despotism. *Frank Leslie's Illustrated* predicted that the draft would turn the Union into "one grand military dictatorship." James McMaster called it the act of a "deluded and almost delirious fanatic." The *Metropolitan Record & New York Vindicator*, a Catholic family paper that was partly funded by Archbishop Hughes after he backed away from McMaster's *Freeman's Journal*, protested in articles with headlines like "Five Hundred Thousand More Victims to Abolitionism" and "The United States Converted into a Military Despotism? The Conscription Act the Last Deadly Blow Aimed at Popular Liberty." The paper's Irish editor, John Mullaly, had originally supported the war, but turned Copperhead with the Emancipation Proclamation, which he had denounced as "a vile and infamous document" that he felt excused the Irish from participating any further in the army. He had also predicted a full-on war between the races.

Dennis Mahony, former editor of the *Dubuque Herald*, a fiercely antiwar and anti-Lincoln Catholic newspaper, had just moved to New York. In 1862, after a barrage of scathing editorials in which he had called for

Lincoln's impeachment and protested "Nigger Suffrage, and Equality, Beecherism, Stoweism, Niggerism, and a dozen isms and Tom fooleries," he'd been arrested by federal marshals and conveyed to the Old Capital Prison in Washington, where he was held four months without any charges ever being filed. Now in New York he put out a collection of his rants in a book titled *The Prisoner of State*.

Clement Vallandigham, king of Copperheads, came to New York as soon as the Enrollment Act was passed to speak to its Peace Democrats. Then he went to Albany to meet with Governor Seymour, who spoke out against conscription as unconstitutional, while hoping to raise enough volunteers to make the draft unnecessary in his state.

This was Vallandigham's last trip to New York for a while. He returned to Ohio, where General Ambrose Burnside now commanded the army's Department of the West, with headquarters in Cincinnati. Disgraced and already in a foul temper after his defeat at Fredericksburg, Burnside quickly discovered that the Northwest—Michigan, Indiana, Vallandigham's Ohio, and Lincoln's Illinois—was a seething nest of Copperheads. There were also many settlers who'd migrated from the South with their sympathies intact. They came to be known as Butternuts, for their faded yellowish clothes and for the uniforms of similar color many Confederate troops wore. It was said that tens of thousands of Copperheads and Butternuts belonged to traitorous secret militias like the Knights of the Golden Circle, in some ways a precursor to the Ku Klux Klan. They were plotting to rise up in armed revolt to establish their own Northwest Confederacy, aligned with the South.

Burnside was having none of that on his watch. On his own authority he issued a decree in April that anyone "declaring sympathy for the enemy" faced arrest and a military trial. Vallandigham, true to character, denounced the decree as tyrannical and unconstitutional, and he openly defied it. One night in May, Burnside sent troops to drag him out of bed. As expected, a military tribunal pronounced him guilty and sentenced him to prison.

Democrats around the Union rose up in protest. In New York, Manton Marble, editor of the *World*, denounced Burnside and the Lincoln administration, while *The Sun* chided, "The Union can survive the assaults of all the armed and disarmed Vallandighams of the South and North, but it cannot long exist without free speech and free press." The Wood brothers staged a large protest rally, at which both McMaster and Mullaly called for all citizens of New York to arm themselves and stand ready to "defend the liberties of their state" against such federal tyranny. Erastus Corning staged a rally in Albany and wrote Lincoln a stinging rebuke. Greeley took Lincoln's side in this fight. He published Lincoln's reply to Corning in the *Tribune*, and had fifty thousand copies printed and distributed as a pamphlet. "I think the time not unlikely to come when I shall be blamed for having made too few arrests rather than too many," Lincoln wrote. "Must I shoot a simple-minded soldier boy who deserts, while I must not touch a hair of a wiley [*sic*] agitator who induces him to desert?"

The protests continued. Lincoln and his cabinet worried that an imprisoned Vallandigham would be a perfect Copperhead martyr, so they banished him to the Confederacy instead. But the South didn't want him either; for all his bitter opposition to Lincoln, he was not a Confederate sympathizer. When Vallandigham requested permission to board a block-ade runner and try to make it to neutral Canada, President Davis happily agreed.

Vallandigham would reach Halifax in early July and head for Lake Ontario, where Toronto and Niagara Falls were crowded with an odd lot of Union deserters and draft dodgers, escaped Confederate POWs, Con-federate and Union spies and counterspies, Copperheads, and assorted adventurers, profiteers, and con men. The neutral Canadians welcomed them all, as long as they paid their bar tabs and hotel bills in gold or silver. From these Civil War Casablancas in 1864 would emanate several Con-federate plots to destabilize and terrorize the Union, including New York City.

In June, Peace Democrats staged a giant rally at Cooper Union that drew an estimated thirty thousand New Yorkers, mostly workers. Lincoln was roundly booed every time his name was mentioned, Vallandigham cheered. Fernando Wood was the star speaker. "We have fallen upon evil times," he declared. "The war should cease, because it never should have been commenced.... Because there was no necessity for it. An amicable adjustment of the questions in dispute could have been, and can be still, procured on terms of fairness and equality.... Because it is made a pre-text for the most outrageous and damnable crimes against the liberty of the citizen.... Because the popular enthusiasm necessary to conduct the war and supply the failing armies has subsided. Force, by a draft, cannot supply the indispensable requisite." The multitude received his remarks with "unlimited cheering and beating of drums," the *Times* reported, and "every species of noise the human voice, feet and hands can make." In an editorial a few days later, Henry Raymond scoffed at "Fernando's Farce," pointing out how ironic it was "to hear a dozen loud-mouthed demagogues denouncing President Lincoln as a bloody tyrant, a vile despot, a monster of arbitrary devices, who would not allow his trampled, trembling subjects to hold, still less to utter, opinions contrary to his own.... Really, the joke is already stale."

It wasn't just among Copperheads that opinions of Lincoln were sinking. "Well, Walt, you and I cannot agree in regard to 'Uncle Abe,'" Jeff Whitman wrote that June. "Everything he does reminds me of an old woman. I hope that the country will last long enough for this damned war to fall through."

CHAPTER 32

Dan Sickles, Hero or Villain?

Robert E. Lee was a close reader of the Northern newspapers that he had smuggled to him. Seeing all the dissent and controversy in the Union that spring, he judged that another demoralizing defeat in battle could tip the scales of Northern opinion in favor of the peace camp, forcing Lincoln to the negotiating table. Lee knew that the Confederacy couldn't keep waging war indefinitely; his men were already bone-weary and deserting in droves. Now was the time for a decisive stroke to end the thing. He proposed a bold plan to invade the North and force peace, and President Davis agreed. He even sent Vice President Alexander Stephens under a flag of truce to the Union-held Fort Monroe in the Potomac, where Stephens wrote Lincoln requesting safe passage to Washington to begin the negotiations.

In mid-June, Lee's Army of Northern Virginia crossed into Pennsylvania, coming within striking range of cities from Washington and Baltimore to Philadelphia and even New York. Sincerely alarmed, Lincoln and Stanton asked nearby governors to rush as many state militia troops as they could to aid in defending Pennsylvania. Governor Seymour sent close to sixteen thousand men, more than any other state. The 7th and many other units marched out of New York City and Brooklyn to the usual huzzahs and hanky-waving. The 7th went first to Harrisburg, but were then rerouted to bolster the defense of Baltimore should that city be attacked or rise up again in revolt.

New York's harbor fortresses and defensive batteries were drained of all but a skeleton force of about five hundred regular troops. Only about that many militiamen were left in the city as well. General John E. Wool, an upstate New Yorker and veteran of the War of 1812 who'd assumed command in January of the army's Department of the East, headquartered in the city, complained to Washington that New York was now "in a defenseless position" should Rebels attack. Mayor Opdyke wrote to Governor Seymour requesting more militia, fretting that the city "was filled with Rebel emissaries" trying to stir up "a revolutionary and treasonable spirit among our people." Neither man was heard.

Joseph Hooker argued that month with Lincoln and Stanton about how to respond to Lee's gambit, and he resigned command of the Army of the Potomac. Given his terrible performance at Chancellorsville, this was received with a general sigh of relief. Dan Sickles's name was among those bruited about as a possible replacement. Even Sickles's old enemy James Gordon Bennett now sang his praises in the *Herald*, pointing out that Julius Caesar and George Washington had also lacked formal military training. On June 28, Lincoln wisely passed over his impetuous friend and gave the command to the experienced West Pointer Meade.

Meade's relations with both Sickles and Butterfield, his inherited chief of staff, had started out frosty and now deteriorated. As Lee's army pushed up into Pennsylvania, Meade had to hurry and shift his forces to meet them. He'd been in command only three days when the two great beasts—roughly ninety-four thousand Yankees and seventy thousand Confederates—faced each other on Wednesday, July 1, around Gettysburg, a Pennsylvania town few had heard of the day before.

Both Sickles and Frank Barlow would commit rash acts on the battlefield the next day, with dire consequences. Sickles either nearly lost the battle for the Union (the official version, and the consensus among Civil War historians today) or saved it (his version, still argued by a few historians). Meade had ordered him to hold the left flank of a long Union line along the slope called Cemetery Ridge, anchored on the right by Culp's Hill and on the left by the two Round Tops. But Sickles was unhappy with the low and soggy terrain he was supposed to occupy. Up ahead of him was an area of high ground known as the Peach Orchard. If the Confederates took it, he reasoned, they could fire down on the whole left side of the Union line. He asked Meade for permission to advance the Third Corps and take that ground before the Rebels got there. Meade, convinced the Rebels would attack on the right, ordered him to stand fast. Sickles worried still. On his own authority he sent out a scouting party, who met up with General James Longstreet's Confederate First Corps as it advanced.

The Confederates had used just such a flanking maneuver to surprise Hooker's army at Chancellorsville, as Sickles knew only too well. Deciding that quick action was needed, he disobeyed his commanding officer and rushed the Third Corps forward to the Peach Orchard, more than half a mile in front of the rest of the Union line. Observing from some distance, Meade and his staff were flabbergasted. Sickles had not only dangerously exposed his own troops but left Little Round Top completely unprotected. The entire Union line was vulnerable.

As the Confederates smashed into Sickles's men, there was nothing for it but to scramble troops to help him and to occupy Little Round Top before the enemy did. Through an afternoon of desperate and hectic slaughter, the Confederates came within an ace of breaking the Union line Sickles had disarranged. He'd lost a third of his men when the rest finally retreated.

Just as the sun was setting, his troops racing for the rear all around him, shrapnel from a twelve-pound cannonball struck Sickles on his horse, shattering his right leg. As he was being lifted onto a stretcher he called for a cigar and was carried into an ambulance puffing away. He later said he did this to keep up his men's morale; this scene of cool courage was one of the major reasons for awarding him a Medal of Honor some thirty-five years later. Sickles was badly wounded enough that Father O'Hagan said the last rites for him.

No show of bravado on Sickles's part could have halted what had become a rout. The remnants of the Third Corps were folded back into the Union line—at Cemetery Ridge where Meade had originally positioned it. Around that night's campfires, with thousands of wounded and dying men moaning and crying out where they still lay across the day's scattered killing fields, the debate began over whether Sickles had correctly foreseen and forestalled a killing blow on the left, or rashly committed "an error which nearly proved fatal in the battle," as the army's official report soon phrased it.

Frank Barlow also pushed his men out in front of the line to take the high ground of Blocher's Knoll, now called Barlow's Knoll. He left the Eleventh open to a blistering flank attack. Roughly half were killed, wounded, or captured, and the rest crumbled and fled. In one of the cannon batteries that Barlow exposed, the young lieutenant Bayard Wilkeson, son of *New*

York Times special Sam Wilkeson, lost much of a leg to Rebel cannon fire. He tied his own tourniquet to the stump and was carried off the field to die nearby. Trying to rally what was left of his troops, Barlow was shot below the armpit. As two of his men lowered him from his horse, bullets ripped through his hat and nipped the tip of a finger. He lay in the grass as whooping Confederate soldiers raced past. A few stopped and carried him into some nearby trees, then left him, presumably thinking he was dying.

Instead, he survived another months-long convalescence, steadfastly refusing to take any responsibility for the fiasco and blaming it all on the Germans of the Eleventh. He railed against them in public and private, writing one friend that "I am convinced we can do nothing with these German [regiments]. They won't fight & the whole history of the war has shown it. I will never set foot in the 11th Corps again." He did not. After recovering, he would join Grant's army as it hounded Lee's in Virginia. In the spring and summer of 1864, Barlow's troops would take heavy losses but acquit themselves with distinction at the gory battles of the Wilderness, Spotsylvania Court House, and Cold Harbor. Arabella was always nearby, working in the field hospitals. Once she bent her ear to the lips of a young soldier to catch his dying words. A Christian missionary anxiously asked what they were and was horrified when Arabella reported he'd gone out singing the minstrel song "Possum Up a Gum Tree." Not long after that, Arabella herself died of typhus. Barlow went home on a furlough. He'd seen the last of the war.

⌒

Luckily for Sickles and Barlow, Robert E. Lee made his own rash decisions at Gettysburg on July 3. Still hoping to exact his war-ending blow, he threw his forces headlong against Meade's center, where they were slaughtered. Sickles's Third saw action again that day and lost more men. Among the dead, the *Times* reported a week later, was a young man from New York City named John Tommy, "the only representative of the Central Flowery Kingdom in the Army of the Potomac"—that is, the only Chinese soldier. Chinese immigrants often assumed Anglo names, thus "John Tommy." He'd come to the city in 1861 and quickly signed up with Sickles's brigade, despite being "a mere lad, entirely ignorant of our language." At Fredericksburg and Gettysburg he "was one of the bravest soldiers in that bravest of brigades, the Excelsior. He seemed not to know what fear was and was the universal favorite of all his fellow soldiers.

He had not been wounded up to Gettysburgh [*sic*—the *Times* often misspelled it in the first few weeks after the battle], but in Friday's fight he was wounded by a shell, which tore off both legs at the thighs, and he shortly bled to death." Sickles's friend Dan Butterfield was also slightly wounded that day, nicked by a shell fragment.

The Garibaldi Guard fought bravely once again at Gettysburg and took heavy casualties. But D'Utassy was not with them. By the start of 1863 the War Department was trying to crack down on the graft and fraud that had riddled army finances for the first two years of the war, and D'Utassy, who had made plenty of enemies among his fellow officers by then, was swept up in a maelstrom of accusations that he was a swindler and a fraud. In April he was brought before a court-martial on twenty-five charges ranging from slandering other officers to forging payrolls to selling government horses and other property for personal gain. He was also accused in the *Tribune* of being an impostor, a Jewish dealer in secondhand clothing from Budapest named David Strasser who'd faked his noble background to defraud New York's elite and debauch its women. Henry Villard called him "nothing but a swaggering pretender." Acquitted on some counts, convicted on others, D'Utassy had passed through New York City in May, in irons, to begin a year's sentence in Sing Sing. He would quietly return to the city afterward, running a photography studio on Broadway and other small businesses into the late 1870s.

What was left of Meagher's Irish Brigade fought without him at Gettysburg. Just before they marched into the killing zone known as the Wheatfield, their chaplain Father Corby stood on a large rock, artillery screaming over his head. His men, Catholic and not, knelt while he blessed them and issued a general absolution, while "urging them to do their duty, and reminding them of the high and sacred nature of their trust as soldiers and the noble object for which they fought." Then more than a third of them fell as they helped to plug a gap in the Union line.

Lee's mangled army, reduced by more than a third, started a long slog of withdrawal, miles and miles of infantry, wagon trains, and tens of thousands of impounded Pennsylvania cattle inching down country lanes toward the Potomac in torrential rain. Union forces, including the twenty-three-year-old Custer, field-promoted to brigadier general just three days before the battle, pursued and harassed them. But Meade, like McClellan before him, failed to deliver the coup de grâce—probably, historians theorize, because his politics were very like McClellan's. Lee would not threaten the North again, but the war would drag on for almost two more years. Lincoln and Stanton were apoplectic. Meanwhile, Lincoln took a moment to write Confederate vice president Stephens and turn down his request for negotiations.

With Sickles out of commission, command of his battered Excelsior Brigade was handed over to another Democrat political officer, Brigadier General Francis Spinola from Brooklyn, who had raised his own Spinola's Empire Brigade in 1862. He would lead the Excelsiors through the rest of the war.

Surgeons amputated Sickles's leg low on the thigh. Severed limbs were usually tossed in piles outside the medical tents for later disposal, but Daniel E. Sickles was not going to let a leg he'd so gloriously sacrificed for his country suffer such ignominy. He instructed the surgeons to box it up and send it to the Army Medical Museum in Washington, which had put out a request for notable specimens. The museum displayed the fractured bones in a glass vitrine. For the rest of his life, he'd go visit them whenever he was in Washington.

Sickles had the rest of himself carried to Washington as well, accompanied by Gus Schurmann. Sickles was anxious to tell the president his side of the story, knowing that Meade's version would be condemnatory. Lincoln, bringing along Tad, came to Sickles's bedside right away and heard him out. He still liked and admired the fiery little gamecock from New York, and he was furious with the dawdling Meade.

CHAPTER 33

The Volcano Erupts

On the morning of Tuesday, July 14, New York governor Horatio Seymour stepped off a ferry from Jersey City onto a dock on the west side of Manhattan. What he saw shocked him. Black smoke billowed from rows of burning buildings. The muggy midsummer air crackled with gunfire and echoed with screams. Phalanxes of policemen and soldiers chased citizens up and down streets littered with smoldering rubble, shards of glass, broken paving stones, and the ruined furnishings of homes tossed out of windows. The most widespread and destructive rioting in the city's long history of mob violence had broken out the day before. It had now escalated into a mad orgy of wanton destruction—of racial murder, drunken hooliganism, arson, thievery, and thuggery. Whole neighborhoods were barricading their streets to keep the Metropolitans and soldiers out. Others armed themselves to keep looters out of their homes and shops. What came to be known as the New York City draft riots were reducing the city to utter anarchy.

The Battle of Gettysburg ended on Friday, July 3. New York papers of Saturday, July 4, were still not quite clear on the outcome of what the *Times* called the "perfectly fearful" fighting. What news had come through in a blizzard of specials' telegrams was, the *Times* said, "of a cheering character, yet not sufficiently definite and decisive to allay the anxieties of the people." The fuller story would come in the Monday editions, along with the news that Vicksburg had at long last surrendered to Grant.

While other New Yorkers celebrated July Fourth with the usual fireworks and cheers, Peace Democrats gathered at the Academy of Music in a more somber mood. Governor Seymour gave a speech characterized not by patriotic huzzahs but by gloom and doom. "I stand before you," he intoned, "not as one animated by expected victories, but feeling...the dread uncertainties of the conflicts which rage around us." Victory and peace could be won only by a united Union, he went on. But how could the Union be united when the Republicans kept trampling on the rights of the citizens? Addressing Republicans, he warned, "Remember this— that the bloody and treasonable and revolutionary doctrine of public necessity can be proclaimed by a mob as well as by a government." That line would soon come back to haunt him.

Definitive news of the Union's victories at Gettysburg and Vicksburg did lighten spirits that following week. "It would seem as though this war might now be brought to an end," Maria Daly wrote, and other New Yorkers let themselves hope that the hated draft would be unnecessary. Then came the staggering lists of the twenty-three thousand Union casualties at Gettysburg. As the collective mood darkened again, Colonel Robert Nugent, late of Corcoran's 69th and Meagher's Irish Brigade, now provost marshal for the city, announced that the first draftees' names would be drawn on Saturday, July 11.

There was every reason to anticipate trouble. In February, speculators on Wall Street had driven the price of gold sky high. A few days later the struggling treasury issued millions of dollars' worth of new greenbacks, and their value slid. Soon, Bryant's Minstrels debuted two satirical new songs, Dan Emmett's "Greenbacks!" and another called "How Are You, Greenbacks." The second, yet another parody of "We Are Coming, Father Abraham," included some rather nasty comments about war profiteers:

> We are coming, Father Abram, one hundred thousand more,
> And cash was ne'er so easily evok'd from rags before;
> To line the fat contractor's purse, or purchase transport craft
> Whose rotten hulks shall sink before the winds begin to waft

Just as bitter was a parody of "Sing a Song of Sixpence" that began:

> Sing a song of greenbacks
> A pocket full of trash
> Over head and ears in debt,
> And out of ready cash

Workers watched the shoddy aristocracy living it up while their own ability to purchase basic necessities declined. With Copperhead newspapers and politicians constantly warning them that freed blacks were about to pour into the city to make things even worse, their anger and anxiety had been erupting in rashes of violence around the city since 1862. In August of that year a few hundred white workers attacked and set fire to a Brooklyn tobacco factory that employed mostly black men, women, and children. Cops dispersed the mob only after a fierce melee, and the owner promised not to hire any more Negroes. Roving white gangs beat random blacks on the streets in the following weeks.

From October 1862 up to July 1863 there were constant, violent strikes on the city's waterfront. Since the mid-1850s most of the city's longshoreman work, done by black men before then, had been in the hands of Irishmen. They jealously guarded those jobs from blacks—not that they were good jobs. Employment was irregular—known euphemistically as "casual labor"—and depended on how many cargo ships were at the docks at a given time. Most longshoremen managed to get only three or four days' work a week. And when the merchants saw how cheaply the Irish would work, they reduced the hourly rate to a pittance.

During the war the longshoremen's position grew even worse. They were still working only a few days a week and still getting their meager 1850s wages, while inflation hiked prices. In February 1863 shipyard and iron workers held a mass meeting at Tammany Hall to denounce their employers for importing "hordes of blacks from the South, as well as whites from Europe" to take their jobs away. The next month a thousand strikers on the Hudson waterfront drove off Negro scabs with sticks and fists. In April hundreds of longshoremen went on a three-day binge of violence, beating any blacks they found on or near the docks, shouting, "Kill the niggers!" and "Drive off the damn niggers!" The Metropolitans barely prevented them from lynching two black men. Another mass strike of longshoremen paralyzed the docks that June, holding up supplies needed on the war front. The federal government stepped in. Soldiers with fixed bayonets kept strikers away from docks while prisoners from Governors Island loaded army supplies. That month barge and railroad workers also went on strike and attacked white and black scabs.

The *Times* claimed at the end of June that the process of building enrollment lists in the city in May and June had gone quietly, and speculated that the violent responses elsewhere must have been "owing to the appointment of insolent or stupid enrolling officers." Shortly after this, however, a construction worker did scuffle with an enrollment officer collecting names at a city construction site; the worker waved a crowbar, and the agent pulled a pistol. The foreman of the site was arrested the following day.

In this extremely volatile setting, the provost marshals proceeded with care. As a Fenian and a Democrat, Nugent had no trouble reading the foul mood of the city's immigrants and workers. He prudently chose to begin the draft in the sporadically developed and sparsely populated zone north of 42nd Street. And in fact the Saturday, July 11, drawing of 1,236 names at the draft office on Third Avenue at 46th Street went surprisingly smoothly. A crowd of some 150 men watched as the slips of papers with names on them were turned in a hand-cranked wooden drum the *Daily News* called the wheel of misfortune. The mood, the *Herald* said, was mostly jocular.

Down at the other end of town, Thomas Francis Meagher was trying to raise troops in a different way that Saturday. He had decided to organize a new brigade, and called for all former Irish officers who wished to volunteer to come meet him that day in his home on Ann Street. Meagher's life was beginning to take on a tragicomic aspect. If trying to raise a new Irish brigade in New York City were not already a fool's errand, events of the following week would certainly make it so.

When newspapermen fanned out to the bars and taverns in working-class neighborhoods on Sunday, they recorded much grumbling that built to anger as the day and the drinking progressed. For Irish Catholics an added irritation that Sunday was Orange Day, when the city's Irish Protestants marched and celebrated.

By Monday morning many workers in the city had decided that the choosing of names would not continue as planned. At eight o'clock a contingent began marching up the west side, gathering hundreds more from their workplaces as they passed—longshoremen, iron workers, machinists, construction workers—beginning what in effect would turn into a citywide labor strike. They included skilled and unskilled laborers, Irish, Germans and nativists, Catholics and Protestants. The one group they did not include was black workers. From Central Park they marched down Third Avenue to the draft office at 46th Street. Massing outside the office, they waved "No Draft" placards and yelled insults at President Lincoln and Horace Greeley.

Then the men of Engine Company 33 arrived with a wagon of stones. By an unfortunate accident of history, they were known as the Black Joke Company. "The name was given her in honor of an Albany sloop which distinguished herself in the war of 1812," Augustine Costello wrote in his 1887 history, *Our Firemen*. "She was painted a 'nigger' black on the body, and had a gold stripe running all the way around." In the 1840s the company allowed "two gigantic negroes," nicknamed Black Jack and Black Joe, to run with them. "Those darkeys made themselves very serviceable around the engine house, and felt themselves highly honored in being asked to do anything. They were not, however, allowed to bunk in the engine house."

A member of the company had been on the Saturday list of draftees. Fire laddies had been exempt from conscription in the state militia, and now felt they should be exempt from the federal draft as well. Stones flew through the office's windows, a pistol shot rang out, and the crowd erupted. They broke in, intending to seize and destroy the draft records. They beat a draft officer and a Metropolitan who tried to keep them out, then trashed the building and set it on fire. Outside, a lawyer named John U. Andrews, originally from Virginia and well known to Superintendent Kennedy's agents as a Confederate sympathizer as well as a consorter with thieves and whores, roused the rabble to fury with a speech exhorting them to "crush this damn abolition draft into the dust." Some in the crowd who were under the impression that he was Benjamin Wood cheered loudly. Their bloodlust up, they looted adjacent tenements. They stopped streetcars on Third Avenue, pulled off any blacks they found, and savagely beat them. They looted hardware stores for ax handles to use as weapons, and for crowbars that were used to pull up the tracks of the Fourth Avenue railway. By noon the mayhem was spreading in all directions through the city in a confusion of flames, screams, and gunfire. Workers by the thousands walked off their jobs and joined either the rioters or the huge crowds who climbed up to rooftops to watch them. Business and transportation shut down. Nugent ordered draft documents carried to Governors Island for safety. The city was under siege from its own citizens.

As soon as he heard of the trouble, Superintendent Kennedy took a couple of men and rushed uptown from Metropolitan headquarters on Mulberry Street. The crowd, which was growing in size and ferocity by the minute, immediately engulfed them and clubbed them nearly to death. Other small squads of Metropolitans ventured out from precinct houses and waded into the crowd, swinging their clubs. The metastasizing mob easily scattered them, chasing them through the streets. They stabbed and beat those they caught. The rioters proceeded to George Opdyke's rifle factory at 21st Street and Second Avenue, where the one thousand rifles he'd manufactured, out of the ten thousand the army had contracted, were stored. The mob battered down the doors, drove off the small contingent of Metropolitans guarding the place, hauled out the rifles, and torched the building. Thirteen people died in the melee, several of them in the fire they themselves had set.

Other rioters gathered outside Mayor Opdyke's home on Fifth Avenue, which Tweed's man Judge George Barnard talked them out of destroying. Opdyke was not at home, nor at City Hall. He had fled up Broadway from City Hall to the St. Nicholas Hotel, where he was firing off panicked tele-grams and messages for help in all directions.

The mob turned to the Colored Orphan Asylum on Fifth Avenue between 42nd and 43rd Streets. Quakers founded the asylum in 1836; since the 1840s its medical director had been the extraordinary Dr. James McCune Smith. Born in the city in 1813 to a self-emancipated black mother and a white father he never knew, Smith was refused admission to study medicine at Columbia and other universities in New York. He sailed to Scotland in 1832 (most likely on a British ship, since blacks couldn't buy tickets on many of the New York–based lines) and graduated first in his class from the University of Glasgow's medical school in 1837, the first black American with an M.D. Back in New York City he practiced medi-cine and opened what's believed to be the first black-owned pharmacy in America, on West Broadway, as well as becoming the staff physician at the asylum. As it happens, Smith was home sick the day the rioters attacked the building. As the 237 children were helped to safety—notably, by Irish firemen—the crowd looted and torched the building, shouting things like, "Burn the niggers' nest!" After the rioting, Smith, like many other black New Yorkers, would move his family to Brooklyn, settling in Williamsburg, where he would die of congestive heart failure in 1865.

Dr. John Torrey, a distinguished botanist and chemist, was at work at the U.S. Assay Office on Wall Street when reports of the trouble reached downtown. He decided to return to his home on 49th Street "to protect my colored servants." He would write several letters to a friend over the next few days. This first day he made his way through the growing mayhem, past "rough fellows (& some equally rough women) who were

tearing up rails, cutting down telegraph poles & setting fire to buildings."
When he got home, "furious bareheaded & coatless men assembled under
our windows & shouted aloud for Jeff. Davis!" He ventured out to speak
with "one of the ring-leaders who told me they would burn the whole city
before they got through."

As the day wore on, roving gangs, from a few dozen to a few thousand
each, rampaged all over the city. They engaged in wide-scale looting of
shops and bars, and the great quantities of free liquor consumed added to
the insanity. They targeted the homes of blacks, and of anyone known to
be or suspected of being a Republican, abolitionist, or prowar. One huge
mob filled Printing House Square, outside the offices of those Republican organs the *Tribune*, *Times*, and *Evening Post*. Anticipating trouble,
Henry Raymond had borrowed three Gatling guns, a recent invention,
from the army. He aimed two out windows, manning one himself, and
placed a third on the roof. He armed his staff with muskets. *Post* staff
armed themselves as well. Across the square, ruffians shook their cudgels and fists at the *Tribune*'s windows and called for Horace Greeley. For
once, Greeley kept his cool. He forbade his staff to arm themselves, then
slipped off to keep a dinner engagement with Theodore Tilton at a nearby
restaurant. His staff armed themselves in his absence. Raymond sent sixteen musket-bearing *Times* staffers across the square to help, and Greeley
biographer James Parton showed up with more rifles. The crowd broke
into the *Tribune* building, piled desks in the middle of the ground floor,
and set them alight. Metropolitans arrived in some force to clear them
out before they could do more damage. Meanwhile, up in Chappaqua,
a drunken mob trying to break into Greeley's farm was rebuffed, while
Mary and their daughters hid.

In the past, mayors had called out militia regiments like the 7th to put
down riots. But all available army and militia troops had been sent for
the defense of Pennsylvania and not yet returned. The seventy-nine-year-
old General John E. Wool—"Granny Wool" to younger officers—struck
other officers on the scene as addled and unable to comprehend the mag-
nitude of what was happening. This may not have been entirely fair. Wool
had, after all, seen trouble coming. Events were now proving him right.
Still, the others judged him incompetent and acted on their own authority to put what troops they had onto the streets. As a result the military
response was not just meager but uncoordinated. Nugent handed muskets to seventy men of the Invalid Corps (wounded or sick soldiers unfit

for battle but able to do light duty in the city's garrisons) and deployed them. They got off a couple of ragged volleys, killing and wounding a few rioters, before the mob overcame them, beating two of them to death with their own muskets. Later in the week Irish rioters would break into Nugent's house, chase off his wife and child, and trash the place. They slashed a portrait of Nugent with Meagher, but reportedly spared one of Corcoran, who was still an unsullied hero in their eyes.

By Monday evening panicked New Yorkers were fleeing the island by any conveyance available. Black New Yorkers fled by foot, following rail lines up to the Bronx, and crowded onto the ferries crossing both rivers. Many would never return, permanently settling in safer areas like the free black community of Weeksville far out in Brooklyn. The city's black population would be 20 percent lower after the riots. In *The Devil's Own Work*, Barnet Schecter points out that one of the lasting legacies of the riots would be the increasing segregation and ghettoization of black New Yorkers. Although some had congregated in certain neighborhoods, like the Five Points and Greenwich Village's "Little Africa" (less kindly known as "Coontown"), other black New Yorkers had always lived among whites throughout the city. They would do so less freely and comfortably now.

Upper-crust New Yorkers who hadn't already gone off to Saratoga or Long Branch also ran. Some stampeded the cab companies, where drivers charged as much as a hundred dollars to carry them through the roiling streets to the Bronx and points north. Others, like the Torreys, stayed in their homes, prepared to flee if attacked. Judge Daly, to Maria's "great distress," "sallied out with his pistol" every night of the rioting to see what was going on.

Edwin Booth and various family members huddled in his town house near Union Square. When his wife had contracted pneumonia and died the previous winter, he fled the Fifth Avenue Hotel, first to East 17th Street, then later in the same year to 28 East 19th Street. John Wilkes happened to be in the city staying with Edwin and the family. Edwin's friend Adam "Vagabond" Badeau was with them as well. When the war started he'd joined the Union army and was serving as a general's aide. Wounded in battle, he'd been laid up in a military hospital and then released to finish convalescing in New York. He arrived on a stretcher, too weak to stand, tended by a black male nurse. The Booths fussed over him affectionately. Hearing the roaring crowds and popping gunfire outside, they worried that rioters would target Edwin's well-known address. Edwin had been a highly visible and active supporter of Lincoln and the war effort, giving benefit performances that raised thousands for Union widows and orphans. The presence of a Union officer and a black attendant added to their peril. Rioters in their area were reportedly going house to house, looking for both. John Wilkes ventured out periodically to scout the streets and search for food. Fiercely anti-Irish, he expressed disgust at the chaos the "ignorant foreigners" were causing. Through the days of the rioting, John Wilkes surprised his family by helping to care for Badeau and even being willing to protect the nurse if necessary. Apparently he surprised himself as well. "Imagine me," he later exclaimed, "helping that wounded soldier with my Rebel sinews!" Badeau would survive the riots, regain his health, and join Ulysses S. Grant's staff in 1864.

Heavy rain Monday night raised some hopes that the violence would cease, but when Tuesday dawned sunny and muggy, the mayhem started early. At 6 a.m. a black sailor stepped off a ship tied up at a lower Hudson dock and innocently asked for directions to a grocery store. A white mob beat, stomped, and crushed him with paving stones. He died in the hospital two hours later.

Governor Seymour arrived midmorning. He had been enjoying a weekend at Long Branch. On Monday morning he was happily riding in a carriage along the strand when mounted officers handed him a plea from Mayor Opdyke to come help deal with the crisis. Seymour was not shocked by the news. Hadn't he just warned of mob violence a little over a week earlier? But he was in no hurry to intervene. He could have taken a steamboat directly from Long Branch to New York and gotten there in two hours. Instead he proceeded by land up through New Jersey and spent the night there, probably hoping the crisis would blow over by the time he arrived the next day.

If one sight heartened Seymour as he stepped off the ferry, it was of the large-bellied man waiting with his hand out. William Tweed, a vigorous forty years old, showed absolutely no physical fear on the anarchic streets, but then he had no reason to. The types of people who were rioting trusted Tammany and liked Tweed. For one thing, when Grand Sachem Fowler had absconded back in 1860, Tweed had convinced the other sachems to elect James Connor to replace him—Tammany's first Irish Catholic grand sachem. It was a brilliant move; Tammany's standing with the community soared. It was a sign of Tweed's influence that two wards everyone would have expected to erupt during the rioting—the heavily Irish, crowded, poor, and working-class Sixth and Fourteenth on the Lower East Side—remained quiet all week. Tweed had sent his men out to keep the peace. The residents, loyal to Tammany, heard and obeyed.

As of the previous April, Tweed was now grand sachem, and more than any grand sachem before him, he had consolidated all of Tammany as his machine, down to his handpicked ward bosses. He still dominated the County Board of Supervisors, and he was also filling key slots around the city with friends. He'd been spending the war years using his power to make boodles of money for himself and his cohort. His grandest boon-doggle was the construction of an opulent new County Courthouse behind City Hall, begun in 1861. Tweed and his cronies, who would come to be known as the Tweed Ring, took outrageous cuts from vastly inflated contracts that eventually drove the price tag from an original $250,000 to around $15 million. In 1867, William Seward would arrange for the United States to buy the entire territory of Alaska from Russia for half that. Building what is still known as the Tweed Courthouse would take so long—it would not be finished until 1881, three years after Tweed's death—that it became a running joke in the city. A backdrop for George L. Fox's comic pantomime *Humpty Dumpty*, which opened on Broad-way in 1867, depicted the incomplete structure with a giant billboard announcing that it would be finished in 1960.

With the Republican Opdyke incapacitated by the riots, Tweed saw an opportunity to shine and expand his power. At the start of the upheaval on Monday morning he had gone into action. He sent Judge Barnard to talk down the crowd at Mayor Opdyke's house. It was Tweed who sug-gested that Opdyke move his operations from City Hall to the more easily defended St. Nicholas. That day, when Opdyke was having trouble calling together a quorum of aldermen for an emergency session, Tweed rounded them up. He convinced the mayor not to declare martial law, arguing that it would only inflame the mob more. As the deputy street commissioner, he put armed street workers at the service of the cops and soldiers. He per-sonally visited riot hot spots and spoke to the crowds.

He now escorted Seymour up Broadway to the St. Nicholas, where they met with Opdyke. After being brought up to date, Seymour decided another speech might help. With Tweed, a phalanx of cops, and a gag-gle of city officials—including Opdyke, whom a reporter described as "ghastly white" and visibly terrified—he walked the ten blocks down war-torn Broadway to City Hall. What the *Times* called "a large crowd of men and boys, numbering 800 or over," watched as the governor mounted the wide front steps. Militiamen ringed the park, bayonets affixed to their muskets. The crowd cheered when they recognized Seymour (or maybe it was Tweed, towering behind him). According to the *Times*, someone cried out, "We want you to stay here." "I am going to stay here, my friends," Seymour replied. He ordered the militiamen to put their bayonets away, and announced that he'd already written the president to ask that the draft be suspended in the city. He implored the rioters to go home, telling them that they should "leave your interests in my hands and I will take care that justice is done you." As the crowd cheered, Seymour and Tweed withdrew into the building. They later toured Wall Street and then the riot-torn west side, and Seymour repeated versions of his speech at both.

Again his words would haunt him. As the substance of his message to the rioters spread around the city, New Yorkers who were not participating in the violence were aghast and outraged. The rioters were his *friends*? He would see that justice was done *them*? Not one word for their victims or other law-abiding citizens? Seymour issued a written proclamation using slightly sterner language and declaring the city in a state of insurrection, but it was his notorious "My Friends" speech people remembered.

The mob may have cheered him, but they didn't heed him. The bedlam on Tuesday and Wednesday was even more widespread and grotesque than Monday's. Outmanned, and in some cases outgunned, police squads engaged rioters in flying battles on the streets, in looted buildings, inside bars and porterhouses, across rooftops. Women and children observing from windows threw bricks, crockery, and pots and pans at the Metropolitans' heads. The savagery on Tuesday achieved truly repellent heights. Above 34th Street, two companies of the 11th New York Volunteers—a newly reorganized successor to Elmer Ellsworth's original Zouaves, who had mustered out of service in 1862—lined up across Second Avenue to face an advancing mob. Their commander, Colonel Henry O'Brien, ordered his men to fire their muskets and a howitzer over the rioters' heads. It worked, and the crowd dispersed. O'Brien lived nearby, and found that his house had been looted. He went off to get a horse-cart and returned to salvage what he could. It was a fatal mistake. Firing over the mob's heads, his men had inadvertently shot a little boy and girl leaning out of upper windows; the girl, only two years old, died. The neighborhood knew who O'Brien was, knew where he lived, and when he reappeared, they pounced. They clubbed and beat him, kicked him, dragged him down the street. Little boys tried to set him on fire. Someone shoved a stick down his throat. Others cheered as men and boys continued to torture and mutilate him. A priest finally intervened and carried him in a wheelbarrow to Bellevue, where he died.

On Wednesday Dr. Torrey wrote his friend:

> This morning I was obliged to ride down to the office in a hired coach. A friend who rode with me had seen a poor negro hung an hour or two before. The man had, in a frenzy, shot an Irish fireman, and they immediately strung up the unhappy African. At our office there had been no disturbance in the night. Indeed the people there were "spoiling for a fight." They had a battery of about 25 rifle barrels, carrying 3 balls each, & mounted on a gun-carriage. It could be loaded & fired with rapidity. We had also 10-inch shells, to be lighted & thrown out of the windows.... The worst mobs are on the 1st & 2nd & 7th Avenues. Many have been killed there. They are very hostile to the negroes, & scarcely one of them is to be seen. A person who called at our house this after-noon saw three of them hanging together.

By Wednesday any black males who had not fled the city risked such gruesome deaths. A white gang beat, stoned, and trampled one man before hanging him. Another was hanged from a lamppost while a crowd gave three cheers for Jefferson Davis. They then hauled the corpse down, and a sixteen-year-old dragged it down the street by the genitals before a laughing, cheering audience. After another man was hanged, they chopped off his fingers and toes. The mob, which had shown a curious chivalry in not attacking black females up till now, began to target downtown brothels known to employ black prostitutes.

In the relative safety of her home, Maria Daly heard the stories of these atrocities with great interest but little sympathy. She recorded that when her father came from his country place to check on his house in the city, he "found fifteen Negroes secreted in it....Father ordered them out. We feared for our own block on account of the Negro tenements [nearby], where the Negroes were on the roof, singing psalms and having firearms."

Although she claimed to be "very sorry and much outraged at the cruelties," she went on, "I hope it will give the Negroes a lesson, for since the war commenced, they have been so insolent as to be unbearable. I cannot endure free blacks. They are immoral, with all their piety."

⌒

Thomas Nast, the German immigrant boy from the Lower East Side who had run behind Tweed's fire engine, drew some of the best-known images of the rioting and brutality. It's not clear how much he actually witnessed himself, however.

In 1856, at just fifteen, he'd started working for *Frank Leslie's Illustrated Newspaper* and was soon hanging out with the journalists and bohemians at Pfaff's. Through marriage he fell in with another literary crowd that included the husband-and-wife team of James Parton and Fanny Fern, with whom he shared strong antislavery opinions.

Twenty when the war broke out, Nast headed for the front, drawing for *Leslie's* and then *Harper's Weekly*. Still small and chubby, Roly Poly was not a physically brave young man and never a true battlefield artist like Alf Waud. He spent most of his time in the camps and drew from what soldiers told him. Much of his wartime work was pure propaganda rather than visual reportage. "Southern Chivalry," for instance, is a multipanel spread in which he depicts Confederates committing beheadings, scalpings, and other atrocities. That one earned him death threats from the South. In his most popular images he combined the propaganda with mawkish sentimentality, as in the one of a stars-and-striped Santa handing out presents to the boys at the front.

Nast was now into a twenty-five-year run as the star of *Harper's Weekly*. Fletcher Harper was quite fond of "Tommy," and of Tommy's very positive impact on sales. Nast had tried to make it to Gettysburg for the battle, traveling there with Brady, but Union soldiers detained him because he wasn't carrying proper papers. So he missed the fighting and returned to New York—just in time for the riots. When rioters massed outside the Harper brothers' building in Franklin Square, employees armed themselves and barricaded the doors and windows. There's no indication that Nast was present. He did make several iconic sketches of the violence in the streets, from a pitched battle between rioters and cops in Printing House Square to a black man lynched from a tree. But like his war work, much of what he drew of the riots was probably based on hearsay. It's known that he spent most of the time with his family far away from danger in their home on 125th Street.

⟶

The first troops from outside started to reach the city Wednesday night. When the 7th Regiment arrived before dawn Thursday morning, it brought the number of fresh troops to four thousand. Marching up the streets and avenues in force, muskets and howitzers blazing, the new units scattered the mobs. In the Booths' neighborhood, soldiers went door-to-door rooting armed rioters out of abandoned homes they'd commandeered. Meanwhile, police entered the home of the antiabolition speaker John Andrews that day and found him in bed—with a black prostitute. He was taken in shackles to Fort Lafayette, where he was held until tried in the winter of 1864—the only perpetrator tried in a federal court. Convicted of treason, he did three years in Sing Sing. He'd return to lawyering in the city on his release, and die in 1883 "forgotten even by his former friends," according to his *Times* obituary.

By Friday morning the city was largely peaceful under its pall of black smoke. Businesses and shops gingerly reopened. That afternoon, Archbishop Hughes, whose health was fading at the age of sixty-six (he would die the following January), addressed a crowd of some five or six thousand from a balcony of his home near his still incomplete St. Patrick's Cathedral on Fifth Avenue. A *Times* reporter described the crowd as "of various ages but of one nationality," that is, Irish. "They were quiet and orderly, but disposed to regard with curious and seeking scrutiny any individual whose taste and purse permitted him the luxury of a whole coat and a clean pair of boots." Hughes had been silent during the week, evidently not wanting to heighten the impression that the rioters were all Irish Catholics. He now gave an odd speech in which he cast Irish Catholics as victims of oppression, denied that they had been involved in the rioting, and yet asked them to stop the rioting (which they already had).

"Men of New York," he began. "They call you riotous but I cannot see a riotous face among you....I have been hurt by the reports that you are rioters. You cannot imagine that I could hear these things without being pained grievously. Is there not some way by which you can stop these proceedings, and support the laws, of which none have been enacted against you as Irishmen and Catholics?...Would it not be better for you to retire quietly?" Ending with a little joke, he said, "I hope nothing will occur till you return home; and if by chance, as you go thither, you should meet a police officer, or a military man, why just—look at him."

The assembled cheered and peacefully parted, though someone reportedly shouted out, "Let the niggers stay in the South!" The next day, McMaster's editorial in *Freeman's Journal* argued that Negroes who "float hither from the South" should be "driven out again, imprisoned or exterminated."

On Saturday the citizens of New York emerged and began, quite literally, to pick up the pieces. Squads of police and soldiers patrolled the littered streets, while poor women and children rooted through other people's tossed-out belongings. Some fifty or sixty buildings had been burned to the ground, and many others trashed and looted. The published death count was 119, which makes these riots still the most deadly in the nation's history, but many New Yorkers at the time were sure that this figure was very low. Jeff Whitman wrote Walt from Brooklyn, "Undoubtedly we shall never know the full number but I have it from the very best authority—an eye witness of most of the fights, that there are now more than 400 rioters that have paid their lives for their plunder. The papers are not allowed to publish this. I suppose it is much better not to let it be known, but the lesson was fearful and thorough to these men. Yesterday I saw them taking coffins out of the shanties on 2nd Av. piling them on carts and driving right to the cemetery. I understand they have been doing this ever since Monday night." In 1864, Jeff's name would come up in the draft, and the Whitman family scrambled to raise the money to pay for a substitute.

CHAPTER 34

Tweed to the Rescue

Southern newspapers reacted to the rioting with expressions of glee. They predicted that more riots would break out in the North, forcing Lincoln to suspend conscription. It took only a few days for their euphoria to fade. There were small outbreaks of violence in towns around New York City, from Long Island to Staten Island and New Jersey, but no other large-scale events. Unhappy Northerners would resist through draft evasion rather than draft riots. The specific combination of conditions that caused the rioting—long-standing Southern sympathies, racial hatred, class conflict, and extreme labor unrest—seemed peculiar to New York City.

New York's Democrats and Republicans blamed each other for the havoc. The *Tribune* accused Governor Seymour of inciting the "incendiaries, thieves, and murderers" with his July 4 speech, then kowtowing to them with the "My Friends" speech. Morgan Dix was convinced that Copperhead conspirators, "the sanguinary fiends in our unfortunate city," were behind the riots. The *Times* believed that Confederate provocateurs had collaborated with them, timing the uprising to coincide with Lee's invasion and the draining of troops from the city. Events a year later would suggest that this was not entirely far-fetched. Democratic newspapers like the *World* countered that it was the *Tribune* and the other "radical journals of this City" that were to blame.

Republicans and their publications, including the *Times*, *Tribune*, and *Harper's Weekly*, singled out Irish Catholics as the only or at least the most vicious perpetrators, a version that continued to hold much currency for decades. Hughes and the Irish papers fired back, but nativist and

Know-Nothing sentiments enjoyed a renaissance in the weeks after the disturbance.

Republicans' calls for harsh punishments ran against the dominant sentiments in the city. Though more than four hundred alleged rioters were rounded up on charges from murder and arson to assault and robbery, half were summarily released. Others jumped bail or plea-bargained for light sentences. Grand juries were reluctant to indict, witnesses to testify, juries to convict. When there were convictions, judges were lenient. Their harshest sentences were not for the brutal beatings and murders of blacks but for destruction of property.

Republicans and Democrats also differed on how to proceed with the draft. Republicans wanted Lincoln to restart it immediately, under martial law if necessary. Seymour and the Peace Democrats begged Lincoln to keep the draft suspended in the city until their challenges to its constitutionality cleared the federal courts—which could take months. Lincoln was in no mood to appease the protesters, and his generals needed troops. He could hardly suspend the draft in one city and continue it in others. He ordered its resumption. He did not quite impose martial law, but he did fill the city with a much stronger military presence. As the military man in charge, General Wool took the fall for failing to quell the riots in the first few days. He was forced to retire, moved to his hometown of Troy, and died there in 1869. He lies in Troy's Oakwood Cemetery under a large obelisk.

The general who replaced Wool was John A. Dix. By mid-August, when the draft was scheduled to resume, he had effectively turned New York into an occupied city, with ten thousand federal troops who maintained a highly visible presence on the streets. He had Lincoln's permission to declare martial law if necessary. He also had a network of spies keeping tabs on anyone suspected of Southern sympathies, including some of his Democrat friends like Richard Lathers.

When the draft started up again that month, the city remained calm. In fact, for all their violent opposition to it beforehand, New Yorkers found the draft very easy to evade. For the city's tens of thousands of immigrant men, the easiest way to stay off the draft rolls was simply to put off becoming citizens. Not surprisingly, naturalizations declined sharply for the rest of the war.

While half the New York City men who entered the army as a result of the draft were immigrants, it appears that few of them were actually *compelled* to go. Historian Tyler Anbinder conducted an intensive study of the available draft records, haphazardly kept as they were, and found some surprising data. For example, of the more than fifteen thousand poor people stuffed into the wretched Five Points slum area, most of them Irish immigrants, only a single man seems actually to have served in the army as a result of being drafted. Four out of five poor immigrants whose names were pulled from the wheel of misfortune managed to evade service, and without paying a penny. A good many simply failed to report to the provost officers when their names came up, hoping not to be hunted down for it. More were granted exemptions for a wide variety of reasons: because they were too young or too old, were convicted felons, or sole supporters of parents or children. And because the army was looking for able-bodied men who could march and fight, and because poor immigrants were prone to all sorts of injuries and infirmities, they got medical exemptions for a very long list of reasons ranging from hernias, "inflamed" testicles, and "tender feet" to syphilis, "excessive obesity," imbecility, and "excessive stammering."

Most of the city's immigrants who did serve from July 1863 on were not draftees, but the draftees' paid substitutes. Few workers could come up with the commutation fees and bounties paid to substitutes, but they could turn to their friend William Tweed. In one of the political masterstrokes of his career, Tweed commandeered the draft issue and devised a plan that satisfied everybody. He proposed exemptions for policemen, firemen, and militiamen, so the city would not be left unguarded again. He also called for a County Substitute and Relief Committee of six Democrats (including himself) and six Republicans, which would review the cases of all draftees who asked to be excused from service. The city would raise $2 million and pay the commutation fees and bounties for all cases found worthy.

To give his proposal bipartisan appeal, Tweed enlisted one of the more malleable Republicans on the Board of Supervisors, a gun-maker named Orison Blunt, to cosponsor the idea. During the war Blunt invented his own, apparently inferior version of the Gatling gun, which he called the pepper-box gun. A prototype he demonstrated for President Lincoln somehow fell into Confederate hands, "and after some strange vicissitudes," according to his 1879 obituary in the *Times*, "Mr. Blunt finally discovered the weapon after the war in a junk shop in this City. He bought it back for $5." Opdyke came aboard as well. In August, Tweed and Blunt met with Stanton in Washington and won his approval.

So it wasn't just General Dix's troops who kept the peace when the draft resumed in the city that month. Tweed dispatched Tammany men to stand with the soldiers at all the draft offices, a reassuring indication to the poor men of the city that their friends at Tammany were looking out for them.

At first Tweed's plan seemed to work brilliantly. With Blunt chairing the review process, almost no draftee from the city of New York was ever forced into uniform. At the end of September, of 1,034 cases reviewed, the committee bought substitutes for 983 and excused 49 others, leaving only two who went into uniform. The army got its new soldiers; the masses got a hero and savior in Tweed; even the *Times* approved.

How well the committee actually served the Union is another matter. Inevitably, the millions being paid out to substitutes invited fraud and corruption. When states had begun paying bounties to fill their volunteer quotas in the fall of 1862, a new industry of bounty brokers and "bounty jumpers" sprang up out of nowhere. Although many brokers worked scrupulously to help recruiters fill their rolls, others brought gullible men to the recruitment office by any means necessary and, with the connivance of corrupt recruitment officers, swindled them of some or all of the bounty. Jumpers made a profession of signing up, then disappearing with the bounty, and repeating the process at another office.

Blunt's committee, and the city provosts with whom it collaborated, relied on brokers and ignored the criminal abuses of the bad ones. Brokers were free to go to any length to bring men in. They prowled the city's waterfront dives, got men drunk, and dragged them insensate to the provosts; the men woke up the next day as new recruits in the barracks on Governors Island. Brokers swarmed aboard ships from Europe the instant they docked and signed up uncomprehending, non-English-speaking immigrants. They rounded up deserters and threatened them with imprisonment if they didn't sign up; brought the lame, the halt, and the aged to the provosts, who turned a blind eye; and resorted to outright kidnapping. Large numbers of the recruits who filled the city's quotas weren't from the city at all, but press-ganged and brought in by brokers from rural counties. Brokers weren't above hiring thugs to beat any man who resisted. One seaman who tried to fight off a gang of broker's toughs in a Hester Street bar died of seventeen stab wounds.

Naturally, men recruited in these ways made poor prospects as soldiers. Many deserted before they could even be put into uniform. But that was the army's problem, not the County Committee's. They were counted toward fulfilling the city's quota.

General Dix found all this outrageous. He demanded that Blunt pay closer attention to the abuses, and when he felt that Blunt's response was insufficient, he began arresting the most crooked brokers and ordering them to repay the money they'd swindled or be confined as military prisoners in Fort Lafayette. He moved against corrupt provosts, court-martialing one recruitment-office doctor for "passing men while in a state of intoxication and perfectly unconscious." He stepped up efforts to find and arrest deserters and bounty jumpers. One of the latter came to an unhappy and very public end on Governors Island in February 1865. New Yorker James Devlin enlisted and deserted twice. Then he deserted his wife and three children as well, shacking up with a woman on Mott Street. Enraged, his wife ratted him out to Dix's office. Dix quickly had him court-martialed and sentenced to execution. His wife, frantic with remorse, tried unsuccessfully to secure a pardon. On February 3, on the beach just outside the circular Castle Williams, Devlin faced a firing squad of ten muskets. A priest and the wailing Mrs. Devlin stood near him. "All of the inhabitants of the island, both male and female, including many children, appeared to have assembled to witness the execution," the *Times* reported. They numbered about a thousand. "Boys and girls, from ten years of age upward, were to be seen passing through the crowd, to obtain a good view of the tragedy.... The eagerness of the women to witness the shooting was most disgusting." Devlin was given a white handkerchief for a blindfold, then a volley of "ten balls sped upon their deadly errand, passed through his body, and sank into the bay. The body stood poised in the air a moment, and then fell forward with a heavy thud upon the sward."

Still, the fraud and abuses continued as long as the draft was in effect. Most New Yorkers shrugged, considering brokers and jumpers a necessary evil.

Ironically, the draft riots and ensuing scramble to find volunteer replacements for New York's draftees led to the formation of the first black regiment of volunteers raised in New York, the 20th Regiment of United

States Colored Troops. They were recruited and outfitted by the wealthy Republicans of the Union League Club. Union Leagues, also called Loyal Leagues, had sprung up all around the North to counter the dismal morale that had spread by the start of 1863. Henry Bellows, Frederick Law Olmsted, the lawyer George Templeton Strong, and other Sanitary Commission leaders started New York City's Union League Club in February 1863, and wooed some five hundred others. Club members were the cream of Protestant, patrician New York, including the influential businessman Alexander Stewart and the shipping magnate William Aspinwall, along with politicians like Dix and the former governor and now senator Edwin Morgan. When the draft riots raged around their posh clubhouse on East 17th Street, near both Union Square and Edwin Booth's home, club members like Strong had seethed helplessly at the "brutal, base, cruel... Irish scum" and the "unspeakable infamy of the nigger persecution." In November they went over the head of the objecting Governor Seymour and won Stanton's permission to recruit black volunteers to help fill New York's quota.

On March 5, 1864, the 20th's 1,020 black soldiers marched from the clubhouse to a waiting steamship while tens of thousands lined their route, some cheering and some just gawking. The club would raise a second regiment, the 26th, and part of a third, the 31st, by which point the city's complement of eligible black men had been largely depleted. Many of the soldiers had left jobs paying up to sixty dollars a month to take ten dollars (three less than white soldiers) from the army. As was customary with black regiments, the officers and noncommissioned officers were all white men, except for the chaplain. Reverend Henry Highland Garnet served as chaplain while the regiment trained on Rikers Island, but he could not go to the front with them because he limped on a wooden leg, the result of a boyhood injury. He was replaced by the Reverend George Le Vere of Brooklyn as the unit prepared to leave the city.

While some New Yorkers cheered the men of the 20th, others went out of their way to discourage them. The brokers through whom they signed up cheated them even more grossly than they did white recruits. Facilities on Rikers Island were abysmal. Reverend Garnet was so badly mistreated on the ferry to the island that the army had to assign him an escort. When Le Vere took over, white officers refused to let him eat with them in the mess; even the club neglected to invite him to a reception for the regiment's officers. Two of the city's most famous marching bands, Harvey

Dodsworth's 13th Regiment Band and Claudio Graffula's 7th, refused to lead "the niggers" on their parade through the streets. The five hundred club members marched with the troops, partly as a sort of honor guard, partly as bodyguards. The *Tribune* and *Times* cheered the event, while the *Herald* moaned that putting "these ex-bootblacks and scrubbers, waiters and whitewashers" in uniform was the "inauguration of miscegenation" (a new coinage in the spring of 1864).

The 20th Regiment was posted to the swamps of Louisiana, where, though they didn't engage in any major fighting, more than two hundred of them would die of disease. The 26th and 31st saw more action and fought, their white officers agreed, with distinction.

In the third week of July, Dan Sickles, on crutches, with Gus Schurmann taking an elbow as needed, hobbled off a ferry onto the island of Manhattan, where the ashes were still hot from the rioting the week before. Reeling and in need of something to celebrate, New York City gave him a hero's welcome. Even the *Times* joined in the huzzahs, declaring that he "has proved what militia are capable of, when led by a brave man, even without the advantages of a regular military education.... Gen. Sickles has literally carved his way to fame with his sword.... When the roll of heroes is written for this war, one of the highest on the list will be that of Gen. Daniel E. Sickles, and New York will justly claim him as her own."

No doubt all the lofty praise speeded the general's recovery. By the fall he was back south to ask Meade if he could resume command. Meade put him off on medical grounds. Privately, he was glad to be through with the man.

But Sickles wasn't through with Meade. Now a regular and welcome guest at the White House, he launched a smear campaign to portray Meade as a cowardly bungler who narrowly avoided defeat at Gettysburg only through the fine soldiering of his subordinates, including of course Dan Sickles. In Congress he made his case to the Joint Committee on the Conduct of the War, led by Radicals ready to denounce anyone they felt was not prosecuting the conflict with proper gusto. Butterfield offered supporting testimony. Bennett's *Herald* joined the attack, running letters signed "Historicus" damning Meade and praising Sickles that were almost certainly written by Sickles himself. The committee urged Lincoln to sack Meade, but in the end he kept his job. Sickles never got his back.

Meanwhile, Gus remained with his family in New York City. Gettysburg had been his last battle. Sickles, with Lincoln's approval, had gotten him an appointment to a preparatory school, with the idea that he'd go on to West Point. Gus didn't stay in school long. He went to work to support his mother instead.

A few weeks after Sickles's visit, New York turned out to cheer an unalloyed war hero, Rear Admiral David Farragut, who brought his flagship the *Hartford* to the Brooklyn Navy Yard for repairs and refitting. Since taking New Orleans he'd gone on to victory after victory on the Mississippi, earning the nickname "the American Viking" for his boldness and courage. Oliver Wendell Holmes would dub him "the Sea King." He looked the part, tall and trim in his admiral's gold-buttoned blues, with gray curls ringing the sober and alert visage of an eagle. He would be off again in January, his most legendary victory still to come.

New York City voters went to the polls that December. Opdyke wisely decided not to run, so the Republicans nominated Tweed's collaborator Orison Blunt. The Democrats, as usual, split. Tammany and Mozart Hall agreed to a temporary fusion and nominated a Tammany functionary. Democrats who opposed them nominated Charles Godfrey Gunther, who'd been Tammany's man in 1861. Raised on Maiden Lane in a prosperous fur-trading family, Gunther was pro-South and very antiwar. He was not in fact German, but the German community thought he was and helped him eke out a victory. His two years in office would prove to be almost as tumultuous as Opdyke's had been.

While New York's Germans were electing a mayor, New York's Irish community lost a hero. That December the much-reduced General Meagher visited his old friend Michael Corcoran where the Corcoran Legion was stationed at Fairfax Courthouse, midway between Washington and Manassas. They got to toasting each other's health, and Corcoran decided he wanted to ride Meagher's horse, a big and notoriously testy brute. The beast tossed Corcoran down a ravine and tumbled on top of him. He never regained consciousness. He was thirty-six. His body was brought back to New York City with all solemn honors. Large crowds came to view it as it lay in state at City Hall over Christmas, then followed it to a funeral Mass at St. Patrick's Cathedral on Mott Street, across the street from the Hibernian House where he'd once worked. He was buried at Calvary Cemetery in Brooklyn.

Stephen Foster had returned to New York just before the start of the war. Hard times had come for him again and again in the second half of the 1850s as his songwriting income dwindled to a pittance. He'd been forced to sell his publishers Firth, Pond & Co. the rights to much of his catalog at a terrible price. When he came back to New York in a last-ditch effort to make a go of it, he brought his wife, Jane, and their daughter, Marion, with him. At one point they were in a boardinghouse on Greene Street in today's SoHo.

Foster had sickened of minstrel songs and wrote parlor ballads at a desperate clip; it showed in their tonal mediocrity and poor sales. The morbid lyrics signaled his increasingly dark mood—"Lizzie Dies To-night," "Our Willie Dear Is Dying," "Farewell Mother Dear," and so on. He wrote his last good parlor song, "Beautiful Dreamer," but failed to publish it.

Within a year Jane had left him, taking Marion with her. He sank deeper into despondency and drifted to the Lower East Side, where he took up drinking bad rum in the backroom grog shops behind grocery stores. People on the Bowery recognized the great songwriter even as his condition deteriorated. Some bought him drinks and asked him to sing "Hard Times"; others mocked his sad condition. When one young woman asked if he was Stephen Foster, he replied, "Yes, the wreck of Stephen Foster."

In the winter of 1862–63 a law student named George Cooper, whose father had a store on the Bowery, screwed up his nerve to approach Foster as he was drinking. He had a poem he thought might make a good song, "Willie Has Gone to the War." According to Cooper, Foster pulled a crumpled sheet of music from a pocket, flattened it on one of the cheese boxes that served as tables in the joint, and jotted down a melody for the poem. Then they headed for Broadway, where Foster's music publisher, now called Wm. A. Pond & Co., had its offices. As they passed Wood's Minstrel Hall near Spring Street, Henry Wood stepped out, recognized Foster, and asked if that was a new song he had rolled up in his fist. He bought it on the spot for twenty-five dollars, the easiest money Foster had made in some time. Pond published the sheet music.

Encouraged, Foster collaborated with Cooper on some twenty more songs. Most were undistinguished wartime ditties no one listened to. Some are utterly unperformable now, like "A Soldier in the Colored Brigade," Cooper's lyrics for which include lines like:

Old Uncle Abram wants us, and we're coming right along
I tell you what it is, we're gwine to muster mighty strong
Then fare you well my honey dear! now don't you be afraid
I's bound to be a soldier in de colored brigade

A soldier! a soldier in de darkey brigade!
I's bound to be a soldier in de colored brigade....

In days ob Gen'ral Washington we fought de British well,
Behind de bales wid "Hickory" I tink we made 'em yell.
I tell you we're de chickens dat can handle gun or spade,
And Greeley he'll go wid us in de Colored Brigade.

Foster continued to decline through 1863. He drifted from one cheap rooming house to another on and around the Bowery, drinking too much, eating too little. Even a backroom bartender commented that he was "not very delectable society." In January 1864, with money from a saloon-keeper fan, he managed to take a room in a relatively respectable location by Bowery standards, the New England Hotel at the northwest corner of the Bowery and Bayard Street. On the morning of Sunday, January 9, Foster stood at his door speaking to a chambermaid, then turned and suddenly collapsed, crashing down into a washing bowl that shattered, gashing his neck. The hotel sent for his friend Cooper, who lived a few blocks away. Cooper found him on the floor, bleeding horribly. As they waited for a doctor, Foster croaked, "I'm done for," and asked for a drink. The doctor crudely stitched the wound and had Foster carried up to Bellevue, where he died on January 13. He was thirty-seven. He'd written some of America's favorite songs, and had thirty-eight cents to his name.

CHAPTER 35

The Fire in the Rear

A Lincoln victory in the 1864 elections was by no means assured. In fact, it was a forlorn hope. The North was winning the war, but slowly and at atrocious cost. Since Gettysburg and Vicksburg the South had been fighting a defensive war and losing, but not giving in. Lincoln had brought all the North's greatly superior numbers and industrial power to bear now. By the start of 1864, Union armies were grinding inexorably into the heart of the Confederacy. Grant's army chased Lee's, both sides taking appalling casualties, while Sherman marched toward Atlanta. Lincoln unleashed his generals to wage all-out war, laying waste to cities, farmlands, rail lines.

But the progress was too slow for many war-weary Northerners, and there were demoralizing setbacks. In May 1864, Benjamin Butler, who was as incompetent in the field as he was tough in urban settings, muffed the opportunity to seize a virtually undefended Richmond and took a drubbing from an inferior Confederate force, losing four thousand men. Franz Sigel suffered a similar thrashing that same month. Lincoln had given in to Germans' call to have Sigel back and sent him to West Virginia. Colonel Strother, who was serving there, grumbled, "The Dutch vote must be secured at all hazards for the Government and the sacrifice of West Virginia is a small matter." Patrolling the Shenandoah Valley, Sigel led a small force to defeat against an even smaller Rebel force, which included cadets from the Virginia Military Institute. He was removed from command and would return to New York City for good.

Lincoln found himself besieged on all sides. He was fighting not just the Confederacy but the Democrats, the Copperheads and Butternuts, many members of his own party, and members of his cabinet. He was so unpopular with so many factions for so many reasons that even he considered it "exceedingly probable" that he would not be reelected.

As before, New Yorkers figured prominently among Lincoln's enemies in the North and vigorously fanned the flames of what he called "the fire in the rear." At the end of 1863 the Nassau Street publishing firm Dexter, Hamilton & Co. published a seventy-two-page pamphlet that appeared on city newsstands and was mailed to various opinion-makers and politicians, including President Lincoln. It was called *Miscegenation*, a new term for race-mixing. The anonymous author expressed a remarkably progressive attitude, predicting that "in the millennial future, the most perfect and highest type of manhood will not be white or black, but brown, or colored." He argued that "whoever helps to unite the various races of men, helps to make the human family the sooner realize its great destiny." He further suggested that the Republicans should add a pro-miscegenation plank to their upcoming campaign platform.

It all sounds reasonable enough today, but in the racial context of the Civil War a pro-miscegenation stand was outrageous and controversial in the extreme. The threat of the amalgamation of the races through sexual union had terrified conservative whites since colonial days, despite the fact that it went on constantly on the plantations of the South and in urban areas in the North like the Five Points, where the poor of all races and types were tossed together and did what came naturally. Most abolitionists had always been chary of the amalgamationist label. Some who were mailed the pamphlet approved of it and ran notices for it in their papers, but others were more circumspect.

It was Copperheads who reacted to *Miscegenation* the most hotly. Democrats thundered denunciations in Congress. *Day-Book* editor John Van Evrie coined a new word of his own, "subgenation," for the natural inferiority of blacks, and frothed that white workers "had better cut the throats of their children at once" rather than let them grow up in a world of "degradation and amalgamation." James McMaster used the opportunity to complain, "Filthy black niggers, greasy, sweaty, and disgusting, now jostle white people and even ladies everywhere." Greeley made note of the "tolerably warm discussion" and of course weighed in, arguing that "if a white man pleases to marry a black woman, the mere fact that she is black gives no one a right to interfere to prevent or set aside such marriage. We do not say that such union would be wise, but we do distinctly assert that society has nothing to do with the wisdom of matches." Manton Marble used this as a pretext for charging that Greeley and his fellow Black Republicans had indeed always been secret amalgamationists.

The pamphlet mailed to Lincoln included a respectful note from "Author of 'Miscegenation'" with the request, "May I ask your permission to dedicate it to your excellency?" Lincoln was wise enough not to respond.

In November, two weeks after the election, Marble's *New York World* would reveal that *Miscegenation* was a hoax, a satire of Republican attitudes toward race. An editor and a correspondent at the *World* had cooked it up. They had intended to trick Republicans into admitting their amalgamationist beliefs, but it was their fellow Copperheads who were most fooled.

A few months after *Miscegenation* first appeared, the *New York World* and the *Journal of Commerce* printed another hoax, this time unwittingly. On the morning of May 18 the two papers published an Associated Press dispatch from Washington reporting that because the war was not going as well as President Lincoln hoped, he was about to order a new draft of four hundred thousand more men. No other papers carried the report. New Yorkers responded with howls of dismay. Fearing the economic effects of the news, investors rushed to Wall Street that morning and sold off their stocks, switching to the comparative safety of gold. The stock market plunged and gold prices soared.

Within hours both the Associated Press and Secretary of State Seward declared the report fraudulent. Irate, Lincoln ordered General Dix to seize the two papers' offices and arrest the editors for "wickedly and traitorously" printing false material "with intent to give aid and comfort to the enemy." Dix wisely chose not to make any arrests, but he did shut the papers down for a few days. Since it was obvious that the two papers had been among the victims of the hoax, Lincoln's already seriously sullied reputation regarding the rights of free speech and a free press took more damage he didn't need in an election year. Democrats denounced the administration's despotism once again; Governor Seymour went so far as to order the district attorney, A. Oakey Hall, to arrest Dix on a charge of kidnapping, but because Dix had not actually jailed the editors nothing came of it.

On Saturday, May 21, detectives did arrest the hoaxer: Joseph Howard, who happened to be the thirty-five-year-old son of Reverend Beecher's friend John Tasker Howard. Joe Howard was a well-known journalist, formerly on the staff at the *Times*, now city editor at the *Brooklyn Eagle*. He was also a notorious practical joker. This time he went too far. He had invested in gold, forged the Associated Press report, then sold his gold when the price shot up. He was promptly sent to Fort Lafayette.

In July the war effort was still progressing too slowly for Lincoln, at least if he had any hope of being reelected. Sherman was bogged down in his siege of Atlanta, and Grant at Richmond. Lincoln did in fact issue a call for more conscripts—five hundred thousand, or one hundred thousand more than "Bogus Joe" Howard had put in his fraudulent dispatch. Lincoln ordered Howard's release after one month. Reverend Beecher had quietly reached out to the president and interceded for his friend's son. Granting Beecher's request was Lincoln's way of thanking him for a service he'd rendered in the spring of 1863. On a trip to England, supposedly to rest, Beecher had given a series of speeches, facing down hostile audiences from Edinburgh and Liverpool to London. The nearly complete shutting down of cotton shipments due to the Union blockade of the South had idled thousands of workers in British textile mills and seaports. The English government, which had always been sympathetic to its major supplier of cotton, was considering intervening in the war against the Union. Beecher spoke out passionately for the Union, against slavery, and against intervention. No one, not even he, believed his talks alone turned the tide, but England did stay out of the war, and Lincoln was very grateful for his effort.

Another newspaperman was thrown in jail the following month. In issue after issue of the *Metropolitan Record*, John Mullaly had been railing against the draft for more than a year. His extremism had prompted Archbishop Hughes to withdraw his support of the paper. Now federal marshals arrested Mullaly in his office on Broadway for his "incendiary, disloyal, and traitorous" editorials. He was released on $2,500 bail put up by a supporter and would continue editing the paper for the remainder of the war and several years after.

⁓

The Republicans held their convention in Baltimore that June. In the months leading up to it, of the New York papers only Raymond's *Times* stood firmly behind Lincoln. "Mr. Lincoln is already beaten," Greeley groaned, "and we must have another ticket." In a February 23 *Tribune* editorial, he damned Lincoln with faint praise as "patriotic, honest, and faithful," but "not infallible—not a genius—not one of those rare great men who mold their age." In the *Herald*, Bennett was back to haranguing Lincoln. His February 19 editorial was an amazing rant: "President Lincoln is a joke incarnated. His election was a very sorry joke. The idea that such a man as he should be President of such a country as this is a very ridiculous joke....His Cabinet is and always has been a standing joke. All his State papers are jokes....His emancipation proclamation was a solemn joke. His recent proclamation of abolition and amnesty is another joke....His intrigues to secure a renomination and the hopes he appears to entertain of a re-election are, however, the most laughable jokes of all."

A week before the Republican convention, Greeley and the Radicals held their own separate gathering and nominated Frémont. Their platform included a proposal for a new amendment to the Constitution abolishing slavery forever. Lincoln's mainstream Republicans responded by renaming themselves the National Union Party. The Baltimore convention was tumultuous, but Lincoln and his supporters held out and trounced Frémont and the Radicals, winning the nomination with 507 votes to 22. Lincoln, seeking any inroad with Democrats, asked Vice President Hamlin to step aside. The party nominated as Lincoln's running mate the only Southern Democrat who had backed him throughout the war, Andrew Johnson.

As chairman of the party now, Raymond—who was running for Congress himself—wrote most of the platform. It included language that opposed the Peace Democrats and any compromising with the Rebels; approved of the Emancipation Proclamation and included its own proposal for an amendment to the Constitution banning slavery for good; and added a plank meant to woo immigrant voters away from the Democracy, stating that "foreign immigration, which in the past has added so much to the wealth, development of resources and increase of power to the nation, the asylum of the oppressed of all nations, should be fostered and encouraged by a liberal and just policy."

A month after the Republican convention, probably seething with envy of Raymond, Horace Greeley made one of his most foolish attempts to grab some political glory for himself: Uncle Horace would single-handedly broker an end to the war.

After the fall of Vicksburg and Lee's failed coup at Gettysburg, Jefferson Davis was forced to admit that the South could not win on the battlefield.

By the end of 1863 he was pinning wan hopes on using terrorism and guerrilla warfare to turn the population of the North against the war. He created the Confederate Secret Service and appointed two politicians with no military or spy experience to be its commissioners. Jacob Thompson was a former Mississippi congressman and Buchanan's secretary of the interior. His assistant Clement Clay had been an Alabama senator before the war. Early in 1864, Davis sent them to Canada with $1 million in gold and silver coin and the vague directive to meet with Copperheads and Confederate exiles and stir up whatever trouble they could in the North.

Setting themselves up at the Queens Hotel in Toronto, they linked up with a Captain Thomas Hines, who'd ridden with John Hunt Morgan's Kentucky cavalry and escaped a Union prison. Hines was one of the more upstanding men in their cabal, which included a number of shadowy and dubious characters. One of them was William "Larry" McDonald, a carriage-maker from New York. In his shop on Broadway he'd done most of his business with Southerners, and when the war cut that off he became an embittered Copperhead. As a sutler with a New Jersey brigade, he deliberately drove his wagons across Confederate lines to defect. McDonald had a sideline that was most interesting to Thompson and Clay: He dabbled in building mines, bombs, and incendiary devices.

Then there was the debonair George Sanders, a former editor at John L. O'Sullivan's *United States Magazine and Democratic Review* and purchasing agent for the Brooklyn Navy Yard. (O'Sullivan had coined the term "Manifest Destiny"; his magazine presented the intellectual high end of Democratic and conservative opinion.) When the war started Sanders had toured Europe trying to raise funds for the Confederacy. His son Reid, who had attended the Free Academy (later City College), became a Confederate officer. In 1862, Reid was captured aboard a Rebel ship bound for Europe with dispatches from Richmond. He died in the Fort Warren POW camp outside Boston.

And there was William Cornell "Colorado" Jewett, scion of a prominent Maine family who'd gotten rich mining gold in Colorado. A pacifist and Peace Democrat, he had traveled to the capitals of Europe and spoken to various heads of state, including Queen Victoria and France's Louis Napoleon III, about moderating a peace conference between the North and South. In 1863 he had gotten Greeley involved, and the two of them convinced the French minister in Washington to try to speak to Seward. Seward rebuffed the offer.

Clement Vallandigham met with Thompson and Clay and convinced them that a vast underground of Copperheads in the Northwest was ready to rise up in armed revolt. The commissioners devised a plan, possibly originating with McDonald, to send terrorist teams to Chicago and New York with incendiary materials. The burning cities would be the signal fires for the start of the uprising.

Captain Hines later testified that Fernando and Benjamin Wood went to Niagara Falls to meet with Thompson. According to Hines, the brothers promised to help raise arms for the revolt and assured the commissioners that if the Northwest rose up, tens of thousands of New York Copperheads would too. Hines also said the commission paid Benjamin tens of thousands of dollars to keep writing his antiwar screeds in the *Daily News*. If Hines's story is true, this was the moment when the Wood brothers crossed the line from opposing the war to actual sedition.

Fernando Wood allegedly put the conspirators in touch with the Copperhead proprietor of a violin shop near Washington Square, who sold them a number of rifles and pistols, ammunition, and the chemicals for making "Greek fire," the phosphorus-based precursor to napalm. These supplies were smuggled into Canada and from there into Ohio and Indiana, where they were hidden in "haystacks, graveyards, and barnyards," to be used in the Northwest uprising.

As spymasters, Thompson and Clay proved to be hopelessly inept. Everyone in Canada—and Washington—was aware of their "secret" service. Stanton and Dana sent double agents who effortlessly infiltrated the group. Thompson and Clay actually hired one of these Union spies to be their courier for secret messages to Davis. On his way to Richmond he'd stop off in Washington, where Stanton and Dana read the messages, resealed them, and sent him on his way. This was how the War Department learned of the plan to set fire to Chicago and New York simultaneously. Dana instantly informed General Dix in New York, who at first was "very unwilling to believe that any such design could be seriously entertained."

Besides plotting guerrilla war, the commissioners also tried their hand at public relations. This is where Horace Greeley got involved. In July, Jewett wrote Greeley, "I am authorized to state to you, for our use only, not the public, that two ambassadors of Davis & Co. are now in Canada, with full and complete powers for a peace." He asked Greeley to intercede for them with the president.

Greeley excitedly dashed off a letter to Lincoln. "Our bleeding, bankrupt, almost dying country longs for peace—shudders at the prospect of fresh conscriptions, of further wholesale devastations, and of new rivers of human blood," he lectured the president. "I entreat you to submit overtures for pacification to the Southern insurgents."

Lincoln didn't believe for one second that the "ambassadors" were bona fide, but he directed his aide John Hay to accompany Greeley to Niagara Falls anyway. Hay carried a letter from the president stating that he was ready to entertain "any proposition which embraces the restoration of peace, the integrity of the whole Union, and the abandonment of slavery." Sanders now admitted to Greeley and Hay that his group had no real negotiating authority from "Davis & Co." Disgusted but not surprised, Hay reported back to Lincoln and the cabinet; Attorney General Bates snorted that Jewett was a "meddlesome blockhead" and "crack-brained simpleton." Lincoln sighed that Greeley was like "an old shoe... so rotten that nothing can be done with him." Andrew Johnson later said that Greeley "seemed to me like a whale ashore. He nearly bothered the life out of Lincoln and it was difficult to tell whether he wanted union or separation, war or peace. Greeley is all heart and no head. He is the most vacillating man in the country."

The story went public and Greeley's competitors had another field day mocking him. Dana recalled that "the poor man...was almost universally laughed at." Greeley expressed no remorse this time, but instead blamed Lincoln for thwarting the peace effort.

———

At their convention, the Democrats were just as divided as the Republicans were. The War Democrats backed the front-runner, McClellan. Moderate Peace Democrats promoted New York's Governor Seymour. Hard-line Copperheads preferred another Governor Seymour, Thomas Hart Seymour of Connecticut. In New York, Fernando Wood, James McMaster, and other Copperheads tried to devise ways to derail McClellan's candidacy. Solidly pro-McClellan Tammany mounted a successful campaign to eject the "dis-unionist" Wood from the Democrats' state convention. He trudged out of the hall to a chorus of "groans and hisses." Having made enemies on all sides yet again, Wood waged a lonely campaign for reelection to Congress. "Fernando Wood," Bennett's *Herald* japed, "is the nominee of Fernando Wood. Fernando Wood is patrolling the district, making speeches for Fernando Wood."

The War Democrats prevailed and McClellan was nominated, but the Peace Democrats got one of their own, Ohio representative George Pendleton, nominated as McClellan's running mate. They also forced the party to accept a platform that included a "peace plank," which McClellan, still clinging to his image as warrior hero, could not accept. The peace plank proposed that "immediate efforts be made for a cessation of hostilities, with a view of an ultimate convention of the States," so "peace may be restored on the basis of the Federal Union of the States." *Harper's Weekly* declared the platform "craven, abject, humiliating," and joked that McClellan was like a trick equestrian trying simultaneously to ride two horses going in opposite directions. In fact, McClellan would ride neither; he sat out the campaign, barely appearing in public.

Vallandigham wrote the peace plank. Finding it impossible to sit on the sidelines across the border at such a momentous political juncture, he had donned false whiskers and sneaked by train back into Ohio in July. Democrats toasted his return. Greeley wrote an editorial advising Lincoln to let Vallandigham stay rather than making a Copperhead martyr of him a second time, and for once Greeley and the president were in agreement. Emboldened, Vallandigham came to New York and did some speechmaking with Fernando Wood, promoting a negotiated end to the war. They traveled together to the Chicago convention.

Despite their internal differences, the Democrats were on a roll and both sides knew it. Then Lincoln's fortunes brightened. In August, Admiral Farragut achieved his last great victory at the Battle of Mobile Bay, a titanic clash of wooden and ironclad warships. With rows of cannons on ship and shore thundering in all directions, banks of smoke so choked the broad and shallow bay that captains and crews could barely see where they were going or what they were firing at. Farragut, who had just turned sixty-three, clambered up the *Hartford*'s rigging and shouted directions down to his officers. They were so frightened for his safety that they sent a man up to lash the admiral to the mast. The Confederates had seeded sections of the bay with mines, called "torpedoes" at the time. A Union ironclad struck one and sank in minutes with most hands trapped inside. When this caused another captain to hesitate, Farragut shouted, "Damn the torpedoes," and gave directions for a full-speed advance. Over time his more detailed instructions were compressed into "Damn the torpedoes, full speed ahead!"

When Farragut returned to New York the following December, the reception was even more jubilant than it had been in 1863. Congress would create a new rank, vice admiral, just for him. He and his wife would tour Europe and be feted everywhere. On his death in 1870, New York City would win the honor of hosting his funeral. The city shut down for the day, and President Grant led a long list of dignitaries who attended. Farragut was buried in Woodlawn Cemetery.

On September 2, Sherman finally took Atlanta. A month later, Phil Sheridan would gouge the last Rebels out of the Shenandoah Valley, which had been both a redoubt and a pantry for the Confederacy. Optimism swept the North. The *Times* crowed and gloated, and even Bennett declared final victory near at hand. Greeley had yet another change of heart, now exhorting everyone in the Union to rally behind the president and the war effort—"a little more energy, a little more courage, and we shall soon see the end of it." August Belmont, who chaired the Democrats' national committee, and the *World*'s Manton Marble, who spearheaded their public relations, desperately tried to play down the Pendleton-Vallandigham wing and focus voters' attention on McClellan the war hero. But the Democrats' moment had passed.

The issue of *Harper's Weekly* that hit the stands the day after Atlanta fell fortuitously included a Nast illustration that may have helped as much to get Lincoln reelected as Brady's portrait had helped elect him the first time. Nast was already the most popular illustrator in the country. He was starting to be the most influential as well. Growing up in the Tammany stronghold of the Lower East Side had marked him with a lifelong distrust of Democrats. He was appalled by the Chicago peace platform. The illustration "Compromise with the South" was his response. Nast drew a haughty Confederate and a wounded, demoralized Union soldier shaking hands over a grave with a headstone that reads, "In Memory of the Union Heroes Who Fell in a Useless War." The female figure Columbia kneels between the soldiers, weeping. In the background, a Negro family in chains grieves. Below the image it reads, "Dedicated to the Chicago Convention."

The timing could not have been better. The issue quickly sold out and a startled and delighted Fletcher Harper rushed to print more to meet the continuing demand. As Lincoln's campaign manager, Raymond had the image printed and distributed as a poster.

By October the momentum was gathering behind Lincoln, and McClellan, as he had on the battlefield, still refused to come out and fight. "The times seem to me so out of joint that I can scarcely bear to write," Maria Daly lamented. "It seems to me that the country is mad....Lincoln, a rail-splitter, and his wife, two ignorant and vulgar boors, are king and queen."

Nast produced one more striking illustration to cap the campaign. For the first time, Union states allowed soldiers to cast absentee ballots. Each state was responsible for sending agents into the field to collect the votes of its men in uniform. In late October the army arrested five of New York's agents, all appointed by Governor Seymour, who were caught forging soldiers' signatures, as well as recording numerous votes from dead or imaginary men. All the fraudulent votes were for McClellan. A military court sentenced three of the men to life in prison, though they were later released. "ASTOUNDING FRAUDS!" the *Times* cried. "Arrest of New-York Voting Agents. Soldiers Proxies Forged by Gov. Seymour's Appointees. FULL PARTICULARS OF THE RASCALITY." Nast's cartoon in *Harper's*, titled "How the Copperheads Obtain Their Votes," shows a pair of agents in a dark cemetery recording a soldier's name off his gravestone, while his ghost looms above and curses them "for making me appear disloyal."

That month the Canada commission struck. Twenty-one young Confederate soldiers, all escapees from Union prisons, wearing new gray uniforms tailored in Montreal, crossed the border into Vermont and, on October 19, laid siege to the small town of St. Albans. It was the northernmost Confederate attack of the war. They robbed three banks of almost $90,000 and tried to set the town ablaze using bottles of Greek fire, which merely sputtered and smoked. Driven off by the locals in a hail of bullets, they filtered back across the border, where Canadian authorities promptly arrested and jailed them. The commission paid for their defense attorneys. To maintain neutrality, Canada decided to release the young men, but returned the confiscated loot to St. Albans.

Through the rest of October, New York buzzed with rumors that the Confederates and Copperheads had more terrorist actions in the works. There were predictions that "rioters would occupy the United States Sub-Treasury on Wall Street; others would seize City Hall for use as a fortress, flying the Stars and Bars from its roof," historian Edward Longacre writes.

They would burn down other federal buildings, release the prisoners at Fort Lafayette, and take General Dix hostage. At the same time, Wall Street brokers acting on the South's behalf were said to be buying and hoarding so much gold bullion that greenbacks "would become virtually worthless."

Democrats like Governor Seymour and Mayor Gunther waved off the stories. But based on the wealth of intelligence Stanton and Dana's spies had gathered in Canada, the Lincoln administration opted for a large military presence in the city to keep the peace on election day. They gave General Benjamin Butler, the Beast of New Orleans, the task. He arrived on November 4 trailing five thousand officers and men. He had such a contingent of staff officers that the Fifth Avenue Hotel couldn't accommodate them and they moved to the larger Hoffman House. Then Butler and Dix spat over how large and visible a show of force was needed. Butler wanted a full New Orleans–style lockdown; Dix thought this unnecessary and provocative. He restricted Butler to putting just two thousand of his men in the city.

Butler moved instantly against the gold speculators on Wall Street, summarily ordering one broker, H. J. Lyons, to an interrogation at the Hoffman House. Lyons was definitely worthy of Butler's suspicions, a Southerner who had come to New York from Montreal less than a year earlier and bought up some $3 million in gold bullion. Butler gave him such a fierce grilling, reminding him that the punishment for treason was death, that the ashen-faced man promised to sell off his gold that very day. Butler repeated this performance with principals of four other brokerages, and the price of gold had eased by November 8.

On his own hook, Butler shocked New Yorkers by issuing a proclamation that in effect declared the city under martial law. His troops were in the city as "safeguards of constitutional liberty," he wrote, "which is *freedom to do right, not wrong*. They can be a terror to evil doers only." Interpreting "do right" as "vote for Lincoln," Seymour, Gunther, and other Democrats protested furiously.

When election day dawned, Butler positioned his troops. As Dix wanted, he did it discreetly, to avoid giving New Yorkers the sense that they lived in an occupied city. The bulk he stationed on ferries in the two rivers, where they were out of sight but could quickly get to any trouble spots. The rest he placed at strategic spots like Wall Street, bridges, telegraph offices (a responsibility handed to Dan Butterfield, who was temporarily serving under Dix), and Mackerelville, the east side neighborhood where many Irish thought to have participated in the draft riots lived.

Either despite or because of all the precautions, it turned out to be the quietest election day New Yorkers had seen in years. The only rumble came late in the day, when a large crowd gathered outside the Hoffman House to heckle Butler. Superintendent Kennedy and his Metropolitans dispersed them. Crisis averted, Dix pressed for the immediate removal of Butler's troops, whom he'd never felt comfortable about. Succumbing to the lure of the metropolis, a number of Butler's soldiers and even a few officers went AWOL and vanished in the city; the rest sailed back to the front. Butler stayed on a few days to be wined and dined by the city's grateful elite, including a gala banquet at the Fifth Avenue Hotel at which Reverend Beecher gave the keynote toast.

Lincoln won the election by a 10 percent margin in the popular vote, roughly 2.2 million votes to McClellan's 1.8 million, and thoroughly trounced him in electoral votes, 213 to 21. He won New York State by a mere 1 percent. Once again, he lost by landslides in both Brooklyn and New York City, where McClellan outpolled him two to one. In Manhattan, only the Fifteenth Ward—the posh, Republican "Empire Ward" around Washington Square—voted for Lincoln.

Governor Seymour was turned out and replaced by a Radical Republican, Reuben Fenton. Fernando Wood lost his seat in Congress as well. The *Herald* jeered, "Fernando is a played-out politician, we advise him to die gracefully." Wood would use his final lame-duck weeks in the House to try to obstruct passage of the Thirteenth Amendment. "The Almighty has fixed the distinction of the races," he declared. "The Almighty has made the black man inferior, and, sir, by no legislation, by no partisan success, by no military power, can you wipe out this distinction." Henry Raymond won election to Congress. In fact, the elections were a disaster for Democrats generally. Republicans came out with a three-to-one dominance in Congress.

Abandoning the country that had rebuffed him, McClellan, his wife, and his children sailed from New York for a long European idyll. He would still be away when the war ended, and would not return to the United States until 1868.

CHAPTER 36

New York City's Burning

At the Winter Garden on the evening of Friday, November 25, which New Yorkers celebrated as Evacuation Day (when occupying British troops left the city in 1783), Edwin Booth staged a one-night-only gala performance of *Julius Caesar*. It was a benefit to help pay for a statue of Shakespeare to go in the still incomplete Central Park. The statue was the brainchild of Judge Daly. He'd laid the cornerstone for the statue's pedestal the previous spring. Although the ticket prices were hiked for the gala—a good seat went for five dollars, when it was usually a dollar—the two thousand seats sold out quickly, and people were standing in the aisles. That was because for the first and only time ever, the three Booth brothers would all be onstage together. Junius played Cassius, Edwin played Brutus, and John Wilkes was Mark Antony. When they marched onto the stage together behind Caesar in act 1, scene 2, the overstuffed house exploded with applause. For Edwin it was another duel of Shakespeareans, but this time his rival was the ambitious John Wilkes. John was determined to grab this one opportunity to upstage his older brother, and according to the *Herald* he gave a performance of "phosphorescent passion and fire."

Act 2 had just begun, with Brutus pacing his orchard and murmuring before a rapt and hushed audience, "O conspiracy, / Shamest thou to show thy dangerous brow by night, / When evils are most free? O, then by day / Where wilt thou find a cavern dark enough / To mask thy monstrous visage?" Suddenly there was a clangor of fire engines out on the street, and volunteer firemen charged into the theater's lobby. They were responding to a fire in a room of the adjacent hotel, the Lafarge House. The *Times* reported the next day that "the panic was such for a few moments that it seemed as if all the audience believed the entire building in flames, and just ready to fall upon their devoted heads." Edwin stepped up to the footlights and quietly, firmly enforced calm. After determining that the theater was in no danger, the brothers resumed the play, and only a handful of audience members missed the thunderous ovations at the end.

What no one in the theater knew at the time was that the fire next door had been no accident. The Canada commission had finally attacked New York City.

A month earlier, on Thursday, October 27, eight young Rebel saboteurs, soldiers in civilian dress, had stepped off a New York Central train from Niagara Falls. They fanned out and took rooms under assumed names at the Metropolitan, the St. Denis, and other hotels around the city. That very day, the *Times* printed General Dix's General Orders No. 80. After the St. Albans raid, Dix was convinced that the Canada commission was planning to disrupt the voting in New York City on November 8. He ordered "all persons from the insurgent states" who were in the city—contemporary estimates put the number of Southern refugees and expats in the city at ten to as many as fifty thousand—to register their names at his Bleecker Street headquarters.

Some actually obeyed. The eight new arrivals, of course, did not. Despite their Southern accents, they apparently met no suspicion as they signed their fictitious names at the hotel desks. Their leaders, Colonel Robert Martin and Lieutenant John Headley, were, like Captain Hines, Kentucky cavalrymen who had ridden with Morgan's Raiders. They were both twenty-four. Forty years later, Headley would write a book on his adventures, *Confederate Operations in Canada and New York*. Still an unrepentant Reb in 1906, he would dedicate it to the "defenseless noncombatant people of the South who suffered the untold horrors of merciless warfare" and to the "persecuted people of the North whose sense of justice and humanity revolted at a crusade for the cause of John Brown, and of Horace Greeley, Gerrit Smith and Cornelius Vanderbilt."

Also notable on the team was the group's loose cannon, the hotheaded Captain Robert Cobb Kennedy of Louisiana. At twenty-nine he was the old man of the group. A wealthy doctor's son, Cobb had been booted out of West Point just before the war for drunkenness, insubordination, and low grades. After signing up with a Louisiana regiment he was wounded in battle, leaving him with a significant limp, then captured and sent north to the POW camp on Johnson's Island in Lake Erie. He'd made a bold escape from there and slipped over into Canada to join the Confederate secret service.

On October 28, Martin and Headley presented a letter of introduction from secret service commissioner Thompson to one of the city's leading Copperheads, James McMaster, at the *Freeman's Journal* offices on the block-long (now vanished) Tryon Row just below Printing House Square. McMaster was aware that both Dix and Kennedy had agents keeping surveillance on him—he even knew some of them by name—but to Headley he seemed blithely unconcerned to be greeting two Confederate spies. Six foot three, now white of hair and beard, with hawk's eyes, a Roman nose, and a deeply rumbling voice, "everything about him denoted strength of intellect as well as body," Headley recalled. McMaster assured the conspirators that when they set their fires, some fifteen to twenty thousand local Copperheads, armed and organized in secret, would rise up and seize the city. Then Horatio Seymour and other Copperhead governors in the region would secede and establish a New England Confederacy. Like the Wood brothers, McMaster had now crossed over from being vehemently against the war to outright treason.

Martin and Headley also met with Gus McDonald, Larry's brother, and Gus's pretty daughter Katie. Gus had a piano shop at 358 Broadway, a few blocks up from City Hall, where he let the conspirators store their luggage. Then, with nothing else to do, the young Rebel spies spent the next six days like any other tourists, sightseeing in the big city. They caught one of Artemus Ward's comical lectures at Henry Wood's theater on Broadway across from the St. Nicholas Hotel; listened to speeches at Tammany Hall; saw a torchlight parade and rally for the Democratic candidate McClellan, which McClellan himself reviewed from a balcony of the Fifth Avenue Hotel. They even took the ferry over to Brooklyn Heights to hear a Beecher sermon.

They were thunderstruck when Benjamin Butler and his occupying army arrived in the city four days before the elections. Two days later, McMaster told them that the local Copperheads had decided to postpone their revolt. Two days after that, the Rebels glumly watched as Lincoln was reelected and Horatio Seymour voted out. Just as demoralizing, Chicago did not burn. Over the following days it became apparent to the Rebels that McMaster's uprising was as much a chimera as the

Northwest one. Frustrated and disgusted, they decided among themselves to go ahead and burn New York anyway, and they chose Evacuation Day weekend for the deed. Meanwhile they went around to nineteen hotels all over the city, booking rooms under various aliases. Kennedy wryly used the name Stanton as one of his. These hotel rooms would be the sites for their fires.

On Thanksgiving Day, Headley went alone to find the chemist who had secretly prepared their Greek fire. Their basement meeting spot was, ironically, just off Washington Square Park in the Fifteenth Ward, the only ward in the city that voted for Lincoln. No one has ever identified this man, who handed Headley a valise loaded with twelve dozen four-ounce bottles of the incendiary concoction. The next day, Headley met up with the others at a remote cottage near Central Park. That evening they stuffed their pockets and small bags with the little bottles and set off for the first sites on their lists.

It was a clear, cool Friday night, and the city was lively with holiday crowds. Carriages, streetcars, and omnibuses rumbled over the paving stones. Throngs surged up and down sidewalks. Restaurants, theaters, minstrel halls, shops, and taverns were packed.

At 7:20, Headley went into the Astor House and up to the room he had booked.

"After lighting the gas jet I hung the bedclothes loosely on the head-board and piled the chairs, drawers of the bureau and washstand on the bed," he recalled in his book. "Then stuffed some newspapers about among the mass and poured a bottle of turpentine over it all....I opened a bottle carefully and quickly and spilled it on the pile of rubbish. It blazed up instantly and the whole bed seemed to be in flames before I could get out. I locked the door and walked down the hall and stairway to the office, which was fairly crowded with people. I left the key at the office as usual and passed out."

He headed quickly for his next target, the City Hotel. At various other hotels around the city—the Metropolitan and St. Denis, the Fifth Avenue and St. Nicholas, the LaFarge and more—Martin, Kennedy, and the rest of the saboteurs were doing the same. On a sudden impulse, Kennedy limped into Barnum's American Museum and started a small fire there. As black smoke filled hotel hallways and flames danced behind windows, panic struck the crowded streets outside the targeted buildings. Fire bells clanged from all corners of the city, volunteer fire companies and police vans raced in all directions, and screaming patrons poured out of the hotels, while huge throngs stood and gawked.

The conspirators wormed in and out of the crowds to see what effect they'd had. They were disappointed to see that none of the buildings they'd hit was truly ablaze. In most cases, as at St. Alban's, the Greek fire produced a lot of smoke but no real damage. In a few hours all the fires had been dealt with and the panic subsided. New Yorkers were angry and outraged, but showed no more signs of the terror the terrorists had hoped to provoke.

Despondent, Headley trudged to his bed after midnight and didn't wake until early the next afternoon. All the newspapers had the story— and hotel clerks' descriptions of suspicious characters, including Headley. When he and Martin went to McDonald's piano store to get their luggage, Katie stood at the window and waved them away; Superintendent Kennedy's detectives were inside interviewing her father. That evening the nervous conspirators slinked onto a New York Central train to Albany, and from there made it safely back to Toronto.

Reading the morning papers over breakfast, the Booth brothers argued. John took the conspirators' side, arguing that the attack was justified retaliation for Sherman's destruction of Atlanta. Edwin, who had just voted for Lincoln, forbade John from speaking that way in his home ever again.

What John did not tell Edwin was that he had gone to Canada himself a month earlier and most likely had his own meeting with the commissioners. He had conceived a bold plan: He would kidnap Lincoln and take him south, to be released in exchange for the roughly two hundred thousand Confederate POWs held in Union prisons. In one stroke he would rejuvenate the Southern cause and revive the hope of a military victory. From Canada he went to New York City, where, according to biographer James Cross Giblin, he had a secret meeting with a Copperhead arms dealer—possibly the same violin shop owner Fernando Wood had identified—and bought "two rifles, several revolvers, three daggers, and two pairs of handcuffs." He had them shipped to Baltimore. Booth and his co-conspirators in Washington would meet numerous times over the coming months, refining their kidnap plan. Once he even arranged for them to take in a performance at Ford's Theatre from the box where the Lincolns always sat.

Edwin's event had been a great success, raising the handsome sum of $4,000 for Daly's Shakespeare statue. It wouldn't be completed and unveiled until after the war, in 1872. The sculptor, John Quincy Adams Ward, also made the statue of Horace Greeley in City Hall Park.

∼

General Dix and Superintendent Kennedy were mortified that the attack had happened on their watch. Dix issued a flurry of new orders promising that the perpetrators would be executed if captured, repeating his directive that all Southerners in the city must register their names with him, and threatening any hoteliers who allowed unregistered Southerners to stay in their establishments. He even informed Union troops on the border that they had his permission to invade Canada in pursuit of the saboteurs. The War Department immediately instructed him to rescind that order.

More practically, a team of Kennedy's detectives, who had ascertained the names of Martin, Headley, and Robert Cobb Kennedy, raced to Toronto and straight to the Queens Hotel, where they infiltrated the Confederate crowd as effortlessly as the War Department's spies had. They easily duped Larry McDonald, the former New York carriage-maker, into telling them everything he knew about the operation. Nevertheless, Martin and Headley eluded them. They walked across the frozen Detroit River by night and made it back to Kentucky. Martin would later be captured there, Headley never.

Robert Cobb Kennedy was reaching for his pistol when agents subdued him on a train heading south through Michigan. He was brought to Fort Lafayette. From his cell he wrote letters to McMaster and Benjamin Wood, asking each to lend him $1,500 for bail. The jailer he handed the letters to carried them straight to General Dix, who opened and read them before they were delivered. McMaster and Wood, of course, denied knowing the saboteur. Under interrogation, the game and cocky Kennedy admitted he'd come to New York from Canada using the name Stanton as an alias, but denied participating in the attack; he said he'd merely come for a little vacation before seeking a blockade runner to take him back to the South.

His trial before a military tribunal began on January 31, 1865, at Dix's Bleecker Street headquarters. It went quickly. Called to testify, McMaster lied cravenly, again claiming he didn't know the saboteurs and saying he believed the fires had been started by "some half crazy women or noncombatants." Kennedy was convicted and sentenced to hang.

As Kennedy awaited his execution in March, a writer for the *Times* visited him in his cell. It was Joe Howard, the hoaxer who had recently spent his own time locked up in Fort Lafayette. Since his release he'd been freelancing for various publications. "The room in which Kennedy sleeps and lives is an ordinary casement, some twenty by twelve feet in size, with two iron-barred loop-holes facing the Narrows, and a third looking into the court-yard," Howard reported. "The furniture consists of an iron bedstead...two camp chairs and small pine table. A roaring anthracite fire blazed at the far end of the room, by which Capt. Kennedy was standing as we entered." Under sentence of death, Kennedy looked "thin and old and nervous." He now spoke freely of his involvement in the fires, and though he'd written to President Lincoln for a reprieve, he knew there was little hope.

A few weeks earlier, another saboteur for the Canada commission, John Yeats Beall, had been taken from his cell at Fort Lafayette over to Governors Island, where he was hanged on the parade ground outside Fort Columbus. Beall, a Virginia seaman and privateer, had been involved in the failed attempts to rouse a Northwest revolt. In December he'd been caught up in the wide-flung manhunt for the New York saboteurs and brought to New York, where Dix, anxious to reclaim some face, wasted no time having him convicted and sentenced. Lincoln had resisted concerted efforts to grant a pardon.

And now it was Kennedy's turn. He was hanged on March 25 in the Fort Lafayette courtyard, the only one of the New York saboteurs to be executed. Martin was brought to Fort Lafayette and held without trial until 1866. Interestingly, in the 1870s he would move to Brooklyn, run a tobacco warehouse there, and be buried in Green-Wood Cemetery in 1901. Headley enjoyed a long and peaceful postwar life, writing several books and serving as Kentucky's secretary of state in the 1890s. He was ninety when he died in Los Angeles in 1930. Gus McDonald was briefly jailed but suffered no other consequences for having helped them; neither did McMaster.

CHAPTER 37

Last Acts

All those goddamned Booths are crazy.

—*Edwin Forrest*

In the first three months of 1865, events rolled swiftly toward a conclusion everyone now knew to be inevitable. At the end of January 1865, after intense backroom deal-cutting, Congress approved the Thirteenth Amendment abolishing slavery. In February, Lincoln and Stanton traveled to Hampton Roads, site of the *Monitor* and *Merrimac* battle, to confer with a Confederate peace commission. With the war nearly won, Lincoln was under no constraint to offer terms and the commissioners trudged back to Richmond empty-handed. That month Union troops took Charleston, where it all began. Grant hounded the tattered remnants of Lee's army.

Lincoln's second inauguration took place on Saturday, March 4. Walt Whitman went to the grand reception at the White House afterward. "Never before was such a compact jam in front of the White House—all the grounds fill'd, and away out to the spacious sidewalks," he recorded. "I was there, as I took a notion to go—was in the rush inside with the crowd—surged along the passage-ways, the blue and other rooms, and through the great east room. Crowds of country people, some very funny. Fine music from the Marine band, off in a side place. I saw Mr. Lincoln, drest all in black, with white kid gloves and a claw-hammer coat, receiving, as in duty bound, shaking hands, looking very disconsolate, and as if he would give anything to be somewhere else." Lincoln was said to shake at least five thousand hands that day. Guards barred obvious prostitutes, criminals—and Negroes, including Frederick Douglass. He got word in to the president, who had him admitted.

The next day, seemingly the whole city of New York turned out for a Union Jubilee. One estimate put the crowd at one million, which was more than the entire population of the city. Never mind that so many New Yorkers had never liked Lincoln, never voted for him, had sometimes been in open revolt against him. The war was nearly over, and besides, it was a great day for a parade, a bright and balmy Sunday. The *Times* said the parade that snaked around and around the streets was seven miles long. It included thousands of blue-coated soldiers, soldiers' orphans, hundreds of red-shirted firemen, sailors carrying models of the *Monitor* and a fully rigged sailing ship, workers from all the different industries in the city, choral clubs, every dignitary in the city in his black frock coat (General Dix, Judge Daly, and others delivered speeches), flags, banners (including one with Dix's famous line, "If any one attempts to lower the American flag, shoot him on the spot"), coaches and wagons, howitzers and other guns, some stuffed animals from Barnum's museum, a few live elephants and camels, and fireworks to finish it off. The mood was entirely festive, as though the previous four years were already passing from memory.

Jefferson and Varina Davis fled Richmond with their children a month later, on Sunday, April 2; Union troops occupied it the next day. Alf Waud was at Appomattox the following Sunday when Lee surrendered to Grant. Waud drew an affecting portrait of the defeated but still proud general riding away on his white charger. Waud would continue to draw for *Harper's* for several more years, traveling through the devastated South and the West, widely recognized and warmly greeted. He designed the invitation to President Grant's 1869 inauguration ball and was one of the star guests. From the mid-1870s on he would freelance for various publishers from a studio at 896 Broadway above Union Square. In April 1891, while touring Southern battlefields for a book project, he took sick and died in Marietta, Georgia, at the age of sixty-two. Although he had many friends in New York and family in New Jersey, his remains were not sent north; he lies under a simple stone in Marietta's St. James Episcopal Cemetery.

When Lee surrendered, Greeley published an editorial titled "Magnanimity in Triumph," urging no reprisals against Confederates:

> In behalf of our country, burdened with a war which is still cost-
> ing her three millions of dollars per day, and which has carried
> mourning to every fireside—in behalf of all downtrodden, suffer-
> ing humanity, we entreat the President promptly to do and dare in
> the cause of magnanimity. What we ask is that the President say,
> in effect, "Slavery having, through rebellion, committed suicide,
> let the North and the South unite to bury its carcass and then
> clasp hands across the grave."

Raymond's *Times* disagreed, arguing that "the hanging of Jeff Davis is
called for.... To let Jeff Davis and his confederates go unpunished would
not be so much an amnesty for the past as a plenary indulgence for future
treason."

A jubilant, drunken crowd gathered on the White House lawn on
Monday, April 10. Lincoln—who Greeley said had been looking "care-
ploughed, tempest-tossed and weather-beaten"—promised them a speech
soon, and asked that the band with them play his favorite song, "Dixie."

He read his speech the next day, standing at the tall window above the
White House portico, addressing a large and festive crowd. John Wilkes
Booth and a co-conspirator were in that crowd. He had appeared as an
actor for the last time on March 18, at Ford's Theatre. It was a benefit for
his friend John McCullough, an Irish-American actor who had developed
paresis, a debilitating condition often associated with syphilis, the great
scourge of the age before penicillin. When Lee surrendered to Grant at
Appomattox, John Wilkes's plan to kidnap the president became obsolete.
He decided to assassinate him instead.

Lincoln sounded nothing like the triumphant leader of a victorious people as he carefully read his speech, dropping each sheet as he finished it.
Tad, kneeling beside him, collected the fallen pages. After thanks that the
conflict was ending, Lincoln launched immediately into a warning that
"the re-inauguration of the national authority—reconstruction—which
has had a large share of thought from the first" would be "fraught with
great difficulty." He did not call for universal suffrage for black males, as
the Radicals had hoped. Noting that it was "unsatisfactory to some that
the elective franchise is not given to the colored man," he said, "I would
myself prefer that it were now conferred on the very intelligent, and on
those who serve our cause as soldiers."

"That means nigger citizenship," Booth growled to his companion. "Now, by God, I'll put him through. That is the last speech he will ever make."

He made good on his word. That Friday, April 14—Good Friday—he sauntered into Ford's Theatre. Laura Keene was finishing a two-week run there, and had decided to end with a special benefit performance of a play everyone knew and loved, *Our American Cousin*. The Lincolns had tickets for a different theater, but when Mary heard of the special performance she changed their plans.

Keene was waiting for her act 3 entrance when there was a commotion out front. Booth had shot the president behind the ear with a derringer and slashed his bodyguard with a knife. Charles A. Leale, a twenty-three-year-old New Yorker, was seated in the orchestra section. "I saw a man in mid-air leaping from the President's box to the stage, brandishing in his hand a drawn dagger," he would write almost half a century later. "His spur caught in the American flag festooned in front of the box, causing him to stumble when he struck the stage, and he fell on his hands and knees. He quickly regained the erect posture and hopped across the stage, flourishing his dagger, clearing the stage before him and dragging the foot of the leg, which was subsequently found to be broken, [and] he disappeared behind the scene on the opposite side of the stage. Then followed cries that the President had been murdered, interspersed with cries of 'Kill the murderer!' 'Shoot him!' etc., from different parts of the building." Others in the audience said they heard Booth shout Brutus's line from *Julius Caesar*, "Sic semper tyrannis!"

Keene strode up to the footlights and urged calm. There were calls for a doctor. Leale was a brand-new army surgeon who had graduated from New York's Bellevue Hospital Medical College only six weeks earlier. He jumped from his seat and forced his way through the crowd and into the Lincolns' box. He eased the stricken president to the floor. Asked to bring some water, Keene made her way up to the box. Mary Lincoln was moaning in grief. There was blood everywhere. Keene knelt on the floor and cradled the president's head in her lap, bathing his temples with water. Leale and others carried Lincoln out of the theater to a house across the street. The young doctor would sit holding the president's hand through the night, until he breathed his last early the next morning. Meanwhile, Keene wandered in a daze down to the theater's lobby, her dress and hands covered in Lincoln's blood.

Not far away, Booth's co-conspirator Lewis Powell entered William Seward's home. He pistol-whipped Seward's son Frederick and stabbed the father repeatedly, but failed to assassinate him. A third conspirator, George Atzerodt, was detailed to kill Vice President Johnson but lost heart and fled.

Ford's Theatre closed that night and wouldn't reopen for a century. Keene and her troupe were briefly detained and questioned. In New York, when the actors John McCullough and Edwin Forrest heard the news of the assassination, McCullough said he didn't believe it.

"Well I do," Forrest snapped. "All those goddamned Booths are crazy."

In Cincinnati, where Junius was performing, an angry crowd threatened his life in the lobby of his hotel. Edwin was in Boston, starring as the black-caped villain in an old potboiler called *The Iron Chest*. He was in his dressing room after taking multiple curtain calls when he heard the news. He later said he felt like he had been hit on the head with a hammer. Despite John's ravings over the years, Edwin had no premonition of this. The manager of the theater canceled the rest of the show's run. Federal marshals questioned Edwin and inspected his luggage, then allowed him to board a midnight train for New York on Easter Sunday night. He arrived in New York before dawn and went straight to 19th Street, where he hid with family for the next few weeks. Hundreds of letters of hate mail poured in. "Revolvers are loaded with which to shoot you down." "Your house will be burnt." "Your life will be the penalty if you tarry heare [*sic*] 48 hours longer."

Lincoln was still on his deathbed when Stanton organized a military commission to investigate the attacks and identify the conspirators. They interviewed a character actor named Samuel Knapp Chester, who had just played King Claudius in Edwin's smash one-hundred-night run of *Hamlet* at the Winter Garden that ended in March. Chester had been friendly with Edwin's brother for more than a decade. In December 1864 or early January 1865 (Chester was unsure of the date), John Wilkes picked him up at his boardinghouse at 45 Grove Street just off Bleecker Street. They walked down to one of several English-themed ale houses on Houston Street, the House of Lords, at Houston and Crosby Streets. (Another was called the House of Commons.) There they spent "I suppose an hour, eating and drinking," then moved on to the Revere House on the corner of Broadway and Houston Street, where they drank some more and ate oysters. As they were walking back toward Chester's boardinghouse, Booth "told me then that he was in a large conspiracy to capture the heads of the Government, including the President, and take them to Richmond." Chester said that Booth pressed him for half an hour to join the conspiracy, offering him the considerable sum of $3,000. When Chester refused, Booth swore him to secrecy, warning that "if I attempted to betray them, I would be hunted down through life."

Chester said that Booth visited him in New York again on Friday, April 7, one week before the assassination. They went again to the House of Lords. Booth told Chester that he'd been at the inauguration, and rued not killing Lincoln then, but according to Chester he said nothing about his actual assassination plans.

Chester went on with his long acting career; on retiring he would live his last sixteen years in the Actors' Fund Home on Staten Island, where he died at the age of eighty-seven in 1921.

Henry Ward Beecher was not at Plymouth Church on Good Friday 1865. He was in the newly occupied city of Charleston. But he'd brought some of Plymouth with him.

After Charleston surrendered in February, Stanton had written to Reverend Beecher and Major General Anderson, asking them to lead a ceremony at Fort Sumter on the second Friday in April, to mark the four-year anniversary of the first shelling. It was another way of thanking Beecher for his England speeches. As news of the trip got around, Beecher biographer Debby Applegate writes, it seemed that "half of Brooklyn and most of Plymouth Church" clamored to be taken along. Theodore Tilton, the Howards and Bowens and Beaches, William Lloyd Garrison, assorted politicians and journalists sailed from New York on two steamers on April 8. They were at sea when Lee surrendered to Grant the next day and didn't get the news until they landed.

They found Sumter largely in ruins. On Good Friday, Anderson raised the torn and tattered flag he'd brought to New York with him in 1861. Beecher delivered a long speech, calling it a "solemn and joyful day" and rejoicing, "[The] long night is ended! And for this returning day we have come from afar, to rejoice and give thanks. No more war. No more accursed secession! *No more slavery, that spawned them both!*" He went on for more than an hour, sometimes allowing his bellicose side to show, sternly warning "peace and protection to loyalty; humiliation and pains to traitors....There may be pardon, but no concession. There may be amnesty and oblivion, but no honeyed compromises. The nation today has peace for the peaceful, and war for the turbulent. The only condition of submission is *to submit!*...One nation, under one Government, without slavery, has been ordained, and shall stand."

Some two thousand local blacks attended the ceremony. They'd been organized by James Redpath. As a special for the *Tribune* and the *Boston Daily Journal* he'd entered Charleston when it fell, and the Union military commander of the occupied city asked him to be the new superintendent of public schools. Redpath intended to fully integrate the system, but after white teachers and parents protested, he separated the classes racially. Still, he soon had a hundred teachers, white and black, instructing students who were, as he put it, "from six to sixty." He was also helping to start a black orphanage—the Col. Shaw Orphan House—and was, most controversially, arming and training a black "home guard."

Two weeks after the Beecher group's visit, some ten thousand Charlestonians, mostly black, would attend a Redpath-organized event at the Charleston racecourse. During the war it had held Union POWs, and 250 of them had been buried in mass grave trenches. Redpath and a committee of local blacks put a white picket fence around the graves, and on May 1 conducted a service that would be emulated around the country as it evolved into Memorial Day. Whites forced Redpath out not long after that and he returned to the North.

After the ceremony at the fort, Beecher's group went into bombed and burned Charleston, a charred husk of the city it once was. They had a grand dinner, followed by a ball and fireworks over the harbor. Five hundred miles north, President Lincoln was assassinated as they partied. Word flashed by telegraph around the rest of the country, but in Charleston and elsewhere in the South the occupying Federals restricted wire access and impounded the weekend newspapers, lest the news trigger a new uprising. It was a couple of days before Beecher and the New Yorkers heard it.

They returned immediately to find New York and Brooklyn gloomily quiet and draped in black. At Plymouth, Beecher preached a sermon comparing Lincoln to Moses, who led his people to the promised land but could not enter it with them. Recalling what it felt like to hear the news, he said, "The blow brought not a sharp pang. It was so terrible that at first it stunned sensibility. Citizens were like men awakened at midnight by an earthquake, and bewildered to find everything they were accustomed to trust wavering and falling."

Whitman was staying with his family in Brooklyn when the news hit. In January he'd finally gotten a government job, as a clerk in the Department of the Interior's Office of Indian Affairs. By his own admission he didn't work at it too hard, and was home on his first extended break in April. On Saturday, April 15, he wrote in a notebook:

> All Broadway is black with mourning—the facades of the houses are festooned with black—great flags with wide & heavy fringes of dead black, give a pensive effect—towards noon the sky darkened & began to rain. Drip, drip, & heavy moist black weather....
>
> Lincoln's death—black, black, black—as you look toward the sky—long broad black like great serpents slowly undulating in every direction.

He immediately wrote the first of his Lincoln elegies, "Hushed Be the Camps To-Day," for insertion into his new book of verses about the war, *Drum-Taps*, which was already at the printer. Walt's wartime experiences, and now Lincoln's murder, profoundly changed his poetic voice. No more barbaric yawp or the visionary leaps of the original *Leaves*; the poet of "Camps," and his two better-known Lincoln elegies "O Captain! My Captain!" and "When Lilacs Last in the Dooryard Bloomed," would be a far more conventional, Emersonian versifier.

⌒

Some New York Copperheads reacted to Lincoln's murder not with grief but with feelings of vindication and satisfaction. Those few who were foolish enough to express these feelings publicly bore the brunt of other New Yorkers' anger. Passengers dumped a man over the side of a Brooklyn ferry for "disloyal and offensive" remarks. A passing boat plucked him out of the East River. A fellow they called Southern George, standing at the corner of Pearl and Chatham Streets, was heard to growl, "Old Abe, the son of a bitch, is dead and he ought to have been killed long ago." A passing Metropolitan knocked him down, then hauled him to jail, where he spent the next six months. An Irish cop "made vulgar comments to fellow officers," who arrested him. He resigned from the force.

The Saturday night after the assassination, three local toughs burst into Castleton Hill, the Gardiners' home on Staten Island, armed with clubs and swords. It was no secret that Julia Gardiner Tyler, still a proud and defiant Confederate, had been living there since the end of 1863. She could have gotten a pass north earlier, but refused to take the required oath of allegiance to the Union. Instead, she had boarded an illegal blockade runner that carried her to Bermuda, after which she sailed on a British ship to New York. She fell in with a small group of Copperhead women on Staten Island, distributing pamphlets that called for peace, shipping care packages to Southern friends, and stumping for McClellan. In the spring of 1864, Union forces once again surged up the Virginia Peninsula, and this time the kid gloves were off. Julia read reports of Negro troops under "Beast" Butler's command ransacking Sherwood Forest and other plantations, jailing or murdering some owners, and turning the homes and land over to the freed slaves. She wrote angry letters of protest to Lincoln as "Mrs. (Ex-President) Tyler." She was equally distressed to learn that her Virginia niece Maria Tyler had married "a little Dutchman" from the occupying Union army, Private John Kick of the New York Mounted Rifles. The entire Tyler family disowned the girl.

The ruffians who broke into Castleton Hill demanded that Julia surrender a Confederate flag she was widely rumored to have displayed in the house. There was none, but they ransacked the house anyway. The papers ran unsympathetic reports of the little fracas, and for some time afterward the Gardiners received anonymous letters threatening to burn the house down.

~

Defiant to the very end and beyond, Confederate colonel Charles Augustus Lafayette Lamar was shot and killed by Union soldiers on a street in Columbus, Georgia, on Sunday, April 16. It was exactly one week since Lee's surrender at Appomattox. Soon afterward, Charles Dana at the War Department ordered the arrest of Charles's father, Gazaway, in Savannah, on suspicion of his having conspired with Jefferson Davis and other Confederate leaders in Lincoln's assassination. Gazaway Lamar did have some cause to wish Lincoln dead. When Sherman occupied Savannah in December 1864 he sent Lincoln a "Christmas present" of twenty-five thousand bales of cotton seized on its waterfront—most of it Gazaway Lamar's stash. The old man was furious. No evidence of a conspiracy materialized, however, and he was released after three months. He was soon arrested again for trying to hide what was left of his cotton from the occupying military authorities. A military court convicted him and briefly imprisoned him once more. He would spend the rest of his life pursuing lawsuits against the federal government, sometimes with the help of New York law firms, and in 1874 would win a half-million-dollar judgment. He died six months later.

CHAPTER 38

A "Hippodrome of Sorrow"

On the morning of Monday, April 24, Lincoln made his last visit to the city that had been more help and more trouble to him than any other in the Union. A vast throng lined the Hudson River waterfront to watch the ferry *Jersey City* bring his coffin over from the train terminal there to the dock at the foot of Desbrosses Street. They were as silent as they'd been the last time he'd visited four years earlier. Some of the women wore full widow's weeds, and everyone wore at least a black crepe armband or one of the memorial badges sold by enterprising street vendors. Men and boys bared their heads and women quietly wept as mournful church bells tolled and cannons boomed, their white smoke rolling out over the choppy water.

The city had been preparing all week. A committee headed up by Tweed, Tammany bigwigs, and various prominent businessmen organized a huge procession. Every building from the grandest hotel to the humblest hovel wore some kind of mournful decoration, "crape or black folds or drapery or black muslin, rosettes, sable emblems," Carl Sandburg would write. "In store fronts and home windows were busts of Lincoln and little paper monuments resembling marble. Medals and plaques of bronze and copper were common, his face outlined on each." A species of grief industry had grown up during the war, mass-producing such memento mori items for retail. Over the entrance of Barnum's museum was a large black urn of smoking incense, with the words "LINCOLN" and *Dulce et decorum est pro patria mori.*" Banners hung everywhere, citing scripture or Shakespeare ("Oh, the pity of it, Iago—the pity of it"). One quoted the new pennies that had appeared in 1864, which used "In God We Trust" for the first time. Another simply read "Death to Assassins."

Lincoln's casket had ridden across the river in a modest hearse; he'd be transferred to a much fancier one for the city's official farewell to him the next day. The 7th Regiment in their crisp grays formed an honor guard around the hearse. They had not fought a single battlefield engagement during the war, but when it came to marching through the streets, no city unit looked finer. General Dix and other officers led the way. The contingent who'd ridden on the seven-car funeral train from Washington came behind the hearse in carriages. Among them were Lincoln's friends Ward Lamon and General David Hunter and his aide John Hay, all of whom had ridden on his train from Springfield to Washington four years earlier. Behind them Mayor Gunther and city dignitaries trod on foot. The procession followed a path up to Canal Street, over to Broadway, and down to City Hall.

City Hall wore black ribbons from the top of its cupola to the ground. Over its entrance a banner proclaimed, "THE NATION MOURNS." On the steps a thousand members of local German musical societies sang the towering "Pilgrims' Chorus" from *Tannhäuser* as the coffin was carried in. The coffin was placed on an elaborate altar and the lid opened. Then some 150,000 viewers, in two very long lines, shuffled past straight through Monday afternoon, straight through the night, right up to noon Tuesday, when another 300,000 were said still to be waiting. Many mentioned with dismay how sunken and shriveled the president looked. Brooklyn's Dr. Holmes had not done the embalming.

A little before one o'clock Tuesday afternoon, the undertaker for the City of New York, a man named Peter Relyea, brought the new hearse to be used in the day's procession. He'd spent the last three days working on it around the clock, out on the street at the corner of East Broadway and Grand. It "just about paralyzed all beholders with its magnificence." It was immense, fourteen feet long and seven wide, and glistening black, with glass walls. Relyea had trimmed the inside with white satin. From the ceiling a golden eagle hung over the casket. Outside on the roof he had affixed a miniature "gold and white temple of Liberty with a half-masted small flag fluttering." Other flags and black plumes fluttered around it. Sixteen horses wearing black cloaks and hoods pulled the grandly gloomy vehicle, each led by a black groom.

The casket was carried out to this enormous catafalque, and the huge procession that Tweed and company had planned slowly unwound. It comprised an astounding 160,000 participants. The whole city, even the bars, had been closed, and the whole population turned out, a sea of humanity that swamped Manhattan below 14th Street. Most contemporary estimates put the crowd at half a million. Few of these people had ever voted for Lincoln. Many had despised him, a good number of them had rioted against his policies, and some had plotted treason against him. A few had even colluded in or at least kept silent about John Wilkes Booth's plans.

So why had this largely hostile city, this city of sedition, massed to pay him their last regards? Historians tend to reason that his murder, the first presidential assassination in American history, shocked and frightened them into this display of respect. A sense of guilt, they say, may also have played a part. In his 1929 *Myths After Lincoln*, Lloyd Lewis, a Chicago newspaperman and friend of Sandburg, took a more cynical point of view. He derided the "show" New York put on as a "hippodrome of sorrow, much of it pure ostentation," "half circus, half heartache." It was a warm, soft spring day; everybody was off work and had nothing else to do. Nineteenth-century New Yorkers loved parades and processions and would turn out en masse at the slightest provocation. In this instance, morbid curiosity may have played as large a part as guilt.

General Dix rode at the head of the procession; Admiral Farragut and the ancient General Winfield Scott were also present. Every city unit of army, navy, and marines marched. Whitman's brother George marched with Brooklyn's 51st. Behind them snaked a seemingly endless line of groups representing all the city's businesses, lodges, labor unions, and civic organizations. "The Henry Clay Debating Society, the German Bakers, the Turner Sharpshooters, the German Carvers, Hose Companies galore, Temperance Cadets, women's clubs, all were in line hoisting mottoes," Lewis wrote. "The children of Brooklyn's Fifth Ward waved the legend 'The hand of the assassin has entwined the name of Abraham Lincoln in a wreath of immortality.'" Some groups had built mourning floats.

Two hundred black New Yorkers brought up the very rear of the line. More had wanted to participate, but Tweed and Tammany, fearing it might set off new rioting, at first banned them. Secretary Stanton, who had the ultimate say, telegraphed General Dix that "no discrimination regarding color should be exercised." Dix provided the black marchers with an armed escort, but it was unnecessary. White onlookers applauded politely as they went by.

Crowds lined the procession route in "a dense human hedge twelve or fifteen feet deep" according to the *Times*. Thousands more, including a six-year-old Teddy Roosevelt, leaned out of every window and watched from every rooftop. Some homeowners and landlords along the route posted handbills outside their doors, charging admission of up to forty dollars; many had removed the window casements so that more heads could crowd the openings. Viewers hung from every lamppost and tree.

Gus Schurmann was in the crowd. He would grow up to hold various civil service jobs, be active in veterans' groups like the Grand Army of the Republic and the Mozart Veterans Association, and serve as the president of the city's Republican Party. He died of tuberculosis in 1905 at the age of fifty-six and was buried in Woodlawn Cemetery. A maker of tin soldiers for collectors recently offered one of Gus as a little bugler.

All over the city, through the whole long march, church bells tolled and cannons boomed. The procession brought the coffin up to the same Hudson River Railroad depot on 30th Street where President-elect Lincoln had entered the city four years earlier. At 4:15 the Lincoln Special, hung with black bunting, chugged out of the station, bound for Albany.

～

John Wilkes Booth died early the next morning. He had fully expected to be cheered for ridding the land of the tyrant Lincoln. Instead, he'd found himself on the lam, hunted and hated, with a bounty on his head. Before dawn on April 26 a detachment of the 16th New York Volunteer Cavalry found him holed up in a Virginia tobacco barn. When he wouldn't come out, they set fire to the barn. They were under strict orders to take him alive; Stanton wanted a trial.

But one man who rode with the 16th answered to a higher authority: Sergeant Thomas "Boston" Corbett, the castrated fanatic who'd upset the businessmen at the Fulton Street prayer meetings before the war. When the war started, he had signed up with the 12th New York Militia—the same regiment Frank Barlow had originally joined, led by Colonel Dan

Butterfield. Carrying his Bible with him everywhere, Corbett continued to make himself a nuisance as he ranted at his fellow soldiers and even Colonel Butterfield about their ungodly speech and actions. He was court-martialed but reenlisted, and was serving with the 16th Cavalry when he was taken prisoner in 1864. He nearly died of scurvy and starvation in the infamous Andersonville prison, from which he escaped twice and was twice recaptured, before being released in an exchange.

On the morning of April 26, Sergeant Corbett aimed a Colt pistol through a crack in the tobacco barn wall and, flagrantly disobeying orders, shot John Wilkes in the neck behind the ear. He later told the *Times* that "it seemed to me that God had directed it, for apparently it was just where he had shot the President." Booth was dragged from the burning barn and died shortly after, muttering, "Useless...Useless."

The officers on the scene arrested Corbett. Secretary Stanton was livid with him. But Corbett was hailed as a hero throughout the North, and Stanton bowed to public sentiment. "The rebel is dead," he said in pardoning Corbett. "The patriot lives."

Corbett returned to New York City, where he was feted as an avenging angel, had his portrait done by Mathew Brady, then went back to his evangelizing. Over the next decade he would wander restlessly from one place to another, made increasingly paranoid by threatening mail from die-hard Confederates. In the 1880s, working as a doorman for the Kansas state legislature, he pulled a gun on legislators he may have believed were mocking God. He was confined to an insane asylum but escaped, to no one knows where, although there were sightings of him in various places for many years. It's possible he went to Mexico to live out his final years in obscurity. Another theory puts him in Minnesota, where he may have perished in the Great Hinckley Fire of 1894.

Union troops caught Jefferson and Varina Davis in Georgia on May 10. Just as they had when Lincoln sneaked into Washington in 1861, newspapers and cartoonists in the North made rich sport of the story that Davis was wearing ladies' clothing when captured. It was Varina's fault. As the soldiers approached, she threw a woman's coat and shawl over her husband as a disguise. (Barnum was soon displaying in his museum what he claimed was this very outfit.) She also probably saved his life. When the soldiers accosted them, she grabbed Davis's arm as he reached for his pistol. Had he pulled it he would almost certainly have been shot, as the soldiers had orders to take him dead or alive. They took him in irons to Fort Monroe. Greeley called for an orderly trial; the *Times* wanted a quick execution. The debate would drag on for two years while Davis was held without bail or trial; Greeley would lead the effort that ultimately sprung him.

That June, in the Traveler's Club on Fifth Avenue at 14th Street, Thomas Francis Meagher attended a lecture on the brand-new Montana Territory and thought he heard a chance for a fresh start. He needed one. He ended the war with his once glittering military career seriously blemished. By appealing directly to Lincoln he had finally managed to get a backwater command late in 1864. It lasted only a few weeks. He was drinking heavily and created such confusion and disorder that Grant removed him. In New York, the Dalys and other leaders of the Irish community had turned irrevocably against him. He needed to aim his life in a new direction, and like many thousands of others he now thought that direction was westward ho.

On July 4 the surviving six hundred members of the Irish Brigade led a parade from 23rd Street up to 42nd and then down to Union Square. The untouched 7th marched with them, along with many other city militia units that, unlike the Irish Brigade, had seen little or no action in the war. Robert Nugent rode at the head of the Irishmen. Thomas Francis Meagher was nowhere to be seen. He left New York for good that month and was in Montana by the fall. It was the lawless, wildest West. The discovery of gold there during the war had drawn a motley assortment of whites into what had been Indian land. By 1865 it was home to some thirty thousand bandits, vigilantes, prospectors, die-hard Rebels, a handful of U.S. cavalry scattered in remote forts, even Fenians. They were generally and often violently hostile to one another, to the Indians, and pretty soon to Meagher as well. With the dilatory territorial governor spending most of his time back east, Meagher became acting governor. He tried his hand at negotiating treaties with the Indians; when that failed, he organized a militia to force them into compliance. He failed at that as well. He tried to organize the rough and wide-flung citizenry to apply for statehood, and failed.

On the evening of July 1, 1867, he went over the rail of a steamboat and the swift Missouri River carried him away. His body was never found. Some thought he had been pushed by one of the many enemies he'd made in less than two years out west. Others said he was drunk. He was forty-three.

~

Edwin Booth stayed out of the public eye for the rest of 1865. In January 1866 he returned to the Winter Garden as Hamlet. The *Herald* expressed outrage that the brother of Lincoln's assassin would show his face, but most of the other papers were supportive. The theater was packed to the gaslights on opening night, and when the moody Dane first appeared in act 1, scene 2 the entire audience stood and applauded. Tears in his eyes, Booth bowed deeply.

When the Winter Garden was gutted by fire in 1867, Booth decided to build his own theater. The opulent Booth's Theatre opened at the southeast corner of Sixth Avenue and 23rd Street in 1869. It was a great artistic and popular triumph at first, but Booth outspent his box-office receipts on lavish productions and lost the space to bankruptcy in 1874. A few years later the building was converted into a dry goods store.

Booth continued to act for other producers, and his fame only rose. He shared the stage with a young man named Maurice Barrymore, patriarch of the acting family. He toured the country, traveling by private train, hailed as the greatest Shakespearean alive, packing houses where ticket prices went as high as one hundred dollars. The one city where he refused to perform was Washington. In the South, people mostly seemed interested in seeing John Wilkes's brother. In Mobile he got a letter from Boston Corbett, asking for free tickets. Edwin groaned and sent them. Performing as Richard II in Chicago on Shakespeare's birthday in 1879, Booth gave in to a sudden urge to stand while delivering a soliloquy he usually recited sitting down. As he rose, a bullet ripped by him right where he'd been seated. Another missed him as well. A dry goods clerk from St. Louis had fired two pistol shots at him from the balcony. Booth claimed his second sight had saved him. The shooter was a mad celebrity stalker.

In 1888, Booth would move to the capacious Greek Revival town house at 16 Gramercy Park South. Putting his wealthy neighbors' noses out of joint, he dedicated the first two floors to the Players Club, a gathering place for men of artistic and literary bent, and the Gilded Age industrialists and politicians who liked to drink with them. Women weren't admitted as members until a hundred years later. Early members included Mark Twain, Grover Cleveland, Nikola Tesla, Astors, Carnegies, and Vanderbilts. William Tecumseh Sherman also joined. He moved to New York after retiring from the army in 1884 and was a devoted patron of the arts. He would die in the city in 1891. Booth presided over club affairs, lived upstairs, and died in 1893 in a room the club still preserves as it was in his day. In 1918 the club donated the statue of Booth as Hamlet that stands in Gramercy Park.

PART III

After

City of Gilt

CHAPTER 39

The Postwar Boom

With the grieving for Lincoln behind them, Northerners returned to the problem of how to treat the vanquished South. Democrats were for letting bygones be bygones and allowing the South to reintegrate into the nation, preserving all its old ways, with the sole exception of slavery. Republicans, especially the Radicals, wanted to seize the opportunity to reconstruct the South, dismantling the plantation system, disenfranchising the leaders of the rebellion, and giving all black males the right to vote and participate in government.

Inheriting a mantle of "Accidency," President Andrew Johnson was also conflicted on how to proceed. He'd grown up dirt poor and functionally illiterate in a log cabin in North Carolina. He despised the old plantation aristocracy, whom he blamed for causing the war, but also deeply mistrusted the Northern elite. A former slave-owner and unregenerate white supremacist, he could accept the end of slavery but was dead set against black equality or black male suffrage. As a longtime states' rightist he wanted to let Southern states plot their own courses back into the nation rather than allow the vengeful Radicals to run roughshod over them. It was soon evident that he and the Radicals were on a collision course. He needed all the friends he could muster as he resisted a Congress where Republicans held a three-to-one dominance.

Dan Sickles was one of those friends. They'd known each other since their days in Congress. In 1865, Johnson sent Dan with seven thousand federal troops to oversee Reconstruction in North and South Carolina. Carolinians were glad and relieved to see Sickles; they remembered him as a friend to the South before the war. He set himself up in Charleston, once the defiant birthplace of rebellion, now ruined. Its harbor, with Fort Sumter flying the same U.S. flag it had displayed in April 1861, was idled. Many of its shops were boarded up. Former Confederate soldiers roamed its dusty streets. Outside of town, untended plantations grew weeds. Sickles showed his flair for leadership and politicking as he toiled to get the area reorganized and back to work.

Meanwhile, the Radicals, led by Sumner in the Senate, kept pressing for black civil and voting rights. In states like South Carolina, where whites were the numerical minority, the prospect of being politically ruled by former slaves was their worst nightmare. At their mildest, whites argued that their former slaves, whom they'd kept illiterate and uneducated, were unprepared as yet for enfranchisement. Sickles agreed, writing to Stanton that "Mr. Sumner would not be in a hurry to confer Negro suffrage if he could see the plantation Negroes and thus Comprehend how hopelessly they lack the Capacity for political franchises." Other whites, joining hooded guerrilla groups like the Klan and the Regulators, turned to terrorist tactics. This Dan could not abide.

His Carolina honeymoon was over by 1866. He declared martial law, made numerous arrests, and banned the carrying of firearms even by law enforcement officials, many of whom supported the vigilantes. As he grew more hot-tempered and autocratic, "King Sickles" alienated his former Southern friends. Insubordinate as ever, he fought with Washington as well. When vigilantes killed three of his soldiers in 1867, four white men were convicted in one of his military courts. They appealed to the U.S. District Court judge for South Carolina, who issued a writ of habeas corpus. Sickles ignored it. The judge bumped the matter upstairs to Johnson, who ordered Sickles to respond. Sickles ignored him too. Johnson already had his hands full dealing with a Congress that was openly at war with him. Republicans passed the Fourteenth Amendment over his objections in 1866, and swept the midterm elections that year, rendering his veto power moot. He didn't need his old pal Dan adding to his troubles. Growling one of the most cutting of all the insults ever hurled at Sickles—"A conceited cuckold is an abomination in the sight of God"— Johnson fired him.

Teresa died that year. Neglected by her husband and shunned by everyone else, she simply faded away. She was only thirty-one. Her funeral was at the Church of St. Joseph in Greenwich Village, where singers from

Lorenzo Da Ponte's opera house had sung for the dedication ceremony in 1829. Sickles took over the parenting of Laura, who was thirteen. He'd do a poor job of it, alienating her over the years and eventually driving her to drink.

New York's business community, not surprisingly, tended to support Johnson's conciliatory attitude toward the South. The end of the war had come as a jolt to the city's economy, though much more so for the city's workers and poor than for their bosses and landlords. Businesses and manufacturers of all sorts, from shipbuilders to bakers to shoemakers to stables, which had been pumped up to produce war products on federal funding, abruptly cut back. Close to three thousand shipyard workers quickly lost their jobs, as did thousands of others who'd done war work. Support for soldiers' widows and orphans ended as the relief agencies shut down. Many were simply thrown out on the streets to fend for themselves. Veterans who'd lost an arm or a leg in the fighting were sent back to the city as the military hospitals shut down; many of them ended up on the streets as well, unable to find jobs. They made sad spectacles all over the city, begging for change and scraps. Muggings, robberies, and other attendant crimes took a sharp rise.

As soon as the war ended, the city was glutted with war surplus. Horses, wagons, and all manner of other military goods went on the auction block at fire-sale prices. For a while the East River was clotted to impassability by all the naval vessels that had been brought back to the city to be auctioned off or scrapped.

In a sense, the end of the war made Mathew Brady's battlefield photographs war surplus as well. He had borrowed and spent a fortune to keep twenty-two photography teams working through the war. Now no one wanted to look at their work and be reminded of the carnage. Brady's hopes that the government would buy his enormous cache of war photos would go unanswered for a decade. Facing debts he couldn't repay, he laid off most of his staff and stored his thousands of glass negatives in warehouses in New York and Washington. Many would be sold over the next few years to pay the storage fees; some went to people who used them as greenhouse panes with odd negative images on them fading away in the sunlight. An exhibition at the New-York Historical Society in 1866 drew lackluster crowds. A generation of younger, more energetic men whom he'd inspired, including Alexander Gardner, photographed the next great chapter in American civilization, the opening of the West.

Brady would declare bankruptcy in 1871. In 1875, Congress finally awarded him $25,000, but it was too little too late. He sank into poverty and obscurity. Mark Twain looked him up in 1891 and discussed the idea of publishing a book of prints, but nothing came of it. In 1895, Brady was struck down by a cart as he crossed a street in the city. He faded away in a cheap rooming house on East 10th Street, and died penniless in a hospital charity ward in January 1896. Veterans of the 7th Regiment paid for his funeral. His body was sent to the Congressional Cemetery in Washington, where the mason who carved his small stone mistakenly gave the year of death as 1895.

The shoddy aristocracy and war profiteers, the industrialists and capitalists and Wall Street sharpers all came out of the war flush with earnings to spend and invest. The Gilded Age dawned. Empires ached to be built in the areas of petroleum and steel. The Republicans in Washington firmly believed that a rising tide of prosperity would help heal the wounds of war. They lavished businessmen with protective tariffs for the manufacturers and generous land grants for railroads and mining operations. The politicians handing out this largesse were often major shareholders and board members of the railroads and mining companies—Republicans practicing Tammany-style graft on a national scale and out in the open. In the postwar pro-business euphoria, no one batted an eye for years.

Vanderbilt, in some ways the first robber baron, died in 1877, but men like John D. Rockefeller, J. P. Morgan, August Belmont, and Andrew Carnegie carried on in his footsteps, amassing gigantic, monopolistic trusts in oil, steel, railroads, and banking. Rockefeller started building his empire in Cleveland, but like so many before him he came to the New York banks for his financing, and eventually he moved his headquarters there. The press loved telling Rockefeller's story, how he started out a lower-middle-class boy and by dint of brains and determination became a tycoon.

Horatio Alger Jr. drilled American boys in the principles of making it in this new corporate world. When he came to New York from New England in 1866, Alger was in his early thirties, a published novelist, also a Harvard-educated Unitarian minister who had lost his church amid charges of "unnatural familiarity with boys," which he did not deny.

Inspired by the flocks of homeless youth around the Five Points and the Bowery, he wrote the first of his rags-to-moderate-riches novels for young readers, *Ragged Dick; or, Street Life in New York with the Bootblacks*. It was serialized in 1867 and published to great success in 1868, leading to a long series. Alger's relentlessly repeated message—that anyone, even a *Ragged Dick* or a *Tattered Tom* or *Ben the Luggage Boy*, could *Strive and Succeed* in America—reached millions and became a foundational tenet of the American dream. It was a distinctly middle-class dream. Alger's street urchins and newsboys don't become Rockefellers. They don't get to be captains of industry themselves, but through hard work and clean living they get to be lieutenants and sergeants, secure and comfortable employees in an increasingly corporate and industrialized world. They stand somewhere between the self-made men of Greeley's generation and the twentieth century's men in the gray flannel suits.

Prosperity was the new evangelism, factories the new cathedrals. Henry Ward Beecher turned to preaching a "Ministry of Wealth." Money was not evil, according to this new gospel; poverty was. Poverty was a sign of sinful ways. The message everywhere in the North was that anybody could make good in America, and any who didn't had only themselves to blame. Even the old bohemian Walt Whitman tried his hand, not very successfully, at penning paeans to industry and commerce.

～

White Southerners in large measure failed to catch this wave. They rode another one, back into nostalgia. New York played a role in this, too.

At first New York's merchants and bankers tried to revive their old relations with the South. They did rebuild the cotton connection, though it was not nearly as integral to the city's prosperity as it had been in the old days. They financed some railroads and new industries in the South, backed cattle ranching in Texas and the birth of the tourism business in Florida. New York's hoteliers and restaurateurs invited Southerners to come back and relive the good old days, and some did; they earned the nickname "Confederate carpetbaggers." Generals Gustavus Smith and Mansfield Lovell, who'd left to go fight for the South early in the war, returned and were welcomed back with open arms by Tammany and the Democracy. Lovell even got his job back as a civil engineer for the city.

But the war had ravaged the South, physically and psychically, far too much for any quick recovery. It had lost two-thirds of its wealth and a quarter of its white men in their prime. While the North went roaring into a period of breakneck industrialization and urbanization, the South remained agrarian and rural. A mythology of the Old South, where happy darkies loved their kindly masters and the sun shone bright all de live-long day, swept through popular culture in the decades after the war. It was fanned by Northerners as much as by Southerners. It was the New York publishing firm of D. Appleton that sought out the Southern writer Joel Chandler Harris to collect his Uncle Remus stories in book form. The huge minstrel troupes that toured out of New York in the decades after the war presented lavish spectacles of purest fantasy, portraying the antebellum South as a preindustrial plantation Eden. The sense of triumph and vindication Northerners might have felt at the end of the war was supplanted by something closer to survivor's guilt.

For the most part, New York's affection for the South went unrequited. New York merchants and business agents traveling below the Mason-Dixon Line found Southerners bitterly resentful, very hostile to carpetbagging Yankees in general and New Yorkers in particular, and violently resistant to Reconstruction. They concluded that the South was not where New Yorkers wanted to be or invest.

Instead, the city continued and expanded the wartime inroads it had made in the West. Just as the slave trade and the plantation South had been sustained by New York before the war, New York and New Yorkers now played central roles in settling the western frontier.

The old dream of a transcontinental railroad could not have been realized in 1869 without New York money and muscle. Lincoln had signed the Pacific Railway Act in 1862, but the work had to wait until after the war. In 1866 the Central Pacific headed east from California and the Union Pacific drove west from Nebraska. Thousands of New York Irishmen went west to lay Union Pacific track. John A. Dix was the first president of the railroad, but its real architect was Thomas C. Durant, another New England transplant to New York. Durant used a dummy corporation, Credit Mobilier, to finance the railroad project. Credit Mobilier was a gigantic scam. It shoveled tens of millions of dollars in Washington subsidies and Wall Street investments into the hands of Durant, other directors, and their Republican backers in Washington.

The second transcontinental railroad, the Northern Pacific, was built by another New Yorker, and a surprising one: Henry Villard. After spending the war reporting as a special for both the *Herald* and the *Tribune*, he returned to New York City and dove into the frothily rising tide of Wall Street. Displaying a genius for making money that had gone untapped during the war, he raised $8 million in a famous "blind pool"—gathering investors on the strength of his good name alone, without telling them what they were investing in—to complete the Northern Pacific in 1883.

———

Ulysses S. Grant emerged from the war vastly more popular with New Yorkers than Lincoln had ever been. The city's relations with him would be a characteristic confusion of support and abuse, honors and humiliation. As early as the fall of 1865, New Yorkers began the push to have Grant succeed the beleaguered Johnson in the White House. That November the city treated the general and his wife, Julia, to a whirlwind week of lavish receptions, balls, and banquets. Wealthy and influential men like A. T. Stewart, August Belmont, Hamilton Fish, John A. Dix, and Cornelius Vanderbilt hosted the celebrations, took his elbow, and showered him with gifts, including a new horse and $100,000 for the mortgage on a home in Washington. At the *Tribune*, Greeley sniffed that all the hero worship and gift-giving were of "pitiable taste."

In December 1867, Thurlow Weed orchestrated a Grant-for-President rally at Cooper Union hosted by numerous local heavyweights. Greeley eventually came over to Grant's camp. Dan Sickles, happy to help sink Johnson, also threw his lot in, even joining the Republican Party. He became one of Grant's most visible and vocal campaigners, addressing large Grant rallies all over the East. When the Republicans held their convention in Chicago the following May, Grant's was the only name on the ballot. Dan Sickles chaired the New York delegation.

Once Grant accepted the nomination, his election was very nearly inevitable. The Democrats had little to put up against him. They'd come out of the war severely tarnished as the party of Copperheads and traitors. It would be twenty years before another Democrat was in the White House.

In New York City, however, Tammany was on the ascendant. In 1867 ground was broken for a lavish new wigwam on East 14th Street. The Democrats held their national convention there in 1868, with Vallandigham and other former Copperheads notably present. They flailed around for a candidate. They let McClellan know they'd run him again if he was interested. He chose not to lose a second time.

The Democrats nominated Horatio Seymour instead. Seymour's campaign was openly white supremacist. He told conventioneers, "It is a very notorious fact that nearly one-half of the people of the [former Confederate] States are negroes; that they are in form, color, and character unlike the whites, and that they are, in their present condition, an ignorant and degraded race." The lyrics of one campaign song went:

Join with a brave intent
To vindicate our Fathers' choice
A White Man's Government!
No Carpet-bag or Negro rule
For men who truly prize
The heritage of glory from
Our Sires, the true, the wise.

In sharp contrast, Grant's campaign slogan was "Let Us Have Peace." Miles O'Reilly wrote daily campaign songs for the *Tribune* with verses like:

So boys! a final bumper
While we all in chorus chant—
"For next President we nominate
Our own Ulysses Grant!"

Grant won handily, 214 electoral votes to Seymour's 80. A striking Nast cartoon in *Harper's Weekly* that November 14 showed Grant on a white charger, holding aloft an American flag emblazoned with the words "Union" and "Equal Rights," driving his sword through the throat of Governor Seymour, who is tumbling off a black horse with a KKK brand.

Seymour won in New York City and State. Tweed and Tammany made sure he did. Though the Democracy sank as a national party in the years after the war, one place where it was still very strong was New York City. Tammany Hall's Democrats emerged from the war more in control of the city than ever, thanks largely to William Tweed's brilliant maneuvering.

Tweed was less interested in Seymour's doomed campaign than in matters closer to home: putting his man John Hoffman, Tammany's grand sachem, in the governor's mansion; his man A. Oakey Hall ("Elegant Oakey") in the mayor's office; and getting himself elected to the state senate and reelected as county supervisor. He did all that by cranking up what's still considered the crookedest election in New York history. To offset the Republicans' dominance in the rest of the state, Tweed looked to the huge cache of potential new voters in the city's estimated seventy-five thousand Irish and German immigrant men who had put off becoming citizens to avoid military service during the war. Tammany naturalized more than forty thousand of them in the weeks leading up to the elections. Judge Barnard, who was up for reelection himself, turned his courtroom into a citizenship mill, with half a dozen or more men crowding around a Bible to be sworn in together. Some were impostors using false addresses, like the forty-two who all gave their address as 70 Greene Street, a famous whorehouse. All would vote as Democrats, of course.

Republican papers cried foul, and the Republican U.S. marshal vowed to put officers at every poll to challenge suspicious activities. Jimmy O'Brien, the city's Tammany sheriff, countered by deputizing up to two thousand Tammany men—roughly the size of the entire Metropolitan Police force—who would do their own poll-watching. On election day the entire Tammany army—new voters, repeaters, ward heelers, "poll inspectors," and O'Brien's deputies—marched to the polling stations. O'Brien's men got right to work. They bullied and arrested Republican poll workers and acted as armed escorts for Tammany repeaters, marching them from poll to poll. The marshal's men made their own arrests, dragging Tammany thugs to jail; in his courtroom, Barnard kept busy that day signing writs of habeas corpus, so they were released and back at the polls within hours.

Meanwhile, Tammany had operatives at the polls in cities and towns throughout the rest of the state. They telegraphed vote counts right after their polls closed. Tammany thus knew exactly how many ballots to stuff into the city's boxes that evening. The unremarkable result was a sweeping Tammany landslide. Seymour beat Grant in New York State by precisely ten thousand votes, a laughably round figure that showed just how brazen and devil-may-care Tammany's fraud had grown by then.

George McClellan, who was just turning forty-two, watched it all from the sidelines. He then settled down to a comfortable life and never lost his celebrity status in New York and New Jersey. In 1870 he would accept a job as the chief engineer for New York City's Department of Docks, a position he kept while becoming president of the Atlantic and Great Western Railroad as well. He remained a glittering fixture in New York society, always an honored guest at the balls and fetes of the winter social season. He'd spend another three years in Europe in the mid-1870s, and on his return, to his surprise, would be nominated and elected governor of New Jersey in 1877, serving a respectable and competent three-year term. He was effectively retired, traveling and working on his memoirs, when he died suddenly of a heart attack in 1885 at the age of fifty-eight. In his obituary the *Evening Post* opined, "Probably no soldier who did so little fighting has ever had his qualities as a commander so minutely, and we may add, so fiercely discussed." His son George Jr. would serve two terms as mayor of New York City, from 1904 to 1909.

CHAPTER 40

Anything to Beat Grant

On the morning after the voting, Grant told Julia, "I'm afraid I'm elected." His reticence was well founded. His dream of bringing the South along with the rest of the nation faded during his two terms. The size of the federal government ballooned, partly because of the giant administrative burden of Reconstruction. The sheer volume offered myriad opportunities for graft. It was the old spoils and patronage system, but now it was so glaring in its excesses and iniquities that it provoked howls of outrage and prompted the eventual creation of the civil service merit system. Grant left himself open to criticism by filling his cabinet and other plum appointments with friends, supporters, cronies, and family. A few proved to be competent and scrupulous, such as Hamilton Fish, his first secretary of state. Many others turned out to be either terrible crooks, the patsies of crooks, or just disasters in their jobs, like Dan Sickles.

As soon as Grant was in, Sickles began lobbying for an appointment. Grant asked Fish to find something for him. Sickles and Fish had known each other for years. Superficially, they had a few things in common. They both practiced law. They both came from old New York City families, though Fish's was older and loftier than Sickles's. Temperamentally, however, Fish and Sickles were opposites. When Sickles had been making a notorious name for himself, Fish had lived the quiet life of a gentlemanly lawyer and competent, unspectacular politician. He'd been appalled and disgusted by the sensational Sickles-Key murder. When Dan went off to make glorious war in 1861, Fish was president of the Union Defense Committee. Fish quietly stuck with Lincoln as the war dragged on and the

Radical Republicans grew frustrated, and after the war he was deeply disturbed by their vindictiveness toward the South. He was sixty, living a comfortable patrician's life, when Grant asked him to be his secretary of state.

Fish thought it best to give Dan a small post somewhere out of the way where he couldn't cause much trouble. He offered him a consulship to Mexico. Dan haughtily refused the backwater post. Then Grant suggested making him minister to Spain. Grant made a number of questionable appointments in his troubled two terms, but few seem so spectacularly woodheaded. The United States and Spain were still vying over Cuba. Insurgents there had fallen into a protracted civil war with the Spanish colonial authorities. With so many Americans living and/or doing business on the island, fighting there could drag Spain and the United States into war. Mild-mannered Fish was the perfect man to deal with the supremely touchy situation. Sending Sickles to Madrid was like throwing a lit torch into an arsenal filled with gunpowder.

Fish sent Sickles to Spain with a delicately worked-out proposal by which Spain would recognize Cuba's independence, Cuba would give up its slaves, and the United States would guarantee a large payment to the critically cash-strapped Spanish government. All sides would come out winners. The general, still not the most diplomatic of men, entangled himself in intrigues both political and personal as soon as he reached Madrid. He found Spanish politics a morass of warring factions and was soon frustrated. He consoled himself by falling back on his old profligate and licentious ways. He scandalized all Europe—and all of his enemies back home—by reputedly taking up with Isabella II, Spain's wanton deposed queen, who was then living the high life in Paris. He simultaneously wooed a pretty woman who'd been an attendant to Isabella's court, Caroline de Creagh, a few decades younger than he. He converted to Catholicism to marry Caroline in 1871. It would be a rocky marriage, as the fiery Caroline refused either to condone his philandering or to follow him when he eventually returned to America.

Meanwhile, James Watson Webb also caused trouble for Grant. He'd been minister to Brazil since Lincoln appointed him in 1861. Early in Grant's first term, he was accused of extorting a small fortune from the Brazilian government. He resigned and came back to New York, where he lived out his last years, dying in 1884.

Although Grant himself was never directly implicated in any of the boondoggles, swindles, and scandals that dogged his two terms—including the Credit Mobilier scam, which reached all the way to his vice president—they did make him look the hapless buffoon. He was "pre-intellectual, archaic, and would have seemed so even to the cave-dwellers," Henry Adams of the Boston Adamses wrote. "He should have been extinct for ages." It was Adams who japed that "U.S." didn't stand for "Unconditional Surrender," as people had said during the war, but for "Uniquely Stupid"; he added that the descent from President Washington to President Grant proved that Darwin was wrong. Most of the political cognoscenti and press agreed that Grant was "an ignorant soldier, coarse in his taste and blunt in his perceptions, fond of money and material enjoyment and of low company," as *The Nation* put it.

A pair of sharp operators from Wall Street, in cahoots with one of Grant's former generals, did their part to craft his poor image. To reduce the inflation left over from the war and put the growing economy on a sound footing, Grant's administration began to buy back wartime greenbacks with gold. That gave Jay Gould, "the Mephistopheles of Wall Street," and "Jubilee Jim" Fisk an idea. They were another of history's Mutt 'n' Jeff pairs. Gould was a small, dour ectomorph, so quiet as to seem sinister. Fisk was a fat, loud howdyboy who wore diamonds on his vest and actresses on his arm and loved nothing better than to gorge on steak and oyster pies at Delmonico's. During the war Gould had speculated in gold and Fisk had smuggled cotton out of the South.

If Grant had been paying any attention to Wall Street he'd have known to be wary of them. With the assistance of Boss Tweed, Fisk and Gould had just hornswoggled Commodore Vanderbilt out of his Erie Railway by flooding the market with watered stock. Tweed calculated that for his efforts he earned a princely $650,000 in just three months. That was nothing compared to the $60 million Gould, as chairman, would wring from Erie's board and common stockholders, while letting the railroad deteriorate to the point that people said it was worth your life to ride on it.

In the summer of 1869, Gould and Fisk began a concerted campaign of showering President Grant with lavish dinners, drinks, trips to the opera, and the finest cigars. Grant, who'd been poor virtually all his life, enjoyed being wooed by the high rollers. They intended to corner the gold market, buying low and driving up the price. For that they needed not only a hoodwinked Grant but the connivance of the assistant secretary of the treasury at Wall Street's Sub-Treasury Building, who was responsible for transacting government sales in gold. That man was another disastrous Grant appointee: Dan Butterfield. Fisk and Gould bribed Butterfield with a check that equaled his annual government salary.

By September they'd driven the price of gold so high that calls came from around the country for Grant to release some of the treasury's bullion to ease it back down. It finally dawned on Grant that he'd been had. On Friday, September 24, 1869, the government dumped $4 million worth of bullion onto the market. The price plummeted in what came to be known as the Black Friday crash. Gould and Fisk were unharmed; they'd sold while the market was still at its peak, just hours before the crash. But they'd ruined many others on Wall Street—a couple of dozen investors committed suicide—and given Grant's reputation a serious black eye.

Butterfield resigned. He sailed on through the rest of his life a prosperous man. After he died in 1901 his widow commissioned a bronze statue by Gutzon Borglum, who also did the statue of Henry Ward Beecher that stands outside Plymouth Church, as well as Mount Rushmore. Butterfield's heroic statue stands in the small Sakura Park in Morningside Heights; wearing his uniform, arms folded across his chest, he gazes across Riverside Drive at Grant's Tomb, his expression inscrutable.

～

With Tweed and Tammany dominating New York City's postwar municipal government, corruption ran amok. In 1866, James Parton had visited the City Council and noted the "absolute exclusion of all honest men" and the "supremacy in the Common Council of pickpockets, prize fighters, emigrant runners, pimps, and the lowest class of liquor dealers, are facts which admit of no question." A joke made the rounds at the time that a newsboy ran into council chambers once and shouted, "Mister, your liquor store is on fire!" Every alderman jumped up and rushed out the door. On the city's payrolls Parton found dozens of men listed as clerks or inspectors of this or that (including a dozen "manure inspectors") who in fact were "bar-keepers, low ward politicians, nameless hangers-on of saloons, who absolutely performed no official duty whatever except to draw the salary attached to their places." City taxes kept climbing, yet so did the city's deficit. The *Herald* declared New York the worst-run city in Christendom.

Tweed had grown not only very fat (nearly three hundred pounds) but very wealthy. Besides the Erie he was a director or president of several banks, the New York Gas Light Company, the New York Mutual Insurance Company, the Third Avenue Railroad Company, and other institutions. He had invested large amounts in real estate and on Wall Street. He owned several homes, including a mansion in Greenwich, Connecticut, and a stable filled with his horses and carriages, and a pair of yachts. He showered his wife and daughters in jewels and swathed them in silks.

By 1870, between the numerous scandals plaguing the Grant administration and the glaringly obvious corruption locally, reform was in the air. After Henry Raymond died, at the age of only forty-nine, in June 1869, publisher George Jones, his longtime partner at the *Times* (and Greeley's before that), decided it was time to attack. Jones began a concerted campaign to expose the gargantuan levels of greed and fraud that the Tweed Ring and their army of fellow travelers had perpetrated.

Tweed's old friends the Irish Catholics compounded his troubles. New York's Fenians had come out of the war battle-hardened and itching for a fight with the British. When small bands of them crossed into Canada and launched ludicrously ill-planned raids on Crown installations in 1866, even Tammany Hall abandoned them. One man took the Fenians' side: Fernando Wood. He'd been languishing in political limbo since losing his seat in Congress in 1864. Now he suddenly popped up at Fenian rallies to deliver stirring speeches on the Irishman's inalienable right to revolt against the British oppressor. Irish New York loved him for it. He agreed to make peace between Tammany and the Irish, for a price: He wanted to go back to Congress. The sachems, gritting their teeth, backed him in his bid for the predominantly Irish and German Catholic Ninth District. He won in a cakewalk. He was still in Congress when he died in 1881.

Relations between the working-class Irish Catholics and the better-off "lace curtain" Protestants in New York, which had never been good, deteriorated into deadly violence. In July 1870, the Irish Protestants' annual Orange Day parade occasioned armed skirmishes with Catholics, and eight people died. The following year, the Tammany trio of Tweed, Mayor Hall, and Governor Hoffman failed to prevent an even larger riot in which more than sixty were killed and hundreds of others wounded.

The city united in blaming Tammany. Tweed's empire collapsed with head-spinning speed. Ten days after the deadly rioting, the *Times* ran a front-page article with column after column of accounts related to the County Courthouse swindle, drawn from a ledger that, for obvious reasons, Tweed and his cronies had managed to keep secret until then. Even the most jaded New Yorkers gaped at the figures. Almost $3 million paid to a plasterer in two years. More than $350,000 to a carpenter. Another $3 million for furniture, more than half a million for carpets, $40,000 for brooms. Thermometers at $7,500 each. On and on the stupefying figures rolled. It's been estimated that the Tweed Ring's rake from these grotesquely padded bills was some $11 million.

At *Harper's Weekly*, Thomas Nast poured all his boyhood hatred of Tammany, the Irish, and Catholics into a barrage of virulent cartoons. People started to see the Boss the way Nast did, as a pear-shaped giant with piggy little eyes and grubby little fingers, or with a bag of money in place of a head. Reaching back into his childhood, Nast popularized the image of the Tammany Tiger as a predatory beast that needed slaying. One cartoon shows a giant thumb pressing down on the city, with the caption, "Well, what are you going to do about it?"

In 1873, Tweed was convicted on multiple charges including larceny and forgery, and sentenced to twelve years. He served one before that decision was overturned, but he came out to face a multimillion-dollar civil suit. Unable to make bail, he went to the dismal Ludlow Street jail, but was allowed out periodically for home visits. During one of those he ran. He made it to Florida, and from there to Cuba, and sailed from there to Spain, working as a common seaman, operating on the mistaken notion that the country had no extradition treaty with the United States. In 1876 he was arrested by Spanish police, who, legend has it, recognized him from one of Nast's cartoons. Back home and back in jail, sick and exhausted, he made a full and voluminous confession. He died behind bars in 1878, soon after his fifty-fifth birthday but looking far older, and was buried in Green-Wood Cemetery.

In 1872, Dan Sickles made a brief return trip to New York to help the state attorney general—Frank Barlow—pry the Erie Railroad away from Jay Gould. Hired as a lawyer by disgruntled shareholders, Dan orchestrated a revolt among the Erie board members, who voted to remove Gould from his chairmanship. He also contacted Barlow and asked if the attorney general would bring a lawsuit against Gould and his cronies. Barlow was preparing his case when Sickles, impetuous as ever, decided to remove Gould from office in his own inimitable way. On crutches, he marched up to the Erie's ornate offices in the Grand Opera House at Eighth Avenue and 23rd Street at the head of a column of a few hundred cops and paid ruffians. He carried papers ordering Gould to resign his chairmanship and leave the premises forthwith.

Gould locked himself in his office. He had hired his own gang of thugs from the Irish west side, nicknamed "Gould's guardian angels." A *Sun* reporter called them "a sorry sight...dirty and unkempt," and depicted them lounging around the Erie offices "lighting their well-stained clay pipes," playing cards on the desks, and generally creating "an atmosphere which was somewhat akin to the foul air of a fourth class Tammany bar-room." With Gould locked in his office, the two camps faced each other in what sounds like a rather lackadaisical standoff, with the cops in the middle. The climax was anticlimactic. Eventually Gould allowed Sickles into his office, Sickles handed him the papers deposing him, and Gould quietly surrendered.

Dan Sickles returned to Spain, and more controversy. A Spanish war-ship captured the *Virginius*, a steamer that had been running arms and supplies to the Cuban insurrectionists. Her captain was Joseph Fry, a for-mer commodore in the Confederate navy, and her crew were British and American mercenaries, plus some Cuban revolutionaries. The Spanish colonial authorities in Cuba executed Fry and fifty-two others for piracy. Some had their heads blown off at close range, their corpses trampled by horses. Reading in all the papers of the "*Virginius* massacre" with its "unparalleled atrocities," Americans screamed for bloody revenge. Grant and Fish had their hands full keeping the country out of war. Having Dan Sickles as their man in Madrid didn't help. He raged at Spanish ministers and told the *Herald* that war was unavoidable. When Fish and his Spanish counterparts worked around the general and negotiated a peaceful resolu-tion, Dan was furious at being upstaged. He resigned, to everyone's relief, and removed himself to Paris. He would not return to New York until 1879.

⁓

Much of 1872 was taken up with campaigning for the fall presidential elections, a mean and ludicrous shambles. For all the abuse he'd been taking from the wonks and cognoscenti, President Grant remained a great hero among rank-and-file Americans. The Democrats, still in the depths of their postwar demoralization, couldn't even scratch up a candidate. Instead, they formed an alliance with a core of disaffected reformers who broke away from Grant's Republican Party and started their own Liberal Republican Party. Their leading light was Carl Schurz, who by then was a senator for Missouri. But they couldn't nominate Schurz for president because he was foreign-born. Another potential candidate was the Missouri governor Benjamin Brown, known as "Boozy Brown." Even against the reputedly boozy Grant that wouldn't fly.

Out of the gloom rode a quixotic figure on a dark horse: Horace Greeley. At sixty-one he was a living legend, still a household name, and still itching for public office. The masses still found him entertaining and lovable, though they had never elected him to public office in his life. As recently as 1869 he'd run for New York's state comptroller and lost—to Franz Sigel, who had returned to the city at the end of the war and would live there another forty years.

Other factors rendered Greeley a less than ideal candidate. He had been railing against Democrats for decades by then, casting the Liberal Republicans' alliance with them in an odd light. And while Greeley the abolitionist was still unloved in the South, Greeley the conciliator had upset many of his longtime fans in the North. In 1867, a Richmond circuit court judge had ruled that the government could not keep holding Jefferson Davis without a trial. He would release Davis on a $100,000 bond, provided that some of the guarantors were Northerners. Greeley had responded instantly, traveling to Richmond with a delegation of New Yorkers including Cornelius Vanderbilt. On Greeley's securing of Davis's release, many Northerners canceled their subscriptions to the *Tribune*.

From a convention that was a frenzy of bickering and balloting—the *Times* dismissed it as "the Bolters' Convention," and characterized Liberal Republicans as "soreheads"—Greeley emerged victorious, with Boozy Brown his running mate. One party member who decided to return to the mainstream fold remarked, "That Grant is an ass, no one can deny, but better an ass than a mischievous idiot." William Lloyd Garrison declared Greeley "smitten with imbecility," while Thurlow Weed thought that no one "outside a lunatic asylum" could take him seriously.

The Democrats gloomily nominated Greeley at their convention several weeks later. Greeley removed himself from the editorship of the *Tribune* and launched into campaigning with his usual windmill-tilting zeal, traveling as far as Texas in his old white coat, giving as many as two hundred speeches in a single month. He called for reconciliation between North and South, black and white, urging all Americans to bury the hatchet and clasp hands "over the bloody chasm of the war." It became a campaign slogan and image, along with the glummer "Anything to Beat Grant." Boozy Brown went on the stump as well, and lived up to his name. At one picnic he was reportedly seen spreading butter on a slice of watermelon, thinking it was a slice of bread. In a speech to graduating students at Yale, barely able to stand, he told them to vote for Greeley because he had "the largest head in America."

Grant the bungler versus Greeley the loony was a rich feast for the press, who delighted in lambasting and lampooning both candidates. At *Frank Leslie's Illustrated*, Matt Morgan, recently brought over from London specifically to go up against Nast, depicted Grant as King Grant, a drunken despot lolling in dissipation, surrounded by sycophants and turning aside the needy commoner. But Morgan's work looked timid compared to Nast's. Nast's weekly barrage of anti-Greeley cartoons—once three in a single issue—was relentlessly vicious and mocking. For accepting the Democratic nomination, Nast drew Greeley as an organ grinder's monkey dancing to Tammany's tune, or showed him whitewashing the Tiger, or shaking hands with Tweed and a long line of classic Tammany thugs and brutes. For Greeley's appeasing attitude toward the South he showed him conspiring with the Ku Klux Klan and shaking hands with John Wilkes Booth over Lincoln's grave. In one illustration Greeley is on his knees praying to Satan.

In the midst of all this, Greeley's wife, Mary, died on October 30. She had been sickly with consumption for years, during which they'd drifted apart as he scurried about pursuing his various causes. He left the campaign trail to sit by her bedside for her last few days and nights. The day she died, *Harper's* hit the stands with a Nast illustration of Greeley himself on a stretcher, dead or dying, being carried off to Chappaqua. Nast was roundly criticized for the ghastly though unintentional timing.

Greeley, and his campaign, collapsed in the final days before the voting. "I have been assailed so bitterly that I hardly know whether I was running for President or the penitentiary," he moaned. Grant was reelected on November 5, with 286 electoral votes to Greeley's 66. Greeley's desolation was complete. Exhausted, shattered by two great losses within days of each other, he tumbled into his last bout of brain fever, a complete mental and physical breakdown, and died, babbling incoherently, on Friday, November 29, just as the electoral college was confirming Grant's win. Thousands passed through City Hall for the viewing; Grant attended the funeral and was in the cortege of some 125 carriages that followed the hearse out to Green-Wood, where Greeley's old nemesis Henry Raymond was also laid.

The Sunday after Greeley died, Henry Ward Beecher mentioned him only briefly in his sermon, and then only to characterize him as "a man of noble ambition, if not always the most wise." Asked to speak at the funeral a few days later, he characteristically rose to the occasion and offered a more glowing assessment.

Beecher's own character was just then coming under intense scrutiny. Plymouth insiders had harbored suspicions since the 1850s that their preacher was having affairs with some of the adoring females in his congregation, including Henry Bowen's wife. Now it came out that he'd dallied with Theodore Tilton's wife as well. Tilton sued Beecher for alienation of affection. The trial, held in the Brooklyn City Courthouse from January into July 1875, was the epicenter of the media circus of the century. It would end in a hung jury, the reverend's reputation dinged but not fatally damaged. After he died in 1887 the public chose to remember him as the great orator and abolitionist, not the philanderer.

CHAPTER 41

Scandals and Scams

Grant's second term was as turbulent as his first. In September 1873 he rushed by train to Wall Street to stave off a new catastrophe, but he could do nothing. It started when banks that had disastrously overextended themselves backing the railroad tycoons started going bankrupt. A run on other banks followed. Pandemonium on Wall Street closed the exchange for an unprecedented ten days. As the Panic of 1873 rolled out across the land, railroads and factories closed and many other businesses failed, throwing the country into a short but deep depression with unemployment of up to 20 percent.

There were no systems in place at the time by which the government might ameliorate the disaster. Republicans were on their pro-business roll and had little sympathy for the unemployed. In New York City, where some one hundred thousand workers lost their jobs, the Republican mayor, William Havermeyer (a former Tammany Democrat who'd gone over to the other side), admonished workers that they should have saved up some of their pay "for a rainy day." The *Times* lectured them that "the natural laws of trade" were "working themselves out," and they must simply persevere. The *Daily Graphic*, a new illustrated paper, sneered, "Whining and whimpering are as useless as they are disgusting." When seven thousand unemployed laborers gathered for a "Work or Bread" protest rally in Tompkins Square Park, the police commissioner—Abram Duryee, who had led the Zouaves of the 5th New York Volunteers in the war—sent almost two thousand cops smashing into them, clubbing heads in what an observer called "an orgy of brutality." Duryee called it "the most glorious sight I ever saw," and Havermeyer judged that "nothing better could have happened." As the go-ahead economics and politics of the Gilded Age made bitter, implacable enemies of capitalism and labor, such scenes and worse would become commonplace.

In 1874, in the depths of the depression, George Armstrong Custer led a fateful expedition into the Black Hills of South Dakota. After the war Custer had become a legend fighting Indians in the West. But had things gone just a little differently, he might have ended up living in New York City instead.

Custer didn't come to his postwar celebrity by chance. He carefully orchestrated his fame. While out west chasing Indians in the late 1860s, he wrote a series of articles for the New York sporting weekly *Turf, Field and Farm*, using the diaphanous pseudonym "NOMAD." They went a long way to establishing his heroic reputation. Despite his constructed image as a man of the frontier, Custer loved New York City. From the winter of 1870 through the summer of 1871, thinking about resigning from the army, he made several extended trips to the city to look into the opportunities for a new career, possibly on Wall Street. The city, fat with Gilded Age spoils, wined and dined him. He squired the soprano Clara Louise Kellogg around, and told her "the most wonderful, thrilling stories...of his earliest fights with the Indians," she later recalled. "He was a most vivid creature; one felt a sense of vigor and energy and eagerness about him; and he was so brave and zealous as to make one know that he would always come up to the mark. I never saw more magnificent enthusiasm." Custer toyed with the notion of taking the stage himself.

Instead, he returned to the Plains, and on that 1874 expedition he discovered gold. Hordes of hungry, unemployed whites raced into what was Sioux land. Despite a high level of sympathy for Native Americans, Grant saw this new gold rush as a kind of economic stimulus plan and directed that the Indians be shoved out of the way. The ensuing tensions led eventually to Custer's death at the Little Bighorn in 1876.

The depression had a dreadful impact on the South. Whites in the North became too concerned with their own well-being to have much of a care for reconstructing the South or guarding the welfare of Southern blacks. Even many of the former white abolitionists, including the Beechers, had lost interest once blacks were enfranchised by the Fifteenth Amendment in 1870, and concentrated on other causes like women's rights. The resistance of Southern whites hardened into outright rebellion, with spreading terrorism, murders, and massacres. Grant sent in federal troops, many of them black, and the situation turned uglier still. Democrats reclaimed control of the South. By the end of Grant's second term, Reconstruction was effectively dead, and Southern blacks were on their own.

"I was never as happy in my life as the day I left the White House," Grant told a reporter after his successor Rutherford B. Hayes's inauguration. "I felt like a boy getting out of school." In 1881, with help from wealthy New York fans, he and Julia bought a brownstone half a block from Central Park at 3 East 66th Street. (It would be torn down in the 1930s for an apartment building.) Grant accepted a spot as a celebrity partner in his son Ulysses Jr.'s Wall Street brokerage, Grant & Ward. Born in the Finger Lakes region of upstate New York, Ferdinand Ward was just twenty-eight and a rising star on the Street, hailed as "the Young Napoleon of finance." He fawned on the older Grant, and the general easily convinced himself that the Young Napoleon was a financial wizard. Along with the whole Grant family, the general got many of his old comrades to invest in the firm; some gave him their entire pensions.

For a few years Ward made them all rich—on paper. It was a Ponzi scheme forty years before Charles Ponzi made the ploy infamous. Ward used later investors' money to pay out dividends to earlier ones in an ever-growing pyramid of fraud, took out bank loans the firm would never pay back, and speculated ineptly. One morning in April 1884 he ran out of funds and panicked. He asked Grant to get a loan from his friend William Henry Vanderbilt, Cornelius's son, the wealthiest man in the world and a prominent Republican. Vanderbilt bluntly told Grant he wouldn't give a dime to Ward, but wrote Grant a personal check for $150,000. Despite Vanderbilt's warning, Grant passed it along to Ward. A few days later when Grant arrived on Wall Street he found the office besieged by angry investors. Ward had vanished with the Vanderbilt loan. Grant & Ward had obligations of almost $17 million and less than $100,000 to cover them. As the firm collapsed it took its largest lender, the Marine National Bank, down with it.

The Grants and many of Grant's friends were ruined. Thomas Nast was among them. He lost his entire life savings when Grant & Ward fell, and his fortunes never truly recovered. Once again Grant had been duped and disgraced. In a rare expression of anger, he told a friend that he wanted to crush Ward "as I would a snake. I believe I should do it, too, but I do not wish to be hanged for the killing of such a wretch."

～

In 1882, Walt Whitman finally achieved a modicum of the success he'd always craved. It came, fittingly, when a new edition of *Leaves* was banned in Boston.

He'd been spending his postwar years trying, with not much luck, to be accepted as "the good gray poet" one of his fans dubbed him. In June 1865 he'd lost his Indian Affairs job after six months, when the secretary of the interior found a copy of *Leaves* on Walt's desk, was scandalized, and fired him as part of a general housecleaning. Walt's friends in the government quickly got him another job, clerking in the attorney general's office, which he managed to keep into the early 1870s.

Whitman's Lincoln elegy "O Captain! My Captain!" made its way into a few poetry anthologies, the only one of his poems to do so during his lifetime. One of the most conventional of his works, its acceptance only made him bitter. "Damn 'My Captain,'" he growled to a friend. "I'm almost sorry I ever wrote the poem." He continued to self-publish various editions of *Leaves*, expanding it further, censoring some of its more scandalous bits. He got some prose published in magazines, gave some lectures on Lincoln with middling success, and earned a cult following in England that counted Oscar Wilde and Bram Stoker among its members. A stroke in January 1873 left him partially paralyzed. He went home to Brooklyn, where his mother died three days after his arrival. His brother George took him in with his family in Camden, New Jersey. They cared for Walt as his health slowly deteriorated.

In 1882 a Boston publisher put out a massive new edition of *Leaves*, with 293 poems. The local district attorney suppressed it as obscene. The resulting scandal and press attracted a new publisher in Philadelphia, and the uproar made this Philadelphia edition the first and only one to see decent sales during Whitman's lifetime. He was able to use the proceeds to buy his own small house in Camden. There a group of disciples took care of him up to his death in 1892, just shy of his seventy-third birthday.

Back in 1855 he had ended "Song of Myself" (as it came to be known) with an invitation:

Failing to fetch me at first keep encouraged,
Missing me one place search another,
I stop some where waiting for you

It would be years before America finally accepted this invitation and embraced Walt's work the way he'd always hoped.

⌒

Herman Melville had died the year before Whitman, in deeper obscurity. In the fall of 1863, a few months after the draft riots, he and his family had moved back to the city, where he spent the rest of his life. In 1866 he had finally gotten his own government appointment, though nothing so lofty or romantic as what he'd sought from the Lincoln administration: an inspector at the Custom House in the city. He trudged back and forth to this quiet, steady job until retiring in 1886. Meanwhile he kept writing, though by then almost no one outside the family circle was reading him. His 1866 Civil War verse collection *Battle-Pieces and Aspects of the War* was ignored. *Clarel*, his epic (six-hundred-page, sixteen-thousand-line) poem using a pilgrimage to the Holy Land as a vehicle for meditations on the world's religions, was published by G. P. Putnam in 1876, with Melville using money left him by an uncle to pay for it. It was barely noticed, its few reviewers professing themselves bewildered and exhausted by what one called its "overwhelming tide of mediocrity." Putnam sold a few copies and Melville recalled the rest.

He published nothing after that. In 1890 an *Atlantic Monthly* writer considering a whatever-happened-to article wrote in a letter to his editor that the once feted author of *Typee* and *Omoo* "is alive still, clinging like a weary but tenacious barnacle to the N.Y. Custom House & very much averse to publicity." Melville had in fact retired four years earlier and was averse to publicity only because it had generally been so very negative for so long.

He turned back to fiction and was working on *Billy Budd* when he died in the city, of a heart attack, in September 1891. Everything he had published was out of print. "He has died an absolutely forgotten man," the *Times* wrote. *Typee* and *Omoo* were reissued a couple of years later, but it wouldn't be until the 1920s that the rest of his work was rediscovered and championed.

⌒

Meanwhile, James Redpath was taking the last and in some ways most curious turns of his career. As the managing editor of the *North American Review*, he engaged many celebrated figures, including his old friend Whitman, to write on current or historical events. In this capacity Redpath, the erstwhile biographer of John Brown, became the ghostwriter for Jefferson Davis. Beginning in 1888, he made a few trips from New York to the plantation near Biloxi where the Davises had settled. He stayed for months at a time; despite some ghosts of old political disagreements, he got along well with both Davis and Varina. Davis started on the autobiography but died in 1889 with much left to do on it. Varina decided to complete it for him as a biography, and Redpath spent more months helping her pull it into shape.

In January 1890 the New York publisher Alexander Belford Company put out Varina Howell Davis's massive two-volume biography *Jefferson Davis*. It sold poorly. *Jefferson Davis* was in effect the final act of James Redpath's long and varied career. In 1891 he was crossing Park Avenue when he was struck down by a horse-drawn trolley and died from his injuries a few days later at the age of fifty-seven.

Despite its lackluster sales, Varina's book was the start of a writing career that brought her with her daughter Winnie to New York City. At the age of sixty-four, the former first lady of the Confederacy settled into New York society with great ease. It wasn't just the presence of many other Confederate carpetbaggers. She'd lived a cosmopolitan life, had always liked cities—New York was one of her favorites, Richmond one of her least—and had always had friends in the North as well as the South. A grandfather had been governor of New Jersey. She liked to call herself a half-breed, since she'd had family and friends on both sides of the war. One of the friends was Joseph Pulitzer, a Hungarian Jew who had come to New York penniless in 1864 and served as a private in Schurz's 1st New York Cavalry. After the war he moved to St. Louis and began to make his fortune in newspapers there. He bought the *New York World* from Jay Gould in 1883. Meanwhile he had married Kate Davis, an in-law of Varina's.

Pulitzer now gave Varina and Winnie jobs, paying them modest annual stipends to write for his paper. Varina wasn't much of a writer, but Winnie wrote a couple of successful romantic novels along with her items for

Pulitzer. Varina took a suite in the Hotel Gerard on West 44th Street, in today's theater district, and filled it with a Victorian profusion of knick-knacks and souvenirs. She was often seen taking carriage rides around Central Park, and became friendly with many of New York's society ladies. She and Julia Grant met and became cool but cordial acquaintances, which press and public cheered as a fine symbol of the nation's having fully healed. Varina resisted persistent overtures from the South to move back, including an offer of a free home from the Richmond city council, and died in New York City in 1906 at the age of eighty. Only then did she return to Richmond, to be buried at Hollywood Cemetery.

CHAPTER 42

Old Soldiers

When Ferdinand Ward's Ponzi scheme collapsed, Grant had two hundred dollars to his name, and, he soon learned, throat cancer. But he also still had many fans and good friends. Dan Sickles, Hamilton Fish, and William Tecumseh Sherman were among the latter. So was Mark Twain. The new monthly *The Century*, an illustrated family magazine, was having great success publishing stories about the war, and it contracted Grant to write a series about some of his battles. The stories went over well and he started getting offers from book publishers for his full memoirs. Twain and his brother-in-law Charles Webster had founded Webster and Company to publish Twain's books, and they were enjoying success with *Huckleberry Finn*. Twain trumped all offers for his friend's book, promising Grant a healthy $10,000 advance and 70 percent of the profits.

Grant raced to complete his two-volume *Personal Memoirs* as his health deteriorated. The *Tribune* and other papers filed regular reports on the progress of both the manuscript and his health. Well-wishers took to gathering on 63rd Street to cheer him whenever he stepped out the door. Webster and Company received an unprecedented sixty thousand advance orders. In June 1885 a new resort near Saratoga Springs, Mount McGregor, offered the Grants a free cottage for the summer. The promoter of the resort later explained, "I thought if we could get him to come here to Mount McGregor, and if he should die there it might make the place a national shrine, and incidentally a success." The woods around the cottage were thick with reporters as Grant pushed himself to the finish, unable to speak, the cancer gnawing him away to less than a hundred pounds. He completed volume 2 on July 18, 1885, and died in his bed, his family around him, five days later.

New York City, Washington, and several other cities appealed to the family for the honor of being the general's final resting place. New York mayor William R. Grace proved the most convincing suitor. Civic leaders in other cities grumbled about "the New York Takeover." The *Times* crowed that it was "A Most Fitting Burial Place: The Nation's Greatest Hero Should Rest in the Nation's Greatest City." Grace organized a Grant Memorial Association of top-tier New Yorkers, including J. P. Morgan, Cornelius Vanderbilt II, Chester A. Arthur, Hamilton Fish, and Joseph Pulitzer. They set out to raise an audacious $1 million. Over the next several years everyone from robber barons to schoolchildren would contribute. After considering Central Park, the Grant family agreed on placing the monument in the new Riverside Park, a sliver of green facing the Hudson on the Upper West Side. It was a rather lonely spot, but a quiet and pretty one.

President Cleveland meanwhile offered the family a state funeral and appointed Major General Winfield Scott Hancock, who'd helped save Dan Sickles's bacon at Gettysburg, to oversee the arrangements. Hancock and a staff of forty set up on Governors Island. It was not an easy task. Every veteran, politician, dignitary, military unit, and civic organization in the country wanted a place in the ceremonies.

After stops in Albany and West Point, Grant's funeral train arrived at Grand Central (the original, one of Commodore Vanderbilt's last achievements) on August 6. A quarter of a million mourners filed past his casket in the black-draped City Hall that day and the next. Grant's funeral procession in New York City on Saturday, August 8, was larger than Lincoln's. It took five hours to pass under the window where his friend Twain watched. Half a million visitors joined the city's million residents in the streets. Twenty years earlier, only the North had mourned for Lincoln. Now, as the *Times* put it, "The Reunited Republic Buries Gen. Grant."

The day dawned "heavy and sullen," according to the *Times*, but cleared and turned hot by afternoon. At City Hall the coffin was placed onto a flat, open horse-drawn cart. The procession included somber marching bands, gray-bearded Civil War veterans both Union and Confederate on horse and on foot, regiments of soldiers and sailors and marines, mounted and foot police, and scores of black carriages carrying bishops and rabbis, President Grover Cleveland, senators and aldermen, mayors and governors from as far away as California. "Gen. Dan Sickles, as erect and soldierly as ever, and with almost all his old-time spirit in his eyes," rode at the head of Third Corps veterans. "His crutches were strapped by the horse's side. His stump was fitted into a socket made on purpose for it in the saddle," *The Sun* reported.

All the windows, doors, and lampposts along the route wore black crepe or flag bunting as the procession wound slowly up Broadway, then Fifth Avenue, then the Boulevard (as Broadway above Columbus Circle was then known) to 72nd Street. The *Times* described how "every balcony, window, and door commanding a view of the line was teeming; the roofs and cornices swarmed; there was not an accessible point, however high and dangerous, but had its observer; men climbed the telegraph poles and clung to the wires; boys were high in the trees…the statues in the squares were black with climbers."

At 72nd Street the procession entered Riverside Park. Grant's temporary vault was a simple brick affair surrounded by hemlocks. A wooden reviewing stand was set up outside. There was an embarrassing crush when it was discovered that the stand could not hold all the gathered dignitaries. In a classic New York City moment, a handful of con artists trying to hawk seats for fifty cents each were chased away by the cops. After funeral services, rifle volleys, and the playing of Dan Butterfield's "Taps," the vault was sealed and its iron gate locked, the key remaining with the Parks Department. By midnight only eight soldiers in blue remained, guarding the site.

Construction of the Grant Monument began in 1892. Grant was moved there in a solemn ceremony in 1897. As he had requested, Julia joined him there when she died in 1902. Into the 1910s the Grant Monument—known colloquially as Grant's Tomb—was the city's most popular attraction, outdrawing even the Statue of Liberty. But Grant's star dimmed as the twentieth century progressed. Lincoln eclipsed him as the great hero of the Civil War, and Grant was increasingly identified as the corrupt bumbler of his postwar years. With Morningside Heights growing up around it, the monument deteriorated into what the *Times* called in 1994 a "graffiti-scarred hangout for drug dealers and muggers." As its centennial approached, plans to clean up and restore the site failed to generate much interest among New Yorkers. Responding to the old joke "Who's buried in Grant's Tomb?" the *Times* columnist John Tierney sneered,

"Who cares?" The restoration was accomplished in time, but the monument remains lonely and remote, a sparsely visited tribute to a poorly remembered hero. There are days when only Dan Butterfield seems to be paying it any attention.

Dan Sickles outlived Grant by nearly thirty years. When he returned to New York from Europe in 1879 he was probably sixty but often shaved a few years off when asked, still an imperious and imposing figure, extravagantly mustachioed, standing ramrod straight in his crutches. He had an artificial leg but preferred the crutches, with the empty pants leg pinned up to make plain just what he'd sacrificed for his country. When Mark Twain met the general, he got the impression that Dan "valued his lost leg away above the one that is left. I am perfectly sure that if he had to part with either of them, he would part with the one that he has got." Sickles took the town house at 23 Fifth Avenue, on the corner of 9th Street, just up from Washington Square, and filled it with military memorabilia. His father died in 1887 and Dan became the executor of his estate, valued at more than $5 million. He would seem to be set for the rest of his life.

Into his seventies, eighties, and nineties he remained a busy and ubiquitous figure, frequently seen around town at gala dinners and first nights at the opera, involved in various civic committees, the old taint of scandal lingering but fading as he became a living monument to a bygone age, the memories of which he refused to let die. In 1890 he was elected sheriff of New York County. In 1893 he was elected to Congress one last time, where he pushed for veterans' pensions and helped spearhead the successful move to have the Gettysburg battlefield made a national park—not least because it afforded him new opportunities to push his version of the battle. He was a familiar figure at gatherings of veterans, and he and General Longstreet, the Rebel who'd cost him his leg, became warm comrades—especially when Longstreet started telling anyone who'd listen that in moving out ahead of the Union line the way he had that day at Gettysburg, Sickles probably saved the day for the North, because he delayed Longstreet's forces too long to capture Little Round Top. He neglected to say that if Sickles had not moved out in front, Little Round Top wouldn't have been vulnerable in the first place. In 1897, Sickles was awarded a Medal of Honor for "conspicuous valor" at Gettysburg, which he felt fully vindicated him. Others did not and still do not. On Memorial Day

1904, Sickles and Oliver Howard, another former Union general, guided an excited President Theodore Roosevelt all around the battlefield sites of Gettysburg for several hours in pouring rain.

In 1906, Mark Twain was renting the town house across 9th Street from the general's. He had not yet met him, but they had a mutual friend in Joseph Twichell. After the war, Twichell became a pastor in Hartford, Connecticut, and a well-known exponent of "muscular Christianity," that Victorian blend of spiritual and physical health. Twain had met him in 1868, and by 1906 they were long and fast friends. It was Twichell who took Twain across the street to meet the general. Twain liked him well enough, although he was faintly disquieted at the way his rooms felt and smelled like a dowdy museum, and admitted dozing off more than once as the old warhorse droned on and on about himself and his escapades.

By 1912, Dan had blown through what his father left him, had narrowly escaped foreclosure on the town house, and was grouchily reduced to renting out the top two floors. On the third floor was an old Tammany pol, William "Plain Bill" Sulzer, who was elected governor that year. The following year, caught in a tangle of scandal and intrigue, he'd be impeached. Bringing things full circle, Mabel Dodge rented the second floor and began holding the weekly soirees, or "Evenings," that made her the doyenne of Greenwich Village's blossoming bohemian scene, which the Da Pontes probably would have enjoyed. She noted in her memoirs that the general once concluded a stiff but polite note to her declining an invitation with the words, "Written in the 93rd year of my life without the aid of spectacles."

He died of a cerebral hemorrhage in May 1914. "Nobody with warm blood flowing through his veins can read the obituary notices of Gen. Sickles without a certain thrill of admiration," the *Times* eulogized. "His was truly the adventurous spirit." He got a grand funeral in St. Patrick's Cathedral, a solemn procession in Washington, and a grave in Arlington National Cemetery. The National Museum of Health and Medicine displays his leg bones to this day. At the Gettysburg national park that he helped to create, his monument, sited where he was wounded, is one of the smallest and plainest of any general officer's. It was placed there during his lifetime. He claimed not to be offended by the apparent slight, declaring that the whole park was a monument to him anyway.

Epilogue

When Dan Sickles was born, New York City was confined to the twenty-three square miles of Manhattan, and had fewer than 150,000 residents. When he died nearly a century later, the city had expanded to include Brooklyn, Queens, the Bronx, and Staten Island, a metropolis of about three hundred square miles, with a population of around five million. In Dan's youth, New York was the biggest, busiest city in America. When he died, it was well on its way to being the capital of the world.

For all that New York's business leaders had initially feared and resisted General Sickles's war, they had seized the opportunities it presented to amass capital, create new industries, and expand their markets, laying the foundation for the city's booming growth in the decades that followed. On balance, the war so many New Yorkers had argued, voted, and rioted against was good for the city.

In the half century since the war ended, memories of New York's highly controversial role in it had faded. The war itself was now more myth than memory. The gray-haired veterans who marched in Sickles's funeral procession celebrated it as a glorious epoch of valor and honor, not a holocaust of hatred and slaughter. Lincoln too was passing into mythology, from the barely elected, widely reviled, and often questioned politician to the giant, godlike figure enshrined in the Lincoln Memorial, construction of which began in March 1914, two months before Sickles died.

In 1914, relations between black and white Americans were reaching a post–Civil War nadir. Jim Crow and segregation laws enforced an American apartheid. New forms of white nativism spread hatred of blacks, as well as Jews, Catholics, and immigrants. Lynchings of blacks reached their peak in this period. Minstrel music, which had once expressed a confusion of love and hate, had devolved in the 1890s into the immensely popular form called the "coon song," which reduced blacks to a small set of repulsively racist signifiers.

Released the year after Sickles's death, *The Birth of a Nation*, produced and directed by D. W. Griffith, son of a Confederate officer, presented a stunningly racist revisionist interpretation of the Civil War that cast the Ku Klux Klan, born during Reconstruction, as white knights who heroically defended the South and Southern white womanhood from evil blacks and carpetbaggers. It prompted a resurgence of Klan activity and popularity. Klansmen actually recruited in some theaters screening the movie. It would remain the most controversial American film of the twentieth century—and one of the largest-grossing.

To the young intellectuals, artists, and radicals who gathered in Mabel Dodge's apartment, Dan Sickles was just the crusty old man who lived downstairs, as much a relic as the memorabilia that surrounded him. This new generation of New Yorkers was entirely focused on its own moment, on the new century and its promises and problems: the modern European art of Picasso, Matisse, and Duchamp, which they introduced to Americans in the 1913 Armory Show; modern theater, music, dance, and literature, all of which they were pioneering; the new psychological theories of Sigmund Freud, who visited New York in 1909; women's suffrage, reproductive rights, and sexual freedom; socialism, anarchism, and organized labor; and the terrible deterioration in race relations.

Starting in July 1914, two months after Dan Sickles died, there was a new war as well. It came to be called the Great War, and opinions about it would be as divided as always in the heterogeneous metropolis.

Acknowledgments

First, heartfelt thanks to my editor, Sean Desmond, and everyone at Twelve for making this book such a joy to work on.

Thanks also to Chris Calhoun and Danielle Lanzet at the Chris Calhoun Agency.

Friends, family, and colleagues helped in myriad ways as I researched and wrote this book. Thanks to: Nick Aumiller, Brian Berger, Lauri Bortz, Russell Boulet, William Bryk, Richard Byrne, Irwin Chusid, Michael Gentile, Tanisha Jones, Lisa Kearns, Don Kennison, Jim Knipfel, Laura Lindgren, Thomas Lisanti, Don MacLeod, Dermot McEvoy, Diane Ramo, Rasha Refaie, Daniel Riccuito, Elliot Rosenberg, Nancy Sherbert, Jane Strausbaugh, Ken Swezey, James Taylor, Tony Trachta, Greg Trupiano, and Christine Walker.

Notes

Complete publication details for each reference are provided in the bibliography following the notes section.

Chapter 1. *My God, We Are Ruined!*

3   Walt Whitman strolled out: Whitman, *Complete Prose*, 1:28.

3   Nearby, a group of prominent businessmen: Dix, *Memoirs*, 2:9.

4   Civil War historian James McPherson argues: McPherson, *Mighty Scourge*, 3–19.

5   Even Whitman, whose vision of America: Kaplan, *Walt Whitman*, 336.

7   After a congressman pulled a pistol: Heidler and Heidler, *Henry Clay*, 469.

Chapter 2. *City of Slavery*

10   "The City of New York belongs": Johnson, *"Vast and Fiendish Plot,"* 62.

10   But by the 1830s shipyards: Bunker, *Harbor and Haven*, 49–50.

11   In 1860 the port of New York: Albion, *Rise of New York Port*, 63–74.

13   As a natural corollary: Burrows and Wallace, *Gotham*, 443–46.

13   "the banking-house of the continent": Browne, *Great Metropolis*, 40.

14   what's now midtown: Cook, *Armies of the Streets*, 5–6.

14   One of the ironies: Lydon, "New York and the Slave Trade."

15   Of the approximately 813,000 people: Hodges, *Root and Branch*, 280.

15   Cotton was the key: Yafa, *Big Cotton*, 78–86.

17   And yet the planters kept buying: Woodman, *King Cotton and His Retainers*, 135 and 3–43.

18   New York City also grabbed: Albion, *Rise of New York Port*, 101–4.

19   Some Southerners deplored: Woodman, *King Cotton and His Retainers*, 129–45.

19   Southerners didn't let that stop them: Johnson, *"Vast and Fiendish Plot,"* 31–37.

20   the *New York Day-Book*: Perkins, "Defense of Slavery."

21   "more than the value of land": McPherson, *Mighty Scourge*, 1.

21   "the sympathy of the Government": "The Execution of Gordon, the Slave-Trader," *Harper's Weekly*, February 21, 1862.

21   As the port of New York grew: Fehrenbacher, *Slaveholding Republic*, 202 and 174–89.

22   Up to 1861, 125 slave ship captains: Soodalter, *Hanging Captain Gordon*, 9.

Chapter 3. *City of Confusion*

25   Its primary targets: Tappan, *Life of Arthur Tappan*, 96.
26   abolitionists such as the Reverend Peter Williams Jr.: Hewitt, "Peter Williams, Jr."
27   the young Horace Greeley: Greeley, *Autobiography*, 41–84.
28   When Hod was fifteen: Williams, *Horace Greeley*, 19.
29   The Collect Pond: Brown, *Valentine's Manual*, 164–65.
29   what passed for milk: Cook, *Armies of the Streets*, 14–15.
29   Even the ferries: Brown, *Valentine's Manual*, 148.
29   The summer after Greeley arrived: Wilford, "How Epidemics Helped Shape the Modern Metropolis."
30   His friend P. T. Barnum: Williams, *Horace Greeley*, 60.
30   "the avowed rustic, the homely sage": Rourke, *Trumpets of Jubilee*, 266.
30   The first half of the nineteenth century: Widmer, *Young America*, 11.
32   Benjamin Day, another young printer: O'Brien, *Story of The Sun*, 1–30.
33   On slavery he wrote: Parton, *Life of Horace Greeley*, 162–63.
34   Early minstrelsy: For a full discussion, see Lhamon, *Raising Cain*.
34   As the numbers of Irish Catholics: Goldfield, *America Aflame*, 24–26.
35   Chatham Gardens Theatre: Henderson, *The City and the Theatre*, 56–57.
35   While the abolitionists were meeting there: Tappan, *Life of Arthur Tappan*, 169–71.

Chapter 4. *The Great Riot Year*

36   the Great Riot Year: Prince, "The Great 'Riot Year.'"
37   The Tappans were again at the focal point: Wyatt-Brown, *Lewis Tappan*, 115–63.
38   a young associate of the Tappans named David Ruggles: Hodges, *David Ruggles*.
40   Traditionally, municipal politics: Mushkat, *Tammany*, 1–7.
42   Tammany might never have developed: Allen, *Tiger*, 1–50.
44   Tammany toughs shoved their way: Headley, *Great Riots of New York*, 71.
46   Greeley would remember him: Greeley, *Autobiography*, 312.
46   A thirty-year-old delegate: Borchard, *Abraham Lincoln and Horace Greeley*, 18.
46   Greeley was disconsolate: Williams, *Horace Greeley*, 45–50.

Chapter 5. *The War of the Pennies*

48   launched by James Gordon Bennett: Seitz, *The James Gordon Bennetts*, 15–27.
49   In 1836, Bennett wrote: O'Brien, *Story of The Sun*, 61–62.
49   "gentlemen were in the almost daily habit": Barnum, *Struggles and Triumphs*, 669.
49   Being a former reporter himself: Seitz, *The James Gordon Bennetts*, 59–78.
50   Greeley made the *Tribune* a platform: Williams, *Horace Greeley*, 56–124.
51   "filth, squalor, rags": Greeley, *Autobiography*, 145.
51   One evening in June 1844: Seager, *And Tyler Too*, 1–47.
52   when Polk welcomed Texas: Williams, *Horace Greeley*, 105–10.
52   He sent himself: Borchard, *Abraham Lincoln and Horace Greeley*, 8–35.
53   In September 1851: Berger, *Story of The New York Times*, 2–17.

Chapter 6. *Immigrants and Know-Nothings*

56   The crush of new Irish Catholics: Morris, *American Catholic*.
56   Called "guttersnipes": Gilfoyle, "Street-Rats and Gutter-Snipes."

57 **exactly the opposite happened:** Man, "Labor Competition and the New York Draft Riots of 1863."

57 **In 1844 the nativist American Republican Party:** Bennett, *Party of Fear*, 105–12.

58 **first great champion, Bishop John Hughes:** Hassard, *Reverend John Hughes*, 9–206.

59 **Even while defending his flock:** Stern, "How Dagger John Saved New York's Irish."

59 **Bishop Hughes reflected the interests:** Andrews, "Slavery Views of a Northern Prelate."

60 **recent convert, James Alphonsus McMaster:** Kwitchen, *James Alphonsus McMaster*, 1–71.

60 **the personages of Thomas Francis Meagher:** Wylie, *Irish General*, 11–97.

61 **Judge Charles Patrick Daly, and his sharp-tongued wife:** Hammond, *Commoners' Judge*, 15–142.

62 **"big words and small deeds":** Hassard, *Reverend John Hughes*, 304.

62 **John Mitchel settled in Brooklyn:** McGovern, *John Mitchel*, 131.

63 **Meagher stood by his outrageous friend:** Wylie, *Irish General*, 95–96.

Chapter 7. *A Trio of Tammany Rogues*

65 **Fernando Wood was born:** Mushkat, *Fernando Wood*, 1–26.

66 **Daniel Edgar Sickles was so gossiped and argued about:** Swanberg, *Sickles the Incredible*, 75–85.

66 **Finally George found a setting:** Acocella, "Nights at the Opera."

67 **In many ways this cultured old reprobate:** Swanberg, *Sickles the Incredible*, 77–81.

68 **when Fanny learned of it:** Hessler, *Sickles at Gettysburg*, 5.

69 **The council was comprised of:** Werner, *Tammany Hall*, 108.

69 **a crooked tradition had been set:** Brummer, *Political History of New York State*, 36–38.

69 **William M. Tweed first learned:** Hershkowitz, *Tweed's New York*, 4–14.

70 **Fire was a constant danger:** Costello, *Our Firemen*, 15–39 and 161–76.

71 **an immigrant boy named Tommy Nast:** Halloran, *Thomas Nast*, 1–40.

71 **Tweed got into politics:** Hershkowitz, *Tweed's New York*, 35–69.

Chapter 8. *Lurching Toward the Precipice*

73 **"the Whig party is not merely discomfited":** Stoddard, *Horace Greeley*, 149.

74 **"The whole process":** Hibben, *Henry Ward Beecher*, 102.

75 **"a thickness of speech":** Beecher and Scoville, *Biography of Henry Ward Beecher*, 95.

75 **Henry was a student at Lane:** Applegate, *Most Famous Man in America*, 104–18.

75 **"His personal appearance":** "The Brooklyn Pulpit—No. 1," *Brooklyn Daily Eagle*, May 10, 1848.

75 **Sinclair Lewis would call him:** Hibben, *Henry Ward Beecher*, vii.

76 **Mark Twain, who caught a Plymouth service:** Applegate, *Most Famous Man in America*, 372.

76 *The Fugitive Blacksmith*: Bland, *African American Slave Narratives*, 2:575.

77 **Henry's sister Harriet:** Stowe, *The Key to Uncle Tom's Cabin*, 324.

77 **The abolitionists' annual meeting:** Sherwin, *Prophet of Liberty*, 211.

78 **"drunkards, thieves, gamblers, and ruffians":** "The Empire Club Chief," *New York Times*, January 14, 1885.

78 **"any number of soap-lock":** "Picture of a Short-Boy," *New York Times*, September 14, 1854.

79 **Frederick Douglass spoke next:** Wilson, *Specters of Democracy*, 28.

79 **Walt Whitman wrote a brief piece:** Holloway, *Uncollected Poetry and Prose of Walt Whitman*, 1:235.

79 **Rynders's gang turned up:** "The Anniversaries," *New York Tribune*, May 9, 1850.

79 **Beecher hastily talked:** Applegate, *Most Famous Man in America*, 253.

79 **Then his sister Harriet upstaged him:** Ibid., 262–63.

80 **a new Stephen Foster song:** Emerson, *Doo-dah!*, 17–23.

81 **Horace Greeley got himself so worked up:** Williams, *Horace Greeley*, 156–59.

81 **At a banquet, Colonel Davis:** "The Great Exhibition," *New York Times*, July 16, 1853.

82 **Barnum blamed the location:** Barnum, *Life of P. T. Barnum*, 386.

Chapter 9. *Riot and Outrage*

83 **the smooth-talking Fernando Wood:** Mushkat, *Fernando Wood*, 26–30.

83 **Jacob Westervelt, one of the city's:** "Death of an Ex-Mayor," *New York Times*, February 22, 1879.

83 **an itinerant street preacher:** "Anticipated Riot," *New York Times*, December 12, 1853.

84 **Fernando Wood saw his opening:** Mushkat, *Fernando Wood*, 94.

85 **A *Tribune* reporter saw one rioter:** "Fourth of July," *New York Tribune*, July 6, 1857.

86 **At one point Isaiah Rynders:** Sante, *Low Life*, 203.

86 **Dan Sickles meanwhile was causing trouble:** Swanberg, *Sickles the Incredible*, 1–25 and 88–100.

Chapter 10. *From New York to Bleeding Kansas*

89 **Greeley railed against the plan:** Williams, *Horace Greeley*, 172–73.

89 **Henry Ward Beecher went up:** Applegate, *Most Famous Man in America*, 201–2.

90 **sent…James Redpath to Kansas:** McKivigan, *Forgotten Firebrand*, 2–18.

91 **Brown was born in 1800:** DeCaro, *John Brown*, 3–42.

92 **Preston Brooks, sought out:** Stampp, *America in 1857*, 11–17.

92 **Greeley was assaulted in Washington:** Williams, *Horace Greeley*, 183.

92 **Preston Brooks was lionized:** Copeland, *Antebellum Era*, 364.

92 **Lucius Quintus Cincinnatus Lamar II:** Wyatt-Brown, *Honor and Violence in the Old South*, 27.

93 **Redpath was already:** Gilpin, *John Brown Still Lives!*, 24–25.

93 **John E. Cook was a slight:** Lubet, *John Brown's Spy*, 12–31.

94 **The *Tribune* was by now:** Williams, *Horace Greeley*, 207–9.

94 **the writer and feminist Julia Ward Howe:** Howe, *Reminiscences, 1819–1899*, 4 and 254–56.

Chapter 11. Leaves of Grass

96   **John Brown Jr. was working:** DeCaro, *John Brown*, 129.
96   **"The hard labor of the farm":** Stovall, *Prose Works 1892*, 580.
96   **Louisa was Quaker:** Kaplan, *Walt Whitman*, 55–70.
97   **the New England Transcendentalist Ralph Waldo Emerson:** "Mr. Emerson's Lecture," *New York Tribune*, February 8, 1843.
98   **In 1849, Whitman walked into:** Greenspan, *Walt Whitman and the American Reader*, 61–88.
98   **"I am the mate and companion":** Whitman, *Leaves of Grass*, 21.
99   **Whitman published *Leaves*:** Greenspan, *Walt Whitman and the American Reader*, 86–98.
99   **"bold, stirring thoughts":** *New York Tribune*, July 23, 1855.
99   **At the *Times*:** Kaplan, *Walt Whitman*, 321.
99   **"Who is this arrogant young man":** "Leaves of Grass," *New York Times*, November 13, 1856.
100   **writing as Fanny Fern:** Kaplan, *Walt Whitman*, 198–228.
100   **Still, *Leaves* didn't sell:** Greenspan, *Walt Whitman and the American Reader*, 176.
101   **as the *Tribune*'s Junius Browne put it:** Browne, *Great Metropolis*, 154.

Chapter 12. *Hard Times and High*

102   **the Panic of 1857:** Calomiris and Schweikart, "The Panic of 1857."
103   **Most New York banks:** Burrows and Wallace, *Gotham*, 845–46.
103   **Mayor Wood responded by proposing:** Mushkat, *Fernando Wood*, 41–81.
103   **In their dismay that fall:** Long, *Revival of 1857–58*, 11–45.
105   **Edwin Booth was dazzling them on Broadway:** Titone, *My Thoughts Be Bloody*, 35–60.
106   **the actor he'd subbed for was…Junius Brutus Booth:** Ruggles, *Prince of Players*, 3–25.
107   **To a young Walt Whitman:** Whitman, *Complete Prose Works*, 1:428.
108   **At eighteen, Edwin sailed:** Ruggles, *Prince of Players*, 26–53.
108   **Laura Keene, a British actress:** Henneke, *Laura Keene*, 1–58.
108   **Keene took Edwin for a lover:** Giblin, *Good Brother, Bad Brother*, 69–70.
109   **When Edwin came to the Metropolitan:** Henderson, *The City and the Theatre*, 107–8.
109   **Booth was billed:** Giblin, *Good Brother, Bad Brother*, 47.
109   **critic and aesthete Adam Badeau:** Badeau, *The Vagabond*, vii and 122.
109   **she debuted *Our American Cousin*:** Henneke, *Laura Keene*, 59–106.

Chapter 13. *Murder and Rebellion*

111   **In February 1859:** "Dreadful Tragedy," *New York Times*, February 28, 1859.
112   **The *Tribune* rendered it:** "Dreadful Affair at Washington," *New York Tribune*, February 28, 1859.
112   **"Is the scoundrel dead?":** Hessler, *Sickles at Gettysburg*, 11.
112   **one of the most sensational murders:** Swanberg, *Sickles the Incredible*, 63.
112   **"intensely exciting":** "The Sickles Tragedy," *New York Times*, April 5, 1859.

112 "the decorum of the Court": Ibid., April 27, 1859.

113 Dan Sickles basked: Swanberg, *Sickles the Incredible*, 47–66.

113 On the night of October 16, 1859: Lubet, *John Brown's Spy*, 60–64.

113 David Hunter Strother wrote: Eby, *"Porte Crayon,"* 104–8.

114 *The Sun* was still reporting: "Insurrection at Harper's Ferry," *The Sun*, October 22, 1859.

115 the twenty-one-year-old actor John Wilkes Booth: Titone, *My Thoughts Be Bloody*, 209–14.

115 After the hanging: DeCaro, *John Brown*, 96–99.

115 Thirty years later: "John Brown's Clothes," *Brooklyn Eagle*, April 6, 1890.

116 Two journalists joined the line: Genoways, *Walt Whitman and the Civil War*, 12–48.

116 The white supremacist *Day-Book*: Conrad, "Whitman and the Proslavery Press: Newly Recovered 1860 Reviews."

117 When Fernando Wood lost: Mushkat, *Fernando Wood*, 82–96.

Chapter 14. *Slave Ships*

119 the *Wanderer* was the most: Wells, *The Slave Ship Wanderer*, 8–52.

119 Charles's father, Gazaway Bugg Lamar: Hay, "Gazaway Bugg Lamar."

121 "a slave-dealer, a kidnapper of negroes": "Chivalric Swindling," *New York Times*, March 21, 1859.

121 The *Nightingale* began life: Sherwood, "Perfidious Albion."

122 The prosecutor argued: Soodalter, *Hanging Captain Gordon*, 139–40.

122 From his long instructions to the jury: "The Slaver Nightingale," *New York Times*, November 15, 1861.

122 "a matter of surprise": "Impunity for Slave Traders," *New York Times*, November 15, 1861.

122 "The prisoner is a young man": "The Slave Trade," *New York Times*, November 25, 1861.

122 he enlisted and served: Phisterer, *New York in the War of the Rebellion*, 1541–48.

Chapter 15. *The Tall, Dark Horse Stranger*

124 "If he had not come to New York": McPherson, *Mighty Scourge*, 199.

124 On Saturday, February 25, 1860: Freeman, *Abraham Lincoln Goes to New York*, 13–18.

125 In the *Tribune*, Greeley exhorted: Harper, *Lincoln and the Press*, 45.

125 Lincoln walked a short way: Freeman, *Abraham Lincoln Goes to New York*, 20–36.

126 Mathew Brady's photography studio: Rosenheim, *Photography and the American Civil War*, 17–32.

128 Fifteen hundred people: Freeman, *Abraham Lincoln Goes to New York*, 89–90.

129 Afterward, Lincoln went: Harper, *Lincoln and the Press*, 45–46.

130 When Lincoln went: Freeman, *Abraham Lincoln Goes to New York*, 94–100.

130 When the Republicans met: Harper, *Lincoln and the Press*, 50–51.

131 It was as big an upset: Borchard, *Abraham Lincoln and Horace Greeley*, 60–65.

133 **"moneybags of Wall Street"**: Burrows and Wallace, *Gotham*, 864.

133 **The squabbling among the various Democrat factions**: McKay, *The Civil War and New York City*, 19.

134 **"The engrafting of negrology"**: "Ratification of Fusion," *New York Times*, October 9, 1860.

135 **called themselves the Wide-Awakes**: Grinspan, "Young Men for War."

135 **Seward addressed a Lincoln rally**: "Gov. Seward in the Metropolis," *New York Times*, November 3, 1860.

Chapter 16. *City of Secession*

136 **newspaper editors throughout the South**: Harper, *Lincoln and the Press*, 66–68.

136 **Correspondents for New York papers**: Andrews, *The North Reports the Civil War*, 14–19.

136 **the erratic Greeley lost heart**: Harper, *Lincoln and the Press*, 101–2.

137 **the May 1859 issue of *De Bow's Review***: *De Bow's Review* 1, no. 5 (May 1859).

137 **On December 15, Richard Lathers**: Garner, *Civil War World of Herman Melville*, 9–10.

137 **Lathers and the meeting's other organizers**: Farrow et al., *Complicity*, 10–11.

137 **Lathers and his wife**: Garner, *Civil War World of Herman Melville*, 68–70.

137 **forty thousand of the city's businessmen**: Johnson, *"Vast and Fiendish Plot,"* 71.

137 **Mayor Wood offered New Yorkers**: "City Government for 1861," *New York Times*, January 7, 1861.

138 **The idea of New York becoming**: Anbinder, "Fernando Wood and New York City's Secession from the Union."

138 **"miserable sophistries and puerilities"**: "Secession Gone to Seed," *New York Times*, January 8, 1861.

138 **"but tarried at the bar"**: Myers, *History of Tammany Hall*, 194–95.

139 **Although Dix's new role**: Leonard, *History of the City of New York*, 368–70.

139 **Rynders and a large group**: "Sympathy for Secession," *New York Times*, January 16, 1861.

139 **Gazaway Bugg Lamar, who made other such purchases**: Hay, "Gazaway Bugg Lamar."

140 **a twenty-five-year-old named Henry Villard**: Villard de Borchgrave and Cullen, *Villard*, 1–94.

140 **"his shameful record as a journalist"**: Villard, *Memoirs*, 1:162.

141 **the Lincoln Special**: Kline, *Baltimore Plot*, 151.

141 **When the train stopped in Albany**: Titone, *My Thoughts Be Bloody*, 241.

141 **Walt Whitman recorded an uncomfortable moment**: Whitman, *Prose Works*, 499–500.

142 **"I can only say that I fully concur"**: Basler, *Collected Works of Abraham Lincoln*, 232–33.

142 **In Philadelphia, Lincoln heard**: Kline, *Baltimore Plot*, 70.

Chapter 17. *The Tempest Bursting*

147 **the plague of office-seeking locusts**: Garner, *Civil War World of Herman Melville*, 80–81.

147 **"Orpheus C. Kerr"—Office Seeker:** Newell, *Orpheus C. Kerr Papers*, 1:37–38.

148 **At forty-one, Herman Melville:** Garner, *Civil War World of Herman Melville*, 82–84.

151 **Greeley met with the president:** Stoddard, *Horace Greeley*, 212.

151 **the stocky, bushy-bearded Albert Richardson:** Carlson, *Junius and Albert's Adventures*, 11–17.

151 **as a secret *Tribune* correspondent:** Richardson, *Secret Service*, 31–42.

152 **Davis hoped the North:** Merrington, *Custer Story*, 9–10.

152 **"a peacetime joke":** McPherson, *Ordeal by Fire*, 168.

153 **The Tuesday, April 9, *Times*:** "Military and Naval Movements," *New York Times*, April 9, 1861.

154 **The *Herald* thought it knew:** Spann, *Gotham at War*, 12.

154 **Bradley Osborn, a reporter for the *World*:** Andrews, *The North Reports the Civil War*, 1–5.

Chapter 18. *War! War!! War!!!*

155 **Laura Keene was starring:** Henneke, *Laura Keene*, 147–54.

156 **historian Mark Caldwell notes:** Caldwell, *New York Night*, 149.

156 **the soprano Clara Louise Kellogg:** Kellogg, *Memoirs of an American Prima Donna*, 1.

156 **He walked into the Metropolitan Hotel:** Whitman, *Complete Prose*, 1:28–29.

157 **"always alive all night":** Caldwell, *New York Night*, 149.

157 **Edwin Booth's brother John:** Giblin, *Good Brother, Bad Brother*, 63–64.

157 **The *Herald* printed 135,000 papers:** McKay, *The Civil War and New York City*, 56.

157 **Beecher preached an abolitionist war sermon:** Beecher, *Writings*, 84–109.

158 **Bennett had hammered away:** Seitz, *James Gordon Bennetts*, 171.

158 **Lincoln summoned Thurlow Weed:** Weed, *Autobiography*, 617.

158 **Bennett asked Henry Villard:** Villard, *Memoirs*, 1:162.

159 **James Jr.'s sailing yacht:** Seitz, *James Gordon Bennetts*, 182.

159 **the *Baltic* reached New York:** "The Heroes of Fort Sumter," *New York Times*, April 19, 1861.

159 **the *Times* called it:** "The Union Forever!," *New York Times*, April 21, 1861.

159 **Orpheus C. Kerr added a poem:** Newell, *Orpheus C. Kerr Papers*, 31.

160 **Gazaway Bugg Lamar would leave the city:** Hay, "Gazaway Bugg Lamar."

160 **Back in Savannah:** Marsh, "The Military Trial of Gazaway Bugg Lamar."

160 **Recalling the martial fever:** Whitman, *Complete Prose*, 30–31.

161 **less courteously as Copperheads:** "The Impending War," *New York Times*, April 10, 1861.

161 **By 1862, Peace Democrats:** Weber, *Copperheads*, 3.

Chapter 19. *New York to the Rescue*

163 **"The condition of Baltimore":** Dix, *Memoirs*, 2:27.

164 **Southerners expected to seize:** Lockwood and Lockwood, *Siege of Washington*, 59–60.

164 **"and his physical infirmities":** Villard, *Memoirs*, 1:179.

164 **To fund the start-up:** Spann, *Gotham at War*, 23–25.

165 **"in almost every street":** Alduino and Coles, *Sons of Garibaldi*, 48.

165 **Tammany Hall put together a regiment:** Hershkowitz, *Tweed's New York*, 82–83.

166 **William "Billy" Wilson, a lightweight boxer:** Stott, *Jolly Fellows*, 222.

166 **Maria Daly, who liked him:** Daly, *Diary of a Union Lady*, 22.

166 *The Sun* **was not buying it:** "The Traitors Among Us—A Warning," *The Sun*, April 16, 1861.

166 **Frederick and Gustav "Gus" Schurmann:** Styple, *Little Bugler*, 10–20.

167 **formed the Union Defense Committee:** Leonard, *History of the City of New York*, 370.

168 **James Stevenson wrote a pamphlet:** Stevenson, *History of the Excelsior or Sickles' Brigade*, 8.

168 **Joseph Twichell, a young abolitionist:** Messent and Courtney, *Civil War Letters of Joseph Hopkins Twichell*, 16–18.

168 **Colonel Billy Wilson's 6th:** McKay, *The Civil War and New York City*, 74–75.

169 **"Colonel Wilson's men":** Blake, *Pictorial History*, 92.

169 **the first New York City regiment:** Emmons, *History of the Second Company*, 290.

169 **Private O'Brien cheered his fellows:** Lockwood and Lockwood, *Siege of Washington*, 183 and 227–48.

171 **the photographers George Barnard and C. O. Bostwick:** Rosenheim, *Photography and the American Civil War*, 63.

171 **The *Times* reported:** "A Sergeant of the McLelland Rifles Shot," *New York Times*, November 8, 1861.

171 **he wrote an extraordinary letter:** "Funeral of Lieut. Fitz-James O'Brien," *New York Times*, April 10, 1862.

172 **New York's harbor defenses:** Spann, *Gotham at War*, 156–57.

Chapter 20. *Immigrants Join the Fight*

174 **New York City fielded more German units:** Keller, *Chancellorsville and the Germans*, 24–27.

174 **the 8th New York Infantry:** Burton, *Melting Pot Soldiers*, 84–85.

175 **were also compelled to volunteer:** Bruce, *The Harp and the Eagle*, 60.

176 **At their head was Colonel Michael Corcoran:** Burton, *Melting Pot Soldiers*, 112–13.

177 **Captain D. P. Conyngham, a journalist:** Conyngham, *Irish Brigade*, 21.

177 **"About 5 o'clock the regiment":** "Off for the War," *New York Times*, April 24, 1861.

177 **Maria Daly recorded with alarm:** Daly, *Diary of a Union Lady*, 18–23.

178 **Meanwhile it took only a week:** Wylie, *Irish General*, 117–22.

178 **Chaplain Mooney got in trouble:** Bruce, *The Harp and the Eagle*, 77.

178 **to be called the Garibaldi Guard:** Alduino and Coles, *Sons of Garibaldi*, 49; Burton, *Melting Pot Soldiers*, 169–72.

Chapter 21. *The First to Fall*

181 **"the name Zouave":** "The Zouaves," *New York Times*, July 20, 1860.

181 **The *Sunday Mercury* joked:** Alice Fahs, *The Imagined Civil War*, 84.

181 **R. H. Macy's Dry Goods:** Morgan, *Civil War Lover's Guide*, 60–61.

181 **Notable among them:** Stott, *Jolly Fellows*, 222.

182 **Henry J. Wisner, a *Times* writer:** "From the Fire Zouaves," *New York Times*, May 11, 1861.

183 **Wisner wrote a detailed account:** "The Death of Col. Ellsworth," *New York Times*, May 26, 1861.

184 **"The faces of all were sad":** "Obsequies of Col. Ellsworth," *New York Times*, May 27, 1861.

185 **As early as May 7 the *Times* was reporting:** "Military and Naval Movements," *New York Times*, May 7, 1861.

185 **"The sides of the awning":** "Remains of Capt. Ward," *New York Times*, July 2, 1861.

186 **Herman Melville happened to be in the city:** Garner, *Civil War World of Herman Melville*, 101–2.

Chapter 22. *Seeing the Elephant; or, The Great Skedaddle*

187 the *Daily News* was more reserved: Weber, *Copperheads*, 38.

189 The volunteers sauntered: Davis, *Battle at Bull Run*, 96.

189 Mathew Brady and a crew: Horan, *Mathew Brady*, 37–38.

189 the thirty-two-year-old Alfred "Alf" Waud: Ray, *Alfred R. Waud*, 13–43.

190 rode up to Colonel William Tecumseh Sherman: Sherman, *Memoirs*, 100–195.

190 "Our men are not good soldiers": Davis, *Battle at Bull Run*, 219.

191 a few Northern specials rushed off: Perry, *Bohemian Brigade*, 31–42.

191 "seeing the elephant": "Seeing the Elephant," *New York Times*, March 1, 1861.

191 One of Corcoran's officers, Lieutenant Colonel James Haggerty: Wylie, *Irish General*, 128.

192 Orpheus C. Kerr claimed: Newell, *Orpheus C. Kerr Papers*, 1:82.

192 "a wild, senseless rabble": Villard, *Memoirs*, 1:192–93.

192 "There was a regular mingling": Conyngham, *Irish Brigade*, 39.

193 Determined not to let that happen again: Rosenheim, *Photography and the American Civil War*, 63–65.

193 Blenker's brigade: Burton, *Melting Pot Soldiers*, 84–86.

193 At least one New York unit: McKay, *The Civil War and New York City*, 89.

194 An engraving made from a Waud sketch: Ray, *Alfred R. Waud*, 27–28.

194 was quoted in the *Brooklyn Daily Eagle*: "The Battle of Bull's Run," *Brooklyn Daily Eagle*, July 24, 1861.

194 William Russell claimed that: Wylie, *Irish General*, 130.

194 In her diary, Maria Daly: Daly, *Diary of a Union Lady*, 40–41 and 271.

195 "This order was received": Stevenson, *History of the Excelsior or Sickles' Brigade*, 9.

Chapter 23. *The Hyenas of War*

196 On July 29 he scrawled an astounding letter: James M. Lundberg, "On to Richmond! Or Not," *New York Times*, July 28, 2011.

197 Dana would write: Dana, *Recollections*, 1–2.

197 Benjamin Wood was now openly calling: Blondheim, *Copperhead Gore*, 14.

198 McMaster, on the other hand: Kwitchen, *James Alphonsus McMaster*, 125–32.

199 "Everything is as clean and bright": "Department of the East," *New York Times*, March 17, 1865.

200 House Republicans looked for new excuses: Blondheim, *Copperhead Gore*, 33–34.

Chapter 24. *The Shoddy Aristocracy*

202 **an open invitation to graft:** McKay, *The Civil War and New York City*, 98–99.

203 **Henry Bowen and Thurlow Weed, already prosperous:** Goldsmith, *Other Powers*, 75; Van Deusen, *Thurlow Weed*, 287–99.

203 **The war was beneficial:** Burrows and Wallace, *Gotham*, 873–79; Spann, *Gotham at War*, 135–45.

204 **speculating on the price of gold:** Browder, *Money Game*, 97–99.

206 **Fernando Wood once again found himself:** Allen, *Tiger*, 78; Mushkat, *Fernando Wood*, 116–32.

207 **the slave ship captain Nathaniel Gordon:** Soodalter, *Hanging Captain Gordon*, 69–243.

Chapter 25. *We Are Coming, Father Abraham*

209 **Elizabeth Blackwell had grown up:** Harper, *Women During the Civil War*, 414.

210 **"The gross perversion":** Blackwell, *Pioneer Work*, 30.

210 **"I took good rooms":** Ibid., 180–209.

210 **They used the same approach in 1861:** Humphreys, *Marrow of Tragedy*, 105–6 and 20–24.

211 **the men brought in Dorothea Dix:** Harper, *Women During the Civil War*, 415.

211 **at least Olmsted was in place:** Maxwell, *Lincoln's Fifth Wheel*, 20–22.

212 **Lincoln called on General George McClellan:** Sears, *George B. McClellan*, 1–146.

213 **At first he lived up to the great expectations:** Bailey, *Forward to Richmond*, 16–22.

214 **It helped inspire one visitor, Julia Ward Howe:** Howe, *Reminiscences*, 271–75.

215 **the boyish-looking Colonel Francis (Frank) Channing Barlow:** Welch, *Boy General*, 19–42.

216 **One of his men, Private Charles Fuller:** Fuller, *Personal Recollections*, 10.

216 **Winslow Homer met up with him:** Downes, *Life and Works of Winslow Homer*, 34–50.

217 **"I don't believe in dilettante nursing":** Daly, *Diary of a Union Lady*, 77.

217 **Whetten described one group:** Hass, "A Volunteer Nurse."

217 **McClellan moved his great force:** Bailey, *Forward to Richmond*, 124–25.

218 **Miles O'Reilly:** Halpine, *Poetical Works*, 286.

218 **All the New York papers:** Andrews, *The North Reports the Civil War*, 189–95.

219 **Julia Tyler put on a brave front:** Seager, *And Tyler Too*, 473–77.

220 **Kearny fumed that he was "feeble":** De Peyster, *Personal and Military History of Philip Kearny*, 333–50.

221 **They sent him Gus Schurmann:** Styple, *Little Bugler*, 83–91.

221 **But the gung-ho sentiment:** Weber, *Copperheads*, 50–52.

Chapter 26. *Three Cheers for Ericsson*

223 **In September 1861:** deKay, *Monitor*, 24–59.

224 **New Yorkers would write Lincoln:** Holzer, *Lincoln Mailbag*, 24 and 76.

225 **Finally, with a crew of fifty-eight:** Livingston, *Brooklyn and the Civil War*, 73–76.

225 **"having no more effect"**: "Desperate Naval Engagements in Hampton Roads," *New York Times*, March 10, 1862.

226 **"Raise your voices everyone"**: Pastor, *Tony Pastor's Book*.

226 **"the marine monster"**: "The Merrimac Menacing the Capital," *New York Times*, March 12, 1862.

227 **Cornelius Vanderbilt answered**: Stiles, *First Tycoon*, 277 and 340–48.

228 **The *Merrimac* steamed out of Gosport**: deKay, *Monitor*, 203–25.

228 **David Farragut was born in Tennessee**: Duffy, *Lincoln's Admiral*, 3–114.

230 **Tony Pastor mocked him**: Pastor, *Tony Pastor's Book*, 66–67.

230 **leaving the occupation...to General Benjamin Butler**: McPherson, *Mighty Scourge*, 231–32 and 266–67.

Chapter 27. *I Goes to Fight mit Sigel*

231 **"one of the most miserable"**: Keller, *Chancellorsville and the Germans*, 35–45.

234 **Michael Corcoran was back in New York City**: "Col. Corcoran in Washington," *New York Times*, August 19, 1862.

234 **That September, D'Utassy**: Alduino and Coles, *Sons of Garibaldi*, 56–71.

Chapter 28. *The Dead of Antietam*

236 **"As soon as my men began to fall"**: Corby, *Memoirs of Chaplain Life*, 113.

236 **"looking so handsome"**: Welch, *Boy General*, 70.

237 **Barlow wrote his mother**: Samito, *"Fear Was Not in Him,"* 116–22.

237 **Private Charles Fuller spoke for many**: Fuller, *Personal Recollections*, 63.

238 **"Mr. Brady has done something"**: "Brady's Photographs," *New York Times*, October 20, 1862.

239 **Gardner was redressing that situation**: Rosenheim, *Photography and the American Civil War*, 7–12.

Chapter 29. *Sambo's Right to Be Kilt*

240 **"one of the great ironies of the war"**: Oates, *Our Fiery Trial*, 78.

240 **After Horace Greeley got over**: Williams, *Horace Greeley*, 227.

241 **"Sambo's Right to Be Kilt"**: Stedman, *American Anthology*, 860.

241 **Lincoln liked and admired Hunter**: Oates, *Our Fiery Trial*, 74–78.

242 **"My paramount object"**: Basler, *Abraham Lincoln*, 652.

242 **he began the momentous meeting**: Fahs, *Imagined Civil War*, 195–96.

243 **In the *Tribune*, Greeley enthused**: "The Proclamation of Freedom," *New York Tribune*, September 24, 1862.

244 **"looking at its possible economical and moral results"**: "The President's Proclamation," *New York Times*, September 28, 1862.

244 **Soldiers deserted in record numbers**: White, *Emancipation*, 69–82.

245 **Michael Corcoran was putting together**: Burton, *Melting Pot Soldiers*, 116–17.

246 **Horatio Seymour, who blamed the war**: Mushkat, *Reconstruction*, 39.

246 **All six of the city's congressional seats**: Spann, *Gotham at War*, 91.

246 **"There has never been so great"**: Daly, *Diary of a Union Lady*, 195.

246 **Benjamin Wood resumed publishing**: Blondheim, *Copperhead Gore*, 44–50.

246 **"Give us back our old Commander"**: McWhirter, *Battle Hymns*, 95–96.

247 **Raymond rallied behind his president**: "The Removal of Gen. McClellan," *New York Times*, November 10, 1862.

Chapter 30. *Burnside Falls, Sickles Rises*

249 **"As we advanced":** Corby, *Memoirs of Chaplain Life*, 131–32.

249 **Walt Whitman saw the name of his younger brother:** Whitman, *Complete Prose*, 1:38–39 and 1:58–59.

251 **Redpath wrote Walt:** McKivigan, *Forgotten Firebrand*, 84–94.

251 **another younger brother, Jeff:** Berthold and Price, *Dear Brother Walt*, 44.

251 **"We can tell the imps of faction":** "The Cry for the Recall of McClellan," *New York Times*, May 9, 1863.

252 **With that, Gus Schurmann became:** Styple, *Little Bugler*, 115.

252 **Sickles and Butterfield threw gala parties:** Swanberg, *Sickles the Incredible*, 170–74.

252 **the young Princess Salm-Salm:** Coffey, *Soldier Princess*, 1–14.

253 **Sickles gave Gus a week's furlough:** Styple, *Little Bugler*, 116–41.

253 **Sickles organized a reception:** Swanberg, *Sickles the Incredible*, 175–76.

254 **whom he christened General Tom Thumb:** "The Loving Lilliputians," *New York Times*, February 11, 1863.

255 **Posted near Newport News, Michael Corcoran:** "The Death of Lieut-Col. Kimball," *New York Times*, April 20, 1863.

256 **The men of the Eleventh Corps:** Burton, *Melting Pot Soldiers*, 122–25.

257 **the "flying Dutchmen":** Keller, *Chancellorsville and the Germans*, 79–121.

257 **Barlow wrote his family:** Samito, *"Fear Was Not in Him,"* 130–41.

258 **Captain Francis Adams:** Hessler, *Sickles at Gettysburg*, 69.

258 **awarded one to Gus Schurmann:** Styple, *Little Bugler*, 148–49.

259 **a committee led by Albert Richardson:** Carlson, *Junius and Albert's Adventures*, 11–218.

259 **Sherman's terse reply:** Perry, *Bohemian Brigade*, 135–55.

260 **Richardson would not be:** Carlson, *Junius and Albert's Adventures*, 250–56.

Chapter 31. *Grafted into the Army*

262 **"The laboring classes":** Daly, *Diary of a Union Lady*, 248.

262 **a large new federal bureaucracy:** Weber, *Copperheads*, 87–105.

263 **Draft dodging was rampant:** Levine, "Draft Evasion."

263 **Dennis Mahony, former editor:** Klement, "Catholics as Copperheads."

264 **Clement Vallandigham, king of Copperheads:** Klement, *Limits of Dissent*, 138–58.

264 **The Wood brothers staged:** Brummer, *Political History of New York State*, 314–15.

265 **Lincoln's reply to Corning:** Holzer, *State of the Union*, 115–24.

265 **Peace Democrats staged a giant rally:** "The Peace Party," *New York Times*, June 4, 1863.

266 **Henry Raymond scoffed at "Fernando's Farce":** "Fernando's Farce," *New York Times*, June 7, 1863.

266 **"Well, Walt, you and I cannot agree":** Berthold and Price, *Dear Brother Walt*, 61.

Chapter 32. *Dan Sickles, Hero or Villain?*

267 **Robert E. Lee was a close reader:** McPherson, *Mighty Scourge*, 78–85.

267 **Governor Seymour sent:** Schecter, *Devil's Own Work*, 18–19.

268 **Sickles either nearly lost:** Hessler, *Sickles at Gettysburg*, 101–234.

269 Frank Barlow also pushed: Samito, *"Fear Was Not in Him,"* 144–67 and 201.

270 a young man from New York City named John Tommy: "China at Gettysburg," *New York Times*, July 12, 1863.

271 But D'Utassy was not with them: Catalfamo, "Thorny Rose."

271 Henry Villard called him: Villard, *Memoirs*, 1:174.

Chapter 33. *The Volcano Erupts*

273 On the morning of Tuesday, July 14: Ackerman, *Boss Tweed*, 13–14.

273 Peace Democrats gathered: "The Fourth of July," *New York Tribune*, July 6, 1863.

274 two satirical new songs: Nathan, "Two Inflation Songs."

275 Workers watched the shoddy aristocracy: Man, "Labor Competition."

275 The *Times* claimed at the end of June: "The Enrollment," *New York Times*, June 30, 1863.

276 a construction worker did scuffle: Schecter, *Devil's Own Work*, 19.

276 Thomas Francis Meagher was trying to raise: Wylie, *Irish General*, 196–97.

276 an added irritation that Sunday was Orange Day: Bruce, *The Harp and the Eagle*, 178.

277 "The name was given her": Costello, *Our Firemen*, 174–75.

277 Stones flew through the office's windows: Bernstein, *New York City Draft Riots*, 18.

278 The mob turned to the Colored Orphan Asylum: Cook, *Armies of the Streets*, 53–78.

278 Dr. John Torrey, a distinguished botanist and chemist: Dupree and Fishel, "Eyewitness Account."

279 As the day wore on: Schecter, *Devil's Own Work*, 242–46.

280 Some stampeded the cab companies: Cook, *Armies of the Streets*, 80–90.

280 Edwin Booth and various family members: Titone, *My Thoughts Be Bloody*, 293–300.

281 William Tweed...showed absolutely no physical fear: Bernstein, *New York City Draft Riots*, 24–25.

282 He'd been spending the war years: Allen, *Tiger*, 89–94.

282 Tweed saw an opportunity: Ackerman, *Boss Tweed*, 15–22.

283 According to the *Times*: "Doings of Gov. Seymour," *New York Times*, July 15, 1863.

283 Their commander, Colonel Henry O'Brien: Cook, *Armies of the Streets*, 110–19.

284 Maria Daly heard the stories: Daly, *Diary of a Union Lady*, 49–251.

285 Thomas Nast, the German immigrant: Halloran, *Thomas Nast*, 74–79.

286 "forgotten even by his former friends": "The Leader of the Riots Dead," *New York Times*, December 8, 1883.

286 That afternoon, Archbishop Hughes: "The Archbishop and His Flock," *New York Times*, July 18, 1863.

287 "Let the niggers stay in the South!": Man, "Labor Competition."

287 "Undoubtedly we shall never know": Berthold and Price, *Dear Brother Walt*, 64–65.

Chapter 34. *Tweed to the Rescue*

288 the *Tribune* accused Governor Seymour: "Our Peril," *New York Tribune*, July 16, 1863.

288 singled out Irish Catholics: Bruce, *The Harp and the Eagle*, 181–84.

289 Republicans' calls for harsh punishments: Cook, *Armies of the Streets*, 177–84.

290 Historian Tyler Anbinder conducted: Anbinder, "Which Poor Man's Fight?"

290 a gun-maker named Orison Blunt: "Orison Blunt," *New York Times*, April 22, 1879.

291 At first Tweed's plan: Ackerman, *Boss Tweed*, 25–28.

291 a new industry of bounty brokers: Murdock, "New York's Civil War Bounty Brokers."

292 New Yorker James Devlin: "Military Execution at Governor's Island," *New York Times*, February 4, 1865.

292 led to the formation of the first black regiment: Jones, "Union League Club."

294 Dan Sickles, on crutches: "What Pennsylvania Has Escaped," *New York Times*, July 6, 1863.

294 meanwhile, Gus remained with his family: Styple, *Little Bugler*, 163–64.

295 New York City voters went to the polls: Brummer, *Political History of New York State*, 554.

295 visited his old friend Michael Corcoran: Burton, *Melting Pot Soldiers*, 118–19.

296 Stephen Foster had returned to New York: Emerson, *Doo-dah!*, 243–305.

Chapter 35. *The Fire in the Rear*

298 Franz Sigel suffered a similar thrashing: Keller, *Chancellorsville and the Germans*, 157.

299 It was Copperheads who reacted: Bruce, *The Harp and the Eagle*, 160–62.

299 Greeley made note: "Miscegenation," *New York Tribune*, March 16, 1864.

300 The pamphlet mailed to Lincoln: Holzer, *Mailbag*, 176–77.

301 Reverend Beecher had quietly reached out: Applegate, *Most Famous Man in America*, 346–50.

301 John Mullaly had been railing: "The Editor of the Metropolitan Record Arrested for Inciting Gov. Seymour to Resist the Draft," *New York Times*, August 20, 1864.

302 After the fall of Vicksburg: Johnson, *"Vast and Fiendish Plot,"* 112–14.

303 One of them was William "Larry" McDonald: "The Rebel Incendiary Plot," *New York Times*, February 8, 1865.

303 Then there was the debonair George Sanders: Mayers, *Dixie and the Dominion*, 65–66 and 160.

304 Captain Hines later testified: Johnson, *"Vast and Fiendish Plot,"* 165.

304 Stanton and Dana sent double agents: Dana, *Recollections*, 242.

304 Greeley excitedly dashed off a letter: Williams, *Horace Greeley*, 247–55.

305 Andrew Johnson later said: Stoddard, *Horace Greeley*, 248.

305 In New York, Fernando Wood: Mushkat, *Fernando Wood*, 133–51.

306 included a "peace plank": Bruce, *The Harp and the Eagle*, 172.

306 **Vallandigham wrote the peace plank:** Klement, "Catholics as Copperheads," 271–87.

306 **In August, Admiral Farragut achieved:** Duffy, *Lincoln's Admiral*, 219–53.

308 **"The times seem to me":** Daly, *Diary of a Union Lady*, 306–7.

308 **"ASTOUNDING FRAUDS!":** *New York Times*, October 26, 1864.

308 **That month the Canada commission struck:** Mayers, *Dixie and the Dominion*, 105–16.

308 **There were predictions:** Longacre, "Union Army Occupation."

Chapter 36. *New York City's Burning*

311 **At the Winter Garden:** Giblin, *Good Brother, Bad Brother*, 97–98.

311 **"the panic was such":** "The Plot," *New York Times*, November 27, 1864.

312 **Edwin stepped up to the footlights:** Ruggles, *Prince of Players*, 163–65.

312 **eight young Rebel saboteurs:** Johnson, *"Vast and Fiendish Plot,"* 166–76.

312 **Headley would write a book:** Headley, *Confederate Operations*, 266–80.

313 **They were thunderstruck:** Brandt, *Man Who Tried to Burn New York*, 89–97.

315 **Reading the morning papers:** Giblin, *Good Brother, Bad Brother*, 93–96.

316 **General Dix and Superintendent Kennedy were mortified:** Johnson, *"Vast and Fiendish Plot,"* 233–48.

317 **It was Joe Howard:** "Department of the East," *New York Times*, March 17, 1865.

Chapter 37. *Last Acts*

318 **Whitman went to the grand reception:** Whitman, *Prose Works*, 110.

319 **turned out for a Union Jubilee:** "The Union Jubilee," *New York Times*, March 7, 1865.

319 **Greeley published an editorial:** Stoddard, *Horace Greeley*, 232–33.

320 **A jubilant, drunken crowd:** Searcher, *Farewell to Lincoln*, 23.

320 **Lincoln sounded nothing like:** Basler, *Abraham Lincoln*, 797.

321 **"That means nigger citizenship":** Giblin, *Good Brother, Bad Brother*, 114.

321 **"I saw a man in mid-air":** Leale, *Lincoln's Last Hours*, 3–4.

321 **Keene strode up to the footlights:** Henneke, *Laura Keene*, 193–208.

322 **when the actors John McCullough and Edwin Forrest heard the news:** Ruggles, *Prince of Players*, 182–98.

322 **a character actor named Samuel Knapp Chester:** "The Trial of the Assassins," *New York Times*, May 17, 1865.

323 **Henry Ward Beecher was not at Plymouth Church:** Applegate, *Most Famous Man in America*, 11–12.

323 **Beecher delivered a long speech:** Beecher and Scoville, *Biography of Henry Ward Beecher*, 453–54.

324 **They'd been organized by James Redpath:** McKivigan, *Forgotten Firebrand*, 98–110.

325 **"All Broadway is black with mourning":** Glicksberg, *Walt Whitman and the Civil War*, 174–75.

325 **Some New York Copperheads:** Searcher, *Farewell to Lincoln*, 39.

326 **Julia Gardiner Tyler, still a proud and defiant Confederate:** Seager, *And Tyler Too*, 473–510.

326 **Charles's father, Gazaway:** Marsh, "Military Trial."

Chapter 38. A *"Hippodrome of Sorrow"*

328 On the morning of Monday, April 24: Searcher, *Farewell to Lincoln*, 124–40.

328 "crape or black folds": Sandburg, *Abraham Lincoln*, 4:396.

329 a man named Peter Relyea: Kunhardt and Kunhardt, *Twenty Days*, 168–69.

330 a "hippodrome of sorrow": Lewis, *Myths After Lincoln*, 119–21.

331 "a dense human hedge": "The Procession," *New York Times*, April 26, 1865.

331 But one man who rode with the 16th: Furgurson, "The Man Who Shot the Man Who Shot Lincoln."

333 Thomas Francis Meagher attended a lecture: Wylie, *Irish General*, 209–315.

333 On July 4 the surviving six hundred: Spann, *Gotham at War*, 189.

334 Edwin Booth stayed out of the public eye: Ruggles, *Prince of Players*, 252–61.

Chapter 39. *The Postwar Boom*

339 Dan Sickles was one of those friends: Swanberg, *Sickles the Incredible*, 279–91.

341 New York's business community: Spann, *Gotham at War*, 190–92.

341 Mathew Brady's battlefield photographs: Horan, *Mathew Brady*, 62–87.

343 Prosperity was the new evangelism: Goldfield, *America Aflame*, 439–57.

344 The second transcontinental railroad: Villard de Borchgrave and Cullen, *Villard*, 289–382.

345 Ulysses S. Grant emerged from the war: Hesseltine, *Ulysses S. Grant*, 54–102.

346 The Democrats nominated Horatio Seymour: Waugh, *U. S. Grant*, 121–23.

346 Tweed and Tammany made sure he did: Ackerman, *Boss Tweed*, 44–56.

347 George McClellan, who was just turning forty-two: Sears, *George B. McClellan*, 387–401.

Chapter 40. *Anything to Beat Grant*

349 Sickles and Fish had known each other for years: Nevins, *Hamilton Fish*, 1–65.

351 Although Grant himself: Waugh, *U. S. Grant*, 104.

351 A pair of sharp operators: Browder, *Money Game*, 164.

352 corruption ran amok: Allen, *Tiger*, 82; Hershkowitz, *Tweed's New York*, 137–62.

353 One man took the Fenians' side: Mushkat, *Fernando Wood*, 160–61.

353 annual Orange Day parade: Burrows and Wallace, *Gotham*, 1003–8.

354 the County Courthouse swindle: Ackerman, *Boss Tweed*, 167–70.

354 At *Harper's Weekly*, Thomas Nast: Halloran, *Thomas Nast*, 119–38.

354 In 1873, Tweed was convicted: Burrows and Wallace, *Gotham*, 1008–11.

354 In 1872, Dan Sickles: Welch, *Boy General*, 209–15.

355 "a sorry sight": "Mr. Jay Gould Resigns," *The Sun*, March 13, 1872.

355 A Spanish warship captured the *Virginius*: "Virginius Massacre," *New York Tribune*, November 13, 1873.

355 Dan was furious at being upstaged: Swanberg, *Sickles the Incredible*, 313–51.

356 "the Bolters' Convention": "The True Voice of the People," *New York Times*, April 27, 1872.

356 Greeley emerged victorious: Williams, *Horace Greeley*, 293–303.

357 Matt Morgan, recently brought over from London: Kent, "War Cartooned."

357 Nast drew Greeley: Jarman, "Graphic Art of Thomas Nast."

358 **Henry Ward Beecher mentioned him:** "Henry Ward Beecher's Discourse—'A Broken-Hearted Man,' " *New York Times*, December 2, 1872.

Chapter 41. *Scandals and Scams*

359 **Republicans were on their pro-business roll:** Fairfield, *The Public and Its Possibilities*, 116–17.

360 **Custer didn't come to his postwar celebrity:** Monaghan, *Custer*, 332–35.

360 **"the most wonderful, thrilling stories":** Kellogg, *Memoirs*, 57–58.

361 **"I was never as happy":** Waugh, *U. S. Grant*, 155–65.

362 **"Damn 'My Captain' ":** Kaplan, *Walt Whitman*, 309.

363 **Herman Melville had died the year before:** Lutwack, "Herman Melville and *Atlantic Monthly* Critics."

364 **Meanwhile, James Redpath was taking:** McKivigan, *Forgotten Firebrand*, 190–91.

Chapter 42. *Old Soldiers*

366 **Grant had two hundred dollars:** Waugh, *U. S. Grant*, 167–201 and 261–75.

367 **the *Times* crowed:** "To Rest in Central Park," *New York Times*, July 25, 1885.

368 **"Gen. Dan Sickles":** "The Hero Laid to Rest," *The Sun*, August 9, 1885.

368 **"every balcony, window, and door":** "A Nation at a Tomb," *New York Times*, August 9, 1885.

369 **"valued his lost leg":** Smith, *Autobiography of Mark Twain*, 1:287.

369 **General Longstreet, the Rebel who'd cost him his leg:** Hessler, *Sickles at Gettysburg*, 386.

370 **"Nobody with warm blood":** "Daniel E. Sickles," *New York Times*, May 5, 1914.

Bibliography

Note: *Period newspaper and magazine articles quoted in the book are cited in the notes.*

Ackerman, Kenneth D. *Boss Tweed: The Corrupt Pol Who Conceived the Modern Soul of New York.* New York: Carroll & Graf, 2005.

Acocella, Joan. "Nights at the Opera." *New Yorker*, January 8, 2007.

Albion, Robert Greenhalgh. *The Rise of New York Port, 1815–1860.* New York: Charles Scribner's Sons, 1939.

Alduino, Frank, and David J. Coles. *Sons of Garibaldi in Blue and Gray: Italians in the American Civil War.* Amherst, NY: Cambria, 2007.

Allen, Oliver E. *The Tiger: The Rise and Fall of Tammany Hall.* Reading, MA: Addison-Wesley, 1993.

Anbinder, Tyler. "Fernando Wood and New York City's Secession from the Union." *New York History*, January 1987.

———. "Which Poor Man's Fight?" *Civil War History*, December 2006.

Andrews, J. Cutler. *The North Reports the Civil War.* Pittsburgh: University of Pittsburgh Press, 1955.

Andrews, Rena Mazyck. "Slavery Views of a Northern Prelate." *Church History* 3, no. 1 (March 1934).

Applegate, Debby. *The Most Famous Man in America: The Biography of Henry Ward Beecher.* New York: Doubleday, 2006.

Badeau, Adam. *The Vagabond.* New York: Rudd & Carlton, 1859.

Bailey, Ronald H. *Forward to Richmond: McClellan's Peninsular Campaign.* New York: Time Life, 1983.

Barnum, P. T. *Life of P. T. Barnum.* London: Sampson Low, Son & Co., 1855.

———. *Struggles and Triumphs.* Buffalo, NY: Warren, Johnson & Co., 1872.

Basler, Roy P., ed. *Abraham Lincoln.* Cleveland: World Publishing Company, 1946.

———. *The Collected Works of Abraham Lincoln.* New Brunswick, NJ: Rutgers University Press, 1953.

Beecher, Henry Ward. *Henry Ward Beecher's Writings.* Boston: Ticknor & Fields, 1863.

Beecher, Wm. C., and Rev. Samuel Scoville. *A Biography of Henry Ward Beecher.* New York: Charles L. Webster & Co., 1888.

Bennett, David H. *The Party of Fear: The American Far Right from Nativism to the Militia Movement.* Chapel Hill: University of North Carolina Press, 1988.

Berger, Meyer. *The Story of The New York Times, 1851–1951.* New York: Simon & Schuster, 1951.

Bernstein, Iver. *The New York City Draft Riots: Their Significance for American Society and Politics in the Age of the Civil War.* New York: Oxford University Press, 1990.

Berthold, Dennis, and Kenneth Price, eds. *Dear Brother Walt: The Letters of Thomas Jefferson Whitman.* Kent, OH: Kent State University Press, 1984.

Blackwell, Elizabeth. *Pioneer Work in Opening the Medical Profession to Women.* London: Longmans, Green & Co., 1895.

Blake, William O., ed. *Pictorial History of the Great Rebellion.* Columbus, OH: Gilmore & Segner, 1866.

Bland, Sterling Lecater, Jr. *African American Slave Narratives.* Vol. 2. Westport, CT: Greenwood Press, 2001.

Blondheim, Menahem, ed. *Copperhead Gore: Benjamin Wood's Fort Lafayette and Civil War America.* Bloomington: Indiana University Press, 2006.

Borchard, Gregory A. *Abraham Lincoln and Horace Greeley.* Carbondale: Southern Illinois University Press, 2011.

Brandt, Nat. *The Man Who Tried to Burn New York.* Syracuse, NY: Syracuse University Press, 1986.

Browder, Clifford. *The Money Game in Old New York: Daniel Drew and His Times.* Lexington: University Press of Kentucky, 1986.

Brown, Henry Collins, ed. *Valentine's Manual of Old New York, No. 5.* New York: Valentine's Manual Inc., 1921.

Browne, Junius. *Four Years in Secessia.* Hartford, CT: O. D. Case, 1865.

———. *The Great Metropolis.* Hartford, CT: American Publishing Co., 1869.

Bruce, Susannah Ural. *The Harp and the Eagle: Irish-American Volunteers and the Union Army, 1861–1865.* New York: New York University Press, 2006.

Brummer, Sidney David. *Political History of New York State During the Period of the Civil War.* New York: Columbia University, 1911.

Bunker, John G. *Harbor and Haven: An Illustrated History of the Port of New York.* Woodland Hills, CA: Windsor Publications, 1979.

Burrows, Edwin G., and Mike Wallace. *Gotham: A History of New York City to 1898.* New York: Oxford University Press, 1999.

Burton, William L. *Melting Pot Soldiers: The Union Ethnic Regiments.* New York: Fordham University Press, 1998.

Caldwell, Mark. *New York Night: The Mystique and Its Mystery.* New York: Scribner, 2001.

Calomiris, Charles W., and Larry Schweikart. "The Panic of 1857." *Journal of Economic History* 51, no. 4 (December 1991).

Carlson, Peter. *Junius and Albert's Adventures in the Confederacy: A Civil War Odyssey.* New York: PublicAffairs, 2013.

Carnahan, Burrus M. *Lincoln on Trial: Southern Civilians and the Law of War.* Lexington: University Press of Kentucky, 2010.

Catalfamo, Catherine. "The Thorny Rose: The Americanization of an Urban, Immigrant, Working Class Regiment in the Civil War; A Social History of the Garibaldi Guard, 1861–64." PhD dissertation, University of Texas, 1989.

Coffey, David. *Soldier Princess: The Life and Legend of Agnes Salm-Salm in North America, 1861–1867*. College Station: Texas A&M University Press, 2002.

Conrad, Eric. "Whitman and the Proslavery Press: Newly Recovered 1860 Reviews." *Walt Whitman Quarterly Review* 27 (2010).

Conyngham, D. P. *The Irish Brigade and Its Campaigns*. New York: William McSorley & Co., 1867.

Cook, Adrian. *The Armies of the Streets: The New York City Draft Riots of 1863*. Lexington: University Press of Kentucky, 1974.

Copeland, David A. *The Antebellum Era: Primary Documents on Events from 1820 to 1860*. Westport, CT: Greenwood Press, 2003.

Corby, W. *Memoirs of Chaplain Life*. Chicago: La Monte, O'Donnell & Co., 1893.

Costello, Augustine E. *Our Firemen*. New York: Augustine E. Costello, 1887.

Daly, Maria Lydig. *Diary of a Union Lady, 1861–1865*. Lincoln: University of Nebraska Press, 2001.

Dana, Charles A. *Recollections of the Civil War*. New York: D. Appleton and Company, 1902.

Davis, William C. *Battle at Bull Run: A History of the First Major Campaign of the Civil War*. Baton Rouge: Louisiana State University Press, 1977.

DeCaro, Louis A., Jr. *John Brown: The Cost of Freedom; Selections from His Life and Letters*. New York: International Publishers, 2007.

deKay, James Tertius. *Monitor: The Story of the Legendary Civil War Ironclad and the Man Whose Invention Changed the Course of History*. New York: Walker & Co., 1997.

De Peyster, John Watts. *Personal and Military History of Philip Kearny*. Elizabeth, NJ: Palmer & Co., 1870.

Dix, Morgan. *Memoirs of John Adams Dix*. 2 vols. New York: Harper & Brothers, 1883.

Downes, William Howe. *The Life and Works of Winslow Homer*. Boston: Houghton Mifflin, 1911.

Duffy, James P. *Lincoln's Admiral: The Civil War Campaigns of David Farragut*. Edison, NJ: Castle Books, 1997.

Dupree, A. Hunter, and Leslie H. Fishel. "An Eyewitness Account of the New York Draft Riots, July, 1863." *Mississippi Valley Historical Review* 47, no. 3 (December 1960).

Eby, Cecil D., Jr. *"Porte Crayon": The Life of David Hunter Strother*. Chapel Hill: University of North Carolina Press, 1960.

Emerson, Ken. *Doo-dah!: Stephen Foster and the Rise of American Popular Culture*. New York: Simon & Schuster, 1997.

Emmons, Clark. *History of the Second Company of the Seventh Regiment*. New York: James G. Gregory, 1864.

Fahs, Alice. *The Imagined Civil War: Popular Literature of the North and South, 1861–1865*. Chapel Hill: University of North Carolina Press, 2001.

Fairfield, John D. *The Public and Its Possibilities: Triumphs and Tragedies in the American City*. Philadelphia: Temple University Press, 2010.

Farrow, Ann, et al. *Complicity: How the North Promoted, Prolonged, and Profited from Slavery*. New York: Ballantine, 2006.

Fehrenbacher, Don E. *The Slaveholding Republic: An Account of the United States Government's Relations to Slavery.* New York: Oxford University Press, 2001.

Freeman, Andrew A. *Abraham Lincoln Goes to New York.* New York: Coward-McCann, 1960.

Fuller, Charles A. *Personal Recollections of the War of 1861.* Sherburne, NY: News Job Printing House, 1906.

Furgurson, Ernest B. "The Man Who Shot the Man Who Shot Lincoln." *American Scholar* (Spring 2009).

Garner, Stanton. *The Civil War World of Herman Melville.* Lawrence: University of Kansas Press, 1993.

Genoways, Ted. *Walt Whitman and the Civil War: America's Poet During the Lost Years of 1860–1862.* Berkeley: University of California Press, 2009.

Giblin, James Cross. *Good Brother, Bad Brother: The Story of Edwin Booth and John Wilkes Booth.* New York: Clarion, 2005.

Gilfoyle, Timothy J. "Street-Rats and Gutter-Snipes." *Journal of Social History* 37, no. 4 (Summer 2004).

Gilpin, R. Blakeslee. *John Brown Still Lives!: America's Long Reckoning with Violence, Equality, and Change.* Chapel Hill: University of North Carolina Press, 2011.

Glicksberg, Charles I., ed. *Walt Whitman and the Civil War.* New York: A. S. Barnes, 1933.

Goldfield, David. *America Aflame: How the Civil War Created a Nation.* New York: Bloomsbury, 2011.

Goldsmith, Barbara. *Other Powers: The Age of Suffrage, Spiritualism, and the Scandalous Victoria Woodhull.* New York: Alfred A. Knopf, 1998.

Greeley, Horace. *The Autobiography of Horace Greeley.* New York: E. B. Treat, 1872.

Greenspan, Ezra. *Walt Whitman and the American Reader.* New York: Cambridge University Press, 1990.

Grinspan, Jon. "Young Men for War." *Journal of American History* 96 (September 2009).

Halloran, Fiona Deans. *Thomas Nast: The Father of Modern Political Cartoons.* Chapel Hill: University of North Carolina Press, 2013.

Halpine, Charles G. *Poetical Works of Charles G. Halpine (Miles O'Reilly).* New York: Harper & Brothers, 1869.

Hammond, Harold Earl. *A Commoners' Judge: The Life and Times of Charles Patrick Daly.* Boston: Christopher Publishing, 1954.

Harper, Judith E. *Women During the Civil War: An Encyclopedia.* New York: Routledge, 2003.

Harper, Robert S. *Lincoln and the Press.* New York: McGraw-Hill, 1951.

Hass, Paul H., ed. "A Volunteer Nurse in the Civil War." *Wisconsin Magazine of History* 8, no. 3 (Spring 1965).

Hassard, John R. G. *Life of the Most Reverend John Hughes.* New York: D. Appleton & Co., 1866.

Hay, Thomas Robson. "Gazaway Bugg Lamar, Confederate Banker and Business Man." *Georgia Historical Quarterly* 37, no. 2 (June 1953).

Headley, Joel Tyler. *The Great Riots of New York, 1712 to 1873*. New York: E. B. Treat, 1873.

Headley, John W. *Confederate Operations in Canada and New York*. New York: Neale Publishing Co., 1906.

Heidler, David S., and Jeanne T. Heidler. *Henry Clay: The Essential American*. New York: Random House, 2010.

Henderson, Mary C. *The City and the Theatre: The History of New York Playhouses*. Clifton, NJ: James T. White & Co., 1973.

Henneke, Ben Graf. *Laura Keene: A Biography*. Tulsa, OK: Council Oak Books, 1990.

Hershkowitz, Leo. *Tweed's New York: Another Look*. Garden City, NY: Anchor, 1977.

Hesseltine, William B. *Ulysses S. Grant, Politician*. New York: Dodd, Mead & Co., 1935.

Hessler, James A. *Sickles at Gettysburg: The Controversial Civil War General Who Committed Murder, Abandoned Little Round Top, and Declared Himself the Hero of Gettysburg*. New York: Savas Beatie, 2009.

Hewitt, John H. "Peter Williams, Jr." *New York History* 79, no. 2 (April 1998).

Hibben, Paxton. *Henry Ward Beecher: An American Portrait*. New York: Press of the Readers Club, 1942.

Hodges, Graham Russell. *David Ruggles: A Radical Black Abolitionist and the Underground Railroad in New York City*. Chapel Hill: University of North Carolina Press, 2010.

———. *Root and Branch: African Americans in New York and East Jersey, 1613–1863*. Chapel Hill: University of North Carolina Press, 1999.

Holloway, Emory, ed. *The Uncollected Poetry and Prose of Walt Whitman*. Vol. 1. Garden City, NY: Doubleday, Page & Co., 1921.

Holzer, Harold, ed. *The Lincoln Mailbag: America Writes to the President, 1861–1865*. Carbondale: Southern Illinois University Press, 1998.

———. *State of the Union: New York and the Civil War*. New York: Fordham University Press, 2002.

Horan, James D. *Mathew Brady: Historian with a Camera*. New York: Crown, 1955.

Howe, Julia Ward. *Reminiscences, 1819–1899*. Boston: Houghton Mifflin, 1899.

Humphreys, Margaret. *Marrow of Tragedy: The Health Crisis of the American Civil War*. Baltimore: Johns Hopkins University Press, 2013.

Jarman, Baird. "The Graphic Art of Thomas Nast." *American Periodicals* 20, no. 2 (2010).

Johnson, Clint. *"A Vast and Fiendish Plot": The Confederate Attack on New York City*. New York: Citadel, 2010.

Jones, Thomas L. "The Union League Club and New York's First Black Regiments in the Civil War." *New York History* 87, no. 3 (Summer 2006).

Kaplan, Justin. *Walt Whitman: A Life*. New York: HarperCollins, 1980.

Keller, Christian B. *Chancellorsville and the Germans: Nativism, Ethnicity, and Civil War Memory*. New York: Fordham University Press, 2007.

Kellogg, Clara Louise. *Memoirs of an American Prima Donna*. New York: G. P. Putnam's Sons, 1913.

Kent, Christopher. "War Cartooned." *Victorian Periodicals Review* 36, no. 2 (Summer 2003).

Klement, Frank L. "Catholics as Copperheads During the Civil War." *Catholic Historical Review* 80, no. 1 (January 1994).

———. *The Limits of Dissent: Clement L. Vallandigham and the Civil War.* New York: Fordham University Press, 1999.

Kline, Michael J. *The Baltimore Plot: The First Conspiracy to Assassinate Abraham Lincoln.* Yardley, PA: Westholme Publishing, 2008.

Kunhardt, Dorothy Meserve, and Philip B. Kunhardt Jr. *Twenty Days: A Narrative in Text and Pictures of the Assassination of Abraham Lincoln.* North Hollywood, CA: Newcastle, 1985.

Kwitchen, Sister Mary Augustine. *James Alphonsus McMaster: A Study of American Thought.* Washington, DC: Catholic University Press of America, 1949.

Leale, Charles A. *Lincoln's Last Hours.* New York, 1909.

Leonard, John William. *History of the City of New York, 1609–1909.* New York: Journal of Commerce and Commercial Bulletin, 1910.

Levine, Peter. "Draft Evasion in the North During the Civil War, 1863–1865." *Journal of American History* 67, no. 4 (1981).

Lewis, Lloyd. *Myths After Lincoln.* New York: Press of the Readers Club, 1929.

Lhamon, William T., Jr. *Raising Cain: Blackface Performance from Jim Crow to Hip Hop.* Cambridge, MA: Harvard University Press, 2000.

Livingston, E. A. *Brooklyn and the Civil War.* Charleston, SC: History Press, 2012.

Lockwood, John, and Charles Lockwood. *The Siege of Washington: The Untold Story of the Twelve Days That Shook the Union.* New York: Oxford University Press, 2011.

Long, Kathryn Teresa. *The Revival of 1857–58: Interpreting an American Religious Awakening.* New York: Oxford University Press, 1998.

Longacre, Edward G. "The Union Army Occupation of New York City, November 1864." *New York History* 65, no. 2 (April 1984).

Lubet, Steven. *John Brown's Spy: The Adventurous Life and Tragic Confession of John E. Cook.* New Haven, CT: Yale University Press, 2012.

Lundberg, James M. "On to Richmond! Or Not." *New York Times,* July 28, 2011.

Lutwack, Leonard. "Herman Melville and *Atlantic Monthly* Critics." *Huntington Library Quarterly* 13, no. 4 (August 1950).

Lydon, James G. "New York and the Slave Trade, 1700 to 1774." *William and Mary Quarterly* 35, no. 2 (April 1978).

McGovern, Bryan P. *John Mitchel: Irish Nationalist, Southern Secessionist.* Knoxville: University of Tennessee Press, 2009.

McKay, Ernest A. *The Civil War and New York City.* Syracuse, NY: Syracuse University Press, 1990.

McKivigan, John R. *Forgotten Firebrand: James Redpath and the Making of Nineteenth-Century America.* Ithaca, NY: Cornell University Press, 2008.

McPherson, James. *Ordeal by Fire: The Civil War and Reconstruction.* New York: McGraw-Hill, 2010.

———. *This Mighty Scourge: Perspectives on the Civil War.* New York: Oxford University Press, 2007.

McWhirter, Christian. *Battle Hymns: The Power and Popularity of Music in the Civil War.* Chapel Hill: University of North Carolina Press, 2012.

Man, Albon P., Jr. "Labor Competition and the New York Draft Riots of 1863." *Journal of Negro History* 36, no. 4 (October 1951).

Marsh, Richard C. "The Military Trial of Gazaway Bugg Lamar." *Georgia Historical Quarterly* 85, no. 4 (Winter 2001).

Maxwell, William Quentin. *Lincoln's Fifth Wheel: The Political History of the U.S. Sanitary Commission.* London: Longmans, Green & Co., 1956.

Mayers, Adam. *Dixie and the Dominion: Canada, the Confederacy, and the War for the Union.* Toronto: Dundurn Group, 2003.

Merrington, Marguerite. *The Custer Story: The Life and Intimate Letters of General George A. Custer and His Wife Elizabeth.* Lincoln: University of Nebraska Press, 1987.

Messent, Peter, and Steve Courtney, eds. *The Civil War Letters of Joseph Hopkins Twichell.* Athens: University of Georgia Press, 2006.

Monaghan, Jay. *Custer: The Life of General George Armstrong Custer.* Lincoln: University of Nebraska Press, 1971.

Morgan, Bill. *The Civil War Lover's Guide to New York City.* Eldorado Hills, CA: Savas Beatie, 2013.

Morris, Charles R. *American Catholic: The Saints and Sinners Who Built America's Most Powerful Church.* New York: Random House, 1997.

Murdock, Eugene C. "New York's Civil War Bounty Brokers." *Journal of American History* 53, no. 2 (September 1966).

Mushkat, Jerome. *Fernando Wood: A Political Biography.* Kent, OH: Kent State University Press, 1990.

———. *Tammany: The Evolution of a Political Machine, 1789–1865.* Syracuse, NY: Syracuse University Press, 1971.

———. *The Reconstruction of the New York Democracy, 1861–1874.* East Brunswick, NJ: Associated University Presses, 1981.

Myers, Gustavus. *The History of Tammany Hall.* New York: Boni & Liveright, 1917.

Nathan, Hans. "Two Inflation Songs of the Civil War." *Musical Quarterly* 29, no. 2 (April 1943).

Nevins, Allan. *Hamilton Fish: The Inner History of the Grant Administration.* New York: Frederick Ungar, 1957.

Newell, Robert Henry. *The Orpheus C. Kerr Papers.* Vol. 1. New York: Blakeman & Mason, 1862.

Oates, Stephen B. *Our Fiery Trial: Abraham Lincoln, John Brown, and the Civil War Era.* Amherst: University of Massachusetts Press, 1979.

O'Brien, Frank M. *The Story of The Sun.* New York: D. Appleton & Co., 1928.

Parton, James. *The Life of Horace Greeley.* Boston: Fields, Osgood, & Co., 1869.

Pastor, Tony. *Tony Pastor's Book of Six Hundred Comic Songs and Speeches.* New York: Dick & Fitzgerald, 1867.

Perkins, Howard C. "The Defense of Slavery in the Northern Press on the Eve of the Civil War." *Journal of Southern History* 9, no. 4 (November 1943).

Perry, James M. *A Bohemian Brigade: The Civil War Correspondents—Mostly Rough, Sometimes Ready.* New York: John Wiley & Sons, 2000.

Phisterer, Frederick. *New York in the War of the Rebellion, 1861 to 1865*. Albany, NY: J. B. Lyon Co., 1912.

Prince, Carl E. "The Great 'Riot Year.'" *Journal of the Early Republic* 5, no. 1 (Spring 1985).

Ray, Frederic E. *Alfred R. Waud: Civil War Artist*. New York: Viking, 1974.

Redpath, James. *The Roving Editor*. New York: A. B. Burdick, 1859.

Richardson, Albert. *The Secret Service, the Field, the Dungeon, and the Escape*. Hartford, CT: American Publishing Co., 1865.

Rosenheim, Jeff L. *Photography and the American Civil War*. Hartford, CT: Yale University Press, 2013.

Rourke, Constance. *Trumpets of Jubilee*. New York: Harcourt, Brace, 1927.

Ruggles, Eleanor. *Prince of Players: Edwin Booth*. New York: W. W. Norton & Co., 1953.

Samito, Christian G., ed. *"Fear Was Not in Him": The Civil War Letters of Major General Francis C. Barlow, U.S.A.* New York: Fordham University Press, 2006.

Sandburg, Carl. *Abraham Lincoln*. Vol. 4. Boston: Houghton Mifflin, 1939.

Sante, Luc. *Low Life: Lures and Snares of Old New York*. New York: Farrar, Straus & Giroux, 2001.

Schecter, Barnet. *The Devil's Own Work: The Civil War Draft Riots and the Fight to Reconstruct America*. New York: Walker & Co., 2005.

Seager, Robert. *And Tyler Too: A Biography of John and Julia Gardiner Tyler*. New York: McGraw-Hill, 1963.

Searcher, Victor. *The Farewell to Lincoln*. New York: Abingdon Press, 1965.

Sears, Stephen W. *George B. McClellan: The Young Napoleon*. New York: Ticknor & Fields, 1988.

———, ed. *The Civil War Papers of George B. McClellan*. New York: Ticknor & Fields, 1989.

Seitz, Don C. *The James Gordon Bennetts*. Indianapolis: Bobbs-Merrill, 1928.

Sherman, William Tecumseh. *Memoirs of General William Tecumseh Sherman*. New York: D. Appleton & Co., 1889.

Sherwin, Oscar. *Prophet of Liberty: The Life and Times of Wendell Phillips*. New York: Bookman Associates, 1958.

Sherwood, Marika. "Perfidious Albion." *Contributions in Black Studies* 13 (1995).

Smith, Harriet Elinor, ed. *Autobiography of Mark Twain*. Vol. 1. Berkeley: University of California Press, 2011.

Soodalter, Ron. *Hanging Captain Gordon: The Life and Trial of an American Slave Trader*. New York: Atria Books, 2006.

Spann, Edward K. *Gotham at War: New York City, 1860–1865*. New York: Rowman & Littlefield, 2002.

Stampp, Kenneth M. *America in 1857: A Nation on the Brink*. New York: Oxford University Press, 1990.

Stedman, Edmund Clarence. *An American Anthology, 1787–1900*. Boston: Houghton Mifflin, 1900.

Stern, William M. "How Dagger John Saved New York's Irish." *City Journal* (Spring 1997).

Stevenson, James. *History of the Excelsior or Sickles' Brigade*. Paterson, NJ: Van Derhoven & Holms, 1863.

Stiles, T. J. *The First Tycoon: The Epic Life of Cornelius Vanderbilt.* New York: Alfred A. Knopf, 2009.

Stoddard, Henry Luther. *Horace Greeley: Printer, Editor, Crusader.* New York: G. P. Putnam's Sons, 1946.

Stott, Richard. *Jolly Fellows: Male Milieus in Nineteenth-Century America.* Baltimore: Johns Hopkins University Press, 2009.

Stovall, Floyd, ed. *The Collected Writings of Walt Whitman.* Vol. 2, *Prose Works 1892.* New York: New York University Press, 1964.

Stowe, Harriet Beecher. *The Key to Uncle Tom's Cabin.* Boston: John P. Jewett & Co., 1854.

Styple, William B. *The Little Bugler.* Kearny, NJ: Belle Grove Publishing, 1998.

Swanberg, W. A. *Sickles the Incredible: A Biography of Daniel Edgar Sickles.* New York: Charles Scribner's Sons, 1956.

Tappan, Lewis. *The Life of Arthur Tappan.* New York: Hurd & Houghton, 1870.

Titone, Nora. *My Thoughts Be Bloody: The Bitter Rivalry That Led to the Assassination of Abraham Lincoln.* New York: Free Press, 2011.

Van Deusen, Glyndon G. *Thurlow Weed, Wizard of the Lobby.* Boston: Little, Brown, 1947.

Villard, Henry. *Memoirs of Henry Villard.* Vol. 1. Boston: Houghton Mifflin, 1904.

Villard de Borchgrave, Alexandra, and John Cullen. *Villard: The Life and Times of an American Titan.* New York: Nan A. Talese, 2001.

Waugh, Joan. *U. S. Grant: American Hero, American Myth.* Chapel Hill: University of North Carolina Press, 2009.

Weber, Jennifer L. *Copperheads: The Rise and Fall of Lincoln's Opponents in the North.* New York: Oxford University Press, 2006.

Weed, Thurlow. *Autobiography of Thurlow Weed.* Boston: Houghton, Mifflin & Co., 1884.

Welch, Richard F. *The Boy General: The Life and Careers of Francis Channing Barlow.* Kent, OH: Kent State University Press, 2005.

Wells, Tom Henderson. *The Slave Ship Wanderer.* Athens: University of Georgia Press, 1967.

Werner, M. R. *Tammany Hall.* New York: Doubleday, 1928.

White, Jonathan W. *Emancipation, the Union Army, and the Reelection of Abraham Lincoln.* Baton Rouge: Louisiana State University Press, 2014.

———. "How Lincoln Won the Soldier Vote." *New York Times*, November 7, 2014.

Whitman, Walt. *Leaves of Grass.* Brooklyn, 1855.

———. *Prose Works.* Philadelphia: David McKay, 1892.

———. *The Complete Prose Works of Walt Whitman.* Vol. 1. New York: G. P. Putnam's Sons, 1902.

Widmer, Edward L. *Young America: The Flowering of Democracy in New York City.* New York: Oxford University Press, 1999.

Wilford, John Noble. "How Epidemics Helped Shape the Modern Metropolis." *New York Times*, April 15, 2008.

Williams, Robert C. *Horace Greeley: Champion of American Freedom.* New York: New York University Press, 2006.

Wilson, Ivy G. *Specters of Democracy: Blackness and the Aesthetics of Politics in the Antebellum U.S.* New York: Oxford University Press, 2011.

Woodman, Harold D. *King Cotton and His Retainers: Financing and Marketing the Cotton Crop of the South, 1800–1925.* Columbia, SC: University of South Carolina Press, 1990.

Wyatt-Brown, Bertram. *Honor and Violence in the Old South.* New York: Oxford University Press, 1986.

———. *Lewis Tappan and the Evangelical War Against Slavery.* Cleveland: Press of Case Western Reserve University, 1969.

Wylie, Paul R. *The Irish General: Thomas Francis Meagher.* Norman: University of Oklahoma Press, 2007.

Yafa, Stephen. *Big Cotton: How a Humble Fiber Created Fortunes, Wrecked Civilizations, and Put America on the Map.* New York: Viking, 2005.

Index